Acknowledgments

My major indebtedness for this book is to the many helpful public, college, and seminary librarians and curators, too numerous to mention, in the Twin Cities area and across the United States and Canada who opened their resources to me for my research. Without them this book would not have materialized.

Also, thanks are due the Tau State Organization, Minnesota, of The Delta Kappa Gamma Society International for their financial grant to complete research for the chapter on Narcissa Whitman.

I am grateful to my son Rick for generating the idea for a book about women in religion and to son Jon for his editing assistance through five years of research and writing.

Grateful acknowledgment is made to the following for permission to reprint material as noted:

Abingdon Press from *The Elusive Mr. Wesley,* vol. 1 by Richard Heitzenrater, 1984; *Here I Stand* by Roland Bainton, 1950; and *Susanna, Mother of the Wesleys* by Rebecca Lamar Harmon, 1968.

Augsburg Fortress from *Luther, the Reformer* by James Kittelson, 1986, Augsburg Publishing House; *Women of the Reformation in Germany and Italy* by Roland Bainton, 1971, Augsburg Publishing House; *God's Court Jester* by Eric Gritsch, 1983, Fortress Press; and *Luther's Works,* vol. 54, 1967, Fortress Press.

The Arthur H. Clark Company from *First White Woman Over the Rockies,* vol. I by Clifford Drury, 1963; and *Marcus and Narcissa Whitman & the Opening of Old Oregon,* vols. I and II by Clifford Drury, 1973.

The Crossroad Publishing Company from *Luther: A Life* by John M. Todd, 1982 by John M. Todd.

Daughters of St. Paul Books & Media (Boston) from *Three Ways of Love* by Frances Parkinson Keyes, 1963 by Frances Parkinson Keyes.

Dover Publications, Inc. from *The People Called Shakers* by Edward Deming Andrews, 1963.

William B. Eerdmans Publishing Co. from *Voices from the Heart* by Roger Lundin & Mark A. Nolls, eds., 1987.

Farrar, Straus and Giroux, Inc. from *The Perfect Life* by Doris Faber, 1974 by Doris Faber.

Fordham University Press (New York) from *The Positio of the Historical Section of the Sacred Congregation of Rites on the Introduction of the Cause for Beatification and Canonization and on the Virtues of the Servant of God Katharine Tekakwitha, the Lily of the Moharks,* 1940.

Fremantle, Anne from *Treasury of Early Christianity,* edited by Anne Fremantle, 1953.

Harper Collins Publishers from *Women and Religion in America,* vol. II by Rosemary Ruether and Rosemary Keller, 1984 by Lillian Webb; and *Sojourner Truth, a Self-made Woman* by Victoria Ortiz, 1974 by Victoria Ortiz.

The Harvard Common Press, Inc. from *The Shaker Holy Land* by Edward R. Horgan, 1982 by The Harvard Common Press, Inc.; and *Forgotten Founders* by Bruce E. Johansen, 1982 by

Bruce E. Johansen.

Henry Holt and Company, Inc. from *Divine Rebel* by Selma R. Williams, 1981 by Selma R. Williams.

ICS Publications (2131 Lincoln Road N.E., Washington D.C. 20002) from *The Collected Works of St. Teresa of Avila, vol. I* translated by Kieran Kavanaugh and Otilio Rodriguez, 1976 by Washington Province of Discalced Carmelites (Washington D.C.); and *The Collected Works of St. Teresa of Avila, vol. II* translated by Kieran Kavanaugh and Otilio Rodriguez, 1980 by Washington Province of Discalced Carmelites.

Little, Brown and Company from *Ann the World: The Life of Mother Ann Lee, Founder of the Shakers* by Nardi Reeder Campion, 1976 by Nardi Reeder Campion.

Macmillan Publishing Company from *Holy Company* by Elliott Wright, 1980 by Elliott Wright; and *The Life and Times of Frederick Douglass* by Frederick Douglass, 1962 by Macmillan Publishing Company.

Harold Ober Association Inc. from *Luther Alive* by Edith Simon, 1968 by Edith Simon.

Paulist Press from *Catherine of Siena: The Dialogue* translated by Suzanne Noffke, 1980; and *Shakers: Two Centuries of Spiritual Reflection* by Robley Edward Whitson ed., 1983.

The Pennsylvania State University Press (University Park and London) from *Black Women in Nineteenth-Century American Life*, pp. 240-41, 235-36, by Bert James Loewenberg and Ruth Bogin eds., 1976 by The Pennsylvania State University.

Random House, Inc. from *A Pictorial History of the Negro in America* by Langston Hughes and Milton Meltzer, 1968 by Crown Publishers Inc.; and *Four Women in a Violent Time* by Deborah Crawford, 1970 by Crown Publishers Inc.

Marian Reiner for the author from *I Became Alone* by Judith Thurman, 1975 by Judith Thurman.

Review and Herald Publishing Association from *The Morning Star of Wittenberg* by Anne Ilgenstein Katterfield, 1956.

Irene Roth from *Dona Gracia of the House of Nasi* by Cecil Roth, 1977.

Sepher-Hermon Press, Inc. from *A History of the Marranos* by Cecil Roth, 1974.

Sheed & Ward (Kansas City, MO) from *Passion of SS Perpetua & Felicity Together with the Sermons of S. Augustine* by W.W. Shewring, translator, 1931; and *Catherine of Siena* by Sigrid Undset, 1954.

The United Methodist Church from "Salute to Susanna" by Frank Baker in *Methodist History*, April, 1989; and "Susanna Wesley's Spirituality" by Charles Wallace in *Methodist History*, April, 1984.

University Press of New England from *The Shakers and the World's People* by Flo Morse, 1980 by Flo Morse.

Upper Room Books (1908 Grand Avenue, P.O. Box 189, Nashville, TN 37202) from *Such a Woman* by Rita F. Snowden, 1962.

Ye Galleon Press from *The Letters of Narcissa Whitman* by Narcissa Whitman, 1986; and *My Journal* by Narcissa Whitman, 1982.

Women of Faith

PORTRAITS OF TWELVE SPIRIT-FILLED WOMEN

by
Grace Stageberg Swenson

NORTH STAR PRESS OF ST. CLOUD, INC.

Design: Corinne A. Dwyer

Library of Congress Cataloging-in-Publication Data

Swenson, Grace Stageberg.
    Women of faith : portraits of twelve spirit-
filled women / by Grace Stageberg Swenson.
    216 p. 253 cm.
    Includes bibliographical references and
index.
    ISBN 0-87839-063-4 : $19.95
    1. Religious biography. 2. Women—
Biography. I. Title.
BL72.S92   1991
270′.092′2—dc20
[B]   91-18687
                                           CIP

Published by North Star Press of St. Cloud, Inc.,
P.O. Box 451, St. Cloud, Minnesota 56302.

ISBN: 0-87839-063-4

Picture Credits:

Perpetua (page 1). The secret sign used by early
Christians to identify themselves to one another in the days of persecution.

Catherine of Siena (page 7). Taken from a wall
painting by 14th century artist Andrea di
Vanni. Courtesy of the Daughters of St. Paul
Books & Media, Boston, Massachusetts.

Katherine von Bora (page 19). Artist's sketch
made from a portrait painted by Louis
Cranach the Elder.

Gracia Nasi Mendes (page 35). The Star of David
is a Jewish symbol. The six points of the star
refers to the six days of creation.

Teresa of Avila (page 47). Reproduction of a
painting of Saint Teresa. Courtesy of ICS Publications, Institute of Carmelite Studies,
Washington, D.C.

Anne Marbury Hutchinson (page 65). A photograph of the statue of Anne Hutchinson on
the grounds of the Massachusetts State House.
Courtesy of the State Library of Massachusetts, Boston, Massachusetts.

Juana Inés de la Cruz (page 83). "The Tenth
Muse." Permission requested from the Organization of American States, Washington, D.C.

Kateri Tekakwitha (page 91). Statue of Kateri
Tekakwitha on the great bronze doors of Saint
Patrick's Cathedral, New York City. Courtesy
of the Blessed Kateri Tekakwitha League,
Auriesville, New York.

Susanna Annesley Wesley (page 107). Artist's
sketch from portrait of Susanna Wesley.

Ann Lee (page 125). A drawing of the Shaker
symbol, the Tree of Life, as originally painted
by Hannah Cohoon in 1854.

Narcissa Prentiss Whitman (page 139). A portrait drawn from memory by an acquaintance
of Narcissa Whitman. Courtesy of Ye Galleon
Press, Fairfield, Washington.

Sojourner Truth (page 165). An engraving show-
ing Sojourner Truth as a young woman.

Dedication
For sons Jon and Rick
who helped me choose and change.

"The Lord doesn't look so much at the greatness of our works
as at the love with which they are done."

Teresa of Avila
from *The Interior Castle*

Contents

Introduction

This volume was developed from specific questions concerning the role of women of past generations in the field of religion. The emerging awareness of the place of females in the Christian and Jewish traditions and the efforts towards ecumenicism and inclusivity led to exploring the personal lives of twelve women who have lived during various historical periods. They represent diverse races, religions, ethnic and cultural backgrounds. They were all spirit-filled women, who, despite male prejudices and attitudes, made worthy contributions in orthodox and sectarian religions.

Despite the many valuable contributions of church fathers and rabbis to religious thought, they have often expressed negative views of women that have prevailed over the ages. For example, Tertullian called females the "devil's gateway" and claimed that all women shared the ignominy of Eve. Thomas Aquinas, as did Aristotle, regarded females as "misbegotten males" who were defective by nature. Luther and Calvin found women useful as mothers and wives, but did not allow them any authority within the church. A rabbi observed, "Eminence is not for women."

With such indoctrination, what channels did these women adopt to break loose from the stereotypes heaped upon them? How did they cope with prevailing attitudes that placed them at the backstage of history and society? How did they maneuver within the framework of theologies formulated over the centuries by men?

For the most part women's histories were written, edited, censored, and preserved in varying degrees by men. Men chose what of their stories to save for posterity and what to discard. For example, Anne Hutchinson's confrontations with the Puritans in the Massachusetts Bay Colony were recorded by Governor John Winthrop in a biased diary that became the basis for judging her for decades following her death. Saint Teresa's writings were considered at times by her male confessors to be inappropriate, and inquisitors were warned that her words and proclamations were inflammatory. While library shelves overflow with the words of Martin Luther, only one of Katherine von Bora's letters appears to be saved. Juana Inés de la Cruz was reprimanded by the priests for being too worldly when she wrote secular prose and poetry and studied nonreligious subjects. She raised a furor when she challenged the tenets of a male theologian.

Although all twelve women developed distinct personalities shaped by the conditions of the times, their lives showed many similarities as they searched for a meaningful existence. Strong-willed females were constantly reminded that their proper place was secondary to males. Susanna Wesley incurred the wrath of her minister husband when during his absence she dared conduct church services and read the sermons in her own kitchen. Ann Lee, the founder of the Shaker movement, was ridiculed and persecuted for her messianic prophecies. Sojourner Truth had to overcome both racial and female discrimination.

Whereas boys and young men were trained for professions in schools and universities, girls and young women had no educational opportunities. With the exception of Narcissa Whitman, all of these women had no formal education. Teresa of Avila, Katherine von Bora, and Juana Inés de la Cruz received religious training in convents. Catherine of Siena taught herself to read, but never learned to write. Her letters and writings were dictated to secretaries. Kateri Tekakwitha, Ann Lee, and Sojourner Truth were illiterate, and their stories were recorded by others. Anne Hutchinson and Susanna Wesley acquired their considerable knowledge of the Bible and theology through their own private study.

These women displayed unusual courage and took great risks. Perpetua, back in the second century, demonstrated leadership and bravery unequaled among the five martyrs who died in the Carthage arena. She wrote her own story up to the time of her martyrdom. Because Gracia Nasi Mendes had the status of wealth and position, she rose above the usual stereotypes of the average Jewish woman. But she displayed unusual bravery as she helped persecuted Jews escaped the Inquisition in sixteenth century Spain and Portugal. Narcissa Whitman, the first white woman to cross the Rockies on the overland route, heroically ventured to Old Oregon where she became a missionary to the Cayuse Indians.

Generally women were considered morally weaker than men and were excluded from active participation in the patriarchal churches and synagogues. Male theologians and scholars interpreted the Scriptures, made the laws, established values, and set controls. The male experience was considered normal; the female was deviant. When women were denied full participation in mainstream churches, they sometimes embraced sectarian faiths and joined heretical movements where they could become preachers and leaders. Anne Hutchinson and Ann Lee found power through their unorthodox beliefs.

Women of royalty, wealth, and noble birth could rise above the status of ordinary females as could abbesses of convents. Through chastity and virginity, celibate women in convents were given more respect than other females. Monastic life offered them alternatives to unhappy marriages and frequent pregnancies. In the convents they found security, independence, and opportunities for spiritual pursuits. The most celebrated ascetics were Catherine of Siena and Teresa of Avila, who were sainted and made "doctors" of the church. By virtue of their holiness and claims of communication with God, they transcended womanhood and sex. Kateri Tekakwitha, the Mohawk holy woman, achieved recognition by leading a saintly celibate life.

In varying degrees the contributions of these women have changed, enriched, and broadened religious life. Susanna Wesley and Katherine von Bora advanced the position of women in the Protestant Church. Ann Lee established Shaker communities, now extinct, which are still respected for artistry, industry, and dedication. The words of Teresa of Avila are studied as models for attaining perfection and holiness. Kateri Tekakwitha's life became an example of supreme Christian devotion. Juana Inés de la Cruz proved that genius can be a feminine attribute. Catherine of Siena showed the power of one female activist to bring about change in the church. The experiences of Anne Hutchinson, Ann Lee, Sojourner Truth, and Gracia Mendes exposed blatant hypocrisy and prejudice. Perpetua and Narcissa Whitman sacrificed their lives to accomplish their goals.

As I researched the lives of these twelve women, I was struck by their humanness, their sincerity of purpose, and their tenacity in clinging to their beliefs. I have tried to portray them, not as high-minded paragons of righteousness, but as women with human frailties who boldly resisted the prevailing attitudes and disparagements thrust upon them. Although I found some of their views puzzling and foreign, I admired the determination with which they forged their credos. They diligently pursued their goals in accordance with God's will as they perceived it. Despite formidable obstacles, they managed to carve out a niche for themselves in religious history.

Here, then, are portraits of these twelve spirit-filled women.

Grace Stageberg Swenson

Chapter 1

Perpetua
(c. 181 - 203)

EARLY CHRISTIAN MARTYR WHO WAS SACRIFICED TO THE WILD BEASTS
IN THE AMPHITHEATER IN OLD CARTHAGE.

AT CARTHAGE in early March 203 A.D. five catechumens preparing for Christian baptism were imprisoned and brought to trial before Hilarian, the Provincial Procurator. Among the five was Perpetua, a young twenty-two-year-old matron from the illustrious Vibii family. She was the mother of a nursing infant and said to be the wife of a wealthy Carthaginian, who was either a timid Christian in hiding, a pagan who had abandoned her when she became a Christian, or a man who had died earlier. Perpetua

and her two brothers had been raised by a pagan father and a Christian mother.

At Perpetua's side were four other converts—her slave girl, Felicity, eight months pregnant, Felicity's husband Revocatus, and two other male catechumens, Saturninus and Secundulus. The Christians were to be brought to trial, and if they refused to recant their new religion, they were to be thrown to the wild animals in the arena at the forthcoming festival honoring Caesar Geta.

What Do We Do with the Christians?

During the first and second centuries pagan rulers subjected Christians to varying degrees of persecution. At times ruthless sovereigns vigorously sought out the Christians and severely punished them; at other times more benevolent monarchs allowed them to co-exist as long as they created no disturbances.

Pliny, the Roman governor of Bethynia in Asia Minor (present day Turkey), confessed his bewilderment at how to treat Christians. Sometime between the years 111 and 113 A.D. he wrote to Trajan, the Roman emperor:

> I have never been present at the trial of Christians, and I do not know what to ask or how to punish. I have been very much at a loss to know whether to make any distinction for age or strength, whether to excuse those who have renounced Christianity. . . . In the meantime this is what I have done. I have asked the accused whether they were Christians.

If they confessed, I asked a second and a third time, threatening penalty. Those who persisted I ordered to be executed, for I did not doubt that whatever it was they professed they deserved to be punished for their inflexible obstinacy.[1]

In his reply Trajan reassured Pliny saying:

You have followed, my dear Secundus, the proper course of procedure in examining the cases of those who were accused to you as Christians. For, indeed, nothing can be laid down as a general law which contains anything like a definite rule of action. They are not to be sought out. If they are accused and convicted, they are to be punished, yet on this condition, that he who denies that he is a Christian and makes the fact evident by an act, that is, by worshipping our gods, shall obtain pardon on his repentance, however much suspected as to the past. Papers, however, which are presented anonymously ought not to be admitted in any accusation. For they are a very bad example and unworthy of our times. . . .[2]

During the waning years of the second century, Christians were largely ignored as the Empire became embroiled in civil wars and the defense of its borders. But at the onset of the third century, Septimius Severus, Emperor of Carthage in North Africa, in an attempt to unite all his subjects and establish religious harmony, declared that worship of all gods would be accepted as long as "Sol Invictus" (the Unconquered Sun) was acknowledged as the Supreme God.

When the Jews and Christians refused to recognize the Sun as their god, the Emperor issued an edict in 202 A.D. that all converts to Judaism and Christianity would be put to death. Because the edict was directed mainly toward the newly-converted and their teachers, famous Christian scholars such as Clement of Alexandria had to flee. It appeared that the Roman magistrate had given up exterminating those who were already professing Christians and Jews, but hoped to stem the spread of these religions by sacrificing the newcomers. He particularly wanted to make examples of those with social status as a warning to others harboring similar ideas.

I Am a Christian.

While in prison Perpetua kept a diary known as *The Passion of Perpetua and Felicity.* The introduction and conclusion appeared to have been written by an eyewitness, perhaps Tertullian (c.160 - c.203), the Roman Christian theologian. Although Perpetua wrote the main part of the work until the day before her death, her brother Saturus added a portion telling of his vision while in prison with her.

The Passion is important as an account of the visions of early Christians and their views of martyrdom. The work, thought to be the earliest piece of literature written by a woman, is remarkable for its simplicity and vividness. Perpetua's sacrifice was often included in the liturgy of the early church. St. Augustine frequently quoted from *The Passion* in his sermons, but warned that the work should not be given importance equal to Holy Scriptures.

In her diary, written perhaps first in Latin, then translated to Greek, Perpetua wrote graphically of imprisonment, trial, sentencing, and the sadness it brought to her family, particularly her pagan father. She related how the five Christians were first placed under guard at a private house. They were soon joined by Saturus, Perpetua's brother and instructor, who voluntarily came to baptize the catechumens and ultimately to die with them.

Perpetua's pagan father visited her hoping to persuade his favorite child to abandon her faith. But Perpetua refused saying, ". . . I cannot call myself by any other name than what I am—a Christian." Her father became enraged at the word "Christian." Perpetua wrote, ". . . [he] threw himself upon me as if he would pluck out my eyes, but he only shook me and in fact he was vanquished." He left in despair.[3]

Shortly they were moved to the state prison above the town, a dark torrid dungeon where the soldiers delighted in subjecting prisoners to the stocks and other tortures. Tertius and Pomponius, two deacons, were allowed to administer to them, and by bribing the guards, the prisoners were released to better quarters for a few hours. Perpetua was granted permission to nurse her child who was weak from hunger. With the infant again in her arms, she said, ". . . my prison suddenly became a palace to me and I would rather have been there than anywhere else."[4]

But realizing what was in store for her, she commended the care of her baby to her mother and relatives.

Her brother Saturus asked Perpetua to pray for a vision to reveal their fate. She answered, "Tomorrow I will tell thee." As she promised, that night she dreamed that she saw a golden ladder reaching to heaven, but on both sides of the ladder were sharp swords, spears, and daggers. Only one watchful person at a time could safely climb up without tearing flesh. At the foot of the ladder lay a huge serpent to frighten away any who might try to mount.

Saturus climbed up first. When he reached the top, he cautioned his sister, "Perpetua I await thee, but see that the serpent bite thee not." She answered, "It shall not hurt me, in the name of Jesus Christ." Perpetua then stepped on the serpent's head, reached the top safely, and was welcomed and fed by a tall white-haired shepherd surrounded by thousands of figures dressed in white garments.

"Welcome child," greeted the shepherd as he gave her a sweet curd of milk to eat. The angels chanted, "Amen." Upon awakening, Perpetua related her dream to Saturus who interpreted it as a sign that they were destined to suffer and would soon leave this world.[5]

Shortly before they were to be cross-examined, Perpetua's father again visited her and pleaded:

> Daughter, pity my white hairs! Pity your father if I am worthy to be called father by you, if I have brought you to this your prime of life, if I have preferred you to your brothers. Make me not a reproach to men! . . . look upon your son who cannot live after you are gone. Lay aside your pride, do not ruin us all, for none of us will ever speak freely again if anything happens to you.[6]

He kissed her hands, knelt at her feet and addressed her as "lady," not "daughter." Perpetua grieved for her father, admitting, ". . . he alone of all my kindred would not have joy at my martyrdom."

Perpetua tried in vain to comfort her father. "It shall happen as God shall choose, for assuredly we lie not in our own power but in the power of God."[7] Her words disturbed her father greatly, and he departed in deep sorrow.

While in prison Secundulus, one of the catechumens, died, or was killed. The other five were summoned to the market place forum for a public examination before Procurator Hilarian. A large crowd had gathered to witness the event. The first ones to be examined professed their Christian faith.

Perpetua's father again appeared, this time carrying her infant son. As he thrust the child toward her, he implored, "Have pity on your child." Hilarian also entreated her, "Spare your father's white hairs: spare the tender years of your child. Offer a sacrifice for the prosperity of the emperors."

When Perpetua refused, Hilarian asked,

"Are you a Christian?" She replied, "I am." When her father again approached her, Hilarian ordered that he be struck with a rod and driven away. Perpetua mourned for her aged father but remained firm in her resolve.[8]

Hilarian then commanded that Saturninus, Revocatus, and Saturus be beaten, and Perpetua and Felicity be struck. All five were then condemned to be thrown to the wild beasts at the garrison games on Caesar Geta's festival. The Christians returned to prison rejoicing that they would be allowed to sacrifice their lives to God.

Perpetua sent for her child, then in her father's care, but he refused her request.

Because it was illegal to execute pregnant women, Felicity prayed that she would deliver her baby early so she could join her companions in the arena. Three days before the festival, she gave birth prematurely to a baby girl. When the jailers heard her cries of pain as she delivered the child, they taunted her asking how she could possibly face the worse torture of the wild beasts.

She answered, as was typical of the martyrs of the day, "I myself now suffer that which I suffer, but there another shall be in me who shall suffer for me, because I am to suffer for him."[9] Felicity's newborn daughter was adopted by a sister.

While in prison Perpetua had another vision. She saw in purgatory her brother, Dinocrates, who had died a horrible death from cancer at the age of seven. When she interceded for him, he appeared in heaven, happy and cured of his disease. Upon awakening, she knew her deceased brother was no longer suffering.

Again her father visited her, this time demented with grief. Perpetua, although filled with compassion for her elderly father, could do nothing to ease his burden.

The day before the games Perpetua had her final vision. She saw herself led to the arena to fight to the death an "ill-favoured Egyptian." In preparation for the duel, Perpetua, then turned into a man, was stripped and rubbed with oil by the attendants. The Egyptian rolled in the dust.

Perpetua then saw a "wonderfully tall" man rising above the amphitheater carrying a green bough laden with golden apples. He announced to the spectators, "This Egyptian, if he overcome her, shall kill her with a sword, and if she overcome him, she shall receive this bough." Perpetua described the fight in graphic detail:

> And we approached each other and began to use our fists. My opponent tried to catch hold of my

feet, but I kept on striking his face with my heels; and I was lifted up into the air and began to strike him as would one who no longer trod the earth. But when I saw that the fight lagged, I joined my hands, linking my fingers. And I caught hold of his head and he fell on his face; and I trod on his head. And the people shouted, and my supporters sang psalms. And I came forward to the trainer and received the bough; and kissing me, he said, 'Peace be with thee, daughter.' And I began in triumph to go towards the Gate of Life.[10]

When Perpetua awoke, she said, ". . . I saw that I should not fight with beasts but with the Devil; but I knew the victory to be mine." Then she added her final words, "I have written this up to the day before the games. Of what was done in the games themselves, let him write who will."[11]

Saturus also had a vision which he recorded at the end of Perpetua's portion of the diary. He saw Perpetua and himself in heaven surrounded by angels and martyrs. They were welcomed, fed, and honored by those martyrs who had gone before. Joyfully, Saturus awoke. The rest of The Passion is chronicled by another writer, perhaps Tertullian, who appeared to have witnessed the event.

The Christians Must Suffer.

The commanding officer of the prison had heard rumors that the Christians planned to escape by some tricks of magic. To thwart any such attempts, he imposed unusual severity on the prisoners.

Perpetua protested saying, "Why do you not at least suffer us to refresh ourselves, 'the most noble' among the condemned, belonging as we do to Caesar and chosen to fight on his birthday? Or is it not to your credit that we should appear thereon in better trim?"[12] The officer, taken aback by Perpetua's boldness, gave orders allowing the prisoners to "refresh themselves" and visit. It was rumored that even the governor of the prison had become a believer.

The day before the games the five martyrs were brought before the public to eat their last meal or the "free feast." The martyrs called it their "agape" or "love feast." The curious people who crowded around them marvelled at their courage and happiness. Many were said to have been converted.

When the final day arrived, the five left prison and walked joyfully to the amphitheater assured that they were on their way to heaven. The three men marched first, followed by the two women. Perpetua "went along with shining countenance and calm step, as the beloved of God . . . putting down everyone's stare by her own intense gaze."[13]

Before entering the arena, the guards ordered the men to don the robes of the pagan priest Saturn, the women to wear the garments of the priestess Ceres. Perpetua refused so forcefully that the guards withdrew their demands. She then broke into a song of triumph. As the five passed Hilarian's box, they shouted the wrath of God down upon the Procurator and the bystanders. The enraged crowd called for the prisoners to be scourged by the gladiators. As the Christians received the lashes, they thanked God for the opportunity to suffer as their Lord had.

Saturninus had hoped to be killed by several different beasts to attain a greater heavenly reward. His wish was granted when he and Revocatus were first attacked by a leopard, then killed by a bear.

Saturus faced a wild boar, but the animal turned, attacked, and killed its keeper instead. Saturus was then bound and offered to a bear, but that animal refused to come out of its den. The third animal, a leopard, attacked and killed Saturus after he predicted, "See, I go forth yonder, and with one bite from the leopard, all will be over."[14]

After being stripped and covered with nets, Perpetua and Felicity were led into the arena to face a mad cow. When the crowd protested their nakedness, they were given loose robes to wear.

Perpetua was the first to be thrown to the ground. She gathered her blood-stained garment around her and retied her dishevelled hair, as loose hair was considered a sign of mourning. Meanwhile the cow had attacked Felicity. Perpetua ran to help the slave girl, and together the wounded women stood waiting for another onslaught from the mad animal.

For a time the crowd was appeased, and the two women were led out the "Porta Sanavivarian," or the "Gate of Life," reserved for victorious gladiators. At the opposite end of the arena was the "Porta Libitinesis," or the "Gate of Death," for the bodies of the slain. Perpetua appeared to have been in a trance and unaware of what had happened to her in the arena until she saw her bloody mutilated robe. The Christians who spoke to her at the gate believed she was in ecstasy as she faced the wild animal.

But the fickle crowd again clamored to see

the two Christian women suffer. To appease them, the guards again led Perpetua and Felicity into the arena to be executed by the gladiators. The two women embraced and exchanged the kiss of peace. When the executioner's first attempt to kill Perpetua failed, she cried out in pain and guided his second stroke to her throat.

God Has Made You Free.

It is not known when the five martyrs and Secundulus were buried in the Confessio of the Basilica Maiorum at Carthage. The remains were later removed to escape destruction by the pagans who desecrated Christian cemeteries and churches. The bodies were never found, but in 1907 Father Delattre in excavating the site of the Basilica, uncovered a memorial stone which appeared to have marked their graves. The inscription on the ancient tombstone in fourth century characters read: "Here are the martyrs Saturus, Saturninus, Revocatus, Secundulus, Felicity and Perpetua, who suffered on the Nomes of March."[15] In the fourth century they were named martyrs of the Roman Church. Perpetua's feast day is observed on March 7, the day of her death.

In the years that followed, persecution of Christians abated for a time, and the edict of Septimius Severus was not strictly enforced. Conversions to Christianity increased, especially among the aristocracy. In succeeding years the Christians were largely at the mercy and whims of pagan rulers.

It is believed that Perpetua and her companions were Montanist Christians. Montanism, a second century schism, began in Phrygia in Asia Minor under the leadership of the prophet Montanus. He was assisted by two prominent women, Maximilla and Priscilla. The rapidly growing charismatic movement, first known as the "New Prophecy," was soon denounced not only by the pagan rulers, but also by the newly-emerging orthodox church in Rome. The early ecclesiastics, fearing any schism that sought to fragment and weaken the church in its infancy, regarded the Montanists as a threat.

The Montanists placed their emphasis on divine inspiration and direct communication with the Spirit of God. Martyrdom was welcomed. Women were allowed to be full participants, often assuming leadership roles. But despite the support of the great Tertullian, Montanism died in the third century except in isolated areas of Phrygia where it continued until the seventh century.

For women professing Montanism, martyrdom was regarded as the ultimate act of heroism and faith. They could demonstrate their resistance to the power of the state which was the embodiment of evil. By suffering, they could identify with the agonies of Jesus, and by rejecting their female roles as daughters, wives, and mothers, they could overcome the stigma of female weakness. Perpetua appeared to be of this persuasion.

For Perpetua and Felicity, the sacrifice in the arena removed all social disparity—they were no longer mistress and slave, but sisters empowered by Jesus Christ. Perpetua spoke authoritatively to the prison guards and refused to succumb to the threats of Hilarian and the pleas of her father. She was the leader of the five martyrs and the one who could speak directly to the Lord and interpret visions. She was fearless in life and death.

A few years after the slaying of the martyrs, Tertullian wrote of Perpetua and her companions, "O most brave and blessed martyrs, you have gone out of prison rather than into one. Your dungeon is full of darkness, but you yourselves are light. Your dungeon has bonds, but God has made you free."[16]

Notes

1   Roland Bainton, *The Horizon History of Christianity* (New York: American Heritage Publishing Co., 1964), p. 66.

2   Anne Fremantle, *A Treasury of Early Christianity* (New York: The New American Library of World Literature, 1953), p. 216.

3   *Butler's Lives of the Saints*, vol. I, (New York: P. J. Kenedy & Sons, 1962), p. 493.

4   Ibid., p. 494.

5   W. H. Shewring, *The Passion of SS. Perpetua and Felicity* (London: Sheed & Ward, 1931), pp. 25-26. Includes complete account of Perpetua's vision.

6   *Butler's Lives of the Saints*, p. 494.

7   Ibid.

8   Ibid., p. 495.

9   Shewring, p. 36.

10 *Butler's Lives of Saints*, p. 496.

11 Ibid.

12 Fremantle, p. 194.

13 Elaine C. Huber, *Women and the Authority of Inspiration* (Lanham, Maryland: University Press of America, Inc., 1985), p. 53.

14 *Butler's Lives of the Saints*, p. 497.

15 Shewring, p. xviii.

16 Edith Deen, *Great Women of the Christian Faith* (New York: Harper & Row, 1959), p. 7.

Chapter 2

Catherine of Siena
(1347 - 1380)

ITALIAN MYSTIC AND SAINT WHO WORKED TIRELESSLY TO CLEANSE
AND UNIFY THE ROMAN CATHOLIC CHURCH IN WESTERN EUROPE.

BLACK DEATH swept through Italy in 1347, the same year that Catherine of Siena was born. Transported to Europe from the Middle East on rat-infested merchant ships, the devastating bubonic plague spread rapidly along trade routes to Italy, Spain, France, England, and Germany, and reached the northern countries and Russia three years later. There was no cure for the contagion that struck down people within three or four days. It was named "Black Death" because of the black hemorrhaging spots which appeared on the skin of the victims. Exact mortality figures were not recorded, but it was estimated that one-third of the population of Europe died of the plague in the three years from 1347 to 1350. Florence, Italy, a city of 100,000 inhabitants, was said to have lost two-thirds of its population in 1348.

The plague was just beginning to infest southern Europe when Catherine and her twin sister Giovanna were born in Siena on Annunciation Day, March 25, 1347. They were the twenty-third and twenty-fourth children of Giacomo and Lapa Benincasa. Lapa, unable to nurse both babies, turned Giovanna over to a wet-nurse. The twin lived just a few days, but Catherine survived and became a precious addition to the large Benincasa family. Another daughter born a few years later was also christened Giovanna, but she lived just a few years. Thirteen children reached adulthood.

Giacomo, aided by his three elder sons and four journeymen and apprentices, managed a successful trade as a dyer of leathers, considered at that time to be an occupation of the lower classes. He conducted his business on the first floor of their dwelling, while the family lived in the crowded, but comfortable, upstairs rooms. Lapa, his domineering, strong-willed wife ruled over the large family, which at times included remote relatives and an increasing number of grandchildren.

Though Catherine was not a pretty child, being slight and pale, her delicate features, luminous dark eyes, lustrous golden hair, and cheerful disposition won much attention from neighbors. Early she showed a precocious nature, learning the "Ave Maria" as soon as she could talk. By five she had taught herself the "Angelus" which she repeated constantly.

One evening when Catherine was about seven years old as she and her older brother, Stefano, were on their way home from a visit to Bonaventura, their older married sister, Catherine halted and gazed up the hill at the massive gray stone walls of Siena's Abbey Church of San Dominic. Over the roof of the church she saw her first vision, so resplendent it remained etched in her memory forever. There on a throne, adorned in royal robes and wearing a crown, sat Jesus surrounded by Peter, Paul, and John. As the Lord smiled and made a sign of the cross, Catherine was overcome with wonder and joy. Stefano, who had bounded on ahead down the brick street, called to her. When he heard no answer, he ran back to arouse the hypnotized girl from her trance. Catherine wept bitterly when the spell was broken, and the heavenly vision, seen only by her, had vanished. Thus began Catherine's unusual encounters with messages from God, which from that point on, directed her life to Christian sacrifice, penitence, prayer, and service.

After the vision at St. Dominic's Church, Catherine vowed to give herself to the Lord. She prayed to the Virgin Mary, "I love Him with all my soul, I promise Him and you that I will never take another bridegroom."[1] From then on Catherine practiced self-flagellation and spent long hours in solitude, prayer, and meditation. In the fourteenth century it was not uncommon for young emotional girls to turn to asceticism.

For a time her family was unaware that she was eating less food and praying for hours at night. She found secret hiding places where she and her friends scourged themselves with rope. Groups of youths, eager to imitate her and charmed by her good nature, gathered about her. But Catherine, searching for solitude, spent long hours in the parish church praying and meditating. Whenever possible she retreated to the family farm a short distance from Siena to contemplate the natural and supernatural world without distraction.

Italian custom dictated that when a girl reached adolescence, she was of marrying age and could no longer go about in public unless accompanied by an older woman. When Catherine turned twelve, Lapa decided that it was time to find her youngest daughter a suitable husband. She enlisted the help of Bonaventura, and together they tried to impress on Catherine the importance of enhancing her physical appearance in every way possible to attract a desirable suitor. But Catherine, resolving to keep her earlier vow of chastity and virginity, refused to consider marriage. The entire family was indignant. In desperation Giacomo and Lapa sent for Tommaso, a Dominican, who earlier had lived with the Benincasa family after his own parents died of the plague. Giacomo and Lapa hoped that Tommaso could counsel Catherine and change her mind. But when the Dominican heard Catherine relate her visions and vows, he sympathized with her and advised her, perhaps in jest, to cut off her beautiful hair to make herself less attractive. No suitors would then be interested, and her family would abandon the idea of marriage.

Catherine, acting upon Tommaso's advice, chopped off her flowing locks. The shocked family descended upon her with fury. They abused and punished her and made her share a room with her unmarried brother, Stefano, thus depriving her of a place for private communion with God. Lapa dismissed the housemaid and assigned to Catherine the menial duties of washing, cooking, and scrubbing for the large family. Catherine accepted her tasks cheerfully and humbly.

One day Giacomo saw a white dove resting on Catherine's head as she prayed, leading him to believe that his daughter was no ordinary girl. He insisted, against Lapa's objections, that Catherine be given a small room of her own and never be forced to marry.

Catherine gratefully moved into a tiny cell-like room, meagerly furnished with a chest, a bed of boards, and a wooden pillow. Continuing her routine of austerity and self-denial, she allowed herself little food or sleep.

I Here Betroth You as My Bride.

In Siena many devout women, widows in particular, had joined the Sisters of Penitence of St. Dominic's Third Order. They wore special habits—white veils with white woolen dresses covered by black capes. They were affectionately known as the "Mantellata," or the Wearers of Cloaks, and were highly regarded in the community. Although most of them continued to live with their families, they dedicated themselves to lives of abstinence, prayer, and sanctity.

For years Catherine had longed to become one of them. One night she dreamed that St. Dominic, holding a beautiful white lily, showed her a robe worn by the Sisters and said to her, "Beloved daughter, take courage. Be afraid of nothing, for you shall surely be clothed in this robe which you desire."[2]

When Catherine announced her wishes to join the Order to her family, they disapproved. But soon her father, who was not surprised at her decision, promised Catherine that because it was the will of God they would no longer oppose her. He then commanded his family, "From now on no one is to tease or annoy my beloved daughter or dare to lay obstacles in her way. Let her serve her Bridegroom in complete freedom and pray earnestly for us. We could never have obtained so honourable a marriage for her, so let us not complain that instead of a mortal man we have been given the immortal God-made-man."[3]

Catherine humbly thanked her father and her Lord, and confined herself to her room for more solitude, prayer, and self-discipline. In imitation of St. Dominic she scourged herself with an iron chain three times a day, one time for her own failings, once for the sins of the world, and a third time for souls in purgatory. When Lapa saw the bleeding wounds, she cried bitterly, "Oh my daughter, my daughter, you will die, you are killing yourself. Oh, who has taken my child from me?"[4]

Lapa soon realized she couldn't deter her strong-willed daughter from castigating herself, or denying herself food and sleep, so she devised another plan. Thirty miles south of Siena was a popular resort, Vignone, where hot sulphur springs were reputed to restore health and vitality. Lapa persuaded Catherine to accompany her there. After a week they returned, Lapa seething with anger and Catherine swathed in bandages. While in the pool, Catherine had gone, intentionally or accidently, to the pipes where the scalding sulphur water poured in. While her body was being painfully burned, she imagined she was experiencing the tortures of purgatory or hell.

After they returned home, Catherine continued to suffer from fever which soon proved to be smallpox. To appease her seriously-ill daughter, remorseful Lapa promised to go to the Mother Superior of the Sisters of Penitence to request that Catherine be accepted into the Order. The Reverend Mother advised Lapa that a girl of sixteen was much too young. Catherine rejected that argument and sent Lapa back a second time, this visit bringing positive results. Before being allowed to join the Order and wear the white habit and black cloak of the Sisters, Catherine was questioned and tested at length.

For three years Catherine withdrew from her family to her tiny room, leaving the house only to go to church for Mass and Confession. During this time it was said she taught herself to read, considered by some a miracle. Visions appeared more frequently as she battled with temptation, doubt, and sin. Some conversations with her Lord were spiritual, some intellectual, some personal, some ecstatic. Catherine absorbed them all, and at the end of her life recorded the experiences in her book, *The Dialogue*.

When she was about twenty, the Lord appeared to her with a beautiful gold ring inset with pearls and a diamond. As he slipped it on her finger, he said, "I here betroth you as My bride in perfect faith, which for all time shall keep you pure and rejoicing. My daughter, from now on you must undertake without protest all the works which I come to demand of you, for armed with the power of faith you shall triumphantly overcome all your opponents."[5] The vision vanished, but the engagement ring, invisible to everyone else, remained there for Catherine to see.

As a young woman just beginning to experience a consecrated life, Catherine never dreamed what works the Lord would eventually demand of her. Nor could she fathom what sacrifices, service, and dedication would be required of her in later years, nor comprehended what power and authority she would command in the political and religious worlds before her death at the early age of thirty-three.

Begin to Serve the World.

During Catherine's lifetime Italy had not yet become a nation. Scores of political, military, family, and religious divisions existed, all of them in hostile competition for recognition, power, and territory. Mercenary armies, hired by princes and popes, plundered cities and towns. The economy was in shambles.

In spite of military and church upheavals, the city of Siena, located in Tuscany in north central Italy, had attained the reputation as a wealthy cultural and spiritual center. Its beautiful cathedrals housed significant religious paintings and statuary, and the city boasted an outstanding school of medicine. The province of Siena had a democratic, but volatile, form of government as did other northern Italian provinces. Pisa and Lucca were independent; Florence, one of the great republics of the Middle Ages, flourished as a center of art and culture; Genoa and Venice, both great independent sea powers, were hostile rivals. Naples, to the south, was ruled by a king, while most of the other Italian provinces were under the Emperors of the Holy Roman Empire who kept residence in central Europe. Pope Clement V had deserted Rome in 1305 to set up papal headquarters in Avignon, France, much to the displeasure of the Italian Catholics. This was the convoluted world Catherine was soon to confront.

Shortly after her mystical betrothal, Catherine had another vision. This time the Lord commanded her to join her family at the table and begin her service to the world, a difficult task for one who had spent the last few years isolated from society. Obediently Catherine rejoined the family circle, delighting them with her loving presence and her willingness to do menial tasks about the house. She roamed the streets and gave away her father's money to the poor. She nursed the sick at the Hospital of Santa Maria della Scala, where she worked untiringly with physicians and priests. Her contacts increased as visitors learned of her and sought her out for various reasons—admiration, curiosity, or skepticism.

Catherine's ecstasies continued, mainly at the communion table where for hours she was oblivious to outside distractions, her body remaining rigid as a statue. At times the church fathers considered her a nuisance and carried her unconscious body to the street outside the church door, where occasionally she was kicked by passers-by.

As the ecstasies continued to confound observers, so did the word of Catherine's miracles. She was said to have given the family's best wine to the poor, yet the home wine barrel never emptied; she cured the ill and cast out demons from possessed souls; she manifested superhuman strength as she worked with the sick day and night without food or rest.

Soon people, including her confessor Tommaso, and other brothers of the Order, began to converse with her, but more often to learn from her. They would come to her little room at night, and forgetting the time, would continue their discussions until dawn. Catherine's critics, ever watchful and ready to condemn her, accused her of being an agent of the devil who conducted orgies with men and women together through the night. Some scoffers confronted her openly, taunting her with jeers and ridicule. Catherine turned them away or converted them with her sincerity, patience, and love.

At Santa Maria della Scalla, Catherine was given a small room in the cellar so she could attend to patients during the night. She willingly nursed the sick that others refused to touch—those with cancer and leprosy. When some ungrateful patients spread rumors discrediting her work and morals, she was summoned before the prioress to defend herself against charges of sin and immorality, Catherine could only answer, "In truth . . . by the Grace of Jesus Christ I am a maiden [virgin]."[6]

Alone in her room Catherine wept bitter tears and prayed fervently. Again Jesus appeared to her, offering her two crowns, one of thorns, the other of precious jewels. She could choose to wear one while she lived, the other she would wear for eternity. Catherine clutched the crown of thorns, placed it hard upon her head. Thereafter she felt sharp thorns press into her flesh, a constant reminder of the difficult tasks facing her on earth.

A Saint, or an Agent of the Devil?

Siena, although in name a republic, was in constant turmoil as political power shifted between various factions representing the citizens, the nobles, the families, or the church. Whoever was in control ruled with an iron fist. Anarchy and violence prevailed. Though independent, Siena still owed allegiance to the Emperor of the Holy Roman Empire, but those opposing the Emperor gave their loyalty to his arch-rival, the Pope. Bands of mercenaries fought bloody wars without conviction or conscience for whatever group could pay them the most money.

In August 1368 shortly before the outbreak of a rebellion against the controlling citizens' party, Catherine's father died. Fortunately, he did not witness the massacre and imprisonment of members of his own party, the one actively supported by his sons.

When Giacomo was on his deathbed, Catherine pleaded with God to restore his health, but she finally realized that his life was finished. She then prayed that his soul not be condemned to the flames of purgatory, asking that she be allowed to suffer for him. Before Giacomo died, Catherine knew that her wish had been granted, because from then on she felt a severe pain in her side, a sign to her that her father had been spared. Giacomo's eldest son became the head of the house, but the family's political affiliation put them in disfavor, and the business suffered.

The anxiety of her husband's death was too much for the aging Lapa, who, fearing that she too would die, begged Catherine to pray for her recovery. After entreaties failed, life seemed to slip away. When Lapa refused Confession and the Last Sacraments, Catherine prayed for her soul and threatened the Lord, "I will not go alive from Your feet until You give me my mother back."[7] The grieving women who had gathered at the bedside heard Lapa gasp for breath and saw her make a slight movement. In a few days she had recovered. Years later Lapa moved from the house in Siena to a little place near Porta Romana. She died at age eighty-nine, outliving most of her children and grandchildren.

When Catherine was in her early twenties, she experienced more visions and ecstasies, many of them witnessed by others. As the trances increased in number and duration, Catherine's physical strength diminished to the point where she lay unconscious for three days. Friends knelt around her bedside grieving over her imminent death. A young friar in the last stages of tuberculosis begged to see her. When he touched her seemingly dead body, his bleeding miraculously stopped. Soon Catherine opened her eyes and wept as though disappointed to be returning to this world. She murmured, "I have seen the hidden things of God."[8]

Another time while meditating, Catherine asked God to take away her selfish sinful heart. The Lord appeared to her in a vision, opened her left side, removed her heart, and carried it away. A day or two later while Catherine knelt at Mass, he appeared to her again, this time returning his own heart to her body. It was said that from that day on Catherine bore a scar under her left breast.

As Catherine's reputation spread and her followers grew in numbers, so did the skeptics and accusers, including at times the sisters and brothers of the Order. Some saw her as an agent of the devil, a demented fanatic, a dangerous meddler in religious and political affairs. But her fame as a saint and spiritual adviser extended to a wide assortment of believers—politicians, noblemen, artists, poets, and priests sought her counsel. Although many were older than she, they affectionately called her "dolce mamma." Her ability as a clairvoyant astounded

them when she could discern what they had said, done, or thought when out of her presence.

Catherine's reputation reached far beyond Siena. To correspond with persons of authority, she dictated her letters to men and women secretaries because she herself had never learned to write. It was said that she could compose two or three letters at a time without losing her train of thought. Her messages were always simple and direct, filled with religious fervor and sage advice.

But there continued to be those who would not accept this woman from Siena. It seemed blasphemous for one so uneducated and ordinary to claim to talk directly to God. Two learned theologians from nearby monasteries, intending to expose her as a fraud, unleashed on her a barrage of profound theological questions. Catherine's replies were so guileless and wise, the men were speechless. But Catherine did not stop there—she accused them of making a mockery of their vows of poverty as they lived in comfort and ease. Both men, in shame, divested themselves of their belongings and gave them to the poor. One of the men later became Catherine's follower and friend.

The Church Has Grown Corrupt and Slothful.

The worsening hostility between the papacy and the tyrannical lords led to bitter conflict over control of the government and land. The entire region was embroiled in hostile quarrels and warfare. The Florentines openly defied the authority of the Pope.

As Catherine grieved over the condition of the church, how it had grown corrupt and slothful, she began to take an active role in trying to correct its abuses and bring it back to its original purpose. She sent letters to government officials, church prelates, cardinals, and the Pope, begging them to establish peace. She often chastised them for their sins and wrongdoings. Pope Gregory XI in Avignon, to whom Catherine had sent a letter, had heard rumors of this woman from Siena reputed to be a saint endowed with extraordinary spiritual powers. He wanted her investigated.

The Dominicans were meeting in Florence in June 1374 and the Pope summoned Catherine to appear before them for questioning. Elias, the Master General, was ordered to guide the Council to a decision concerning this presumptuous woman who had the audacity to correspond with prominent politicians and advise even the Pope, most inappropriate acts for a female.

In the band of six that traveled with Catherine to Florence were two Sienese Dominicans who were going to attend the Council, one of them being Tommaso, Catherine's foster brother and confessor. Among the three women in the group, all members of the Order, was Catherine's sister-in-law, Lisa, who wanted to go to Florence to see her husband, Bartolommeo Benincasa, who had fled to Florence with his brother, Stefano, during the Siena uprising.

Although the travelers had to pass through the war-ravaged districts of Tuscany, the fifty-mile trip in late May was generally pleasant. When they tired of walking, they took turns riding the donkeys. Along the way they stopped at convents and monasteries for food and lodging. When they arrived in Florence, Catherine and Lisa were reunited with Bartolommeo and Stefano. Catherine quickly made friends with other Florentines, among them a wealthy member of the government, who offered her luxuriant quarters.

The Council had assembled early to learn something of Catherine before the inquisition. Some protested that they were wasting their time on such an unimportant matter, but Master General Elias was determined to secure as much information as possible about this sister from Siena. He conferred with the two Dominicans who had accompanied her, and read the documents that Tommaso had recorded of Catherine's past activities. Elias also sought the advice of Raymond of Capua, a respected scholar, writer, and theologian, who had heard of Catherine, but had never met her. Raymond welcomed the opportunity to meet Catherine and judge for himself whether or not she was a saint. After talking with her, he was convinced of Catherine's sincerity and integrity. Elias ordered a monk, a specialist in sorcery and witchcraft, to interrogate Catherine. After questioning her, the monk reported that she was no witch and was possibly a saint.

Elias convened the Council in the magnificent chapter house of Santa Maria Novella, where the 500 members were seated in rows on either side, the Master General on a throne at the far end. Catherine entered, a slight solitary figure in her black and white habit. One council member stood and fired one accusation after another at her. Another member rose to defend her. Catherine, deep in prayer, stood before

them erect and calm, oblivious to the heated debate surrounding her. Then followed the inquisition. Any council member could ask her the most penetrating, difficult, or humiliating questions. Catherine answered each question with composed directness, astounding the entire Council with her wisdom. When she was dismissed, both the prosecution and defense asked to be excused from their summations, as each Council member had heard for himself all the evidence. Elias then called on Raymond of Capua, who reported that he found the accusations against Catherine to be false. After judging her not guilty, the Council adjourned.

Because she had aroused many enemies, Elias, in concern for her safety, assigned Raymond to be her confessor and spiritual adviser when he assumed his new position as lector at St. Dominic's Church in Siena. Throughout their association Raymond kept detailed notes, and after Catherine's death compiled an extensive biography that became the most important source of information on her life.

In late June the travelers set out on the journey back to Siena. They were accompanied by Raymond, who was taking up his new post at St. Dominic's, and Catherine's brother Bartolommeo. As they neared Siena, the air hung heavy with the stench of decay and death. A cart loaded with dead bodies was on its way to a burial ground outside the city. The Black Plague had struck the city again.

Catherine and her women companions went immediately to the Misericordia Hospital to care for the great numbers of victims of the pestilence. Catherine also nursed members of her own family, many of whom died. Bartolommeo was struck down, as was an older sister and eight nieces and nephews. Later it was learned that brother Stefano had died in Rome and another brother in Florence.

Catherine worked with little rest, occasionally being summoned to the bedside of some important citizen who pleaded to be restored to health through her intercession. Raymond observed and recorded the so-called miracles. After he himself fell ill and manifested all the signs of the plague, Raymond attributed his recovery to Catherine's prayers.

When summer ended, the plague had abated, but the town and church had been decimated. It was reported that one-third of Siena's citizens had died. To add to the suffering, food was scarce and famine followed. By this time Catherine's endurance had been expended, and she collapsed from exhaustion. She prayed to be removed from this world, but the Virgin Mary appeared to her in a vision saying that she must live to accomplish the work yet to be done.

I Now Bear His Stigmata on My Body.

In the autumn of 1374 Catherine went on a pilgrimage to Montepulciano, a Dominican monastery some forty miles south of Siena, to recover her health and pay homage to St. Agnes, who had died in 1317. When Catherine and her entourage arrived at Montepulciano, they went immediately to the bier. As Catherine knelt to kiss the feet of St. Agnes, one foot from the lifeless body appeared to raise up to meet Catherine's lips. The next day the nuns who had witnessed the incident reported it to Raymond. "Another miracle," they said. Raymond had no reason to dispute it and recorded it as such in his biography.

When Catherine reluctantly left the peace of Montepulciano to return to Siena, she was drawn immediately into the religious and political upheavals of the day. Pope Gregory XI sent an emissary from Avignon requesting her to support his plans for a holy crusade against Islam. The crusade would unite the feuding Tuscan princes against a common enemy, the Muslim forces which were plundering and enslaving Christians and threatening to destroy the holy places where Jesus and the disciples had once lived. Catherine, usually an advocate of peace, was convinced of the value of a crusade for religious and political reasons. She fired off a stream of letters to powerful government, military, and church leaders throughout the region. She even wrote to King Charles V of France urging him to give up his war against England and join the crusade. She advised Pope Gregory to end corruption within the church, to leave France, and return the Papacy to Rome where it rightly belonged.

In February 1375 Catherine accepted an invitation to go to Pisa to help unify that city behind the Pope. Accompanying her were Raymond and two other clerics assigned by the Pope to hear confessions and give absolution to her many converts. Catherine was particularly pleased that her mother, Lapa, had become a Mantellata and was among the sisters who accompanied her on the week-long journey.

At Pisa they received a royal welcome from the Governor, the Archbishop, and other dignitaries. Cheering crowds lined the streets hoping to get a glimpse of the woman from Siena. As in Florence, the travelers were given lodging at the home of an influential family, the Buonconti brothers, who had heard of Catherine and wanted to meet her. The Buoncontis introduced Catherine to many of the elite to whom she preached unity and allegiance to the Pope. Some listened and agreed with her, others favored an alliance with Bernabo Visconti, the ruthless Duke of Milan, who was seeking to woo the Tuscan republics away from the Pope.

Near the Buonconti home was the small church of St. Christina where Catherine chose to worship. On April 1, the fourth Sunday in Lent, Raymond officiated at Mass. After Catherine received communion and prostrated herself, she rose to her knees, lifted her arms upward, and with closed eyes and radiant face remained frozen in that posture for a long time. Suddenly she collapsed on the floor as though struck down. When she regained consciousness, she reported to Raymond, "Father, know that by the grace of Our Lord Jesus I now bear His stigmata on my body."[9]

Catherine related how she had seen five streams of blood come toward her from the Lord on the cross. The blood turned to beams of light which entered her body at five points. No visible scars showed during her lifetime, but witnesses testified that they saw the marks on her body after her death. From that date forward, artists always painted her with the scars.

After receiving the stigmata, Catherine was gravely ill for a week, and her followers feared for her life. But on Easter Sunday, she arose and walked to St. Christina's Church for Mass. Catherine spent the rest of her time in Pisa advocating peace.

The political situation steadily worsened with all the Tuscan republics taking sides for or against the Pope, who stubbornly continued to keep his headquarters in Avignon. To make matters worse, Pope Gregory XI and the corrupt Duke of Milan had joined forces to control the city-states by force. Sir John Hawkwood was camped with his mercenaries near Pisa awaiting offers from the highest bidder for his services. Raymond visited Hawkwood with a request to defend Pisa, an offer Hawkwood at first rejected because he had been offered more gilders to protect the Florentines. Raymond then handed him a letter from Catherine, a plea for him to give up his sinful ventures and join the Christian crusade against the Muslims. Hawkwood, to the surprise of the priest, consented to defend

Pisa and promised to go on the crusade when plans were definite. To show his sincerity Hawkwood took communion, but his promises were soon forgotten, and the crusade never materialized.

Politics, Piety, and Peace.

The years 1374 and 1375 marked Catherine's official entry into public affairs. After her visits to Florence and Pisa, she focused her attention on four public issues: the need for a unified crusade against the Muslims; the reform of the church and the clergy; the return of the Papacy to Rome; and the end of the bitter conflict between the Tuscan republics and the Pope. To achieve her goals, she corresponded frequently with religious and political leaders.

When Catherine had concluded her work in Pisa, she returned to Siena to prove to her critics that she had not abandoned her own city. After a few days of quiet, she was visited by a wealthy man who offered her a valuable parcel of land near Siena where stood Belcaro, an old, but solid, castle. Catherine, at first reluctant to accept such an extravagant gift, changed her mind when Raymond suggested that this would be an ideal location for a convent for the Dominican nuns. Catherine immediately began to plan for its development.

But an urgent matter interrupted the opening of the convent. A young man, a newcomer to Siena, was accused of being a spy and was thrown into the dungeon. Here he raged violently, professing in vain his innocence. Catherine's attempt to change the judge's verdict failed, but she received permission to visit the prisoner and prepare his soul for death. She fearlessly entered the dungeon against the advice of the guard, calmed the young man with her loving and compassionate words, and offered to arrange communion for him. On his last day she accompanied him to the block, heard his final words of faith, and caught his head in her hands after the execution.

Catherine's respite in Siena lasted but a few months. She received another order from Pope Gregory, this time to go to Lucca, a small republic a short distance north of Pisa, to persuade them not to join the anti-papal league. When in Lucca, Catherine wrote a long letter to Gregory warning him that unless he took a courageous stand against the abuses within the Church and weeded out corruption and evil, the Church would not prevail. She urged him to nominate worthy legates and cardinals who were men of God. Again she cautioned that his refusal to move to Rome would continue to infuriate the Italians. Although the authorities at Lucca promised to remain loyal to the Pope, she knew that when it was advantageous, they would join Florence and the other rebellious republics.

After she left Lucca, Catherine and her company stopped for a short time at Pisa, where she found the city in revolt against the corrupt French ecclesiastics Gregory had sent them. She feared both Lucca and Pisa would soon be lost to the Pope.

The Pope then hired Sir John Hawkwood and his mercenaries to put down the Florentines and other rebels. In response Florence elected a new government, the Eight of War, which ordered that a red flag bearing the word "LIBERTAS" printed in white letters be flown over the city, evidence of their open defiance of the Pope. As violence and terror reigned, more cities and towns joined the anti-papal league.

As Catherine returned to Siena just before Christmas in 1375, her heart sank. There flying over the Siena tower was a red flag bearing the word "LIBERTAS." Her own city had joined the rebels!

The Pope had made numerous mistakes in dealing with the Italians, and he soon made another with the appointment of nine new cardinals, only one being an Italian. Except for one Spaniard, the rest were French, three of them related to the Pope. The Italians were furious.

Early in 1376 Pope Gregory ordered the leaders of the Florentine government to appear before him in Avignon or face censure. Upon learning of this threat, Catherine wrote several letters to the Pope begging for patience and forgiveness toward the rebels. At the same time she wrote the Florentines urging them to ask the Pope's forgiveness and seek reconciliation. The letters were ineffective. The Florentines had suffered indignities and casualties from Hawkwood's mercenaries, and they refused to go to Avignon. In anger the Pope declared Florence under an interdict which excommunicated the government officials, withdrew the sacraments and Christian burial from citizens, and threatened confiscation of personal property. The interdict would be lifted only if the rebels surrendered and sought reconciliation with the Pope through a mediator. Catherine was the logical person to intervene for them.

The woman of Siena was sent to Florence

for the second time. The Florentines had suffered grievously during the interdict and were eager to do whatever was necessary to establish peace with the Pope, at least so they said. They gratefully accepted Catherine's offer to mediate and sent her on her way to Avignon with a pledge to dispatch their official representatives immediately to seal their covenant with the Pope.

In the spring of 1376 Catherine and twenty-three companions left Florence for the long trip on foot and by boat to Avignon in southeastern France. She would finally come face-to-face with the powerful man to whom she had written so many urgent letters. When she arrived in the magnificent city, she was given luxuriant quarters, much too pretentious for her simple tastes.

Within two days she was summoned to appear before the Pope and the official papal body. The slight, frail woman approached the Pope seated on his throne, knelt to kiss his ring, and began to state her mission in her own Tuscan dialect with Raymond by her side as interpreter. After pleading the cause of the Florentines and assuring the Pope of their desire for reconciliation, she accepted Gregory's proposal to act as the intermediary. The French cardinals objected, thinking this too formidable a task for a mere woman, but Gregory insisted that she mediate the dispute.

While she anxiously awaited the arrival of the promised ambassadors from Florence, Catherine was followed wherever she went by a wide assortment of believers, curiosity seekers, critics, and skeptics. Her harsh words condemning the decadence of Avignon's society and the "stench of sin" that pervaded the clergy earned her more enemies.

She aroused further suspicion as she continued her ecstasies at Mass. One young noblewoman, a relative of the Pope, set out to prove that Catherine was a fraud. When Catherine was at the communion rail in one of her trances, the woman drew from her belt a long needle and drove it deep into Catherine's left foot. When Catherine did not move, the woman hastily left the church. After regaining consciousness, Catherine needed assistance walking because of the painful wound.

In Avignon three French prelates who feared her influence with the Pope accosted her. They questioned her right to represent Florence, challenged her ecstasies and miracles, and cross-examined her theology. Catherine's direct and guileless answers astonished them, and they were convinced of her veracity.

In September the Florentine ambassadors finally arrived, but there had been another change of government in Florence, and these men no longer wanted Catherine to mediate for them. As they attempted to confer with the Pope's representatives, negotiations broke down, and in anger the Florentines returned home. Florence continued its defiance of the Pope and attempted to draw Venice and Genoa into the anti-papal league.

Catherine's work in Avignon was finished except to try to persuade the Pope, as she had done numerous times by letter, to go to Rome. This time she was successful. Despite attempts by the Frenchmen to keep him in France, Pope Gregory and his cardinals finally left Avignon for the Vatican. On October 2 he boarded a ship at Marseilles bound for Genoa and Italian soil, marking the end of a seventy-year absence of the Holy See from Rome.

Catherine and her party set out on the long journey home, preferring to go most of the way by foot rather than by sea. When they arrived in Genoa, they rested from the strenuous journey and the press of crowds that had gathered around Catherine at every stop.

While they were in Genoa, the Pope's ship docked after weathering heavy seas for sixteen days. The disgruntled seasick cardinals again urged the Pope to return to Avignon.

One night at the palace room where she lodged, Catherine was awakened by a visitor who demanded to see her. A man wearing a priest's robe entered. When Catherine recognized the huge ring on his finger, she fell on her knees before him. The Pope had come to her in disguise to seek her advice on matters of grave concern to him. No longer in need of an interpreter, Pope Gregory poured out his problems: Genoa had given him a cold reception; Florence, still in open rebellion, might imprison him; Rome, in revolt, might even kill him; and his cardinals had voted to return to Avignon. What should he do? Catherine's exact words were not recorded, but the Pope left with renewed resolve to proceed to Rome despite the dangers.

Catherine continued on her journey home, returning to Siena in early 1377. There she learned that the Pope had arrived safely in Rome and to his surprise had been given an enthusiastic welcome by the Italians.

At Siena Catherine worked to complete her plans for the Dominican convent in the old Belcaro fortress bequeathed to her. One night while in the seclusion of her fortress room, she, who had never been able to write, was said to have penned a prayer to the Blessed Trinity. Another miracle, some claimed.

In October 1377 the Florentine army won an important victory over the Pope's mercenaries. When the clergy at Florence openly defied the interdict imposed on them, the Pope again sought Catherine's help. He ordered her to go again to Florence as his ambassador at a peace conference between five Florentines and three Roman cardinals. Negotiations were about to begin when word arrived that Pope Gregory had died! The cardinals left immediately for Rome to elect a new Pope, and the Florentines returned to their own city. Peace was not yet a reality.

To the displeasure of the Romans, an archbishop from Naples was elected Pope. The new papal head, Urban VI, was an austere, strong-willed, arrogant man, a marked contrast from his predecessor. Urban considered the situation in Florence to be intolerable and demanded compliance on his terms. As a result, civil war broke out in Florence between the Pope's sympathizers and his enemies.

After the aborted peace conference Catherine chose to stay on in Florence, but as fighting, looting, and burning threatened, she retreated for a time to the countryside. She again took up her correspondence, dictating several letters to Pope Urban pleading with him to be patient and forgiving toward the Florentines. Her words may have had some effect on this resolute man, for on July 28, 1378, a peace treaty was signed.

Catherine again returned to Siena where she spent a few days recovering from her travels at the Benincasa farm, her happy childhood sanctuary. She soon moved to a secluded retreat twenty miles from Siena where she could meditate, pray, and prepare herself for a task she had long hoped to accomplish. She summoned three secretaries and ordered them to take down all the words she spoke. For five days without stopping, she dictated her thoughts and convictions. When it was completed, she apologized to Raymond, "Pardon me for writing too much, but my hands and tongue go along with my heart."[10] Catherine called it *The Book* —Raymond renamed it *The Dialogue*. It appears today in many editions and translations and is considered her masterpiece.

The Dialogue, a weighty complex work, was Catherine's conversation with God. In it she made four supplications for mercy: for herself, for the world, for the church, and for individual souls. Existence on earth, she said, was a gift from God. She acclaimed the sanctified life, fearless and unafraid of adversity, always fighting against the sins of the world.

In addition to *The Dialogue*, her prayers and nearly 400 letters were published in other volumes. Although some present-day scholars are hesitant to give much credence to her mystical experiences, they find Catherine's universal message, her inner vision, the manifestation of the Holy Spirit in her life, expressed as it was in the fourteenth century framework, still pertinent today.

Beloved, You Call Me and I Come.

With the book completed, Catherine was ready to obey Pope Urban's urgent order to come to Rome. Catherine had advised him frequently to be temperate and forgiving, but Urban, bent on bringing order, discipline, and cleansing to the church, had alienated the cardinals and church officials with his harsh, merciless demands. Those who had voted to elect him began to regret their choice. Thirteen cardinals left Rome and made a declaration that Urban had been unlawfully elected and was therefore not the real Pope. On September 20, 1378, the dissenting cardinals elected Robert of Geneva, a brother of the prince of Genoa and a member of French royalty, to be the true Pope. Robert took the name of Clement VII and set up headquarters back in Avignon as the counter-Pope. The Great Western Schism had begun.

Before leaving for Rome, Catherine, saddened by the worsening state of affairs, wrote numerous letters to those involved with the breach in the papacy. She urged dissenters to remain loyal to Urban, whom she believed to be the true head of the Church, and she encouraged Urban to persevere. But the schism was of such a serious nature, she felt compelled to take the long journey to Rome to help heal the wounds. This was to be her last trip.

Accompanied by a large family of friends, she set out for Rome. To ease the load, they carried no provisions, so begged for food and alms along the way. Upon arriving in Rome on November 28, 1378, Catherine and her companions settled in lodgings near the Church of Santa Maria Sopra Minerva. Pope Urban, fearful for his life, had left the Vatican to live in a monastery nearby.

To help his cause, Urban arranged for Catherine to address the assembly of cardinals. A far more confident woman than had addressed Pope Gregory in Avignon two years earlier, she told the eminent body that they should not waver in doing God's work. Her message of hope pleased Urban, and he declared, "See, brothers, how guilty we must appear to God because we are without courage. This little woman puts us to shame . . . see how we tremble while she is strong and calm, and see how she consoles us with her words."[11]

Catherine grieved when Urban dispatched her trusted friend and adviser, Raymond of Capua, to King Charles of France to urge him to disavow Clement and the schismatics. As Catherine bade Raymond farewell before boarding his ship, she uttered prophetic words, "Son, go in safety, protected by the holy sign of the cross, but in life you will never see your mother again."[12]

In early 1379 Catherine's mother, Lapa, came to Rome to be with her daughter. Although in weakening health Catherine continued to receive visitors, administer to the needy, and write letters urging support of Urban. Clement, the rival Pope in Avignon, with the support of King Charles, gathered his forces intending to secure military domination of Italian strongholds. But Urban's army rallied and defeated the Clementists at the fortress of St. Angelo outside Rome. Clement withdrew to Naples under the protection of Joanna, the unprincipled Queen of Naples. Catherine wrote a scathing letter to the Queen, chastising her for her immoral life, and warning her of the physical and eternal dangers of supporting the heretics. When Clement's forces were defeated in Naples, Joanna hinted that she intended to support Urban as Pope.

In the spring of 1380 the French finally surrendered to the Romans, and it was safe for Pope Urban to return to the Vatican. He followed Catherine's suggestion to walk barefoot through the streets, a symbol of humility and penitence. Joyful crowds cheered and celebrated the victory. A degree of peace and stability had finally arrived in Rome.

Although only thirty-three years old, Catherine's health was broken, and she was soon too weak to walk to St. Peter's for Mass. As she lay on her hard bed, her body paralyzed and wasted, friends gathered about to hear her final words and prayers. At noon on April 29, 1380, she spoke for the last time. "Beloved, You call me

and I come. . . . Father, into Your hands I commit my spirit."[13] She made the sign of the cross, folded her hands, and as radiance flooded her face, she died in the arms of one of her faithful sisters. Her body lay in state at Santa Maria Sopra Minerva.

Raymond, her close friend and spiritual adviser, had kept a chronicle of Catherine's life. When he wrote her biography, he gathered information from Lapa and her friends to leave a complete record of Catherine's life, thoughts, visions, and ecstasies. He also wanted to document evidence supporting her canonization. Fortunately, his work remains a perceptive revelation of this remarkable woman, and to him goes credit for preserving *The Dialogue* and her other works.

Catherine was canonized in 1461 by Pope Pius II. She was known, thereafter as St. Catherine of Siena, and along with St. Francis of Assisi, is Italy's principal patron saint. Her feast is celebrated on April 29, the day of her death. She is immortalized further in various paintings which hang in galleries and churches across Italy. The Roman Catholic Church in all its history has bestowed the title of "Doctor of the Church," (meaning "teacher") on only two women, Catherine of Siena and Teresa of Avila. Pope Paul VI thus honored these two female saints in October 1970.

The Roman Catholic Church has canonized saints who have possessed unusual capacities to lead godly lives and demonstrated their holiness through extraordinary documented acts. For believers and hagiographers, who study the saints, acceptance of sainthood is a matter of faith, conviction, and evidence. For unbelievers the claims of direct communion with God through ecstasies and visions, and testimonies of miracles, locutions, levitations, and stigmata, appear to be abnormal exaggerations or products of lively imaginations. Apart from the disparity between the two camps, all agree that "official" saints had some ennobling characteristics in common. They all possessed a consuming love and commitment to Jesus Christ, an intense faith in God, a steadfast devotion to the living Word, and a passionate search for the holy life.

Catherine of Siena demonstrated all of these qualities. She searched for truth in her own life and condemned untruth wherever she found it. Although at times she claimed to be only a "mere woman" with feminine weaknesses, her actions belied that she held that perception of herself. Supported by her own profound faith and her intimacy with God, she boldly chastised popes and kings, rebuked immorality and sin in people of all rank and status, and scolded war-makers into ways of peace. She urged the Church to be militant and its Fathers to "enter the battlefield manfully." At the same time she urged the Church to nurture its children as a mother loves and nurtures her own. She preached obedience to the Church, but insisted that the Church must earn obedience by first being obedient to God.

Catherine was a medieval woman who gained her power through a pursuit of holiness and a claim of direct communication with God. She was regarded by men, not as a woman, but as a divine ambassador. To her, love was para-mount and was to be attained through discipline and obedience. She hated sin, but loved the sinner.

Personally Catherine had great charisma and gifts of persuasion. She was a mystic who effectively used rational arguments, sound theology, and logic coupled with wit, humor, and sarcasm to support her convictions. Above all she sought Christian perfection in herself through obedience to God. All this she accomplished during her short life while remaining selfless, humble in spirit, and fully aware of her human frailties. She believed that the true Christian "must burn up self-love and self-will and let the soul appear, beautiful and full of grace, as it was meant to be when God created us."[14]

Notes

1 Sigrid Undset, *Catherine of Siena* (New York: Sheed & Ward, 1954), p. 22.

2 Ibid., p. 32.

3 Ibid., p. 34.

4 Ibid., p. 36.

5 Ibid., p. 50.

6 Ibid., p. 77.

7 Ibid., p. 89.

8 Francis Parkinson Keyes, *Three Ways of Love* (New York: Hawthorn Books, 1963), p. 178.

9 Undset, p. 160.

10 Catherine of Siena, *The Dialogue* (New York: Paulist Press, 1980), p. 22.

11 Ibid., p. 241.

12 Ibid., p. 250.

13 Keyes, p. 265.

14 Edith Deen, *Great Women of the Christian Faith* (New York: Harper & Row, 1959), p. 59.

Chapter 3

Katherine von Bora
(1499 - 1552)

A FORMER NUN WHO AS THE WIFE OF MARTIN LUTHER BECAME KNOWN AS THE "FIRST LADY OF THE REFORMATION."

IN NOVEMBER 1524 Martin Luther wrote to a friend, "I have not been and am not now inclined to take a wife . . . because I daily expect the death decreed to the heretics."[1] Three years earlier Luther had been condemned by the Imperial Diet of Worms subjecting him to the death penalty. In May 1525 after a change of heart about matrimony, he wrote in a confidential letter, "If I can manage it, I will take Kate to wife before I die, to spite the devil."[2]

What happened to alter the plans of this forty-two-year-old church rebel and bring him to a public betrothal ceremony with twenty-six-year-old Katherine von Bora on June 13 of that same year? Was he really marrying to spite the devil, to make the angels laugh, to vex the pope, to make a personal declaration advocating the marriage of priests, or to fulfill his father's wishes that he marry and produce offspring? Did he envy the rich family life of some of his University colleagues, or did he need a sexual partner in bed, or a housekeeper to care for him? At any rate, the marriage was not a love match as much as one of duty, practicality, and a way out of the perplexing dilemma of trying to marry off a willful runaway nun who had refused other suitors. Shortly after the wedding Luther admitted, "I am not madly in love, but I cherish my wife."[3]

Unfortunately Katherine's letters have not been preserved, so we have to gather information about her from Luther's voluminous writings and those of his male contemporaries. At best the information is filtered through male eyes and does not reveal much of Katherine's personal thoughts and feelings as the wife of the greatest and most influential church reformer of his time.

We do know that Katherine was born in Lippendorf, a small town near Leipzig, on January 29, 1499. Her father, Hans von Bora, a descendant of an old family of West German nobles, was a man of modest means. He owned two properties, the home at Lippendorf and a farm at Zulsdorf which was later purchased by the Luthers.

As a young child Katherine had a sparse home life. Her mother, Katherine von Haubitz, had died when her daughter was about five. Her father, no longer able to care for his young child, sent her to a Benedictine convent boarding school at Brehna near Bitterfeld. Here she stayed and studied until her father was no longer able to pay the boarding school fees.

In 1505 Hans von Bora remarried, but his new wife felt no compulsion to mother young Katherine. So at age ten the girl was sent to a Cistercian convent, Marienthron (Mary's Throne), at Nimbschen, a short distance from the town of Grimma. Nuns, many from the nobility, were secluded in the large wealthy cloister. The massive buildings and stately church lay in a pleasant valley surrounded by rolling hills and fields. Margaret von Haubitz, Katherine's aunt, was the abbess, and Magdalene von Bora, another aunt, cared for the sick. Life at the cloister was strict, but not severe. The young girls spent much time in prayer and devotions, but also learned reading, writing, sewing, and Latin.

On October 15, 1515, after a period of training and preparation Katherine, then sixteen, took her vows before the abbess. On the day of her ordination she stood at the altar steps and repeated her vows of chastity, poverty, and obedience. Her hair was shorn, and she received the white gown and black veil of the order. From then on her life was one of ritual, prayer, meditation, silence, and service.

Outside the secluded walls of the Nimbschen Convent, rumblings against the abuses in the Roman Catholic Church had increased in intensity. For decades the church had been striking back with excommunication, exile, imprisonment, burning at the stake, and other tortures. John Wyclif, the English reformer, had been condemned as a heretic before he died of natural causes in 1384. John Huss, the Czech reformer, was burned at the stake in 1415. After the publishing of the Gutenberg Bible in 1455, scholars were beginning to question the teachings of the church in light of what they were finally able to read for themselves in print.

Since the early 1500s the brash, outspoken Augustinian monk, Martin Luther (1483-1546), had been stirring up the people with his doctrine of justification by faith and the priesthood of all believers. On the eve of All Saints' Day, October 31, 1517, Luther nailed his "Ninety-five Theses" to the door of the Castle Church in Wittenberg, the city where he had been exiled for six years. In the Theses, Luther stated his opposition to the sale of indulgences, which were being solicited throughout Germany by Johann Tetzel, a Dominican priest, to help finance the building of the Sistine Chapel at St. Peter's Church in Rome. With the blessing and under the protection of Pope Leo X, Tetzel was begging ". . . for a quarter of a florin [to] receive these letters of indulgence through which you are able to lead a divine and immortal soul safely and securely into the homeland of paradise."[4]

Luther condemned the practice. The Theses, written originally in Latin for scholars, was soon translated into German, widely circulated and discussed throughout Germany. In addition Luther's tracts and pamphlets had been printed and were inflaming controversy among the people. His debates with opponents angered his enemies and led to threats on his life.

In June 1520 Pope Leo issued a bull, "Exsurge Domine," giving Luther sixty days to recant his position. When the sixty days had expired, Luther had not yet recanted. His refusal led to an order that his books should be burned throughout Europe. As burning took place in Cologne, Mainz, and other cities, Luther's supporters had their own bonfire outside the Elster gate at Wittenberg. The University professors and students lit a fire and threw in the papal books. Luther drew the Pope's bull from his robe and tossed that into the fire. The crowds paraded in the streets singing and shouting.

On January 3, 1521, the Pope issued the final bull excommunicating Luther and his followers. He demanded that Emperor Charles V declare Luther an outlaw who could be killed without fear of recrimination.

But at that time the Emperor had worries of his own. Charles V, a young man of slight stature who carried two titles, had problems on many fronts. As the King of Spain, he was expanding the Spanish Empire into the New World (Mexico, Latin and South America), and as the Emperor of the Holy Roman Empire, he was trying to head off the Turks who were threatening Austria. Furthermore, in Germany he had to deal with the tempermental German princes, electors, and prelates without being able to speak their language, and now Pope Leo, who had opposed his election in the first place, was demanding action on the heretic Luther. Charles was aware of Luther's growing popularity in Germany and of the support of the powerful Elector Frederick the Wise in Saxony.

After vascillating for some time, Charles called together the Diet of Worms. In April 1521 Luther, with assurances of safe conduct, appeared before an assembly of Spanish and German officials. Luther had hoped to be able to debate his position, but instead was asked only to acknowledge that a pile of books on a bench were his and select those he wished to recant.

He was given one day to reply. At the final hearing, Luther, visibly angered, made his famous declaration, ". . . I cannot and will not recant, because it is neither safe nor wise to act against conscience." He added, "Here I stand. I can do no other. God help me! Amen."[5]

On the trip back to Wittenberg, Luther was kidnapped by men sent by Elector Frederick, who was concerned for Luther's safety. He was brought to Frederick's castle, the Wartburg, where he stayed for ten months disguised as a knight. Although he wrote to his friends of his discontent with the forced withdrawal from action, this period proved to be one of the most productive times in Luther's life. At Wartburg he wrote a dozen books which later were published, and he completed the entire New Testament translation into German.

A Wagon Load of Vestal Virgins.

By the early 1520s Luther's writings had filtered into the convents and monasteries. Although reading such inflammatory literature was forbidden, the nuns at Nimbschen gathered secretly at night to ponder Luther's tracts which had been smuggled inside the convent walls. They had also heard of Wolfgang von Zeschau, an Augustinian prior at Grimma, who had renounced his vows and with other monks had left the church and joined the Lutheran priesthood. Some of the Nimbschen nuns began to question their vows, their teachings, and their seclusion from the world.

They were on a dangerous course and were well aware of the risks, being so-warned by the abbess of the severe punishment meted out to Florentina von Oberweimar at a convent near Eisleben, Luther's birthplace. When Florentina was caught writing to Luther, she was sentenced to remain in an unheated cell for a month, laid prostrate on the floor while the other nuns walked over her on their way to devotions, and forced to eat off the floor. When she attempted to smuggle yet another letter out, she was whipped, chained, and locked in a cell. She escaped when the jailer forgot to lock the door.

But in spite of the consequences, twelve restless nuns decided they wanted to leave the convent. Their first course of action was to write home for permission. When they received little or no support or encouragement from their families, their next and more dangerous move was to write to Luther himself pleading for his help. Aided by Katherine's Aunt Magdalene, they smuggled the letter out of the convent. Luther received the message at his residence at the Black Cloister, a monastery no longer in use at Wittenberg.

Escaping Nimbschen was a formidable challenge. The women had no money, no vocations, no clothes, and no place to go. Furthermore, the convent lay in Albertine Saxony under the control of Luther's enemy, Duke George, who had recently executed a man for helping nuns escape. But Luther, who was no stranger to risk-taking, disregarded the consequences of aiding their escape. When his reply arrived at the convent, the nuns were jubilant, but apprehensive.

Luther enlisted the help of Leonard Koppe, a sixty-year-old merchant from Torgau, who delivered barrels of smoked herring to the convent. Koppe knew that Duke George was enforcing the church and civil laws that imposed the death penalty on anyone assisting nuns to escape the convents. Henry Kelmer, a resident in Duke George's territory, had just been beheaded and his head was impaled on a pole as a warning to anyone attempting to aid other escapes.

On Easter Eve it was customary for the sisters of the convent to gather at midnight to begin the Easter vigil after they had rested in their cells. It was April 5, 1523, and the escape was planned for 10:00 P.M., reportedly from a window in Katherine's room on the secluded south side of the building. In the dark of night twelve nuns stole from the cloister, were helped over the convent wall by Koppe's nephew and a friend. The women hid between the empty herring barrels in the wagon under a canvas. They were on their way to Wittenberg located in Electoral Saxony ruled by Frederick the Wise. At the border they were stopped by a guard who asked what was in the barrels. Koppe answered, "Can't you smell? Herring."

On Easter Monday they arrived at Torgau just across the border into friendly territory. At a lodging the women rested, took baths, and were given a change of clothes. They were reluctant to show their shorn heads, but happy to be clean and free. At an evangelical service at St. Marien's Church, they heard for the first time the Gospel read in German from Luther's recent translation. After the service they feasted on lamb and Torgau beer. Three nuns left the group to join their families, nine went on to Wittenberg.

Their wagon lumbered northward along the great river Elbe, a principal source of navigation, fish, and water. On the Tuesday after Easter, they crossed the drawbridge and entered the walled city of Wittenberg, the residence of the great Martin Luther and the seat of the noted University where Dr. Luther taught and lectured. The women were astonished at the drabness of this city of 2,500 residents with its plain brick buildings, high smoking chimneys, and tiled roofs. Professor Phillip Reichenbach, the mayor of the city, greeted them, then brought them to the Black Cloister where they were to be housed until Luther could find other accommodations for them.

Though Koppe preferred to remain anonymous, Luther made a public announcement declaring him a hero, "You have done a good work. Would to God we could free in the same way the many thousand other souls whom the Pope still holds captive."[6]

But now Luther's problems loomed—what to do with nine homeless nuns! The immediate concern was for food, clothing, and money. Luther wrote to his friends, "Pray beg some money for me, to enable me to keep these poor girls for a week or a fortnight, until I can send them to their relations or if these reject them find friends who will receive them."[7]

A student at Wittenberg made a wry comment: "A wagon load of vestal virgins has just come to town all more eager for marriage than for life. May God give them husbands lest worse befall."[8]

Luther enlisted the help of his colleagues to find employment or husbands for the runaways. His friend, Dr. Nicholas Amsdorf, began an advertising campaign. He wrote to a likely candidate:

> They are beautiful and ladylike, all of noble birth and under fifty. The oldest of them, sister of my gracious lord and uncle Dr. Staupitz, would I suggest suit you well; then you might boast of your brother-in-law as I boast of my uncle! But if you would prefer a younger one, you can take your pick. Or if you desire to give something to the poor, give to them, for they are destitute and friendless, and they have no shoes. Do please if you can beg something for them from the court, any scrap of food or clothing will be appreciated, only hurry, for they are in great distress, but very patient. I pity the creatures; I wonder they can be so brave and merry as they are.[9]

Luther's efforts to find a place for the nine "vestal virgins" were largely successful. Some were claimed by their relatives, one was placed as a teacher, others were taken in by families, and a few married. Magdalene von Staupitz, the oldest of the nine and the one Amsdorf had written about, had no interest in marriage, so was sent to a family in another town.

Katherine could not go home because her father had died, and her step-mother would not welcome her. She went to live with the mayor and his family, where for two years she helped with the housework, prepared meals, and tended the garden. Undoubtedly she learned much from Elsa Reichenbach about running a household and managing domestic economics.

Wittenberg, with its University and illustrious faculty, was a center of culture and learning. Katherine attended St. Mary's Church where Luther often preached rousing sermons. She also was introduced to some of the influential people of Wittenberg including one of Luther's colleagues, Philip Melanchthon, a twenty-five-year-old professor of Greek, who had taught at the University since he was eighteen.

At the Melanchthon home she joined other young people in a Latin class and in performing plays. One evening she met Jerome Baumgaertner, the son of a wealthy Nuremberg family, a graduate of the University, and a former student of Melanchthon. The two were immediately attracted to each other, and after a brief courtship, Jerome proposed to Katherine and left for his home in Nuremberg. He promised to return after receiving his parents consent to the marriage.

Katherine waited anxiously to hear from Jerome. When he did not write or return, Luther wrote to him, "If you wish to keep your Kate, be quick about it before she is given to another, who is at hand. She has not overcome her love for you. I would rejoice mightily if you two were united."[10]

Luther's plea was futile. Jerome's parents had not consented to the marriage, no doubt being frightened by King Charles V's threat of the death penalty to anyone who married an escaped nun. Some reports indicated that Jerome soon married a wealthy woman chosen by his parents, but other sources claimed that he did not marry until 1526 after Katherine's wedding to Luther.

I Would Not Say "No."

While recovering from heartbreak and disappointment, Katherine lived at the luxurious mansion of Lucas Cranach, the famous German artist whose name is signed on several paintings and woodcuts of the Luthers. In addition to household duties, Katherine had the opportunity to make social contacts, even meeting King Christian II of Denmark, who had been exiled from his country after becoming a Protestant. The King was so impressed by the former nun, he gave her a ring.

But Luther, still searching for a suitable spouse for Katherine, found another candidate—Dr. Kaspar Glatz, a pastor from Orlamuende. Glatz soon proposed marriage, and Luther, thinking this a fine match, urged Katherine to accept. Katherine, however, had other ideas. She sought the help of Luther's friend, Dr. Nicholas Amsdorf, then a rector at the Wittenberg University. She said she didn't want to be unreasonable or ungrateful, *but* under no circumstance would she marry Glatz, a person she despised. Then she added, "If I were asked by you or Dr. Luther, I would not say 'no.' "[11] Was she serious, or just jesting in the belief that both men were much too old to even consider marriage?

One cannot believe that as Luther urged priests and monks to marry, it had not at times crossed his mind. But because his life was in constant danger and he had no argument with priests remaining celibate if they could resist fornicating, he had put marriage out of his thoughts. He wrote:

> It is not that I do not feel my flesh or my masculine sexuality, since I am neither wood nor stone, but my mind is far removed from marriage, since I daily expect death and the punishment due to a heretic, so I shall not limit God's work in me, nor shall I rely on my own heart. Yet I hope God does not let me live alone.[12]

When Amsdorf told Luther of Katherine's presumptuous proposal, one can only surmise what he thought or said. But the idea germinated, and in April 1525 just one month after Katherine had offered her proposition, this monk, then forty-two, visited his parents at Mansfeld to ask their advice. His aging father, Hans Luther, was delighted at the news having been disappointed when Martin in his youth had chosen the priesthood instead of law. The idea of progeny to carry on the Luther name also pleased him. Luther's friends, however, were not so enthusiastic about the match. Some thought Katherine much too forward and stubborn, and they worried that there would be damage to Luther's reputation.

Dr. Jerome Schurff, Professor of Law at Wittenberg, wrote, "Should this monk marry, the whole world and the devil himself will laugh, and Luther himself will destroy all that he had been building up."[13] But Luther had made up his mind to take a wife, and he didn't need advice from friends or colleagues. Furthermore, he wanted it done quickly so as not to alert his enemies and fan rumors that he and Katherine were living together "in sin," a situation some thought preferable to a monk marrying a nun.

On June 13, 1525, he and Katherine were married in a private ceremony at the Black Cloister with only four close friends as witnesses. The ceremony was performed by Johann Bugenhagen, pastor of the City Church. The pair spoke their vows, exchanged rings, and sat down for a simple meal. Dr. Justus Jonas, one of Wittenberg's first priests to marry and Luther's good friend, wrote of their wedding night, "I was present yesterday and saw the couple on their marriage bed. As I watched this spectacle I could not hold back my tears!"[14]

Although Luther did not look upon marriage as a sacrament, he and Katherine decided to celebrate publicly with a special church service two weeks later. Luther sent out most of the invitations himself, each one containing an explanation or apology for his decision. To Koppe, Katherine's accomplice in the Nimbschen escape, he wrote:

> Suddenly and unexpectedly God has taken me captive in the bonds of holy matrimony, which is to be confirmed with a banquet on Tuesday. That my father and mother and all my good friends may be the merrier, my lord Katharina and I beg you will send us as soon as possible, at my expense, a keg of the best Torgau beer you can find. If it is not good, I shall punish you by making you drink it all yourself. . . .[15]

On June 27 the bells chimed, a band played, and a host of friends and townspeople processed to the church for the public ceremony which was followed by a feast at the Black Cloister for fifteen special guests including Luther's parents, Hans and Margaretha Luther. Dancing and another feast ended the day-long celebration. A bewildered but joyful Luther wrote, "I myself can scarcely believe it; nevertheless, the witnesses are so many that I am honour bound to believe it."[16] One can only guess how Katherine felt as she greeted her former companions from Nimbschen.

There were many gifts for the newlyweds—a silver tankard lined with gold plate from the city of Wittenberg, a large barrel of beer from a city magistrate, and a purse of twenty gulden from the Archbishop of Mainz, one of Luther's adversaries. Luther wanted to return the money considering it "tainted" because it had been received from indulgences. Katherine immediately opposed the idea, establishing early her control of the family finances. She also hid some of the wedding gifts that her too-generous husband wanted to give away.

The largest gift came from Elector John Frederick who had just before the wedding succeeded the deceased duke, Frederick the Wise. The Elector gave them the sprawling Black Cloister for a home and provided money to renovate parts of the aging building. He also gave them some adjoining land and 100 gulden.

In Wittenberg criticism of the marriage spread rapidly. Philip Melanchthon, who had not been invited to the private ceremony, grudgingly attended the public celebration. In a fit of resentment and pique he wrote:

> Luther has married the woman Bora, without letting one who is his friend know of his intention. He only invited Bugenhagen, Cranach, and R. Apel to a supper in the evening and went through the usual forms. You may perhaps wonder that at a time like this, when the good are suffering at every hand, he does not suffer with them but rather, it seems, devotes himself to revelry and compromises his good name, at the very moment when Germany is in especial need of all his mind and authority. I think the explanation is this: the man is extraordinarily easily influenced, and so the nuns, who chased him in every way, ensnared him. Perhaps having so much to do with the nuns softened him up, ... and caused the fire to flare up in him.... The talk that he had already slept with the woman Bora is however a lie. Well, now that it is done, we must put a good face on

it. ... I dare hope that matrimony will make him more dignified, so that he may now give up that buffoonery which we have so often tried to get him out of.[17]

For years Katherine was subjected to ridicule from both friends and enemies. Two years after the wedding a pamphlet chastising her was circulated. It said:

> Woe to you, poor fallen woman, not only because you have passed from light to darkness, from the cloistered holy religion into a damnable, shameful life, but also that you have gone from the grace to the disfavor of God, in that you have left the cloister in lay clothes and have gone to Wittenberg like a chorus girl. You are said to have lived with Luther in sin. Then you have married him, forsaking Christ your bridegroom. You have broken your vow and by your example have reduced many godly young women in the cloisters to a pitiable state of body and soul, despised of all men.[18]

A Pair of Pigtails Lying Beside Him.

When they were united, Katherine understood some of the risks in marrying this controversial man. Luther had warned her that if he were burned as a heretic, his enemies would not spare her. In the early spring, just before the wedding, Luther had taken an unbelievable and unpopular stand in the Peasants' War which found heavily-taxed peasants revolting against the feudal landlords. The peasants issued "The Twelve Articles" listing their demands in religious matters, land reform, and taxation. They had appealed to Luther believing that he would support their cause. Luther first tried to mediate, but the unrest had progressed too far. The peasants pillaged towns in Thuringia and Franconia, leaving cloisters, castles, villages, and countryside in ruin. Although he was sympathetic to the cause of the peasants, Luther believed they were violating their allegiance to the divinely instituted government, destroying property not owned by them, and using the gospel to sanction revolt and violence.

In May 1525 Luther issued an inflammatory treatise, "Against the Murderous and Thieving hordes of Peasants." The princes, George of Saxony and Philip of Hesse, encouraged by Luther's support, gathered their armies and at a battle at Frankenhausen on May 15, killed thousands of peasants, captured and beheaded Thomas Muntzer, their fanatical leader. Luther was condemned by both friends and adversaries, and his followers began to question his leadership. Friends urged him to retract the treatise. Instead Luther issued another paper explaining his position. He said: Both sides were guilty of violence; rebellion was a crime; the gospel should not be used in a political crusade; and Germany was riddled with disrespect for law and order. The Catholic princes held Luther responsible for the outbreak, and the peasants were angry and alienated. One month before the wedding Luther had many distractions on his mind apart from marriage.

For years Luther suffered criticism for his decision. Eight years later he was still trying to vindicate his position. In one of his "Table Talks" he said, "I, Martin Luther, slew all the peasants in the uprising, for I ordered that they be put to death; all their blood is on my neck. But I refer it all to our Lord God, who commanded me to speak as I did."[19]

Into this upheaval, just another of many in Luther's career, Katherine was thrust, perhaps at an opportune time to become a moderating and healing influence on her depressed and often ill husband. Luther's opponent Erasmus observed, "Doctor Martinus has become more gentle after his wedding."[20]

The new bride was confronted immediately with making a habitable home in the living quarters of the austere rundown Black Cloister, which until 1522 had housed forty Augustinian monks. After the monastery was closed, Luther and a friend had lived there, neither of them fastidious housekeepers. Luther admitted that at night he was so tired he fell into his decaying straw bed which was not made from one year to the next.

In the Black Cloister complex, located near the Wittenberg University, was the three-story monks' residence that was to become their home. On the ground floor were forty rooms including the kitchen, storage, and assembly rooms. On the second floor were the cramped cells where the monks had slept. Luther often sequestered himself in his study in the tower where he wrote, meditated, prepared sermons and lectures, and received visitors in a clutter of manuscripts and books.

With the cloister came Wolfgang Sieberger, who had stayed on with Luther as a servant after failing courses at the University. In spite of "Wolf's" physical disability and his penchant for building bird-traps, Luther assigned him to odd jobs about the premises. Wolf regarded Katherine as an intruder, and Katherine complained of Wolf's laziness and dullness. In time

they learned to tolerate each other.

Katherine discovered quickly that she would have to manage the household finances and curb the generosity of her open-handed husband. At their wedding the new Elector, John Frederick, had given them a monthly salary of 200 gulden. Luther's salary for teaching at the University was only 400 gulden a year. He refused to take exemption from taxes granted the clergy and declined payment for the publishing of his books, which earned handsome profits for the printers. He routinely acquired debts and habitually gave away gifts and worldly goods to those more needy. Luther admitted:

> God is the guardian and steward of the poor. I know this for certain from my experience, for I spend far more than I get from my stipend. So far I've not written anything, lectured, or preached for compensation. The two hundred gulden that I get from the prince I have and receive by his indulgence. He who has Christ has enough. I have not wanted to do anything for money, although I might have become rich.[21]

The Black Cloister, or "Lutherhaus" as it was known, was open to student boarders, visiting clergy and professors, dignitaries and royalty from abroad, the sick, the homeless, the poor, refugees, escaped nuns, and anyone who needed help. Elector John Frederick claimed Luther was running an asylum for renegades. Besides Luther's own children, there were living with them six nieces and nephews, four children of a friend whose wife had died in the plague, servants, tutors for the children, and Katherine's aunt Lena.

Feeding and housing the large assortment of people were costly, and whenever there was something to celebrate—a doctorate, a wedding, or a baptism—the Black Cloister was the gathering place. Katherine resolved to make the cloister self-supporting in spite of Luther's cavalier remark. "I'm rich," he said. "My God has given me a nun and has added three children. I don't worry about my debts, for when my Katy has paid them there will be more."[22]

Katherine, a shrewd manager with a keen sense of business, did not intend for the family to be always in debt. She tried to convince Luther that he should do something about the students who were in arrears in their payments for lodging and food, and even suggested, obviously in jest, that they should pay for all the free lectures they were given at the Luther table.

When Martin married, he made no pretense that this was a romantic union. He could have been impressed more by Katherine's character than by her appearance, which from paintings by Lucas Cranach the Elder show her to be quite plain, with high cheek bones, almond-shaped eyes, reddish hair parted in the middle and severely pulled back. But those who knew her said there was a sparkle and vibrancy to her demeanor. Katherine, too, would have been more influenced by Luther's reputation and intelligence than by his romantic nature or handsome appearance. Cranach's portraits show him to be a stocky, large-featured, heavily-jowled, serious man. Luther's words showed clearly how over the years he grew to love his Katie and indicated Katherine's developing admiration and concern for him.

Martin reflected on the changes that marriage brought to his life. "Man has strange thoughts the first year of marriage. When sitting at table he thinks, 'Before I was alone; now there are two.' Or in bed, when he wakes up, he sees a pair of pigtails lying beside him which he hadn't seen there before."[23] Later he confessed, "I would not change Katie for France or for Venice, for God has given her to me. . . ." He added, no doubt with a grin, ". . . and other women have worse faults. She has a few but her virtues outweigh them."[24] Another time he reflected, "The glory of motherhood justly covers and balances all the weaknesses of wives. . . . I love her more than I love myself, for I would die rather than that any harm come to her or to her children."[25]

Katherine usually addressed her husband as "Herr Doktor" in deferrence to his position. But Herr Doktor had many epithets for his wife—some humorous, some barbed. He called her the "morning star of Wittenberg," "my lord Kate," "my rib," "kette" (meaning chain), "my master Kate," "Grand Wizard, our lord Kate," "the rich lady of Zulsdorf," "crafty Katie," "Domina Kate," and others.

Go Forth and Multiply.

In April 1523 Luther wrote a small tract dedicated to Leonard Koppe entitled "Basis and Rationale for Permitting Young Women to Leave the Convent." He argued that life in a nunnery was not natural because women were not made to remain virgins, but to bear children. In a Table Talk nine years later he said, "Many good things may be perceived in a wife. First, there is the Lord's blessing, namely, offspring.

Then there is community of property . . . Imagine what it would be like without sex. The home, cities, economic life, and government would virtually disappear. Men can't do without women."[26]

After he married, Luther acted on his beliefs—Katherine bore six children in eight and one-half years. On October 21, 1525, he made an early announcement, "Katie is fulfilling Genesis 3:8 where the Lord says to woman, 'In pain shall you bring forth children.' "[27] On June 8, 1526, one year after the wedding, Luther reported, "At two o-clock yesterday my dear Kate, by God's grace, brought into the world a little son, Hans (John) Luther. I cannot write more; sick Katie is calling me."[28] After watching Hans's first movements, Luther said, "Kick, little fellow. That is what the pope did to me, but I got loose."[29]

With the birth of Hans, named after Luther's father, life took a domestic turn with intimate homelife and the ordinary trials accorded concerned parents. Hans was making a "joyous nuisance of himself"; Hans was cutting teeth; Hans was scolding everyone; Hans said "Daddy"; Hans was relieving himself in every corner; Hans annoys with his loud singing; Hans needs chastising. Poor firstborn Hans!

On December 10, 1527, Elisabeth was born, but died in August 1528 before reaching her first birthday. Luther wrote to a friend, "My little daughter Elisabeth is dead. I am left as weak as a woman. I would never have believed that the hearts of parents are so moved toward their children."[30]

Their third child, Magdalene (nicknamed Lenchen), arrived on May 4, 1529. Two days later Luther reported, "Katie is as well as if she had never had a baby."[31] Thirteen years later on September 20, 1542, after a painful illness, Magdalene died in Luther's arms. As the distraught parents laid her in her coffin, Luther said, "This parting grieves me beyond measure. Kate, dear, we should not mourn; we have dismissed a saint, a living saint for heaven."[32] But before Magdalene's death, three other children had been added to the family.

On November 9, 1531, one day before Luther's birthday, Martin Jr. arrived. Of him Luther said, "My Martin is my dearest treasure. Hans and Lenchen can talk now and don't need so much care."[33]

It wasn't long before Katherine was pregnant again. Paul arrived on January 28, 1533. Luther wrote to a friend, "This night my Katie has born to me a son. I hope you will assist to bring him from old birth in Adam to the new Birth in Christ. . . . I'd like to have the baptism at vespers that he may be no longer a heathen."[34] Paul was baptized immediately after he was born, as were all the Luther children.

Their sixth and last child, Margaretha, named after Luther's mother, was born on December 17, 1534. It is believed that Luther was inspired to write the hymn "From Heaven Above" as he watched his little "Margaretula" on Christmas Eve. Luther said of his children, "God has given me greater gifts than to any bishop in a thousand years. . . . They are more precious to me than all the kingdoms of Ferdinand."[35]

Half a Doctor.

Children were not Katherine's only contribution to Luther's well-being. She gave him warmth, humanness, compassion, and tenderness, as well as wifely reprimands when his language became too coarse, or his writing too harsh. She also reminded him that he was mortal and must learn to say "No" to the demands made upon him.

Luther's life was one of constant tension. The Peasants' War had turned into bloody confrontations, both sides holding Luther responsible. Protestant mercenaries were attacking clergy, looting and burning churches, and taking hostages in Rome. From May to December 1527 the protesters held Pope Clement in prison. Erasmus lamented: "This is not the ruin of one city, but of the whole world." Luther found no joy in being declared "the new pope" by the rebels. He wrote, "I am sorry Rome was sacked, for it is a great portent. I hope it may yet be inhabited and have its pontiff before we die."[36]

One of Katherine's most consuming and nagging concerns was for her husband's health. Throughout his adult life Luther suffered from a host of illnesses, some of them major. He had periodic attacks of painful kidney and gall stones. He complained of severe headaches and ringing in the ears and often endured hemorrhoids, catarrh, stomach disorders, dizziness, feverish rheumatism, vertigo, and insomnia. He had one heart attack, and in later years suffered from phlebitis in his left leg. At the end of his life, he was often in stages of acute depression, fatigue, and exhaustion.

Despite the maladies, Luther did not stop his activities. Rather he looked upon his suffering as akin to that of Jesus, and he maintained a busy schedule of writing, lecturing, preaching, and traveling, along wth taking out time for family and friends. Some of Luther's associates gave Katherine credit. "Thanks to her care his life will be spared for the church."[37] With her extensive knowledge of herbs and medicines, diets, massages, and poultices, she nursed him during his many illnesses and depressions.

On July 6, 1527, just two years after their wedding, Luther collapsed in Katherine's arms from what appeared to be a serious heart attack. With the doctor and pastor at the bedside, they read Scriptures and prayed. As Luther prepared to die, Katherine said to him, "I commend you to His will, but I hope and trust in God that He will graciously preserve you."[38] Luther recovered in time to help Katherine care for the victims of plague which broke out in August of the same year.

Elector John Frederick ordered the University to move to Jena until the plague was over, but Katherine and Luther refused to leave. Their home became a hospital as they took in victims of the dread disease. Katherine, then pregnant with Elisabeth, dressed boils and nursed sick patients daily. Little Hans, less than two years old, was stricken, but recovered. Luther marvelled at Katie's strength and resistance. He said, "Her escape from death seems almost a miracle."[39] It was during this turbulent time that Luther composed "A Mighty Fortress," the Reformation hymn.

In 1539 another plague devastated the city taking entire families and almost wiping out the food supply. Luther begged grain from the Elector. Again the Black Cloister became the hospital with Katherine the nurse. But this time overwork and exhaustion caught up with her. In January 1540 she became seriously ill and was pronounced beyond recovery by the doctor. Now it was Luther's turn to stay by her bedside day and night. Luther feared he would lose her, but she clung to life and in a few weeks began to recover. Her favorite Psalm 31, which she repeated often, had comforted and strengthened her.

In 1544 an epidemic of measles spread to all the Luther children being especially severe in nine-year-old Margaretha. Katherine was again the nurse. Years later, when her son Paul was appointed Professor of Medicine at the University of Jena, he said in his inaugural address that his mother had helped and healed many. He called her "half a doctor."

I Wish You Would Eat Now.

Katherine was not only "half a doctor" and a loyal wife, but also an able parent, a knowledgeable gardener and farmer, and a tireless worker. She was up before dawn earning her the name "morning star of Wittenberg." After family devotions, the day's activities began. At 7:00 A.M. Luther started his lectures and classes, the older children went to their lessons with the tutors, and Katherine was off to her many domestic duties—caring for the babies, supervising the servants, tending the garden and the animals, brewing the beer, preparing the food, and doing whatever else needed to be done. At 10:00 A.M. they ate their morning meal. When home, Luther spent the afternoons in his tower study, preparing sermons or lectures, writing, or receiving visitors. If there were any free hours, he could be found puttering in the garden, grafting fruit trees, watching birds, or playing games with the children.

At 5:00 P.M. friends, visitors, and students, sometimes numbering twenty or more, joined the family around the table for a simple supper and stimulating conversation. Luther made it known, "I favor good nourishing plain food" which meant sour peas and herring, or pork and apples washed down with plenty of beer. It was up to Katherine to provide the food for the many mouths, a problem she wrestled with their entire married life. The students arrived with their notebooks in hand ready to copy down Luther's observations and comments, which were later compiled in his *Table Talks* with 6,596 entries.

The spirited conversations at the table were in either German or Latin, Luther and Katherine being fluent in both. (Katherine was so proficient in German that Luther recommended she teach a visiting Englishman the language.) At times when Luther was depressed, the meals were eaten in silence, but usually the talk was so animated Katherine had to interrupt. "I wish you would eat now, and not talk forever."[40] Discussions often went on through the evening hours, but bedtime for adults was observed at 9:00 P.M. Luther sometimes played with the children before they were put to bed or sang them to sleep.

When disagreements arose, Katherine did not hesitate to express her opinion. She found Luther's dog Tolpel to be an annoying member of the family, but her husband insisted on keeping the creature believing that he would meet the animal someday in heaven. He wrote, "Oh if I could only pray the way this dog watches the food! All his thoughts are concentrated on the chunk of meat."[41]

Although Luther loved his Katie, at times he found her too willful and independent. He approached some of his annoyance with humor, calling her pet names with a touch of sarcasm, but at other times he said it plainly. "If I can put up with battles with the devil, sin and a bad conscience, then I can also put up with the irritations of Katie von Bora."[42] He quipped, "If I should ever marry again, I would hew myself an obedient wife out of stone. . ."[43]

Train Up a Child.

Religious training and education played an important part in the household. All the Luther children and those staying with the family studied the catechism, sang hymns, prayed, and attended daily devotions. When Luther was home, he led the family worship, but Katherine heard the children's daily prayers and taught them Bible lessons. University students were hired as tutors for special subjects.

Discipline in the family was firm, but tempered with love and kindness. Luther believed "an apple should always lie beside the cane,"[44] and he was not above a little bribery. While he impatiently waited at the Castle Coburg for a decision on the "Augsburg Confession," he wrote home to four-year-old Hans: "I am pleased to hear that you are doing well in your lessons, and that you are praying well. Go on like this, my son, and when I return home I shall bring you a nice present from the fair."[45]

Hans was sent off to school to be away from the noise and confusion of the busy Luther household. At fourteen Hans studied at the University, but when his work there was not satisfactory, Luther sent him to Torgau to the schoolmaster Markus Krodel with the instructions: "Tell him . . . he has been sent to strangers for the purpose of learning and the process of toughening."[46]

At times Katherine found that child-bearing and child-rearing, added to all the other duties, proved too much. In November 1531 just after Martin was born and with Hans and Madalene underfoot, Luther observed Katherine's frustration and commented, "God must be friendlier to me and speak to me in friendlier fashion than my Katie to little Martin."[47]

Four Luther children grew to adulthood. Hans studied law and became the Councellor of State for Elector John Frederick II of Saxony and Duke Albert of Prussia. Martin Jr. studied theology, but because of ill health never entered the clergy. Paul became a Professor of Medicine at the University of Jena and Court Physician to Elector John Frederick. Three years after her mother's death, Margaretha married George von Kunheim, a young Prussian nobleman. She died prematurely at age thirty-six.

Between Times She Reads the Bible.

When Katherine moved into the dirty, run-down, inconvenient Black Cloister, she began a routine of cleaning, furnishing, and re-modelling. She added a bathroom and a cellar under the house to eliminate dampness from the nearby moat, and she planted a vegetable garden that produced a large variety of edibles. Luther, interested in the outdoor venture, or-dered seeds from friends at Nuremberg and Erfurt, famous for their gardens. Katherine, with occasional help from Luther, cultivated an orchard that produced pears, apples, peaches, cherries, grapes, mulberries, and nuts. She re-opened the small brewery at the back of the premises to make their own beer; later she ac-quired land to grow hops for the operation. And she tended chickens, geese, pigeons, pigs, and cows and did the slaughtering herself. She also milked and made butter and cheese. Of his wife's industry Luther wrote, "My lord Kate drives a team, farms, pastures, and sells cows . . . and between times reads the Bible."[48]

But Katherine needed more land. In the early 1530's she persuaded a reluctant Luther to buy a large plot of ground near the Witten-berg Sow Market which became their "swine-market garden." Luther looked more kindly on the purchase when he learned that the brook on the property offered up pike, trout, perch, and carp. Katherine also rented from the Elector a farm and meadow outside the city where her animals could graze.

To manage the household and the many enterprises, the Luthers hired servants. They had a cook, maids, day laborers, a driver, and swineherds. Some of the workers were unreli-able, and a few were downright dishonest as was the "unchaste" maid who masqueraded as an escaped nun and stole from them. Wolf was made the supervisor of the servants, a function he could execute with some degree of proficien-cy.

In 1540 Katherine fulfilled a dream when she was able to purchase the von Bora home-stead in Zulsdorf south of Leipzig. Because it was a two-day journey away, Katherine stayed at Zulsdorf for three weeks at a time. There was plenty of work to do, repairing the rundown buildings and planting gardens. She found the farm to be a stimulating release from the bustle of the Black Cloister. Luther called her "the rich lady of Zulsdorf, Frau Doktor Katherine Luther, who lives in the body at Wittenberg, in the spirit at Zulsdorf."[49]

Our Dear Lord has Taken This Dear and Precious Man.

Throughout his adult life Luther was con-stantly aware of his mortality, but as he grew older he decided he must prepare for the future of his wife and children if he should die. Saxon law gave the inheritance from a father to his chil-dren, not his wife, on the grounds that if wives inherited property and money and later remar-ried, the children would be left destitute. Luther thought the law unfair to wives, an opinion not endorsed by the legal profession and most men of the day. In January, 1542, he made out a will, though not a formal one, leaving all his worldly possessions to Katherine. He made her execu-trix of the estate and guardian of the children.

Luther grew increasingly bitter as he dis-agreed with the Pope, Charles V, the Turks, the Jews, and individual opponents. He grieved as he witnessed the degradation and moral decay in Germany and his town of Wittenberg. He lamented, "I am fed up with the world."[50]

While in neighboring towns for a wedding and an ordination in July 1545 a depressed Lu-ther wrote to Katherine that he would not be returning to Wittenberg, that "Sodom of sin and immorality." He advised her to sell every-thing and move to the farm at Zulsdorf. He did return, however, but not for long.

In early January 1546 in foul winter weath-er, Luther reluctantly set off for Eisleben, his birthplace, eighty miles distant. He had been asked to settle a family feud between two broth-ers, each bearing the title of Count of Mansfeld. Although he was in poor health, Luther felt duty-bound to help the counts, his friends. With him were his three sons, Dr. Justus Jonas, and his secretary. Luther became severely chilled when at Halle they were held up by a flood for three days. Upon finally arriving at Eisleben, he recovered enough to negotiate a settlement of the Mansfeld feud and to preach several sermons. He corresponded regularly with Katherine, advising her of the state of his health and making light of her letters of concern. On February 14, 1546, he wrote her the cheerful words, "God willing, we expect to come home this week."[51]

The next day he began to preach a sermon to a large crowd in an icy church, but illness and age had taken its toll, and he was too weak to finish. For two days he suffered from chills and acute chest pains in addition to the recurrence of his old maladies. In vain physicians tried various remedies along with massages and warm blankets while his sons and friends gathered at his bedside. Jonas asked the dying man, "Reverend Father, do you die firm in the faith you have taught?" The weak reply came, "Yes."[52] Early on February 18 he slipped into a coma and died. The official cause of death was recorded as a heart attack. He was sixty-three.

Luther was honored with a funeral usually reserved for royalty. One day after his death, Dr. Jonas delivered the sermon to a large crowd at a memorial service at Eisleben's St. Andrews Church. The next day a local pastor officiated at another memorial service. It was first planned to bury Luther at Eisleben, his birthplace, but the Elector of Saxony demanded that the burial take place at Wittenberg, Luther's adopted home.

An honor guard escorted the pewter coffin back to Wittenberg, the roads lined with mourners and the bells tolling along the way. Elector John Frederick and his cavalry met the entourage at the border. On February 22 the procession arrived at the Elster Gate at Wittenberg where Katherine joined them and rode in a carriage behind the coffin. At the funeral service at the Castle Church, Luther's friends, John Bugenhagen and Philip Melanchthon, delivered the eulogies. The entire town of Wittenberg turned out to honor their Dr. Luther. The body was buried beneath the church floor in front of the pulpit where Luther had preached numerous sermons. A tablet bearing the epitaph marked the grave.

In one of the few letters written by Katherine which has been preserved, she wrote to her sister-in-law, Christine von Bora, "Wherefore I am truly so heart-broken that I cannot tell my great sorrow to anyone, and hardly know what to think or how to feel. I cannot eat or drink or sleep. . . our dear Lord has taken this dear and precious man not only from me but also from the whole world."[53]

Fallen Asleep in God.

Katherine had often worried about what would happen to her and the children if Luther should die. She had bought property thinking it would give her some security when she no longer had Luther's university salary, no student boarders, no stipend from the Elector, and no costly gifts from visitors. Luther's legacy included a farm, Wolf's cottage, an assortment of gold medals, jewelry, silverware, and a debt of 450 gulden.

Luther's will bequeathing everything to Katherine was contested by a chancellor who ruled the document to be invalid because it had not been made out by an attorney. Furthermore, he said, the law stated that widows and children needed a guardian, and he proceeded to remove the sons from Katherine's care and place them with strangers. Thanks to the intervention of Elector John Frederick, Luther's wishes were honored, and Katherine retained the property and custody of the children. The Elector gave her an annuity of 2,000 gulden drawing five percent interest and helped her purchase Wachsdorf, an estate adjoining her farm at Zulsdorf, a piece of property Katherine had long wished to acquire. She hoped to sell the Black Cloister and move to Zulsdorf as she and Luther had planned to do some day.

The next days and months were difficult and lonely times for Katherine and the children. The Black Cloister that once radiated with Luther's personality was silent, and the endless stream of students, friends, and guests had dwindled to a trickle. To make matters worse, lies were being circulated about the circumstances of Luther's death, and people who had once been friends or recipients of Luther's favors turned away from his widow. She had property and some valuable possessions, but no money. King Christian of Denmark and the Counts of Mansfeld pledged contributions, but the money was late in arriving.

In 1531 The Schmalkald League had been formed to unite and protect Lutheran states and cities against Emperor Charles V and the Roman enemies. During the first summer following Luther's death, the Schmalkald War broke out, and enemy troops, no longer fearing Luther's leadership, threatened Saxony, the stronghold of the Reformation. On November 9, as Charles's forces drew close to Wittenberg, a large caravan of frightened citizens, including Katherine and the children, left for the fortress city of Magdeburg to the north, then went on to Braunschweig fifty miles to the west.

In April 1547 Charles V was victorious at the battle of Muhlberg. Wittenberg was occupied and soon surrendered to the merciless Duke of Alba. Elector John Frederick, a Lutheran, was captured.

The Schmaldkald Wars finally subsided when Charles's troops were defeated at Innsbruck in 1552. Although Charles continued his relentless persecution of Protestants for four more years, he realized that he could no longer hold back the tide of reform. In 1556 he gave up his throne and entered a Spanish monastery, a sick and defeated man. He died two years later.

During the wars, Katherine had hoped to go to Denmark, but the road was blocked by the Emperor's troops. When it was safe to return to Wittenberg, she found the Black Cloister had been ransacked and looted. Fortunately Luther's resting place at the Castle Church had not been desecrated, but nothing remained of the farms at Zulsdorf and Wachsdorf after the fields and buildings had served as a battlefield.

Again Katherine began to work on the Black Cloister. When it was in suitable condition and the University open again, she began to take in boarders, this time insisting the students pay for their food. The table, which Luther had once dominated, was again bubbling with conversation, but the focal point was gone.

Life seemed to settle down for a time. The Duke of Prussia offered to educate Hans at the Koenigsberg University, an offer Katherine gratefully accepted because she didn't have the money to send him to school.

Stability was short-lived. In July 1552 the dreaded plague returned, and bodies of the dead lined the streets. Fortunately the Luther children escaped, but the boarders all left town. When the plague subsided, Katherine found Wittenberg was no longer a pleasant place to live. Only a few friends remained loyal to her; a new elector had made changes; the church was in disarray; and money was scarce. Katherine, herself was often ill and depressed.

She and the children left Wittenberg, hoping to go to Zulsdorf to restore the farm and to live there in peace. As they traveled south by carriage toward Torgau, their horse was frightened and bolted, the carriage lurched, and Katherine was thrown out onto the rocky roadside into a puddle of water. She was soaked and in pain as the children helped her back into the coach. They stopped at Torgau where at the home of a friend she remained in bed for three months with fever and paralysis.

Knowing it was near the end, Katherine gathered her three children around her bed and gave them the only treasures she had saved. To Martin, the theology student, she gave Luther's doctoral ring which he had received in 1512. Margaretha received her father's seal with the coat of arms, a gift from Elector John Frederick. To Paul she gave her wedding ring, no doubt with the intent that he give it to his intended bride, Anna von Warbeck. Hans, away at the Koenigsberg University, was not able to be with his mother.

During her last days Katherine repeated the words of her favorite Psalm 31 over and over. She made one final request that her children sing Luther's cradle hymn, "From Heaven Above," composed when Margaretha was one-week-old. Katherine died on December 20, 1552, one month before turning fifty-four. Her last words were, "I will stick to Christ as a burr to a topcoat."[54]

She was buried at St. Marien's Church at Torgau, the same church she had attended on Easter Monday twenty-nine years earlier as she escaped from the Nimbschen convent. Philip Melanchthon and Rector Paul Eber issued an invitation to her funeral "out of respect to her outstanding godliness and in memory of the distinguished and praiseworthy services rendered by her husband."[55]

Katherine's children placed a marker over their mother's tomb that read:

December 20, 1552:
Fallen asleep in God here at Torgau
lies Dr. Martin Luther's pious, surviving widow
KATHARINA VON BORA.[56]

To a degree Martin Luther had elevated the status of women. He gave the common women options, though limited. If they wished, they could remain celibate in cloisters, (Luther considered this abnormal), or they could marry, raise children, and manage households with some degree of respectability. Women were not to be regarded as temptresses and seducers of men but as legitimate and vital partners in marriage. Divorce was even possible for women under certain conditions—adultery and dissertion. Luther viewed marriage as a deterrent to lustful sin and a school for building character and patience. He saw the home as the rightful place for children to receive a Christian education. Although Luther held the patriarchal view of the day that the husband was the head of the family and as such ruled over the wife, he grew to love and respect his independent wife. He called her "his dearest friend" and feared that at times he loved her more than God. He admitted that the union of flesh was nothing unless there was a union of manners and mind.

Thanks to Luther the Protestant minister's wife became an active participant in the cultural and intellectual activities of the parsonage. But he stopped short of opening the church to women, claiming that females should not be allowed to preach, be ordained, or participate in governing.

Some theologians and historians assess Katherine's life only as it relates to Luther—the devoted wife of a great man, the prototype of the ideal pastor's wife, the nucleus of the first Protestant parsonage, and the "First Lady of the Reformation." Unfortunately we do not have Katherine's own words to relate her story, her thoughts, and her feelings—her numerous letters were not considered worth saving.

Undeniably, Katherine was a dedicated wife and mother. She patiently endured life with the enigmatic and tempermental Luther for twenty-one years, tended to his physical needs, nursed him through his many illnesses, raised his children, and was a gracious hostess to hundreds of guests. She ran the Black Cloister with efficiency and was adroit at managing the family finances. She worked untiringly to make the somber cloister a place of warmth and congeniality for her husband and children and a place of refuge for the troubled and the needy. Her spirited tongue, often directed at her husband and children, was tempered with wit and sparkle.

It took courage for Katherine von Bora, the runaway nun, to marry Martin Luther, the middle-aged rebel. She had left the safe confines of Nimbschen for an uncertain future with a man whose life was in constant danger. When widowed she proved that even in the sixteenth century women could lead independent lives. As we look at her many accomplishments, we see an unusual woman who in her own right was a person of many talents. She had great strength of character, superior intelligence, and to her death held unwavering faith in her God.

Notes

1   C. V. Eckermann, *Mistress of the Black Cloister* (Adelaide, South Australia: Lutheran Publishing House, 1976), p. 18.

2   John M. Todd, *Luther, a Life* (New York: Crossroad, 1982), p. 261.

3   Roland H. Bainton, *Women of the Reformation in Germany and Italy* (Minneapolis: Augsburg Publishing House, 1971), p. 26.

4   James M. Kittelson, *Luther, the Reformer* (Minneapolis: Augsburg Publishing House, 1986), p. 103.

5   Ibid., p. 161.

6   Eckermann, p. 14.

7   Edith Simon, *Luther Alive; Martin Luther and the Making of the Reformation* (Garden City, New York: Doubleday & Co., 1968), p. 327.

8   Bainton, p. 24.

9   Simon, p. 327.

10   Eckermann, p. 16.

11   Ibid., p. 18.

12   Todd, pp. 259-60.

13   Eckermann, p. 19.

14   Richard Friedenthal, *Luther: His Life and Times* (New York: Harcourt Brace Jovanovich Inc.,

1970), p. 438.

15   Simon, p. 333.

16   Eckermann, p. 21.

17   Simon, pp. 331-32.

18   Bainton, p. 27.

19   Martin Luther, *Luther's Works*, volume 54 (Philadelphia: Fortress Press, 1967), Table Talk No. 2911b, p. 180.

20   Anna Ilgenstein Katterfield, *The Morning Star of Wittenberg* (Washington, D.C.: Review & Herald Publishing Association, 1956), p. 48.

21   Luther, Table Talk No. 2931, p. 181.

22   Luther, Table Talk No. 1457, p. 153.

23   Luther, Table Talk No. 3178a, p. 191.

24   Bainton, p. 26.

25   Eckermann, p. 30.

26   Luther, Table Talk No. 1658, pp. 160-61.

27   Bainton, p. 34.

28   Eckermann, p. 26.

29   Roland H. Bainton, *Here I Stand: A Life of Martin Luther* (New York: Abingdon Press, 1950), p. 293.

30   Bainton, *Women of the Reformation*, p. 34.

31   Ibid., p. 36.

32   Eckermann, p. 60.

33   Bainton, *Women of the Reformation*, p. 36.

34   Ibid.

35   Ibid.

36   Charles Ludwig, *Queen of the Reformation* (Minneapolis: Bethany House Publishers, 1986), p. 128.

37   Katterfield, p. 49.

38   Eckermann, p. 57.

39   Ibid., p. 34.

40   Katterfield, p. 93.

41   Todd, p. 327.

42   Ibid.

43   Friedenthal, p. 446.

44   Eckermann, p. 70.

45   Todd, p. 309.

46   Katterfield, p. 162.

47   Todd, p. 326.

48   Eckermann, p. 46.

49   Bainton, *Women of the Reformation*, p. 33.

50   Eric W. Gritsch, *Martin—God's Court Jester* (Philadelphia: Fortress Press, 1983), p. 83.

51   Katterfield, p. 173.

52   Simon, p. 352.

53   Eckermann, pp. 81-82.

54   William J. Petersen, *Martin Luther Had a Wife* (Wheaton, Illinois: Tyndale House Publishers Inc., 1983), p. 37.

55   Katterfield, p. 191.

56   Alice E. Walter, *Katharine Luther, Liberated Nun* (St. Louis: Clayton Publishing House Inc., 1981), p. 75.

Chapter 4

Gracia Nasi Mendes
(c. 1510 - 1569)

JEWISH PHILANTHROPIST WHO AIDED THE SPANISH AND PORTUGUESE
MARRANOS ESCAPE THE INQUISITION.

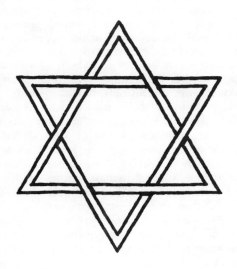

THE THREE SAILING SHIPS of Christopher Columbus (1451-1506) lay anchored at the port of Palos, Spain, awaiting orders to leave for the Indies. By midnight August 2, 1492, the sailors were aboard, the cargo loaded, the maps checked, and the navigating instruments in place. The next morning Columbus gave the orders to hoist the sails and leave Spanish shores.

Earlier King John II of Portugal had rejected Columbus' request to commission such an expedition. In 1486 the explorer secured an audience with King Ferdinand and Queen Isabella of Spain. He hoped to convince them of the value of discovering a water route to India. To the religious Isabella he spoke of the benefits to the Catholic Church in spreading Christianity; to the more practical Ferdinand he described the riches and gold to be reaped from opening a sea-lane to the Indies.

The monarchs listened, but at that time their treasury was depleted from the costly war against the Moors still entrenched in parts of Spain. In addition their majesties faced the onerous problem of ridding their country of heretical Jews, a situation they hoped finally to resolve by issuing a decree of expulsion stating that no Jews could remain in Spain after midnight August 2, 1492.

While searching for backers for his expedition, Columbus had aroused the interest of wealthy Jews who were hoping to find a safe haven for their people away from persecution and death. They offered the explorer their financial support. Ferdinand and Isabella, relieved of the monetary burden, finally approved the expedition, and in April 1492 they signed a contract with Columbus.

It is believed that Columbus, himself, had descended from a family of Jewish converts, and it is known that he had Jewish seamen and an interpreter who spoke Hebrew in his crew. When the inquisitors began to enforce the royal decree after midnight on August 2, Columbus' ships were primed to sail. Was this coincidence, or was Columbus anxious to remove himself and his crew from the grasp of the Inquisition?[1]

Among others expelled from Spain in the fateful year of 1492 was a respected Jewish man with his two sons Francisco and Diogo. They were descendants of the illustrious ancient house of Benveniste and had taken the family name of Mendes. They were probably among the 600 fortunate Jewish families allowed to re-settle in Portugal.

After the Portuguese explorer Vasco da Gama had opened a sea route to India around the Cape of Good Hope in 1497-98, the luxuries of the Far East were available to be shipped to the untapped markets in northern Europe. In 1503 the Portuguese sent the first spice fleet to the Flemish port of Antwerp. After that date the King of Portugal had a virtual monopoly on pepper, cinnamon, cloves, ginger, exotic woods, and luxury goods from the Orient. Through the years the market flourished in northern Europe and brought in substantial revenues to the royal treasury. Spices were in demand not only for royal tables, but for well-to-do citizens who could pay the price.

In Portugal Francisco and Diogo Mendes, who had become dealers in precious stones, seized the opportunity, and expanded their commercial enterprises to the lucrative spice market. With their profits they soon opened a banking house in Lisbon. For safety the Mendes brothers had converted to Christianity, but Francisco Mendes dared to conduct Jewish services in secret.

It was customary even among converted Jews to marry one of their own. Francisco chose for a bride the eighteen-year-old sister of Dr. Miguez, the court physician. She was a descendant of the noble House of Nasi. Before her wedding she was known as Beatrice de Luna; when she married she was called Gracia Mendes; still later she adopted the name Gracia Nasi when she reverted to Judaism. In the Jewish community she was esteemed for her beauty, her exceptional ability, her forthright character, and her compassion for unfortunate victims of the Inquisition.[2]

Isabella and Ferdinand, an Unholy Alliance.

Isabella (1451-1504) of Castile, an ambitious woman of great virtue and religiosity, had married in 1469 the young and equally ambitious Ferdinand (1452-1516) of Aragon. This wedding united two of the most powerful kingdoms in Spain. When they mounted the throne in 1474, they ruled as "the Catholic sovereigns" over all of Spain except Moorish Granada, which fell to them in 1492. Their great achievements for Spain and the Catholic Church were dishonored by the cruelty and suffering they inflicted on their subjects in the name of religion.

Jews had lived in communities in the Iberian peninsula for centuries. Generally they had not been absorbed into the Spanish population, so had kept their identity and religion as Jews. In Spain they had developed the richest, strongest, and most influential Jewish community in Europe. Their successes as physicians, scientists, astronomers, map-makers, financiers, lawyers, craftsmen, scholars, and royal advisers had drawn envy and anti-Semitic sentiments from the jealous public and the Christian clergy.

Isabella, eager to bring unbelievers into the faith, instituted a body of Spanish clerics who were instructed to force Jews and Muslims to convert to Catholicism. Isabella also ordered the clerics to weed out heretics and apostates. The Pope, who opposed forced conversion, challenged the authority of the Spanish Crown to meddle in religious matters. Impatient with interference from Rome, Isabella continued to empower her own inquisitors to use methods that became increasingly harsh. Wealthy Jews paid judicious bribes to the Vatican to forestall the Pope's sanction of an official Inquisition.

The Spanish inquisitors disregarded the Pope's orders and began to force Jews to become "New Christians" through mass conversions. The "Old Christians," those of the general population and Jews of past generations who had become true converts, were suspicious of the motives and sincerity of the newly-converted. The Jews who outwardly accepted Christianity but lived secretly as Jews were especially despised. They were given the name "Marranos," a derogatory term originally meaning "swine." In time this name became acceptable even to the Jews. Those Jews who had been converted and assimilated into Christian society were known as "Conversos."

The forced conversion of the Jews created a problem for the Spanish court and clergy. Before the Jews had been "converted," they were identifiable as a homogeneous group, but as pseudo-Christians their real identity and religious persuasion were obscured. How could one distinguish between the sincere Catholic Jews and the apostates still practicing Judaism in secret?

In 1478 Pope Sixtus IV reluctantly issued a Bull giving Ferdinand and Isabella the authority to establish an Inquisition to root out heretics and sinners. While Jews who had not converted were allowed to live virtually undisturbed, the inquisitors bore down on the backsliding Marranos. A list of thirty-seven clues indicated how informers could recognize Judaizers. The New Christians were suspect if they wore clean clothes on Fridays in preparation for the Saturday Sabbath, or if no smoke came from their chimneys on Jewish holy days, or if they ate certain foods, or were overheard saying Jewish prayers.

Informers were offered incentives to report suspicious behavior. "Come, tell me what you know of these men and women," they were urged. "Give me a good case against them, and in exchange you shall receive the indulgence you crave."[3] The informants were excused from taxation and promised a share of confiscated Jewish property and wealth. Old Christian Jews who reported Judaizers were promised leniency in court.

Those Jews accused of heresy were forced to wear the "sambenito," the garment of shame, so they could be easily recognized. The sambenitos were tunics, usually yellow, bearing red or green crosses or symbols indicating the degree of the victim's sin. The accused ones were forced to parade through the streets and were often flogged at the church doors. The penalty for victims who did not confess to heresy was imprisonment, torture, expulsion, slavery, or at the worst burning at the stake.

After Rome officially approved an Inquisition, Ferdinand and Isabella appointed in 1483 their fanatical confessor, Thomas de Torquemada (1420-1498), as Inquisitor General. He had authority over all Spanish inquisitors and was granted immense power.

Torquemada, obsessed with preserving Catholicism, enforced cruel and harsh measures on the victims and ordered public "autos-de-fé" (acts of faith) where as many as fifty suspected Judaizers were burned alive in one day. The public burnings began at dawn, usually held on Sundays when a large number of people could witness the event. Clergy in resplendent robes and bearing crosses led the procession of victims to the town square. Friars, for the last time, exhorted the heretics to confess. The Grand Inquisitor then led in the celebration of the mass and preached a sermon. So as not to be found guilty of violating the Catholic Church's stand against the shedding of blood, the Inquisitor General then turned the proceedings over to the state to complete. As each victim was led to the "quemadero," or the place of fire, his or her crime was read. Some victims were strangled before burning, others were burned alive. Those fortunate ones who had escaped were burned in effigy. As the burnings proceeded and the screams of the tortured rent the air, the inquisitors feigned shock, and the spectators cheered. Burning incense did not disguise the stench of burning flesh. The autos-de-fé became the mark of Torquemada's Inquisition at its worst.

The Inquisitor General was largely responsible for the royal Edict of Expulsion that led to the exodus of thousands of Jews from Spain before the deadline of August 2, 1492. Ferdinand and Isabella were tempted to accept money from wealthy Jews who wanted to stay in Spain, but Torquemada shamed them into refusing "Judas money." Torquemada continued his vendetta against Christian heretics, Jews, and Muslims until his death in 1498 at the Dominican monastery he had built in Avila with money from repentant heretics. He had erected there a statue dedicated to "limpieza," or purity of blood, a forerunner of the ideology of Nazi Germany. Ironically, Torquemada was himself a descendant of a Jewish grandmother.

Fortunes to be Made in Portugal.

In haste the expelled Spanish Jews had to dispose of their property at ridiculously low prices, leave behind their businesses and their gold, and pay an emigration fee. Unscrupulous sea captains often collected exorbitant sums for passage to some safe port only to change courses and bring unsuspecting victims to Africa to be sold as slaves. Many boarded ships to Italian seaports, were robbed of all their possessions, and set adrift. Other exiles began the torturous overland journey westward to Portugal, the only neighboring country open to them. They carried with them their sole belongings. It was a pitiful exodus.

Upon entering Portugal the emigrants were forced to pay a poll-tax and were granted only eight months to remain in that country. About 100,000 Jews took advantage of King John's offer of sea transportation to other countries such as the Netherlands, Italy, or Turkey. With an eye on the profits to his treasury, the King allowed the wealthy Jews to stay and settle wherever they chose to conduct their lucrative businesses. About 600 wealthy Jewish families believed they had found a safe sanctuary where they could reestablish their homes and professions. Among the fortunate Jewish families welcomed by the King were members of the Mendes family.

As New Christians, Francisco and Diogo Mendes found unlimited opportunities in Portugal. The spice trade had flourished, and the Mendes brothers established a growing trade with Antwerp. Ever alert to new possibilities, Francisco Mendes sent his brother Diogo to Antwerp to open a branch of the family business. With his financial acumen Diogo soon had almost total control of spices exported to Italy, France, Germany, and England, and the King of Portugal had become financially dependent on the Mendes operation. Diogo also expanded the banking enterprise, loaning money to a vast assortment of debtors.

In 1536, after eight years of marriage, Francisco Mendes died in Portugal leaving his young widow with an infant daughter named Reyna. According to his will the vast family fortune was to be administered equally by his widow Gracia and his younger brother Diogo who had by that time become one of the wealthiest men in Antwerp. Gracia and her daughter soon joined Diogo in Antwerp where jointly they ran the family's many enterprises.

Persons Dragged by the Hair to the Font.

When Francisco Mendes died, Lisbon had become a dangerous place for Jews. Shortly after the emigration of the Spanish New Christians to Portugal in 1492, King John II had died and in 1495 was succeeded by his young cousin Manuel I. At the beginning of his reign Manuel the Fortunate, as he was known, had been tolerant of the Spanish Jews. But when he wished to marry young Isabella, daughter of Ferdinand and Isabella, the Spanish monarchs insisted that Manuel first "purify" his country from the curse of the heretic Jews. Young Isabella was even more emphatic. She wrote Manuel stating that she would not set foot in Portugal until it was "cleansed of the presence of all infidels."[4] The marriage agreement was signed on November 30, 1496, and a week later a royal decree banished Muslims and Jews from the country.

Manuel had acquired a bride, but he soon regretted losing the wealth and talents of the Jews. Against the advice of his council and ad-

visers, he devised a plan to force Christian baptism on the Jews. He would then keep them in his domain and at the same time save their souls from eternal damnation.

On March 19, 1497, Manuel issued an order that all Jewish children between the ages of four and fourteen were to be baptized on the following Sunday. Those who did not come voluntarily were dragged to the font, sprinkled with holy water, and declared to be Christians. The parents who refused had their children torn from their arms and sent to distant Christian homes. Some Jewish parents chose death for themselves and their children. One eye witness wrote:

> I saw many persons dragged by the hair to the font. Sometimes, I saw a father, his head covered in sign of grief and pain, lead his son to the font, protesting and calling God to witness that they wished to die together in the law of Moses. Yet more terrible things that were done with them did I witness, with my own eyes.[5]

Contrary to Manuel's hopes, the baptism of children did not draw many of the parents to the font. As an enticement the King offered New Christians immunity from punishment for twenty years, but before the time had lapsed, mob uprisings had escalated into wholesale slayings. By 1506 massacres had begun in Lisbon where on one day over 500 New Christians were put to death. A German Christian wrote of the horrors:

> On Monday, I saw things that I would certainly not have believed had they been reported or written, or unless I had witnessed them myself. Women with child were flung from the windows and caught on spears by those standing underneath, their offspring being hurled away. The peasantry followed the example of the townspeople. Many women and girls were ravished in the fanatical pursuit. The number of New Christians slain is estimated at between 2,000 and 4,000 souls.[6]

During Manuel's reign there were waves of persecution followed by periods of leniency. Upon his death in 1521, Manuel's eldest son John III inherited the throne. The reign of John, a young man of limited intelligence, was marked by intolerance and oppression. In 1525 he married Catalina (or Catharina), granddaughter of Ferdinand and Isabella and sister of Charles V (1516-1556), then King of Spain. The religious, strong-willed Catalina wielded great influence as Queen and as a member of the

Council of State. She saw only one solution to the duplicity of the Portuguese Marranos—the establishing of an Inquisition similar to that in Spain.

King John's application to Rome for permission to set up an office of Inquisition was met with hesitation and delay by Pope Clement VII, who did not condone forced baptisms. In addition, the Pope was eager to continue receiving the lavish bribes from wealthy Jews for his opposition to an Inquisition. Through the ensuing years there were increasing conflicts of authority between the Portuguese royal couple, the Holy Roman Emperor, and the Pope. Abuses, torture, and treachery followed on all sides.

In 1536 the Inquisition was established in Portugal, but not until 1547 did the Pope issue a Bull sanctioning it. By this time a new generation of Jews had intermarried into influential Portuguese families, had become advisers and physicians to nobility, and had established profitable commercial enterprises. But the Inquisition bore down on any persons suspected of having even a small amount of Jewish blood, including those who had become sincere Catholics. There were arbitrary arrests, tortures, imprisonments without trial, and confiscation of property. Promiscuous burnings claimed the lives of both New and Old Christians for the honor of the Inquisition and the glory of God.

The Inquisition continued to wield its terrible power in the Peninsula through the sixteenth, seventeenth, and eighteenth centuries. Autos became as popular as bullfights and were often offered as "entertainment" for royal visitors. During the three centuries it was believed that more than 30,000 Judaizers were put to death.[7]

Antwerp, a Temporary Haven.

During the oppression of Jews in Portugal, scores of New Christians had relocated in Antwerp where for a time there was temporary freedom from persecution. Here the Jews contributed substantially to the economy and professions. Publicly Diogo Mendes continued to attend Roman Catholic mass and observe the necessary rituals, but secretly and cautiously he practiced Judaism. While many of his compatriots left Antwerp for safer locations in the eastern Mediterranean or Turkey, Diogo continued to conduct his expanding business in Antwerp. At the same time he set up an elaborate network of sanctuaries and funds for Marranos escaping from Spain and Portugal.

By this time the Low Countries were under the same rule as Spain and Portugal and owed allegiance to the Holy Roman Emperor. In spite of the Emperor's promises of protection, the New Christians in Antwerp felt the hot breath of the inquisitors drawing ever closer. Even the bribes to the papal treasury did not eliminate the danger.

Suspicions soon were aroused concerning the activities and religious leanings of Diogo Mendes. In 1531 he and three others were arrested for heresy. They were soon released, but one year later Diogo was imprisoned again for assisting the escape of Marranos from Spain and Portugal. He was sent to a Brussels prison without benefit of bail. Diogo's imprisonment raised an outcry from Antwerp's magistrates, consuls, and even from European monarchs who had benefited from the spice trade and had borrowed huge sums from the Mendes bank. After two months in prison Diogo was released and charges dropped with the payment of substantial amounts of money.

Back in Portugal it became increasingly more dangerous for the New Christians to escape from the country. In 1536, the same year the Inquisition was established in Portugal, Gracia Mendes, then a twenty-six-year-old widow, escaped to Antwerp by way of England. With her she brought her infant daughter Reyna, her high-strung younger sister Brianda, and her nephew Joseph Miguez Nasi. With shrewd maneuvering she managed to remove most of her wealth from Portugal. She also brought to Antwerp her great business expertise and a burning passion to help the other New Christians left behind. She also hoped some day to be able to shed the facade of conversion and return to her Jewish traditions and beliefs.

Soon after Gracia and her relatives arrived in Antwerp, her younger sister Brianda married Diogo Mendes. Shortly they had a baby daughter they named Gracia after their illustrious aunt. Diogo continued to assist escaping Spanish and Portuguese whose property and money were in danger of being confiscated. He set up machinery whereby they could transfer their funds to his agents outside the Peninsula.

By this time Antwerp had become an unsafe and inhospitable location for Jews. Although the business had prospered under their joint management, Diogo and Gracia decided to settle their affairs and leave the city. But plans were stopped short when Diogo died in late 1542 or early 1543.

In his will Diogo left a substantial amount of his personal wealth for charity to the poor, the imprisoned, and the orphaned. One-half of the business assets belonged to Gracia from her deceased husband's will, and Diogo named her administrator of his half of the firm's capital with responsibility for the welfare of his wife and young daughter. In view of Brianda's irresponsible nature, Diogo left to his wife only the original dowry she had brought to the marriage. Brianda's bitter resentment of Gracia's control over one of Europe's most successful businesses and largest fortunes caused a lifetime of conflict between the sisters. Gracia's nephew Joseph, a competent young man with a keen sense of finance, soon became her able business associate. But the plans to leave Antwerp were delayed by other developments.

It appeared that at the time of Diogo Mendes' death, Charles V, then Holy Roman Emperor, was collecting evidence to support the confiscation of the entire Mendes fortune. Fearing the loss of such a windfall, the Emperor brought posthumous proceedings of heresy against Diogo. Gracia fought the charges by every means at her disposal—she cited Diogo's devotion to the Christian faith (obviously a falsehood) and offered lavish gifts to the officials. The charges were dropped when she agreed to extend the Emperor an interest free loan of 100,000 ducats for two years. The large sum did not substantially deplete her assets, but it did set a risky precedent. It also exposed the Emperor's true motives for confiscating Jewish property to be financial, not religious.

During the years in Antwerp, Gracia's daughter Reyna had grown into a beautiful young girl in her mid-teens. As an heir to the Mendes fortune she was courted by a host of aristocratic suitors. The most persistent was the aging Francisco d'Aragon, an illegitimate descendant of Spanish royalty. He elicited the aid of the Queen Regent Mary of Netherlands and offered a loan of 200,000 ducats (from the anticipated Mendes fortune) to the Emperor if the marriage took place. When the Queen Regent approached Gracia Mendes with the proposal for her daughter's hand, Gracia was incensed and stated bluntly she would rather see her daughter dead. The Queen Regent and the Emperor, coveting the promised loan, continued by every possible means to press the cause of the rejected suitor.

One day toward the end of 1544, the Mendes mansion stood empty—its female occupants had fled the country on the pretext of a visit to a health spa. To avoid suspicion the Mendes women took with them only what they could carry. Prior to this they had arranged secretly for safe passage to Venice.

Joseph was left back in Antwerp to answer charges of heresy against the Mendes women and to forestall the seizure of their property. Through long and involved negotiations with the Queen Regent, the rejected suitor, and the Emperor, who was furious at losing the Mendes fortune, Joseph tried to placate all parties with monetary inducements. Whether or not he accomplished his goal is not clear, but he too suddenly left Antwerp for Italy where he had transferred a considerable portion of the Mendes assets.

Venice, an Exciting Way-Station.

Once Gracia and her companions were out of the reach of Antwerp officials, they traveled with a large entourage, taking the long route across France and northern Italy to avoid the usual trouble-spots for escaping Jews. When they arrived in Venice, the Mendes family did not settle in the ghetto where Jews were required to live. Instead they took up residence in a mansion in the center of the exciting canal city. Here they lived as Christians enjoying Venetian culture and gentility. At the same time their house became a stopping point for escaping Marranos.

Trouble came from an unforeseen source. Brianda, resentful at being shut out from her husband's inheritance and envious of her sister's authority, demanded her half of the family fortune. Gracia's refusal to turn over the control of money to her volatile and extravagant sister led to a bitter dispute. Brianda used the most dangerous weapon at her disposal—she denounced her sister as a secret Judaizer and informed the court that Gracia planned to move her household and her assets to Turkey where she could revert to the Jewish faith. In a lawsuit against her sister, Brianda asked to be made guardian of her daughter, young Gracia.

The Venetian magistrates, fearful that such a vast fortune should slip away from them, prohibited the removal of the Mendes property and put Gracia under house arrest. The pope's envoy removed the two daughters from their mothers and placed them in a convent where they would be given Christian instruction.

Brianda, through an anti-Jewish agent, also demanded a share of the banking interests in France. The King of France, who had borrowed extensively from the Mendes bank, used Gracia's Judaizing as a guise and eagerly placed an embargo on the Mendes assets in France. The duplicitous agent turned on Brianda and also denounced her as a Judaizer, thus doubling the available funds to be appropriated.

Again Gracia had to fight court battles, produce evidence of true Christian conversion, and offer gifts and bribes to appropriate authorities. With Joseph's help she had been transferring portions of her business to her agent in Constantinople (now Istanbul), the splendid capital of the Ottoman Empire. Here she had the support of Moses Hamon, the Sultan's Jewish physician, who had aroused the interest of his master Suleiman I (1494-1566) in the Mendes fortune.

Although Gracia welcomed the support of the Turkish ambassador in Venice, she was reluctant to transfer all her assets to Turkish protection. She had learned the hard lesson of dealing with royal houses, governments, and clergy that coveted her fortune. By 1549, after negotiations, affirmation of her Christian conversion, and lavish gifts to officials, Gracia was released from confinement in Venice and reunited with her daughter Reyna. In 1550, after a promise of safe-conduct from the liberal-minded duke of Ferrara, she and her daughter moved to that city on the Adriatic just south of Venice. They were still in a land that had not become a papal state, so were allowed to declare their true religion. Unexpectedly Brianda and her daughter soon joined them.

Ferrara, a Short-Lived Sanctuary.

Ferrara, a thriving city under the enlightened rule of Duke Ercole II, had become an asylum for Spanish and Portuguese Marranos who could live openly as Jews. Several cultured and influential Jewish women supported philanthropic, literary, and religious activities which no doubt sparked Gracia's interest in Hebrew culture and literature. One of the important works, probably financed by Gracia, was the translation of the Hebrew Bible which after its publication in 1553 became known as the Ferrara Bible. There were two editions: The Spanish version for Christians was dedicated to the Duke of Ferrara; the Hebrew edition was inscribed to "the Very Magnificent Lady: Doña

Gracia Naci." In a flowery prologue were the following words written by Yom Tob Atias and Abraham Usque:

> Therefore we desired to direct it to Your Honor, as being a person whose merits have always earned the most sublime place among all of our people—both because your greatness deserves it, and because your own birth and love of your land imposes this well-deserved obligation upon us.[8]

In 1553 a volume, the *Consolation for the Tribulations of Israel*, written in Portuguese by Samuel Usque, reviewed Jewish martyrdom in Christian Europe. Usque dedicated the book to Doña Gracia and lauded her for "what you have done and still do to bring to light the fruits of those plants that are buried there [in Portugal] in darkness."[9] One entire section was devoted to Gracia's work in helping the refugees escape Portugal. No exact details were given, but Usque eulogized her in glowing generalities. He wrote:

> She it is who at the beginning of their journey greatly helps your necessitous sons, who are prevented by penury from saving themselves from the pyre and undertaking so long a road, her hope giving them strength. As for those who have already left and have arrived in Flanders and elsewhere overcome by poverty, or who stand distressed by the sea in danger that they will not be able to fare further, she helps these her dependents with a most liberal hand, with money and many other aids and comforts . . . . she brings them to safe lands and does not cease to guide them, and gathers them to the obedience and precepts of their God of old. Thus she has been your tried strength in your weakness; a bank where the weary rest; a fountain of clear water where the parched drink; a fruit-laden shady tree where the hungry eat and the desolate find rest . . .[10]

The Mendes mansion in Ferrara became the most secure haven in Italy for escaping Marranos. But in 1551 the plague struck the city, and the Italians blamed the Portuguese refugees for bringing in the contagion from Germany and Switzerland. When the newcomers were threatened with violence, the Duke of Ferrara was forced to issue an order for all recent Marrano emigrants to leave the city. The helpless outcasts wandered about Italy trying to find a place of safety. Again Gracia came to their rescue. She supplied the refugees with money, supplies, and river boats for their flight. Gracia herself left Ferrara to return to Venice, where it appeared she again was charged with

Judaizing and threatened with arrest. Once more her Turkish connections came to her rescue, and when the plague had passed, she returned to Ferrara.

In Italy the Counter-Reformation was underway, and the powerful and intolerant Cardinal Caraffa in the papal court had laid a heavy hand on those who were not Roman Catholics. A papal Inquisition was established to question and prosecute all heretics. As it became evident that freedom to practice Judaism was again threatened, Gracia completed the transfer of her property to Turkey. In 1552 Gracia Nasi Mendes and her daughter Reyna left for the Ottoman Empire.

Constantinople, a Mecca for Displaced Persons.

The Mendes entry into the glittering capital was a triumphant affair. The large party riding in four magnificent coaches was escorted by forty armed men who had guarded them on the dangerous route across the Balkans. They were welcomed enthusiastically by the Marranos who had settled in Turkey and by the Sultan who was delighted with the financial advantage for his treasury.

For centuries the Muslim forces of the Ottoman Empire had been advancing into Christian Asia and Europe. By the mid-1400s the Ottomans had conquered the entire Byzantine Empire except the capital city of Constantinople. In 1453, after fierce fighting, the majestic Christian city was captured and made into the Muslim capital. By the mid-1500's the Ottomans ruled Asia Minor, the Balkans, part of northern Africa, and the Middle East. The Empire reached its peak under the reign of Sultan Suleiman I, called Suleiman the Magnificent, who ruled from 1520 to 1566. Suleiman was distinguished not only for his military prowess, but for his educational and legal reforms. As a lavish patron of the arts and literature, he made Constantinople a center of opulence and glitter. He indulged his many wives, especially his favorite wife, the tricky and powerful Khurrem Sultana, also known as Roxelana, the daughter of a Russian priest.

When the Jews were expelled from Spain in 1492, they were welcomed in the Ottoman Empire. At that time the ruling Sultan remarked, "How can you call this Ferdinand 'wise'—he who has impoverished his dominions in order to enrich mine?"[11] As the Jews settled in Turkey, they brought with them their religion, money, crafts, professions, and diverse languages and cultures. However, they were heavily taxed, and resentful Turkish citizens often burned the homes and synagogues of the Jews. One German visitor made some uncomplimentary observations in his travel diary. "In Constantinople," he wrote, "the Jews are thick as ants ... The Jews are despised in Turkey as they are anywhere else. ... The Jews lend nothing to the Turks."[12]

A French official was more charitable:

> At the present day they have in their hands the most and greatest traffic of merchandise and ready money that is in the Levant. And likewise the shops and warehouses, the best furnished with all rich sorts of merchandises, which are in Constantinople, are those of the Jews. Likewise, they have amongst them workmen of all arts and handicrafts most excellent, and especially of the *Maranes*, of late banished and driven out of Spain and Portugal, who, to the great detriment and damage of Christianity, have taught the Turks divers inventions, crafts and engines of war, as to make artillery, harquebuses, gunpowder, shot and other ammunition; they have also there set up printing, not before seen in those countries. . . .[13]

When Gracia arrived in Constaninople in 1553, she took up residence with the Europeans in the wealthy suburb of Galata overlooking the Golden Horn, an inlet of the Bosporus strait. She lived a life of luxury with loyal Jewish attendants serving her every desire. She and her household did not adopt Muslim customs or dress, but continued to practice their Spanish language, culture, customs, fashions, and food. Her generous work of charity often found up to eighty needy ones eating at her table.

Soon the festering financial dispute with her sister again erupted. Brianda and her daughter young Gracia, who had married her cousin Samuel Nasi, reopened their claim to Diogo Mendes' share of the fortune. Gracia insisted that the law of Portugal where her husband Francisco had died prevailed over the law of Flanders where Diogo had died. Therefore the original estate should be left in her control. Furthermore, she claimed that she had spent a large portion of Diogo's estate in fighting the confiscation of his property in Antwerp.

When the problem was turned over to the rabbis in Turkey to settle, they judged that the laws of Portugal were to be honored, and Gracia maintained control of the entire Mendes fortune. Though the decision appeared to be weighted unfairly in Gracia's behalf, Brianda and her daughter had ample personal funds and did not suffer. It was believed that Brianda spent her last days in Turkey, and young Gracia and her husband also took up residence there.

In Constantinople Gracia expanded her shipping enterprises, even to building her own sailing vessels. She exported wool, pepper, wine, and grain to markets in Venice and other Italian ports. In early 1554 her nephew Joseph Miguez Nasi joined her and helped manage the business. In an elaborate wedding ceremony he married Gracia's daughter Reyna. From then on Joseph's career had a meteoric rise as a diplomat, politician, and court favorite.

Before Gracia's husband had died in Portugal, he had requested that he be buried in the Holy Land. To honor his wishes Gracia had his remains exhumed from the cemetery in Lisbon and reburied in the Valley of Jehoshaphat outside Jerusalem. Gracia hoped to fulfill her dream to be buried beside her husband and to establish a homeland for the Jews in the land of her ancestors.

In Constantinople Gracia continued to assist the poor and the helpless, often feeding scores of unfortunates at her own table and giving generous support to hospitals. Wherever there was misery, enslavement, or illness, there was Gracia's open hand.

Although she herself had no formal education, she turned her attention to the support of scholary establishments. In Constantinople she founded an academy for rabbinic studies and a synagogue for worship. In Salonica, Greece, then a haven for over 10,000 Marranos, she established the "Wayfarers' Synagogue" and a "Midrash" for the study of rabbinic literature.

As a wealthy woman accustomed to having her own way, Gracia was impatient with anyone opposing her. At times she was angry with the religious leaders who disagreed with her decisions, but most of the rabbis and theologians praised her charitable works, her religious dedication, and her scholarly benevolences.

Failure in Ancona.

One of the cities that benefited from trade with the Mendes exporting business was the ancient Italian port of Ancona on the eastern coast of the Adriatic. Unlike Spain and Portugal, Rome had been receptive to the emigration of New Christians to Italy. In 1547 Pope Paul III had declared the papal city of Ancona open to Marranos, even guaranteeing them a safe refuge and exempting them from excessive taxes and the wearing of special identification as Jews. In exchange for a payment of money, Pope Paul's successor Julius III continued the policy and promised that the Ancona Jews would not be prosecuted for practicing their Jewish faith.

Ancona became a veritable haven for Marranos and benefited greatly from their financial and professional expertise. But the Pope's lenient policy and acceptance of money was soundly criticized outside of Italy. As a member of the papal court, Cardinal Caraffa, an avowed anti-Semite, had begun to burn Hebrew books in Rome. In 1555 when Caraffa was elected Pope under the name of Paul IV, he issued edicts against all heretics, including Lutherans and New Christians. The former guarantees to the Marranos were withdrawn, restricted ghettos were established, and identifying badges of shame were again to be worn by the Jews.

In response to Pope Paul's policy, at least one hundred Ancona Jews were thrown into prison. After bribing one of the Pope's unprincipled commissioners, about fifty Jews managed to escape, but the rest were tortured to extract confessions. Those who refused to disavow their faith, about twenty-five in number, were burned in autos-de-fé similar to those held in Spain and Portugal. These victims included some of the most learned and honored Marranos in Ancona. An agent of the Mendes enterprises committed suicide to escape the burning.

When reports of the Ancona arrests reached Gracia, she was shocked and incensed. The guarantees of safety and freedom of worship had been violated. The Sultan sent his envoy to Ancona demanding the release of the prisoners, but the Pope remained unyielding, and the burnings proceeded.

It was too late to save the victims, but it was not too late to avenge the heinous acts. Gracia ordered her ships to abandon Ancona and deliver cargoes to the rival port Pesaro. Ancona soon felt the loss of the Mendes trade while Pesaro prospered. In 1556 Gracia attempted to align the Jewish merchants and religious leaders behind her in a boycott of Ancona, but there were those who feared reprisals toward Jews in Ancona and Pesaro. When some rabbis in Turkey strongly objected to the measures, the boycott failed. This was one of the few failures in Gracia's business career. In Italy the persecution of the Jews continued.

Crown of the Glory of Goodly Women.

After the defeat of the Ancona boycott, Gracia lost her appetite for running the family business. She turned over the management of the Mendes enterprises to her nephew Joseph Nasi, who had become a court favorite. In 1561 as a reward for his services, Sultan Suleiman I gave Joseph control of the city of Tiberias in Palestine then under the Ottoman Empire. Later Suleiman's son and heir, Sultan Selim II (c. 1524-74), known as The Sot or The Drunkard, gave the favored Jew a cluster of small islands with considerable commercial and strategic importance in the Aegean. Selim then bestowed on Joseph the title of Duke of Naxos. Joseph developed a network of diplomatic and commercial contacts in Poland and gained a monopoly of wine imports from Constantinople. Throughout his lifetime Joseph harbored an intense hatred of the Catholics in the Mediterranean. Upon the death of Sultan Selim, Joseph's influence waned, and he retired to "gilded obscurity" in his castle on the Bosporus.

It was now time for Gracia, in her late fifties, to turn her efforts to fulfilling her vision of creating a Jewish homeland in Palestine. In exchange for 1,000 decats a year, she obtained permission from the Sultan to open an independent Jewish settlement in Tiberias. Although in ruins, Tiberias appeared to be an ideal location—it had historical significance and had been mentioned in the Talmud as a location for establishing a Jewish settlement. It was surrounded by fertile land that would be suitable for agriculture.

Much work was needed to make the run-down city liveable. A protective wall had to be built, homes restored, the ancient synagogue reopened, and mulberry trees planted to support the raising of silkworms. Gracia had a mansion built for herself outside the city where she planned to spend her last days. It is not known if she ever fulfilled her dream, but her absence from Constantinople for a time before her death led to the belief that she may have spent some of her remaining days in her new homeland.

When she died in 1569, the Jewish communities the world over mourned her death. She was commemorated and eulogized by rabbis and scholars, honored in Turkish mosques, and grieved in private by the multitude of unfortunates she had helped. Eloquent tributes extolled her "excellent virtues and noble deeds." She was called the "crown of the glory of goodly women" and "the heart of her people." A poet of Salonica thought to give her the ultimate testimony. He wrote, "Like a man, she girded her loins with might and strengthened her arms . . . making a name like unto the names of the great and holy ones. . . . Verily, there was the garment of a man on a woman."[14]

Gracia Nasi Mendes could not stem the tide of oppression of the Jews in Spain and Portugal, but by her efforts thousands of her compatriots escaped the terrors of the Inquisition. At the end she was remembered not so much for her financial genius, her proficiency in business, and her immense wealth as for her great compassion and love for humanity. With her dedication to establishing a homeland for her people, she could be considered a pioneer of the modern Zionist movement.

Notes

1 Simon Wiesenthal, *Sails of Hope* (New York: Macmillan Publishing Co., Inc., 1973), pp. 3-6. Wiesenthal supports the theory that Columbus had Jewish blood in his ancestry. He further claims that Columbus was financed by Jewish money and supplied with maps from Jewish cartographers.

Henry Kamen in *The Spanish Inquisition* (New York: New American Library, 1965) also contends that Columbus probably descended from a line of Catalan converts and that his crew included Jewish seamen and a Jewish interpreter.

2 Cecil Roth, *Doña Gracia of the House of Nasi* (Philadelphia: The Jewish Publication Society of America, 1977), pp. 12-16. The practice of Jews to change their names when converted or when reverting to Judaism makes consistent identification difficult. To avoid confusion they will be referred to here generally by the last names they assumed. Before her marriage Doña Gracia was known as Beatrice de Luna. When she married, she was known as Gracia Mendes, and when she later returned to her Jewish faith, she adopted her maiden name Gracia Nasi. She will be referred to here by her married name Gracia Mendes or Gracia Nasi Mendes. Her daughter, first known as Brianda, will be referred to by the name her family used, Reyna, and by her married name Reyna Nasi.

Gracia's sister, first known as Brianda, adopted the name Reyna when she returned to the Jewish faith. To distinguish her from Gracia's daughter Reyna, she will be referred to by her original name or her married name Brianda Mendes. Gracia's nephew, known first as João Miguez, will be referred to by his adopted name Joseph Miguez Nasi.

3   Jean Plaidy, *The Spanish Inquisition; Its Rise, Growth, and End* (New York: The Citadel Press, 1967), p. 149 in volume I.

4   Cecil Roth, *A History of the Marranos* (New York: Schocken Books, 1974), p. 56.

5   Ibid., pp. 58-59.

6   Ibid., p. 65.

7   Ibid., p. 145.

8   Roth, *Doña Gracia of the House of Nasi*, p. 74.

9   Ibid., p. 76.

10   Ibid., p. 77.

11   Ibid., p. 90.

12   Ibid., pp. 94-95.

13   Ibid., pp. 96-97.

14   Ibid., pp. 132-33. All quotations in this paragraph are found here.

Chapter 5

Teresa of Avila
(1515 - 1582)

SPANISH MYSTIC, SAINT, FEARLESS REFORMER OF THE CARMELITE
RELIGIOUS ORDER, AND WRITER OF RELIGIOUS LITERATURE.

IN THE UPLAND PLATEAU of Old Castile in central Spain stands the walled city of Avila renowned as the birthplace of St. Teresa, religious reformer, mystic, and writer. Avila, a formidable bulwark, ascends from the barren plains and rocky foothills of the mountain ranges which surround it on three sides. The city, entirely enclosed by walls laid in a hexagonal pattern, is guarded by ninety granite towers and bastions.

In 1090 when construction of the fortifica-

tions began, Christians were gaining control of Avila after centuries of struggle against the Moors. A city of narrow winding streets lined with stone houses, churches, and monasteries, Avila earned the name "town of saints and stones." This was the place where Teresa, the frivolous adolescent, lost her virtue and where Teresa, the mature God-fearing crusader, found respite after exhausting travels across the Castilian plains during spring floods, summer heat, and winter cold.

In 1515, Teresa's birth year, the Catholic monarchs, Ferdinand and Isabella, ruled Spain, then one of the world's greatest powers on both the continent and the sea. Spain's mighty armada had crossed the ocean to reach and claim territories in the Americas. The country was caught up in the religious fervor of the Counter Reformation stirred up by the Protestant movement. At the same time the Inquisition was ruthlessly purging Jews, Turks, and heretics.

Heritage Renounced.

Teresa, the fourth child in her father's large second family of ten, was born on March 28 at her mother's farm in Gotarrendura, a village north of Avila. She was baptized at the Church of San Juan in Avila where her parents worshipped and where one can still see the massive stone baptismal font.

Very early Teresa exhibited an extroverted personality being cheerful, friendly, and outgoing. As she matured, her outstanding physical features—fair skin, lively dark eyes, sparkling white teeth, lustrous black hair, and graceful figure—drew much attention, particularly from the opposite sex. Her natural spontaneity and charm attracted admirers as a magnet.

Of Don Alonso, her strict but adoring father, Teresa admitted, ". . . I was the most loved of my father." Of Dona Beatriz, her mother, Teresa wrote, ". . . she suffered much sickness during her life. She was extremely modest. Although very beautiful, she never gave occasion to anyone to think she paid any attention to her beauty. . . . She was gentle and very intelligent. Great were the trials she suffered during her life."[1]

Don Alonso had wholeheartedly adopted the beliefs of the "Old Christians," trying to leave behind his Jewish heritage and the humiliation of his early childhood. He had raised his large family as devout Catholics, a natural persuasion in a city of monasteries, convents, and churches. Throughout her life Teresa kept secret her Jewish ancestry, as did the relatives who testified at her beatification and canonization. Her early biographers wrote only of her aristocratic Old Christian lineage.

Teresa's grandfather, Juan Sanchez, a successful Jewish merchant of silks and wools in Toledo, had for expedience and safety become a "Converso," or "New Christian." During the Inquisition hundreds of Conversos accused of Judaizing (observing Jewish customs) were put on trial, imprisoned, tortured, publicly humiliated, and often burned at the stake. Juan Sanchez confessed to "having committed many grave crimes and offenses against our Holy Catholic faith."[2] As penance he was forced to parade for seven Fridays wearing the "sambenito," a yellow tunic marked with large red or green crosses on front and back. This garment of shame bearing the victim's name and sins was then displayed in the parish church for all to see.

After changing his name to Juan Sanchez de Cepeda, he began to rebuild his reputation and fortune. When he moved to Avila, Juan Sanchez became a successful financial manager and for a price purchased a title of nobility. He lived in style, brought up his sons to be loyal Catholics, and hoped to marry them to women of status. Before he died, he had the satisfaction of witnessing in 1505 the marriage of his son Alonso, Teresa's father, to Catalina del Peso y Henao, a high-born woman. Two years later she died leaving Alonso with two children, Maria

and Juan de Cepeda.

Trained by his father, Alonso pursued a business in taxes and finance and was keenly interested in maintaining his persona as a man of honor, dignity, and religious conviction. He also loved fine clothes, jewels, and luxuries befitting a man of wealth and station. In his thirties he illegally adopted the name Don Alonso de Cepeda; later he made it his legal name. In her autobiography Teresa wrote of him, "My father was a man very charitable with the poor and compassionate toward the sick, and even toward servants. . . . He was very honest. No one ever saw him swear or engage in fault-finding. He was an upright man."[3]

In October 1509 two years after the death of his first wife, Alonso married Dona Beatriz de Ahumada, the fourteen-year-old cousin of his deceased wife and the daughter of a well-to-do landowner of Gotarrendura. Dona Beatriz brought to the union a large dowry of land and money. The couple settled in Casa de la Moneda, a sprawling mansion in Avila where Dona Beatriz soon gave birth to their first son, Hernando.

Don Alonso's life was interrupted when the "hidalgos," belonging to Spain's lower nobility, were called into service by King Ferdinand in his conquest of the small neighboring kingdom of Navarre. The campaign was successful. Alonso honorably discharged his duties, earned his title as a true hidalgo, and soon returned home to his growing family.

In quick succession came two more sons, Juan de Ahumada and Rodrigo, followed by Teresa, Lorenzo, Antonio, Pedro, Jeronimo, Agustin, and last Juana, on whom Teresa lavished much love and attention. Of her two half-siblings and nine brothers and sisters Teresa wrote, "I was very attached to them all, and they to me."[4]

Hardly Any Virtue Remained.

At age seven Teresa and her favorite brother Rodrigo, after reading about martyrs and saints, set out for the land of the Moors to have their heads cut off so they could gain quickly the wonders of heaven. An uncle found the runaways and brought them home to their anxious parents.

When dying as martyrs did not succeed, the two children planned to be hermits in the stone hut they built in the garden of their summer home. This too failed when the stones tumbled down. Teresa delighted in playing "nuns in a monastery" with her girl friends, but often sought solitude for prayer. Maturity brought on a change of heart when she discovered more exciting pastimes.

For distraction from child-bearing and frequent illness, Teresa's mother found escape in reading the then-popular adventure tales of chivalrous, but immoral, knights. She shared these books with her impressionable daughter, being careful to keep them hidden from Alonso who despised such literature favoring instead devotional and theological reading. Teresa and Rodrigo even authored their own tale of chivalry which was applauded by the few who read it before it was hidden or destroyed. Teresa admitted, "I was so completely taken up with this reading that I didn't think I could be happy if I didn't have a new book." What for Dona Beatriz was mere entertainment, became for her daughter an obsession.

As she matured, Teresa became especially fond of fine clothing, jewelry, and perfume. She was fastidious about her dress and basked in the admiring glances she provoked. She wrote, ". . . when I began to know of the natural attractive qualities the Lord had bestowed on me (which others said were many), instead of thanking Him for them, I began to make use of them all to offend Him . . ."

Alonso had forbidden young men to come to their home to court Teresa, but he could not stop the visits of her male first cousins, who, being older than Teresa, wielded a powerful influence on her. Teresa wrote, "I listened to accounts of their affections . . . not the least bit edifying; and, what was worse, I exposed my soul to that which caused all its harm."

Alonso's attempts to guard Teresa from worldly influences failed again when another relative, a young female, frequently visited their home. Teresa was particularly fond of the "frivolous" companion and "imitated all that was harmful . . . for she encouraged me in all the pastimes I desired."

In her autobiography Teresa warned parents of the harm done by "bad companions" as she herself was so affected that "hardly any virtue remained to my naturally virtuous soul." She admitted that "with the thought that my deeds would not be known, I dared to do many things truly against my honor and against God."[5]

Dona Beatriz bore her tenth and last child, Juana de Ahumada, in 1528. She recorded her last will in November of that year and died soon after at Gotarrendura. She left a lavish wardrobe of beautiful dresses, gifts from Alonso which she no longer wore during the last years of her life. She requested that her body be brought back to Avila at night and secretly buried. Teresa wrote of her mother's death, "She died most Christianly."[6]

Teresa was left motherless at age fourteen (Teresa mistakenly claimed she was twelve). Soon her pious half-sister, Maria de Cepeda, who could have been a stabilizing influence, married and moved to her husband's estate near Castellanos de Canada.

Teresa continued to flirt with temptation and for a time managed with the aid of servants to steal from the house at night without her father's knowledge. She wrote, "So excessive was the love my father bore me and so great my dissimulation that he was unable to believe there was much wrong with me, and so he was not angered with me. . . . I feared so much for my honor, I used every effort to keep my actions secret. . ."[7] Some biographers assume that Teresa lost her virginity at this early age but was circumspect enough not to bring dishonor to the family.

Alonso, concerned for his daughter's reputation and future, sent her to an Avila boarding school at Our Lady of Grace Convent run by Augustinian nuns. Here girls of nobility were educated and prepared for marriage, Alonso's hope for his well-favored daughter.

Servile Fear, Not Love.

At first Teresa disliked Our Lady of Grace with its spartan routine and strict discipline. She feared that the nuns had learned of her indiscretions, but was relieved to discover that they were unaware of her past. In time she gained their love and respect. A tolerant confessor eased her conscience by assuring her that there had been nothing wrong in the close friendship with her male cousin because she had believed it would lead eventually to marriage.

At the convent boarding school girls were subjected to the same restraints as the nuns. There was a strict regimen of silence, prayer, study, and work. Visitors were allowed, but had to sit behind an iron grille. Private conversations were not possible, and messages from the outside were intercepted.

Teresa took a special liking to Dona Maria Briceno, a virtuous nun who supervised the girls' dormitory. Although she listened carefully to Dona Maria's persuasions to seek a religious life, Teresa was not convinced that it was for her. She said, "I asked God not to give me this vocation; although I also feared marriage."[8] She did, however, decide that if she became a nun it would not be at the restrictive Our Lady of Grace, but rather at the more relaxed Carmelite convent of Incarnation in Avila where her good friend Juana Suarez had taken vows.

Teresa's decision was delayed when she became seriously ill with fainting spells and fever, the beginning of a heart condition and rheumatoid arthritis that plagued her the rest of her life. Alonso took his daughter home to recover. After a time her half-sister, Maria, invited Teresa to convalesce at her country home. On the two-day trip to Castellanos, Teresa stopped to visit her uncle, Don Pedro Sanchez de Cepeda, a widower and an intensely devout man who spent his time immersed in religious books that chastised sinners and condemned the vanities of the world.

As Teresa read these books aloud to him, she found them disagreeable, and the harsh message raised fears in her mind. Her uncle gave her *The Letters of St. Jerome*, written by the fourth century scholar, to read at Maria's farm. St. Jerome convinced Teresa that if she should die, she would go straight to hell. She began to admit that religious life was the best and safest state for her. She forced herself to consider it seriously, but admitted she was moved more by "servile fear than by love."[9]

After two weeks with her sister and brother-in-law, Teresa suffered a relapse and returned to Avila. When she told her father of her decision to become a nun, he could not bear the thought of giving his favorite daughter to the church. His only concession was that she could do as she wished after he died. But Teresa, fearing for her own frailty, dared not delay her decision.

A Religious Life, a New Joy.

Determined to enter religious life in spite of her father's objections, Teresa made secret arrangements with her friend Juana Suarez to enter the Carmelite convent of Incarnation. But to become a nun one must have a dowry, and under the circumstances her father would not offer such. Teresa had always been close to her older brother Rodrigo, and he knew her dilemma. Before he set sail for the Indies, he made out a will leaving to Teresa what little he

then owned and whatever fortune he would earn in the New World. Unfortunately, Rodrigo left behind a mistress and a baby daughter with little provision for their welfare. Conflicting reports told of his death either by drowning in the Plata River in southeast South America, being killed by the Aztecs in Peru or by pagan tribes in Chile. The amount of his will or his anticipated fortune were never recorded.

To accomplish her escape to Incarnation, Teresa persuaded her younger brother Antonio, an unstable fellow, to accompany her and at the same time seek entrance to the Dominican monastery of St. Thomas. Early one morning in November the two stole from their home. Antonio stopped at St. Thomas while Teresa went on to Incarnation, a few miles out of town. Juana Suarez was there to greet her.

Teresa wrote of her struggle to leave Casa de la Moneda, ". . . when I left my father's house I felt that separation so keenly that the feeling will not be greater, I think, when I die. For it seemed that every bone in my body was being sundered." How her father felt when he discovered his two missing children can only be surmised.

Antonio's stay at St. Thomas was brief, because he needed and didn't get his father's approval. Later he tried to join the Jeronimites, but was rejected when his "impure" heritage was discovered. He then joined the army and was killed in a battle at Quito, Peru.

The convent at Incarnation, a dilapidated farm-like building, was run under the "mitigated rule" which did not impose severe conditions on the Carmelite sisters. Teresa was given a warm welcome. Life at Incarnation agreed with her, prompting her to write, "All the things of religious life delighted me, and it is true that sometimes while sweeping, during the hours I used to spend in self-indulgence and self-adornment, I realized that I was free of all that and experienced a new joy which amazed me."[10]

Alonso did not share his daughter's newfound joy, but he accepted her decision. After Teresa had served a year's apprenticeship as a postulant, her father signed papers that spelled out the agreements of her dowry. He pledged to supply the convent with 25 measures of grain or 200 gold ducats every year. He also promised to provide Teresa with a bed, linens, clothing, and books. In addition he was to pay for a supper on the day she took her vows, and supply every nun with a new coif or its equivalent in money. In return the nuns pledged "to accept

Dona Teresa de Ahumada and to give her board and lodging all the days of her life."[11] Two days after the signing of the document Teresa donned the habit and white veil of the novice; one year later on November 3, 1537, she took her vows as a Carmelite nun.

Teresa was given a two-room suite, a special dispensation granted well-to-do nuns. The relaxed rules at Incarnation allowed the sisters to enhance their drab habits with colorful accessories and jewelry, use perfumes, and even keep little lap-dogs. They received visitors in the parlor and were free to leave the convent. Nuns were encouraged to give spiritual guidance to "devotos," men from the town who considered this a rare opportunity.

Teresa was one of the most popular nuns at the convent and was sought out by many devotos. But she became too fond of a man she called "a certain person," admitting that, "He was the one who most disturbed my soul . . . because I felt so much fondness for him."[12] Teresa lamented that she received no spiritual counsel from her "misguided confessors" who were only "half-educated."

Again fainting spells and fever plagued her, due to the change in food and life-style. When the best doctors in Avila found no cure, Alonso removed her from the convent and arranged to bring her to a "curandera," a naturpathic healer at Becedas, a small town fifty miles southwest of Avila. Her friend Juana Suarez accompanied her.

On the way to Becedas they stopped again for a short visit with Teresa's uncle, Don Pedro. This time he gave Teresa a book written by a Franciscan friar, Francisco de Osuna—*The Third Spiritual Alphabet* which described the stages of contemplative prayer or "the prayer of quiet." The treatise had a profound effect on Teresa leading her "to follow that path with all my strength" and take "the book for my master."[13]

Teresa stayed with her sister Maria while awaiting the spring when the curandera could find the necessary herbs and potions. A village cleric came to hear her confessions, but soon found himself confessing to Teresa how he had "lost his honor and reputation and no one dared to admonish him about this." Teresa boldly pointed out his sinful ways leading the cleric to give up his mistress, but he then transferred his affection to Teresa. She confessed fondness for him because "it seemed . . . a virtue to be grateful and loyal to anyone who loved me." One

year later the cleric "died a very good death."[14]

When spring arrived, the curandera, obviously a quack, treated Teresa with weird concoctions and ointments that caused her extreme pain and almost killed her. After three months the healer diagnosed her condition as rabies and sent her home.

Alonso brought his daughter back to Avila on a litter. Teresa prepared to die but when she asked for a confessor, Alonso refused thinking it would hasten her death. Her temperature soared, she went into severe convulsions, then a coma that kept her unconscious for four days. In anguish Alonso finally sent for a priest to administer Extreme Unction, the family recited the creed, and sealed her eyelids with wax in preparation for burial. The prioress of the convent ordered a grave dug, and funeral rites were held in a nearby monastery.

To everyone's amazement Teresa gained consciousness, but lay paralyzed and wracked with pain. When she insisted on returning to the convent, she was transported there on a sheet. It was Palm Sunday 1537. For eight months she lay in the infirmary, and for the next three years remained in her cell partially paralyzed. She bore her suffering with serenity and resignation, but confessed:

> Since I saw myself so crippled and still so young and how helpless the doctors of earth were, I resolved to go for aid to the doctors of heaven that they might cure me. For I still desired my health, even though I bore the illness with much happiness. And I thought sometimes that if in being well I were to be condemned, I would be better off this way. But nonetheless I thought I would be able to serve God much better if I were in good health. This is our mistake: not abandoning ourselves entirely to what the Lord does, for He knows best what is fitting for us.[15]

The Most Sinful Year of My Life.

Teresa's recovery was considered a miracle, Teresa giving credit to the intercession of St. Joseph after whom she named several of her foundations. Although she suffered some pain and illness her entire life, she was happy to resume a normal routine at Incarnation. She regained her former beauty and became a celebrity not only in the convent, but in the city. The number of visitors in the parlor increased, and the prioress welcomed the extra income brought in as alms. Teresa readily gave advice on mental prayer, spiritual life, and religious matters, even instructing her own father in the practice of contemplative prayer.

Teresa soon became uneasy with her role as counselor because she herself had given up prayer. She recognized how deceitful and vain she had become and worried about the temptations surrounding the other vulnerable young women in the convent. She wrote, ". . . it seems to me that a monastery of women that allows freedom is a tremendous danger. And, what is more, it seems that for those who desire to live miserable lives it is a step on the way toward hell rather than a remedy for their weaknesses."

Teresa herself had not yet built up an immunity to temptation. A frequent visitor, whom she did not identify, disturbed her. She said, ". . . no other friendship was as much a distraction to me as this one . . . for I was extremely fond of it." The man was probably Garcia de Toledo, the Sub-Prior of the Dominican house of St. Thomas in Avila, a man of noble, but questionable birth.

After one such visit Teresa had her first vision. She wrote, "With great severity, Christ appeared before me, making me understand what He regretted about the friendship. . . . I was left very frightened and disturbed, and didn't want to see that person any more."[16] A short time later when the "same person" visited her again, a large ugly toad suddenly appeared— another signal, she said of God's disapproval.

As Teresa counseled her father, she found him receptive to the practice of mental prayer, but she confessed to him that she, herself, had given it up because of her illness. She wrote, ". . . my father because of his esteem and love for me believed everything I said; in fact he pitied me. But since he had already reached so sublime a state, he did not afterward spend as much time with me but would leave after a brief visit; for he said it was time lost. Since I wasted time on other vanities, I cared little about losing time."

Alonso fell seriously ill, and Teresa left the convent to care for him. "I suffered much hardship during his sickness," she wrote. "When I saw him coming to the end of his life, it seemed my soul was being wrenched from me, for I loved him dearly."[17]

Her father died on December 24, 1543, looking "like an angel." Alonso's confessor, Father Vincente Barron, a scholarly Dominican from the St. Thomas monastery, observed that Alonso was such a true Christian that he had gone "straight to heaven." In accordance with his will, Alonso, just as his wife, was buried in secret.

Alonso left behind a legacy of debt and a bevy of creditors clamoring for payment. As executrix of her father's estate, Teresa called on her skills as mediator to settle the bitter quarrels that broke out among male in-laws. The will was contested, and most of the small inheritance which remained was eaten up by court costs and lawyers fees. Teresa moved her younger sister Juana to Incarnation to live with her.

Distressed by her spiritual laxity, the deception she perpetrated on others, and what she termed "the most sinful year of my life," Teresa turned to her father's confessor, Vincente Barron, for help. He warned her of the "perdition" she was bringing on herself and advised her to take communion every fifteen days and resume her prayer life. Unfortunately, Father Barron left Avila to take another position, and Teresa, then in her early thirties, took other confessors who saw nothing wrong with her "vanities." She criticized her confessors for failing to understand her personal conflict. "I consider it now a pity," she wrote, "that so much happened and so little help was found anywhere, except in God, and that they [the confessors] gave it a great pretext for its pastimes and satisfactions by saying these were licit."[18]

Pedro de la Purification, one of her confessors, recorded a testimony for her beatification which is still preserved in the archives. He said, "One thing worried me about that glorious Mother which I noted many times, and it troubled me to think about it; and that was that when a visitor had to be with her on business, she would talk with him for three or four hours at a time, quite as often in private as in company." Lest his statement be misconstrued, Pedro hastened to add, "Her conversation was so sublime, her words so sweet, her mouth so full of laughter that one never grew weary or could make oneself go away from her."[19]

Second Conversion.

For over ten years Teresa struggled with the conflict between friendship with God and friendship with the world. Her torments reached new depths during Lent 1554 when one day upon entering the oratory, she gazed upon a statue borrowed for a feast to be celebrated that day. She wrote, "It represented the much wounded Christ . . . I felt so keenly aware of how poorly I thanked Him for those wounds that, it seems to me, my heart broke. Beseeching Him to strengthen me once and for all that I might not offend Him, I threw myself down before Him with the greatest outpouring of tears."[20]

Another awakening came as she read *The Confessions of St. Augustine*, recently translated into Spanish. Women were forbidden to read the Latin version, but Teresa had received a copy of the new translation. As she read *The Confessions*, Teresa felt a special affinity for the once-wayward saint, who at an unholy period in his life had prayed, "Lord, grant me chastity and continence—but not yet." St. Augustine, like herself, had been a sinner and had been brought to the Lord. As she compared herself to Augustine and the other saints, she found herself wanting. "But there was one thing," she wrote, "that left me inconsolable . . . that the Lord called them only once, and they did not turn back and fall again; whereas in my case I had turned back so often that I was worn out from it. But by considering the love He bore me, I regained my courage, for I never lost confidence in His mercy; in myself, I lost it many times."[21]

After what is called her "second conversion" at age thirty-nine, Teresa began to forsake worldly pursuits she considered harmful and give herself more to prayer. Gradually she withdrew from the social activities in the parlor and retreated to her cell for hours of meditation. She described the experience: "It used to happen in His presence, or even while reading, that a feeling of the presence of God would come upon me unexpectedly so that I could in no way doubt He was within me or I totally immersed in Him. This did not occur after the manner of a vision. I believe they call the experience 'mystical theology.' "[22]

Teresa's mystical experiences multiplied, and she became a firm believer in mental prayer. This was a dangerous development in Spain where inquisitors were suspicious of ascetics and were purging heretics, reformers, and those of "impure" blood from the land. Women were particularly vulnerable. Furthermore, Teresa was becoming vocal about the abuses, hypocrisy, greed, and laxity that existed within the church and the religious houses. She became convinced that reform was essential.

Mystical Betrothal.

Teresa longed to find confessors who could guide her on the unchartered course she was entering, but she found little encouragement from those men who professed to be her intellectual superiors and claimed authority over her soul and the souls of others. At Incarnation the confessions she had made in confidence regarding her spiritual experiences soon became gossip among the other nuns. Some sisters venerated her and believed her sincerity, but others viewed her new spirituality with suspicion, accusing her of parading as a saint. Teresa began to doubt her own motives, questioning whether her actions were inspired by God or by the devil. She wrote, "His Majesty began to give me the prayer of quiet very habitually—and often, of union—which lasted a long while. Since at that time other women had fallen into serious illusions and deceptions caused by the devil, I began to be afraid."[23]

More confusion arose in her mind when she began to hear inner voices, or locutions, which sometimes encouraged her, at other times warned or scolded her. Were these the voices of God or of Satan? She admitted, ". . . I saw danger everywhere. I was like a person in the middle of a river trying to get out; wherever he goes he fears greater peril there; and he is almost drowning."[24]

Some confessors warned that she was indeed an instrument of the devil; others thought she was hallucinating. Some refused to have anything to do with her.

For a time Teresa found encouragement from the Jesuit confessors who had come to Avila to establish a college. At that time, their order, founded by Ignatius of Loyola, looked upon mystical prayer with favor. One fervent young Jesuit advised her to continue her prayers, but unfortunately he was soon assigned to another post. Again Teresa was back with the two confessors who had renounced her as a vehicle of Satan.

As rumors of Teresa de Ahumada's newborn sanctity spread through the city, and gossip at Incarnation grew more malicious, Teresa's fragile health again reached the breaking point. She was allowed to leave the convent for three years, staying part of the time with Dona Guiomar de Ulloa, a wealthy young widow who, despite her extravagances and love of luxury, had taken up religion and had become a Jesuit patroness.

Dona Guiomar's household gave Teresa the peace and tranquility she needed, and the widow introduced her to Father Juan de Pradanos, the Jesuit Vice-Rector of the College of San Gil, who became Teresa's confessor. He advised her firmly, but kindly, that she must practice self-denial, particularly regarding personal relationships that still distracted her from complete dedication to God. He further advised her to recite the hymn "Veni Creator."

One day while praying and repeating the hymn, Teresa related, ". . . a rapture came upon me so suddenly that it almost carried me out of myself. . . . It was the first time the Lord granted me this favor of rapture. I heard these words: 'No longer do I want you to converse with men but with angels.' "[25]

This experience, though frightening, consoled her and strengthened her resolve to sever her dangerous worldly relationships. The Church recorded this first rapture and locution as her "mystical betrothal." She was then forty-one.

When Father Pradanos was transferred from Avila, Teresa was assigned another confessor, Father Baltasar Alvarez, newly-ordained into the Castilian order. In spite of his twenty-four years, he was reputed to be a wise, but austere, priest. When Teresa had another experience, one she called an "intellectual vision," she hurried to confess it to Alvarez, who questioned her intensely. In what form was He? How do you know it was He? Teresa struggled to put her vision into words:

> The splendor is not one that dazzles; it has a soft whiteness, is infused, gives the most intense delight to the sight, and doesn't tire it; neither does the brilliance, in which is seen the vision of so divine a beauty, tire it. It is a light so different from earthly light that the sun's brightness that we see appears very tarnished in comparison. . . . God gives it so suddenly that there wouldn't even be time to open your eyes. . .[26]

Only when Alvarez himself had a similar vision could he begin to understand Teresa.

Transverberation of the Heart.

As Catholic Spain continued its struggle against Jews, Protestants, and heretics, the Inquisitor General in 1559 issued a long list of forbidden books, among them "spiritual books written in the vernacular that he thought could be harmful to simple souls." Extensive book burnings followed in convents and monasteries. When some of Teresa's books were burned, she wrote, "I felt that prohibition very much because reading some of them was an enjoyment to me, and I could no longer do so since only the Latin editions were allowed. The Lord said to me: 'Don't be sad, for I shall give you a living book.' "[27] From then on she learned directly from her Lord who had become her "true book."

Even Teresa's friends feared that her visions and inner voices might be messages from the devil as her accusers claimed. As they tried to shelter her, the inquisitors pressed for information from the confessors concerning this woman who practiced "mystical theology." A "holy committee" was ordered to interrogate and expose her. As the questioning proceeded Teresa admitted:

> . . . if the Lord hadn't favored me so much, I don't know what would have happened to me. There were enough things to drive me insane. . . . For the opposition of good men to a little woman, wretched, weak, and fearful like myself, seems to be nothing when described in so few words; yet among the very severe trials I suffered in life, this was one of the most severe.[28]

One member of the committee advised her to resist the devil, who was coming to her in the guise of the Lord, by making the gesture of scorn called "the sign of the fig." He promised that the devil would not return. Teresa, obediently but reluctantly, followed the order, but the visions increased accompanied by alternating waves of excessive pain and indescribable happiness.

One of these visions, or transports, had particular significance two and three centuries later when Teresa's remains were examined and found to bear mysterious evidence of a physical miracle. The event, known as the "Transverberation of the Heart," occurring at the home of Dona Guiomar, was described by Teresa:

> I saw close to me toward my left side an angel in bodily form. . . . the angel was not large but small; he was very beautiful, and his face was so aflame that he seemed to be one of those very sublime angels that appear to be all afire. They must belong to those they call the cherubim, for they didn't tell me their names. . . . I saw in his hands a large golden dart and at the end of the iron tip there appeared to be a little fire. It seemed to me this angel plunged the dart several times into my heart and it reached deep within me. When he drew it out, I thought he was carrying off with him the deepest part of me; and he left me all on fire with great love of God. The pain was so great that it made me moan, and the sweetness this greatest pain caused me was so superabundant that there is no desire capable of taking it away; nor is the soul content with less than God. The pain is not bodily but spiritual. . .[29]

The vision left Teresa bewildered and speechless for days. At the sacred shrine of relics in Alba de Tormes where Teresa's heart is preserved, examiners in the eighteenth century discovered in the organ a hole with charred edges, supposedly made by the flame-tipped lance. One century later another examination revealed that a circle of thorns had grown around the heart.

The Transverberation is immortalized in a marble sculpture by Bernini, the famous Italian sculptor and architect. The work entitled "St. Teresa in Ecstasy" was first seen in 1651 when the Cornaro Chapel designed by Bernini at Santa Maria della Vittoria in Rome was completed. Although it has been criticized for its sexual and erotic overtones, the statue is regarded as a supreme example of Roman baroque sculpture.

All the Trials Suffered Were Well Worth It.

While tormented by inner struggles with the devil and outward hostilities, Teresa found a fortunate ally. Dona Guiomar invited Teresa to meet Friar Pedro de Alcantara, a Franciscan mystic whose life had been dedicated to bringing his degenerating order back to the original practices established by its founder, St. Francis of Assisi. Pedro lived a life of sanctity, harsh austerity, and poverty, denying himself sleep, food, and warm clothing. He reassured Teresa that her visitations and voices were certainly from God, and she should remain steadfast in her beliefs. He talked to the two men, Francisco de Salcedo, a pious layman, and Gaspar Daza, an ascetical priest in Avila, who had most adamantly accused Teresa of being in league with the devil. Alcantara was so persuasive the two men were won over.

As Alcantara talked of renouncing worldly possession, self-denial, and reform, Teresa paid rapt attention. She, too, had become increasingly distressed with the Carmelites at Incarnation who had strayed far from the original purpose established by the hermits of Mt. Carmel. She believed the mitigated rule under which Incarnation operated was dangerous as it aimed to please both God and the world.

One night in September 1560 as a few nuns gathered in Teresa's spacious cell, the talk turned to reform of the order and a return to the simple life envisioned by the founders. In spite of the enthusiasm of her companions, Teresa had reservations. Reform movements were not new

in Spain, but most reforms were carried out in monasteries for men. There had been a few attempts in women's houses, but the instigators had been labelled as "lunatic women." Teresa was not afraid of such indictments—she was familiar with name-calling—but she wanted to be assured it was God's will.

One day after communion, Teresa received her summons:

> . . . His majesty earnestly commanded me to strive for this new monastery with all my powers, and He made great promises that it would be founded and that He would be highly served in it. He said it should be called St. Joseph and that this saint would keep watch over us at one door, and our Lady at the other, that Christ would remain with us, and that it should be a star shining with great splendor.[30]

Immediately there were hurdles to overcome. One of the first was the financing of such a venture. Dona Guiomar offered to help endow it, another nun impulsively volunteered 1,000 ducats from her dowry, but more would be needed.

Because they had to secure approval from the hierarchy, Teresa went first to her confessor, Father Alvarez. When he was indecisive and evasive, she went to other learned men, among them her friend Pedro de Alcantara who offered spiritual support and gave practical advice from his experience with religious foundations for men. He suggested that Teresa stay in the background and let Dona Guiomar, who had noble status, make the requests.

Dona Guiomar did exactly that, first sending a petition directly to the Pope in Rome, then approaching Angel de Salazar, the Carmelite Provincial, for permission to locate a convent in his jurisdiction. The influential Father Pedro Ibanez, theology professor at St. Thomas, gave his blessing and offered to be the advocate for the two women. With this encouragement Teresa located a suitable house for her new convent. To avoid public attention the house was purchased by her sister Juana and her husband supposedly for their own dwelling. It appeared that Teresa's dream would be realized.

But then the storm broke. Teresa described it. "Hardly had the knowledge of it begun to spread throughout the city when the great persecution that cannot be briefly described came upon us: gossip, derision, saying that it was foolishness . . . with regard to my companion

[Dona Guiomar], there was so much persecution that she became very upset."[31]

The prioress and nuns at Incarnation were indignant and insulted that one of their own should betray them. The prioress stormed over to Provincial Salazar to protest. In response to the outrage, Salazar changed his mind, refused to accept the foundation in his jurisdiction, and forbade Teresa to go forward with her plans. His excuse—she did not have sufficient funds to open a convent.

Teresa, though frightened and disheartened, was not willing to abandon her project. She turned to Father Alvarez for support, but he reprimanded her for stirring up a scandal. She then appealed to Father Ibanez, still her staunch ally, but unfortunately he was shortly transferred from Avila. Everyone seemed to abandon her, but Teresa was convinced that God was still on her side. Two more visions reaffirmed her faith in the project.

A reply from the Pope arrived, but it was invalid because it did not specify under whose jurisdiction the convent would be built. Immediately Dona Guiomar sent another request, asking that the house be under the Bishop of Avila, not the Carmelite Provincial. After the Pope's consent arrived, the Bishop fell "conveniently" ill and left Avila for his country estate.

In the meantime the necessary repairs on the house had been halted for lack of money. Juana and her husband had no resources of their own, Dona Guiomar had pawned her last possessions and was in debt, and the modest contributions of a few relatives were not sufficient to cover the expenses. One day a package containing 200 ducats arrived from Teresa's brother, Lorenzo, in South America. Work on the house went forward—in secrecy.

Teresa hoped to open the convent as soon as the house was habitable and the briefs had arrived from Rome. She feared that a delay would jeopardize the project.

Again her plans were altered. Dona Luisa de la Cerda, a daughter of a Toledo nobleman, had been plunged into inconsolable despair after the death of her husband. Dona Luisa had heard of the nun of Avila, and she made a request to Provincial Salazar that Teresa be sent to live with her in Toledo to comfort and console her. Salazar could not refuse this respected woman, and he was happy to remove for a time the troublesome "holy woman" from his jurisdiction. He ordered Teresa to leave immediately—no matter that it was Christmas (1561)

and the dead of winter. With reassurances from God, Teresa began the long hard journey to Toledo, traveling for four days in a small cart over icy roads, through treacherous mountain passes, facing howling winds. She arrived in Toledo frozen and travel-weary.

The luxury of Dona Luisa's palace distressed Teresa, and she begged for simple food and modest living quarters. However there was one advantage—Teresa learned how to deal with the superficial world of the nobility to whom she had always felt inferior. She observed, "I conversed with those noble ladies, whom it would have been an honor for me to serve, with the freedom I would have felt had I been their equal."[32] Teresa realized that Dona Luisa, though wealthy, was a woman as "subject to passions and weaknesses" as she was. The widow grew deeply fond of Teresa, a situation not unnoticed by envious servants.

While at Toledo "a certain religious came to that city, a person from nobility" who had visited Teresa as a "frequent visitor" back at Incarnation. This man, Garcia de Toledo, convinced Teresa that she should write her own story. In the undisturbed moments at the palace, Teresa wrote the first draft of her *Vida* or *Life*, a long rambling discourse addressed to her confessor. Unfortunately the original manuscript has been lost. When Teresa gave the pages to Garcia, he returned them urging her to make revisions and additions. This she did later during a tranquil period at her new convent, adding twenty new chapters on prayer and the founding of St. Joseph's.

Another visitor at Toledo made a profound impression on Teresa. Maria de Jesus, a Carmelite widow from Granada, who against great odds had founded a house where strict penance and absolute poverty was observed. Maria convinced Teresa that financial security was unnecessary and would be downright dangerous. If one had faith, God would provide. Teresa claimed that she was ashamed to stand in Maria's presence because Maria was far ahead of her in serving the Lord. Teresa was inspired and regenerated.

In June 1562 Teresa felt compelled to return to Avila despite Dona Luisa's angry protests. On the day she arrived in Avila, the second papers from Rome arrived authorizing the convent to be established under the Bishop of Avila. Civic and church authorities were forbidden to interfere with the founding.

Finally everything appeared to be in place thanks to Pedro de Alcantara's persuasion. The key figures were all assembled including the reluctant Bishop who had returned from his summer home. Teresa, using all of her persuasive powers and charms, won the Bishop's approval and his lasting friendship. Pedro de Alcantara, nearing death, was there to support her. Approval was granted to open her first convent.

Teresa was given permission to move from Incarnation to the new house, supposedly to "care for her sick brother-in-law" but actually to oversee the final preparations. Teresa wrote, no doubt with a smile, "When there was need that he get well so that I could be free and that he could leave the house empty, the Lord immediately brought this about; at which my brother-in-law marvelled."[33]

On August 24, 1562, the reformed convent of St. Joseph was consecrated. Along with Teresa there were four novices and two nuns from Incarnation. One room served as the chapel with a small statue of the Virgin Mary at one entrance, St. Joseph at the other. A second-hand cracked bell tolled the event. Father Gaspar Daza, priest of Avila, led the first mass. The nuns took their vows, sang the "Te Deum," and donned their coarse sackcloth habits.

The convent was founded under the order of the Discalced Carmelites. It was to be run on uncompromising poverty with no endowments or begging of alms—providing for their simple needs was up to God, the charity of the townspeople, and whatever could be raised by selling the sisters' handiwork. Their cells were bare and cold, their food sparse, but to Teresa it was a great delight.

Peace at St. Joseph's was short-lived. When the news flashed through the town that a handful of penniless nuns, led by the one thought to be possessed of the devil, had opened a convent, Avila was aroused to action. The prioress at Incarnation in rage ordered Teresa back to the convent to answer for her misconduct. Teresa, who had taken vows of obedience, was accused of deception, conceit, and disobedience.

After Teresa gave her account, the prioress was somewhat placated and turned the matter over to the Provincial. He ordered Teresa to appear before the nuns at Incarnation to answer the accusations. Teresa, assured that she had committed no offenses, calmly and confidently answered the charges, but the Provincial reprimanded her and ordered her to remain back at Incarnation until the uproar in the city died down.

Meanwhile angry citizens had gathered outside St. Joseph's shouting insults and threats. The town council sent the constable to shut down the convent, but the determined women inside barricaded the door and refused them entrance. They said they were under the authority of God, not the constable.

The mayor and council convened and plotted to close down the convent in any way possible. Citizens appeared to voice their protests, among them the water vendor who claimed that the newly-added extension to the house threatened the fountains from which he drew water to sell to the neighborhood.

The governor called together a junta of influential laymen and clergy. Father Baltasar Alvarez, Teresa's former confessor, was there, but he remained tight-lipped throughout the proceedings. Teresa's "special friend," Garcia de Toledo, was absent, perhaps by his own choice.

Charges were numerous: the nuns had been deceitful and disobedient; they were a danger to the state; they would become a drain on the city's budget with no funds of their own; they were instruments of the devil. The convent must be closed.

Only Father Domingo Banez, a learned Dominican who had only heard of Teresa, defended her. In an eloquent and sarcastic speech he asked, "Could these poor sisters possibly pose such a threat?" He recommended turning the matter over to the Bishop in whose jurisdiction the convent lay. The junta adjourned only to reconvene nine days later.

At the second gathering Father Gaspar Daza represented the Bishop and defended St. Joseph's. The junta appeared to be appeased for the time being, but Daza suffered persecution in the city because of his defense of Teresa and St. Joseph's.

The town council continued the pressure, levelling charges through the Royal Council, the king's legal body. The negotiators proposed a compromise—if Teresa would accept endowments, the convent would not become a liability to the public purse, and the suit could be dropped. For a time Teresa wavered, but after prayer and a vision of then-deceased Pedro de Alcantara advising her not to capitulate, she refused to sign the agreement. The lawsuit continued until the city ran out of funds.

The clerics, offended that the matter had been taken out of their hands by the Royal Council, secured another papal order from

Rome granting the nuns permission "to possess no goods, either individually or collectively, but to maintain themselves freely from the alms and charitable assistance which pious Christians may offer and bestow."[34]

On December 29, 1562, Teresa and four nuns from Incarnation were permitted to move back to St. Joseph's. Even though the lawsuit dragged on until the following June, tempers cooled. A few sympathetic citizens left food and money in the "torno," a small revolving door built into the wall of the convent.

When the controversy was over, Teresa wrote:

> It seems to me that all the trials suffered were well worth it. Now, although there is some austerity because meat is never eaten without necessity and there is an eight-month fast and other things, as are seen in the first rule, this is still in many respects considered small by the sisters; and they have other observances which seemed to us necessary in order to observe the rule with greater perfection. I hope in the Lord that what has been begun will prosper, as His Majesty has told me it would.[35]

The Tranquil Years.

The next five years at St. Joseph's were what Teresa called the most restful of her life. In time the citizens of Avila accepted her house, and the postulants grew in numbers, but never allowed to exceed thirteen. Some were relatives, some wealthy patricians, others penniless women with no other place to live.

In early 1563 Teresa was made the official prioress of St. Joseph's, remaining in that position for five years. Immediately she drew up a constitution of rules for the institution. The Carmelites of St. Joseph's were to be known as the "discalced," or shoeless ones, though they usually wore hemp sandals over their bare feet.

Life at the new convent was one of austerity and piety. The day began at dawn with private prayers, followed by mass at 9:00 A.M. Next came the assigned duties of the day. At 10:00 or 11:00 they sat down to their main meal, usually bread, cheese, or fruit, if any had been left in the torno. Eggs and fish were rare treats, and meat was usually forbidden. After the meal, the women were allowed time for recreation—sewing, spinning, or talking. Following two o'clock vespers they read religious books and meditated. After the eight o'clock compline (the seventh canonical hour of the day), there was silence and prayer. Nine o'clock brought evening matins, and at 11:00 the nuns retired to their straw pallets in their bare cells.

Once a week the nuns gathered for a disciplinary session where penalties were meted out to those who were guilty of misdemeanors, conducting themselves in an unseemly or discourteous manner, using abusive or slanderous language, or in some fashion breaking the rules. Teresa's punishment was usually gentle and tactful, but she didn't hesitate to impose severe measures when the situation warranted it.

Life at St. Joseph's was not always austere. Teresa herself had a humorous streak, and she encouraged the women to laugh, sing, and dance. Those with creative talent composed songs and verses, as did Teresa. At no time were they allowed to complain, "display melancholy," or forget that their first calling was to spiritual perfection.

During these tranquil years Teresa wrote the second draft of *Life*, adding eleven new chapters on the four degrees of prayer (chapters 11-22), five chapters on the founding of St. Joseph's (chapters 32-36), and four additional chapters on the "great favors the Lord granted her" (chapters 37-40). In 1565 when the completed second draft of *Life* reached the hands of Domingo Banez, Teresa's confessor and professor of theology at St. Thomas College in Avila, he viewed it as unsuitable reading for her nuns or anyone else.

Teresa disagreed with Banez's criticism, but when he threatened to burn the manuscript if she insisted on its being circulated, she received his permission to "write some things about prayer" just for her sisters. The result was *The Way of Perfection*, the first draft probably completed in 1566, followed later by many revisions before permission to print it was granted in 1580.

When Teresa finished the work, she gave it to Garcia de Toledo and Domingo Banez to read and censor. They made extensive corrections and deleted Teresa's forthright statements about women being equal to men in the eyes of God, a heretical thought in the sexist world of sixteenth century Spain. Fortunately, her original manuscript was preserved and is now housed at the royal monastery of the Escorial. Teresa obediently made the suggested revisions so the book could be printed and given to women to read.

Teresa addressed her book to the "discalced nuns who observe the primitive rule of our Lady of Mount Carmel." In the prologue to *The Way of Perfection*, Teresa wrote:

> Not long ago I was ordered to write a certain account of my life, in which I also dealt with some things about prayer. It could be that my confessor would not want you to see this account, and so I shall put down here something of what was said there. I shall also write of other things that to me seem necessary. May the Lord's own hand be in this work, as I have begged Him; and may He direct the work to His glory, amen.[36]

At the beginning of the first chapter Teresa stated that her reasons for the foundation were not only to retreat to a life of solitude and consecration, but to answer a call to battle against the forces of evil in the world. She wrote:

> At that time news reached me of the harm being done in France and of the havoc the Lutherans had caused and how much this miserable sect was growing. The news distressed me greatly, and . . . I cried to the Lord and begged Him that I might remedy so much evil. . . . All my longing was and still is that since He has so many enemies and so few friends that these few friends be good ones. As a result I resolved to do the little that was in my power; that is, to follow the evangelical counsels as perfectly as I could and strive that these few persons who live here do the same. I did this trusting in the great goodness of God, who never fails to help anyone who is determined to give up everything for Him.[37]

During the bitter winter days, Teresa must have been warmed by an inner fire as she knelt on the stone floor to write with frozen fingers on the small ledge of the room's paneless window. Only a canvas at the window halted the icy winds. A straw pallet for sleeping was the room's only furniture.

During the years at St. Joseph's, Teresa experienced a profusion of locutions, raptures, and visions both "imaginary" and "intellectual." She also wrote of being embarrassed by her levitations as she struggled to keep her body from physically rising into the air before curious on-lookers. She was also credited with effecting several miracles.

Inquisitors and Foundations.

At the Council of Trent, held in three sessions between the years 1545 and 1563, the Catholic Church drew up practical reforms to correct the abuses that had developed over the centuries. One concern was the laxity in the religious houses, particularly among the Carmelites, Franciscans, and Trinitarians. Giovanni Battista Rossi, the Italian Carmelite General, known in Spain as Rubeo, was dispatched to Spain to set the Carmelite foundations in order. After a disastrous visit to the Andalusian monasteries in southern Spain, he arrived in Avila in April 1567 with his lavish entourage (he professed dedication to poverty) to visit the houses there. After examining Incarnation, he accepted Teresa's invitation to inspect St. Joseph's. Here he found a captivating, beautiful foundress, looking twenty years younger than her fifty-two years, who poured out the story of her life and her ardent wishes to expand the reform movement.

Rubeo, impressed by all he saw at St. Joseph's and won over by Teresa's charms, gave her the authority to open houses in all of Castile. Andalusia, however, was forbidden territory. Teresa was also given permission to open two priories for men, an extraordinary concession to a woman without funds or rank.

The next four years from 1567 to 1571 were unusually active for Teresa as she traveled about Castile opening seven foundations for women and two monasteries for men. She was not always welcome. Opposition came from many sources—angered citizens, jealous nuns, fearful clerics, pampered princesses—but armed as she was with authorization from the Carmelite General and orders direct from God, she continued undaunted. As her fame and reputation spread, and her acquaintances grew to include important persons of wealth and prominence, her work became easier. Although some opposition still persisted, she no longer was relegated to dilapidated houses and forced to beg for funds.

One of her closest associations was formed with a young sensitive "artist-friar" who was "small in stature" but "great in the sight of God." After he was canonized in 1726, he was known as St. John of the Cross. His sanctity and sensitivity appealed to Teresa, and she described him as a "man celestial and divine." St. John's verses are considered some of Spain's greatest mystical and visionary literature.

In 1571, nine years after Teresa had left Incarnation, she was ordered by Father Salazar and a representative of the Pope, to return to that convent to reform it and remedy the laxity that existed. Teresa was installed as prioress amid angry confrontations between the women who openly rebelled against her appointment and those who welcomed her back. Although

Teresa was forced to abandon her other work, she tackled the job of reform at Incarnation with humility, discipline, shrewdness, and a large measure of love. She invited John of the Cross to become the chaplain at Incarnation, a wise move for Father John soon became a favorite with the sisters who found they had much to confess.

A few months after her return to Incarnation, Teresa wrote:

> The Lord be praised for the change he has wrought in them. The most recalcitrant are now more contented and get on better with me. This Lent no visitors have been allowed, either women or men—not even parents—which is something quite new for this house. They put up with everything and are very peaceful. Some of them are really great servants of God, and almost all are better than they were.[38]

But all was not going well at the other houses. Teresa's foes had used the time she was at Incarnation to campaign against her. The mitigated Carmelites plotted and spread scandal about her, and a tempermental princess was making life intolerable for the women in the convent at Pastrana. When Teresa's term as prioress at Incarnation ended in September 1574 she set out to visit the other foundations, often traveling in severe physical pain under extreme conditions.

The next three years brought both pleasure and agony to Teresa, now entering her sixties. She opened a foundation at Beas de la Segura, a pleasant location by a small river, but one which later became a source of trouble as it lay in the ecclesiastical jurisdiction of Andalusia, a territory she had been warned by General Rubeo to avoid. At Beas a vision renewed her waning strength. The Lord placed a beautiful ring on her finger, culminating the spiritual marriage she had experienced two-and-a-half years earlier.

Father Jeronimo Gracian, a young Carmelite reformer, came to Beas to meet Teresa. He soon became her confessor, confidant, and companion, prompting her to write that she had never met anyone so perfect and so gentle. Teresa's infatuation with the young friar half her age gave her enemies more ammunition. They spread scandal about her "affairs." But Teresa, assured in another vision, put complete faith in Gracian and his advice.

At the young friar's urging, Teresa set out for the bustling city of Seville to set up another reform foundation there. After traveling for a week in excessive heat and under exhausting conditions, they arrived at the inhospitable city where Teresa soon discovered she was unwelcome. In addition Carmelite General Rubeo in Rome had changed his mind about the reform movement and had issued a harsh decree excommunicating Teresa and ordering her back to Castile. Meanwhile copies of her autobiography *Life* had fallen into the hands of the inquisitors who were examining it for heresy.

In 1544 Magdalena de la Cruz, a nun from Cordoba who had been recognized nationally for her great gifts of prophecy, was called before the Inquisition. She confessed that she had been guilty of practicing witchcraft, that her visions and ecstasies were a fraud. From then on the Inquisitors looked on all mystics, particularly women, with distrust.

Teresa had often aroused their suspicions, and when the inquisitors scrutinized her autobiography, they concluded it espoused "new and superstitious doctrines . . . full of frauds and deceits, and [was] most harmful to the Christian commonwealth."[39] A delegation arrived in Seville to interrogate her. Again she was summoned before the authorities to defend herself and her writing. During the days of questioning, Teresa conducted herself "like a saint." The inquisitors concluded that the charges against her were malicious lies, and she was allowed to continue her work in Seville.

To prepare the house for its opening, Friar John de la Miseria, an amateur artist, was summoned to decorate the chapel. Gracian also ordered him to paint a portrait of the founder, despite Teresa's protests that it was a show of vanity and a waste of time. Besides, she asked, who would want a picture of her? Reluctantly, she posed while the friar made a rapid sketch intending to complete the portrait later. When he showed her the sketch, Teresa said with feigned disgust, "God forgive you, Friar John. You have made me look ugly and blear-eyed."[40]

Although the portrait bore a passable resemblance to Teresa, Gracian disliked it for it showed none of her magnetism and radiance. However, it is the only portrait made while she was alive. The great El Greco arrived in Toledo in 1577 to work on the altar of the Church of Santo Domingo el Antiguo, but unfortunately he did not paint Teresa while in Spain.

In June 1576 the new house was opened with uncharacteristic pomp and celebration with the Archbishop himself leading the parade through the streets of Seville. During the ceremony he blessed Teresa, then knelt before her and asked her to bless him, an unusual turnabout. Teresa wrote, "Just imagine how I felt when I saw such a great prelate kneeling before this wretched old woman and refusing to get up until I gave him my blessing, and in the presence of all the Orders and Confraternities of Seville too!"[41]

After the ceremonies Teresa left Seville to go to more familiar and friendly territory in Castile. She settled for a time at the house in Toledo where she revised her *Book of Foundations* and at the urging of Gracian began a new work, *The Mansions of the Interior Castle*, a description of the seven successive stages or "mansions" through which a soul travels to God. She continued to carry on a stream of correspondence with people of high and low rank. Over 450 letters are still preserved today, including many personal letters to family members with whom she kept in close touch. Her letters to young Gracian portray her as a woman of passion, sometimes humanly jealous and sensual.

In Avila at Christmas 1577 on her way to mass, Teresa slipped on a stairway and broke her left arm, an accident that caused her partial paralysis and pain the rest of her life. She complained to Gracian, "I am nothing more than a poor old hag."[42]

No Longer Needed in This World.

Although suffering from exhaustion, paralytic fits, fevers, sore throats, and heart spasms, Teresa still managed to criss-cross Castile to inspect established houses and open new ones. She traveled in primitive carts that jolted and bumped over the rough roads. Only her indomitable spirit kept her from succumbing to the tortures of the weather and her failing health.

In the spring of 1582 Teresa, Gracian, and companions were on their way to Burgos when the torrential rains came. The carts skidded, lurched, and sank deep into the mud. Just outside Burgos the caravan came to a halt at the Almazon River where the pontoon bridge was covered by swirling rushing waters. Teresa set out alone on foot to lead the way across the icy waters. When she reached the other side, she waved the others across. A story persists that Teresa complained in a prayer, "Oh, Lord, why do you put such difficulties in our way?" When the Lord answered, "It is thus I treat my friends," Teresa replied wryly, "Ah, my Lord, that is why you have so few."[43]

At Burgos, her last foundation, the all-too-familiar difficulties arose—finding a suitable house, securing funds, obtaining a license from the recalcitrant Archbishop, overcoming opposition from the Calced Carmelites. One month after the house finally opened, the river overflowed its banks flooding the first floor of the convent and forcing the nuns to the attic. When the water receded, Teresa, then very ill, directed the restoration of the damaged building from her bed. Two months after the flood, she again set out on the road to visit the other houses which seemed to be in constant need of help. She had said her final goodbye to Gracian, who had left for a round of visits to Andalusia.

When she finished inspecting her houses, Teresa longed to return to her first love, the convent of St. Joseph's in Avila. But an order from her superior, Father Antonio, forced her to take a detour to Alba de Tormes to attend the election of a new prioress and to be in attendance at the birth of the grandchild of the Duchess of Alba, an old friend. The Duchess' carriage awaited her, and Teresa, too weak to protest, obediently left for Alba.

After a difficult journey, the carriage lumbered into the town. As the nuns helped Teresa to her bed, she complained, "I haven't a sound bone left in my body." Nine days later she suffered a hemorrhage of the lungs. She was carried to the infirmary where she could watch the celebration of mass. Father Antonio heard her weak confession and begged, "Do not leave us so soon!" Teresa murmured, "Hush, Father. How can you say this? I am no longer needed in this world."[44]

Teresa knew she was close to death. She repeated over and over her favorite psalm from David, "A humble and contrite heart, O Lord, thou wilt not despise." She then exhorted the few nuns gathered about her to remain faithful to the rules and constitution. After she received the last communion, she clasped her hands in prayer and whispered, "Lord, I am a daughter of the Church."[45]

At nine o'clock that evening, October 4, 1582, she received the last rites and died in the arms of one of her faithful companions. The mourners reported a mysterious fragrance pervading the entire convent.

Two sisters washed Teresa's body and dressed it in a clean habit. No undertaker was called. That evening a wake was held at the convent followed by a funeral the next morning. The church was filled with nuns, clerics, and royalty. As there was no coffin, the body lay on a litter covered by a white brocade cloth. No funeral mass was said, a ceremony not granted to nuns. During the service, clerics moved to the front of the church to kiss Teresa's "alabaster feet" reporting later on the unusual fragrance.

After the funeral a hasty pine coffin was hammered together to enclose the body. The Duchess of Alba, fearing that the remains would be stolen, had the coffin cemented securely in a deep grave dug in the wall crypt.

A controversy arose between Alba and Avila over which city owned Teresa's body. The Bishop of Avila insisted it should be sent back to Avila, Teresa's birthplace and the site of her first foundation. Juana de Ahumada, Teresa's sister, called the hasty burial at Alba "indecent."

Nine months later Gracian, then the Discalced Provincial, came to Alba on an official visit. With the help of nuns sworn to secrecy, Teresa's body was exhumed and inspected. They found the clothing had rotted, but the body remained intact. Gracian cut off her left hand, which later was placed in a sealed casket in Avila. He kept the little finger for himself as a relic. The body, wrapped in new clothes, was returned to the coffin and the tomb resealed.

Three years later a commission made up of Gracian and three other clerics arrived in Alba to complete an unfinished task. They confided their mission to a stunned prioress, who dared not disobey the orders of her superiors. The body was again exhumed and found to be still well-preserved, though the clothing again had rotted. They wrapped the body in a sheet, carried it to a nearby inn where it remained under guard until the next morning. Hidden in straw, the body was transported on muleback to St. Joseph's in Avila.

The nuns at Avila were overjoyed at receiving the remains, which were displayed in an elaborate casket. But when the Duchess of Alba learned of the theft, she was infuriated. She screamed, "They have stolen my saint!" Her husband sought the help of the Pope who ordered that the remains be returned to Alba. Again the body was loaded onto a mule and brought back to Alba where it was examined and closely guarded for fear of more trickery by Avilans and mutilation by relic-hunters.

By the middle of the eighteenth century, when the remains were publicly exhibited, many parts of the body had been removed as relics and had found their way to various locations. Portions of her body and the heart with its seraph's wound were encased in a sacred shrine at Alba de Tormes; the right foot was preserved in Rome; a part of her cheek was at Madrid; the left hand, removed first by Gracian, became a treasured talisman for Generalissimo Franco of Spain. When Franco died, the hand was returned to the Carmelites in Rondo.

In 1614 after three decades of controversy, investigation, and testimony, Teresa was beatified. She was canonized eight years later and declared a patron saint of Spain. In 1970 Pope Paul VI declared her a "Doctor of the Church," a singular honor granted only one other woman, Catherine of Siena. Teresa's feast day is celebrated on October 15.

Although she is recognized for the seventeen religious houses she founded and for her mystical revelations, Teresa is venerated more today for her writings. The three classics, *Life, The Way of Perfection,* and *The Interior Castle,* have been translated into twenty-two languages and published in over 1,000 editions. Her other works, *Meditation on the Song of Songs, Confession, Book of Foundations,* copious verses, meditations and letters, testify to the life and abilities of a remarkable woman, who with no formal education became one of Spain's foremost religious writers, mystics, and spiritual reformers. Her profound words are recognized today as models for the practice of mental prayer and contemplation which Teresa called "friendly conversation, frequently conversing alone, with One who we know loves us."[46] To this day theologians and scholars study and analyze her life and her works, drawing varying conclusions as to the authenticity of her many ascetic experiences. Those who do not believe in visions, locutions, raptures, transports, or levitations have no disagreement with Teresa's sincerity and depth of Christian faith, her devotion to God and humankind, and her immense capacity to further the kingdom of God.

Notes

1 Teresa of Avila, *The Collected Works of St. Teresa of Avila,* vol. 1 (Washington, D.C.: Institute of Carmelite Studies, 1976), p. 33.

2 Stephen Clissold, *St. Teresa of Avila* (London: Seabury Press, 1979), p. 3.

3 Teresa of Avila, vol. 1, p. 33.

4 Clissold, p. 15.

5 Teresa of Avila, vol. 1, pp. 33-37. Five prior quotations found in this reference.

6 Victoria Lincoln, *Teresa: A Woman* (Albany, N.Y.: Twayne Publishers, 1969), p. 11.

7 Teresa of Avila, vol. 1, p. 37.

8 Ibid., p. 39.

9 Ibid., p. 40.

10 Ibid., p. 41. Prior quote also found here.

11 Clissold, p. 25.

12 Lincoln, p. 24.

13 Teresa of Avila, vol. 1, p. 43.

14 Ibid., pp. 47-49.

15 Ibid., p. 53.

16 Ibid., pp. 57-59. Three prior quotations are found on these pages.

17 Ibid., p. 61. Prior quotation is also found on this page.

18 Ibid., p. 70.

19 Lincoln, p. 36.

20 Ibid., pp. 70-71.

21 Teresa of Avila, vol. 1, p. 72.

22 Ibid., p. 74.

23 Ibid., p. 152.

24 Ibid., p. 156.

25 Ibid., p. 161.

26 Ibid., p. 183.

27 Ibid., p. 172. Prior quote found here.

28 Ibid., p. 188.

29 Ibid., pp. 193-94.

30 Ibid., p. 217.

31 Ibid., p. 218.

32 Ibid., p. 228.

33 Ibid., p. 241.

34 Clissold, p. 100.

35 Teresa of Avila, vol. 1, p. 250.

36 Teresa of Avila, *The Collected Works of St. Teresa of Avila,* vol. 2 (Washington, D.C.: Institute of Carmelite Studies, 1980), p. 40.

37 Ibid., p. 41.

38 Clissold, p. 155.

39 Ibid., p. 189.

40 Ibid., p. 191.

41 Ibid., pp. 192-93.

42 René Fülöp-Miller, *The Saints That Moved the World* (New York: Thomas Y. Crowell Co., 1945), p. 410.

43 Ibid., p. 411.

44 Clissold, p. 250.

45 Lincoln, p. 421.

46 Elliott Wright, *Holy Company* (New York: Macmillan Publishing Co., 1980), p. 28.

Chapter 6

Anne Marbury Hutchinson
(1591 - 1643)

PURITAN WOMAN WHO WAS BANISHED FROM THE MASSACHUSETTS BAY
COLONY FOR HERESY DURING THE ANTINOMIAN CONTROVERSY.

AS THE 300-ton sailing ship *Griffin* approached the Boston harbor in New England, the spirits of some one-hundred passengers lightened. They finally knew they would soon set foot on the solid ground of the New World. After leaving London in July 1634, they had been buffeted about on the high seas for eight weeks. They had been plagued by severe storms and dead winds and had survived a narrow escape from a plundering pirate ship.

The passengers shared cramped quarters below deck with trunks that held family possessions and crates of salt pork, fish, hard bread, and beer. There was no escaping the stench of their own excrement and the constant bawling and smell of the one hundred cattle to be delivered to Governor Winthrop of the Massachusetts Bay Colony.

Among the passengers were Anne and William Hutchinson who anticipated bringing up their large family in this New World colony. Here they hoped to be free from the persecution that had haunted them in Old England. Anne looked forward to hearing again the inspiring sermons of the Reverend John Cotton who had left London on the *Griffin* one year earlier. She was eager to be reunited with her eldest son Edward, then twenty-one, who had sailed with Cotton.

Aboard the *Griffin* were two men who had already learned of Anne Hutchinson. They feared that her boldness meant trouble for the new colony. In England William Bartholomew had overheard Anne say that she had received revelations directly from God, a blasphemous statement. While on board Bartholomew shared this news with the Reverend Zechariah Symmes who, himself, had become incensed with Mistress Hutchinson. During the voyage Anne had forsaken his shipboard sermons and had gathered groups of women below deck at the same hour to hear her own lectures. The husbands, too, were disturbed as their wives disregarded Apostle Paul's admonition to let the women take instructions from their men. Furthermore, Anne had predicted to all on board that they would arrive in New England in three weeks. When they landed on September 18, the very day she had forecast, Symmes and Bartholomew concluded that she must be a witch to be reported to the authorities as soon as they reached the colony.

Her Father's Daughter.

Anne Marbury was born in the tiny English market town of Alford in Lincolnshire, some 140 miles north of London and six miles inland from the North Sea. She was the second child and oldest daughter of the fourteen children born to Francis Marbury (1556-1611) and his second wife Bridget Dryden. Marbury's first wife, Elizabeth Moore, had borne three children before she died. From his first marriage only one child, Susan, survived her father.

The Marburys traced their lineage back to 1420 when the family received property which gave them the status of landed gentry. The Dryden ancestors had signed the Magna Carta in 1215, and Anne's mother claimed England's poet laureate, John Dryden (1631-1700), as a grand-nephew.

When Anne was born, presumably three days before her recorded christening date of July 20, 1591, her father had just been removed from his post as schoolmaster at the Alford Grammar School and curate of the Church of St. Wilfrid, Alford's 250-year-old parish, the center of the town's activities and culture. The bishops of the Church of England had long been troubled by Anne's father whom they believed had Puritan leanings. In their view Francis Marbury was a young upstart, who at age twenty-three had dared to chide the Church for failing to educate the clergy properly. For a time Marbury's rebellious voice had been silenced by three imprisonments. Now at age thirty-five he had raised his voice again to call the bishops "self-seeking soul murderers."[1] When he lost his teaching and preaching position, he was bereft of activity except to supervise his property and teach his children, principally his precocious daughter Anne who early became his most devout and adoring pupil.

Marbury finally declared that he was *not* a Puritan and submitted to Queen Elizabeth's chief counselor and treasurer, Sir William Cecil (Lord Burghley) a request and petitions for his reinstatement from preachers in the area. In 1594, after three years of waiting, Marbury finally recovered his license to preach in Alford.

During Francis Marbury's early life, Queen Elizabeth I was guiding England through one of its greatest periods in history. During her reign England had become a major European power with a great navy, prosperous commerce and industry, and expanding colonization. In 1588 the great Spanish Armada under King Philip of Spain had been defeated through the skill of John Hawkins and Francis Drake who were aided by fierce storms at sea.

Queen Elizabeth, herself a linguistic scholar, spoke flawless English and had mastered Latin, French, Italian, Spanish, and Welsh. She inspired both men and women to great literary and artistic accomplishments. During the Elizabethan age England produced such literary giants as William Shakespeare, Edmund Spenser, and Francis Bacon. With Good Queen Bess as a model, female literacy flourished, and the status of women reached new heights.

Elizabeth, daughter of Henry VIII and Anne Boleyn, had been proclaimed Queen of England in 1558. When her Catholic half-sister, Mary Queen of Scots (Bloody Mary), daughter of Henry VIII and Katharine of Aragon, had been forced to abdicate the Scottish throne, plots to murder Elizabeth and to seat Mary on the English throne led to Mary's imprisonment and execution in 1587. To purge Catholicism from England, Elizabeth had passed the acts of Supremacy and Uniformity in 1559. However, when she established the Church of England, she effected a compromise which instituted the reforms of the Protestants but also retained some of the Catholic structure, ritual, and ceremony. This caused much criticism among the growing body of English Puritans who despised any Papist practices.

Upon the death of Queen Elizabeth in March 1603, James VI (1566-1625) of Scotland, the son of Mary Queen of Scots, mounted the British throne as James I. James had little regard for the role of Parliament and was especially intolerant of the Puritans who by 1604 had become the dominant party in the House of Commons. Wealthy Puritan merchants controlled the country's purse strings. The Puritans challenged the King's right to rule by divine authority and demanded a voice in the government. In a confrontation with King James, known as the Hampton Court Conference, they begged the King to consider the reforms requested by the Puritan clergy. The intransigent

King made few concessions, but did allow them to revise and "purify" the Holy Bible which was completed in 1611 and became known as the King James Version. That same year James dissolved Parliament and for ten years ruled as an absolute monarch.

During this religious and political upheaval, Francis Marbury's once-defiant voice was silent on sectarian matters, and his spirit was quashed by the misfortunes of the day. The dreaded plague took three of his children, rampant inflation ate up his inheritance, and storms and droughts destroyed his crops. Money from his wife's family helped the family survive.

Despite the difficulties, Anne's formative years were pleasant. She had the daily task of caring for her younger brothers and sisters, a usual assignment for older children in the large families of the day. While her brothers went to the local grammar school, Anne learned to read, write, and figure at home. But her real education came from her father whose scholarly writings she devoured and whose religious philosophy she adopted without question. The Bible became her hand-book, and she studied it from cover to cover.

London, the City of Contrasts.

Every Tuesday the sleepy little town of Alford awoke to the cry of vendors who flocked to the marketplace to sell their wares. The market square was the place to hear news of the day and exchange pleasantries and bits of gossip. At the week-long fairs in May and October, merchants came from all parts of England to sell their goods. Alford citizens welcomed the contact with the outside world.

One of Anne's acquaintances was Will Hutchinson whose father owned a dry-goods store. Occasionally Will's father would bring a piece of cloth to Anne's mother to sew into a dress or a coat for one of her daughters. Anne, then thirteen, paid little attention to young Hutchinson, five years her senior, but Will did not forget this fresh-faced, cheerful girl when the Marbury family packed their belongings and moved to London. Francis Marbury, then a subdued forty-nine, had been appointed as preacher in the prestigious Church of St. Martin's in the Vintry on Thames Street.

For ten days the Marbury's carriage and wagon train bumped over 140 miles of rough dusty roads and forded swollen streams. They were ever fearful of falling prey to the numerous highwaymen who looted and stole from travelers. After lodging in wayside inns where they were given food and shelter in crowded quarters, they arrived safely in London and moved into the comfortable rector's house near St. Martin's Church.

For the Marbury's, accustomed to clean air, sun, and windmills and trees scattered in open fields, the dirty crowded streets of London were vile and distasteful. Carriages jammed the narrow crooked roadways lined by small shops, stalls, and tall houses reaching up to four or more stories. Sunlight rarely filtered through the blanket of black coal smoke pouring from the high chimneys of dwellings and factories. Garbage and chamber pots were emptied out the windows to the streets below to be swept up by the street cleaners.

Life in England's capital city and thriving industrial port did have its amenities, however. Exotic treasures and foods were imported from distant places, and culture and wealth thrived shamelessly alongside poverty and degradation. The great literary figures of the day strutted in and out of the coffee houses. Often raucous laughter burst out from the bawdy playhouses where Shakespeare's dramas played. From the bridge spanning the sparkling Thames River, the main artery for passenger boats, citizens could watch foreign ships and browse for merchandise in the vendor's stalls. Massive cathedrals, Parliament buildings, and King James's royal court represented majesty and power.

In London Francis Marbury discreetly refrained from adding his voice to the protests of the Puritan rebels who often gathered at his table to criticize the Established Church, its bishops, ceremonies, vestments, and the rituals that all-too-closely resembled the Catholic Church. Marbury's rewards for his restraint were appointments to more prestigious positions.

After Queen Elizabeth's enlightened reign, King James again succeeded in relegating women to their "proper roles" as lesser individuals. With the blessing of the church, he made decrees against female preaching and participation in church affairs and imposed severe penalties, usually hanging, for the practice of witchcraft. Women often suffered this fate.

England was fast becoming a cauldron of religious dissent as increasing number of radical sects were transported from the Continent. One such was Familism, or the Family of Love, which supported equality of the sexes and allowed women to participate actively in religious functions. The Familists further believed that men and women could communicate directly with God without benefit of the clergy, and they rejected the theories of predestination and Original Sin with Eve as the root of all evil.

Anne Marbury and a growing number of women found nonconformist and sectarian beliefs attractive and often risked excessive fines and imprisonment for participation in such groups. When she was eighteen, Anne met a young woman, Mary Dyer, who was inclined toward Quakerism and its unlimited opportunities for women to participate in the lay ministry of the church. Years later in New England Mary Dyer was a supportive ally when Anne's religious beliefs were under fire.

While the Puritans hoped to effect changes in the Church of England from within, the Separatists broke all connections with the Established Church and after several aborted attempts and imprisonments were able to leave England for Holland. One group of Separatists, discontent with life in Holland, returned to England and obtained a charter from the King to leave for New England. They adopted the name "Pilgrims" and were led by William Bradford to the "Plimouth Plantation" in 1620.

Will Hutchinson, Marriage, and Children.

In early 1611 Francis Marbury's death at the age of fifty-five left Anne, then approaching twenty, without the inspiration of her beloved father. The large Marbury family had to evacuate the rectory, but was sufficiently well-to-do to live comfortably elsewhere. In his will Francis Marbury left each of his twelve children 200 marks upon attaining age twenty-one. Three of Anne's brothers received Oxford educations and were allowed to leave home when of age, but the girls remained home-bound until suitable husbands claimed them. During these years Anne cared diligently for her younger siblings, and showered motherly affection on little Katherine born just one year before her father's death. Anne had earlier assisted at the births of her numerous brothers and sisters, a skill which led to a successful practice of midwifery in New England.

Will Hutchinson from Alford, still a bachelor at age twenty-six, journeyed to London and proposed to Anne, then twenty-one. The two were married on August 9, 1612. Will had made a considerable fortune as a sheep farmer and textile merchant, and he brought his bride back to live as comfortably as was possible in the large house in isolated Alford. Edward, the first of their fifteen children, was baptized on May 28, 1613, at St. Wilfrid's Church where Anne's father had served.

During an age when deaths of mothers and babies often accompanied childbirth, Anne relied heavily upon her religious beliefs and the support of her patient loving Will to sustain her during her numerous pregnancies. She was particularly attracted to the Familists who had settled in the community of Ely some sixty miles south of Alford. Anne often spoke of the unnamed "Woman of Ely" whom she called "a woman of a thousand, hardly any like her."[2] The Familist sect died out during the seventeenth century after strong opposition from Elizabeth I, James I, and the orthodox church, but their influence remained on other radical sects. The beliefs of the Familists appealed to independent women such as Anne Hutchinson, who found themselves shut out from the Anglican Church.

In Alford Anne soon found that the preachers who occupied St. Wilfrid's pulpit were dull and uninspiring, and she began to invite neighbor women to her own home to discuss religion. The women welcomed the opportunity to speak and ask questions they had not dared utter even to their husbands. And they trusted Anne Hutchinson, the woman who dispensed her own religious views as she delivered their babies and treated their maladies with herbal medicines, ointments, and remedies learned from her mother.

John Cotton of St. Botolph's.

Word reached Alford that the Reverend John Cotton, a new preacher had arrived to occupy the pulpit of St. Botolph's, the wealthy thirteenth century church in Lincolnshire's city of Boston twenty-four miles south of Alford. John Cotton's illustrious academic training and career at Cambridge, Trinity, and Emmanuel Colleges had garnered nothing but admiration and praise from professors and colleagues. By age twenty-nine he had earned an enviable reputation as a wit, a colorful preacher, a skilled orator, and an innovative thinker, but his superiors, the conservative Anglican bishops, feared that Cotton leaned too much toward radical Puritanism. After coming to St. Botolph's in

Boston in 1612, Cotton's reputation spread rapidly. This short, stout, pleasant-faced man with the booming voice attracted so many parishioners that he soon had to add another sermon on Sunday afternoons and others on weekdays. He refused to wear ecclesiastical vestments, removed some of the church's ornamental trappings, and simplified some of the sacramental ceremonies.

Cotton's appearance was as a breath of fresh air to Anne's withering spirits. Whenever possible she and William made trips on horseback to Boston to combine William's business affairs with spiritual refreshment at St. Botolph's. William was soon invited to join Cotton's elite "inner circle," a singular honor and an aid to his business connections.

For over a dozen years Cotton cautiously edged St. Botolph's closer to Puritanism, but guarded his rhetoric so as not to arouse the bishops. Some parishioners objected to Cotton's departure from the ceremony of the Established Church, but others approved. In his sermons Cotton often informed his congregation of the opportunities afforded in the New World where the red "savages" were being tamed by the Spirit.

At the heart of Cotton's theology lay the Covenant of Grace whereby only God could bring a soul to salvation, and God alone could bestow the gift of free grace to humans. This was not unlike the doctrine preached by Martin Luther who believed that a person was "justified," or saved, not by works or adherence to laws, but by faith in God and the unconditional promise of grace. The advocates of grace found support in Romans 3:28 where Paul states, "For we hold that a man is justified by faith apart from works of law."

On the other side were the ministers who preached the Covenant of Works, a doctrine whereby persons could gain their salvation by following God's laws and doing works thus becoming "sanctified" or saved. They believed there was no assurance of God's salvation without first earning it.

Anne had often heard about the Covenant of Works from the pulpit, but seldom did the preachers talk about the Covenant of Grace. The concept of grace appealed to her because she recalled several instances when she was certain that God had spoken directly to her through Bible passages, thus preparing her for tragedies to come. The difficulty was that even the Reverend Cotton claimed that only the *men* of God could interpret the will of God as written in the Bible. When Anne dared tell of her experiences, Cotton was taken aback, and William Bartholomew was downright indignant that she would admit to such heresy.

The parishioners at St. Botolph's who were not included in Cotton's "inner circle" soon complained to the church authorities of the pastor's bias toward the elite and his departure from Anglican practices. John Williams, the new and moderate Bishop of Lincoln, repeatedly intervened on Cotton's behalf, temporarily delaying action on Cotton's nonconformity. But a series of events proved calamitous for Cotton and all nonconformists.

In early 1625 upon the death of James I, his son Charles I (1600-1694) succeeded to the throne. Eight years later the conservative William Laud, Charles's favorite religious adviser, became the Archbishop of Canterbury. Laud took an uncompromising stand against all Separatists and Puritans and ordered their imprisonment or expulsion from the church. Cotton, by then an avowed Puritan, was on the list of suspects, as was the Reverend John Wheelwright, Anne's outspoken forty-one-year-old Puritan brother-in-law who had married William Hutchinson's youngest sister Mary.

After a serious bout with ague and the death of his first wife from the same disease, Cotton decided to leave England for freer shores. With the aid of sympathizers, Cotton, with an assumed name and in layman's clothes, escaped the authorities and in July 1633 was able to board the *Griffin* bound for New England. With him was his second wife Sarah, a widow whom he had recently married. Their son born at sea was appropriately named Seaborn.

Leaving England's Shores.

After Cotton's illness and departure from St. Botolph's, Anne was as a rudderless ship floundering at sea. Not only was the religious inspiration gone, but England itself under Charles I and his inept advisers had suffered humiliating naval defeats, exorbitant taxes, and economic chaos. The plague had devastated the population, and intermittent droughts and floods had ruined crops.

Personal tragedy struck the Hutchinsons. Their eighth child, William, had died earlier, shortly after his baptism on June 23, 1623. Seven years later they lost two daughters. Their eldest daughter, Susanna, just turned sixteen, died on

September 8, 1630, followed one month later by eight-year-old Elizabeth. Both daughters appeared to be victims of a plaguelike epidemic that struck down numerous Alford citizens. As Anne and William grieved over their loss, they were forced to display outside their home a brilliant red cross bearing the words, "Lord have mercy upon us,"[3] a warning to all that disease and sin lurked within. Amidst the grief and shame Anne delivered her thirteenth child, baptized September 28, 1631, and renamed William for the baby who had died earlier.

Upon the orders of Charles I, William Laud was ridding the pulpits of all Puritan ministers. Fortunately Cotton had escaped the tentacles of Laud's men who reached ever closer to Alford. But Charles's tax collectors threatened to tap William's inheritance from his recently deceased father. Anne and William made their decision to leave England, but Anne's fourteenth pregnancy delayed their departure for one year. After the birth of another Susanna in November 1633, they made plans to set sail for New England. Anne terminated her women's meetings, and Will turned his business over to his brother John. They gave away their possessions, all except the most essential items to bring with them to the new land.

For some time the Hutchinsons and their ten children (Edward had left earlier) stayed with William Bartholomew and his wife in London while they waited for repairs to be made on the *Griffin* and for the King's permission to leave. It was here that Anne spoke freely to Bartholomew of her communications with God.

When the *Griffin* finally set sail in July 1634, about 100 passengers were allowed to board after being searched by the King's men and ordered to swear allegiance to Britain. Two strong-minded passengers, the Reverend Symmes and Mistress Hutchinson, were soon at odds with each other. Symmes, an Oxford graduate, tolerated no nonsense from this woman even though she was eight years his senior. His was the ministerial calling, and she was dangerously threatening his domain. She must not be allowed to import her heretical ideas to the new colony. When the passengers disembarked at Boston on September 18, Symmes and Bartholomew headed straight to the authorities to report her.

A City on a Hill.

When John Winthrop (1588-1649) and other well-established Puritans managed to secure a royal charter from the King allowing them to form the Massachusetts Bay Company, they intended to set up a self-governing colony in the New World independent of British authority. They hoped to escape the tyranny imposed upn Puritans in England by William Laud, then Bishop of London, and they envisioned a colony where they would be free to worship. The stockholders of the Company, a civil corporation, had been granted unusual autonomy in establishing a colony in the vicinity of Salem. Winthrop was to be the first colonial governor, a position he maintained intermittently for the next twenty years.

In March 1630 eleven ships led by the flagship *Arabella* set sail for New England. John Cotton preached a farewell sermon to the departing company, and Winthrop addressed the group advancing his dreams for the new colony. He warned his compatriots that they must "follow the counsel of Micah, to do justly, to love mercy, to walk humbly with our God." To do otherwise, he said, would bring disaster. "We must consider that we shall be as a city on a hill. The eyes of all people are upon us, so that if we shall deal falsely with our God in this work we have undertaken, and so cause Him to withdraw His present help from us, we shall be made a story and a by-word through the world."

The governor foresaw "a place of cohabitation and consortship under a due form of government both civil and ecclesiastical" paving the way for establishing a theocratic society in early Massachusetts where "public and private piety were one." In the glow of anticipating such a Puritan utopia, Winthrop said, "we must love one another with a pure heart fervently. We must bear one another's burthens."[4] Some seven years later Winthrop's vision of brotherly love had become tarnished by the dissension of one courageous woman.

The original stockholders of the Massachusetts Bay Colony were highly educated clergymen, landed gentry, and men accustomed to positions of authority. John Winthrop came from a notable family which owned a manor near Groton, Suffolk, England. He attended Trinity College, Cambridge, where his father, a lawyer, held a post as auditor. At age eighteen Winthrop served as justice of the peace at Groton, a title often conferred on country gentlemen. It was natural for John Winthrop and the other stockholders to believe that God had ordained them to rule, and they intended to maintain total control for the success and well-being of the Boston community.

Before the end of 1630 about 900 colonists had landed on the Massachusetts peninsula and had settled around Boston harbor. Living conditions were severe while they built shelters from the cold damp weather and tried to provide food and supplies. In 1633 Archbishop Laud's persecution of Puritans, Calvinists, Quakers, and Separatists led to the great migration from England and in 1642 was one of the causes of the English Civil War. By that time some 15,000 English emigrants had settled in the Bay Colony.

Here It Be Tactful
to Hold One's Tongue.

The same ship that brought the Hutchinson family to the colony also carried a document from King Charles demanding that the colony relinquish its royal charter of independence. Prior to this the King had had little time from his domestic troubles to give attention to the colony 3,000 miles across the Atlantic. But rumors had reached him that outspoken critics such as the Reverend Roger Williams and John Endecott, both of Salem, has overstepped royal authority. It was time to tighten the reins on dissenters abroad.

Oblivious to the King's dispatch, Anne eagerly awaited meeting her son Edward and her religious mentor John Cotton. Unlike bustling London, Boston's modest log cabins and frame houses were scattered on the pastures and marshes east of the three hills that rose above the bay of the Charles River. More consoling to Anne and William was the sight of the square one-storied church meeting-house, the most prominent building in the four-year-old town. Here the Hutchinsons hoped to worship in peace.

After his arrival in the colony in 1633, Cotton had established himself as an influential religious and political leader. He had been appointed "teacher" in the Boston Church where the authoritarian Reverend John Wilson, one of the original colonists, held his congregation in firm control as the senior pastor. Although the teacher's duties were to preach the sermons and supervise church doctrine while the pastor tended to congregational matters and conducted the sacraments, their duties often overlapped.

William Hutchinson was admitted immediately to membership in the First Church of Boston as "a visible saint," but when Zechariah Symmes and William Bartholomew reported

Anne Hutchinson's heresy to Thomas Dudley, who had just defeated John Winthrop as governor, and recommended she be barred from membership, Dudley called for an interrogation. John Cotton gave Anne disquieting advice stating, "Here it be tactful to hold one's tongue." He explained that the charter of the colony declared that all residents "shall practice no other form of divine worship than that of the Reformed (Puritan) religion." Every colonist had to become a member of the church or suffer banishment from Boston. Anne would have to make her confession for "wrong thinking" and offer an apology for claiming that the Holy Spirit spoke directly to her. Cotton warned her, "Here members of the Church have suffered whippings for having a whim of their own."[5]

When Anne appeared at the church meeting-house to make her confession, she found four somber interrogators assembled to question her. Before her sat the presiding officer, Governor Dudley, and with him were three ministers—John Cotton, John Wilson, and her chief accuser, Zechariah Symmes, newly installed at the neighboring Charlestown church.

During the long grilling, Anne's articulate and intelligent responses led Governor Dudley to conclude that "she held nothing different from us."[6] Wilson, representing the clerics, ruled that she had given "full satisfaction." One week later she was admitted to membership in the Boston Church.

Because of William's status and wealth, the Hutchinsons were granted a half acre lot on Sentry Lane and High Street where most of the illustrious citizens lived. Just across the street lived the Winthrops and a short ways away were the Cottons and other colonial leaders. The location was ideal—near the church and the market place and close to the spring where pure drinking water could be drawn. The family lived with friends and relatives while William supervised the construction of a large frame home. He had brought with him from England panes of glass for small windows and textiles which he planned to sell in the lean-to at the side of the house. In deference to his position he would be addressed as "Mister," not "Goodman" as lesser individuals were known, and Anne would be "Mistress" or "Mrs." Hutchinson.

Anne was happy to gather her family together in the new house, and for the first time in years she was not pregnant. She soon become accustomed to cooking the foods that were available—plenty of fish, clams, oysters, and lobsters, then considered inferior. Animal meats were rare, but wild turkeys lurked in nearby woods. The Indians had introduced the colonists to corn, a versatile food that could be used in a variety of menus combined at times with maple syrup. Beer was not available so water was the beverage to wash down beans, squash, and pumpkins at the two daily meals. There were fifteen at the Hutchinson table—eleven children ranging from twenty-two-year-old Edward to one-year-old Susanna, and William's two unmarried cousins, Anne and Frances Freiston, who helped with domestic work.

Anne felt secure during her first winter in Boston despite the severity of the weather. She was able to listen to the preaching of John Cotton, who alone tended to the congregation at the Boston Church while Wilson was back in England coaxing his wife to join him. Three prominent neighbors, William Coddington, the colony treasurer and owner of the only brick house in town, Captain John Underhill of the Massachusetts militia, and John Winthrop had paid her a friendly call.

The harsh restrictions imposed by the church had not yet bothered her. The order to wear only plain, simple clothing with no ornaments or accessories had been made just before she arrived, and she didn't mind that church attendance was mandatory and work or frivolities were not allowed on the Sabbath. At the meeting-house, the men entered and sat on one side of the church, while the women came in another door and sat on the opposite side. Highly respected individuals occupied the bare benches at the front of the unheated church; lesser members sat in the rear. Christmas, or "Christ's Mass" associated with Catholicism, was not celebrated. They observed Lent and Easter with fasting and additional church services.

With few pleasures to enjoy during the winter months, the men began to hold weekly meetings to discuss the previous Sunday's sermon. But whenever the subject arose of loyalty to the King and the pros and cons of the Puritan rebellion in England, the meeting disintegrated into arguments and fights. Anne, disturbed that women were excluded from the men's discussions, invited the neighborhood wives to her house on Thursdays to discuss the Sunday sermon and read passages from the Bible. She found a ready audience among the women she had nursed and whose babies she had delivered, and by spring there were as many as sixty women crowding into her home. As they listened to Anne's intelligent observations and enlightening talk, they sewed quilts or made rugs.

The aroused husbands called on John Cotton to investigate this woman who was threatening the peace and tranquility of their hearths. When Cotton confronted Anne, she answered his questions willingly and admitted that "most of the women are in agreement, that of all the ministers we have heard, none preaches the Covenant of Grace so sweetly as does Mr. Cotton." She continued to complain to the uncomfortable Cotton that the Reverend Wilson preached "naught but the Covenant of Works."[7] When Cotton pressed her further, she explained that each woman had the Spirit of God within herself, that God could speak to each one directly through the Holy Word. Even the liberal ears of John Cotton had heard enough. He gave Mistress Hutchinson stern instructions that she must stop her meetings and the preaching of such heretical ideas.

Anne was disheartened and perplexed to hear her idol chastise her for something she had considered a natural extension of the pastor's own nonconformity. The Puritans had left England because of the oppression meted out to them for their dissent from the Established Church, yet the colonial leaders themselves were following the same course but in a different context. There appeared to be little allowance for variant thought and opinion.

Unlike in England, colonial women were protected from physical abuse at the hands of their husbands, and the men could not treat their wives as servants. But just four months after Anne's admission to the Boston Church, females were again reminded that they were inferior persons. To counter King Charles's threat to rescind the colony's charter, the General Court (the legislative and judicial body) sought to increase the number of men who would swear allegiance to the colony. The age for males allowed to take the Freeman's Oath was lowered to sixteen and often younger. Thus Anne's husband, her nineteen-year-old son Richard, and even fourteen-year-old Francis took the oath and were able to vote and hold public office if they chose. The women of the colony were denied that privilege.

A Woman of a Haughty and Fierce Carriage.

From his front window John Winthrop could easily spy on the activities going on at the

Hutchinson home across the street. He saw groups of women, most of them from Boston, enter the house on Thursdays and leave after a considerable time. As the numbers increased and began to include women from neighboring villages, Winthrop became alarmed. He feared that Mistress Hutchinson was becoming a threat to the well-being of the colony and was endangering the utopia he had dreamed of establishing.

Winthrop was a man who cherished order and stability. During his lifetime he was to marry four times and sire sixteen children. He brought strict discipline into his personal life—romance was to be accomplished on schedule. He and his beloved third wife Margaret "thought of each other" between five and six o'clock every Monday and Friday. Even though Margaret had used the services of Midwife Hutchinson, Winthrop found the developments at the house across the street disquieting. He was sure Anne Hutchinson was using her practice of midwifery to ingratiate herself with women and had ensnared them when they were most vulnerable. In his daily journal Winthrop complained, "As soon as she was admitted into the church, she began to go to work, and being a woman very helpful in times of childbirth and other occasions of bodily infirmities, and well furnished for means of those purposes, she easily insinuated herself into the affections of many."[8]

In England the practice of midwifery had long been a target for the authorities, at times with deserved criticism of the unscrupulous who abused their profession. The New England founders continued to be watchful of these women who had "familiarity with the Devil, but also in that service commit devilish malefices."[9] Winthrop found a ready ally in the Reverend Thomas Weld, a minister in neighboring Roxbury, who had often preached that like Eve, the root of Original Sin, women were easy targets for Satan.

Winthrop found Mistress Hutchinson to be more than an ordinary midwife—she was "a woman of a haughty and fierce carriage, of a nimble wit and active spirit, and a very voluble tongue, more bold than a man, though in understanding and judgment inferior to many women."[10] His barbed pen described her husband William as "a man of very mild temper and weak parts and wholly guided by his wife."[11] (Winthrop's journal, where he always referred to himself in the third person, is one of the most quoted accounts of Anne Hutchinson's troubles in the colony.)

Winthrop, Weld, and other authorities found willing support among the husbands who feared their wives had fallen prey to this "she-devil." John Cotton withdrew to his study hoping to avoid direct confrontation, but had been urged by the other men to send spies to Anne's meetings. He wrote, "I sent some sisters of the Church on purpose to her repetitions so that I might know the truth. But when she discerned any such present, no speech fell from her that could be excepted against."[12]

Tradesmen, angered that they were excluded from leadership in the colony and upset by heavy taxes and stringent wage and price controls imposed by the magistrates, soon began to attend the Hutchinson meetings. To accommodate the increasing numbers, Anne added a Monday gathering. In the meantime another election had ejected Thomas Dudley from the governor's office in favor of the wealthy John Haynes. Winthrop and Dudley, both rejected by the Freemans' vote, could concentrate on Mistress Hutchinson.

In the fall of 1635 Anne temporarily withdrew from the public eye. While she was discouraged by developments in the colonies, her husband had risen to positions of importance—he had been elected to the General Court and was on a committee of merchants assigned to work out satisfactory controls on the prices of goods and merchandise. And Anne, at the age of forty-four, found she was into her fifteenth pregnancy.

Arrivals of Many Cloths.

Events in Boston brought rapid change. The Reverend Wilson arrived back from his second trip to England, this time accompanied by his reluctant wife Elizabeth. Wilson had to reestablish his authority in the Boston community where Cotton had gained considerable religious and political status.

In October another ship docked carrying a young gentleman of the English aristocracy—Henry Vane, age twenty-two, son of Sir Henry Vane, the King's controller. Young Vane, with his trim beard, plumed tricorne hat, and elegant clothes, was given a warm reception despite his reputation in England as a troublemaker. Perhaps his royal connections could be used to advantage with the King on the matter of rescinding the charter.

Winthrop and the other leaders of the colony, however, were not prepared for the meteoric rise of young Vane in politics. Shortly after his arrival Vane was admitted to the church, and he soon headed a committee that was to hold public hearings on disputes, particularly the contention that had arisen between Dudley, a strict disciplinarian, and Winthrop, who favored a more lenient approach to offenders. Winthrop lost the decision and bitterly acknowledged that he had failed by "over much leniency and remissness, and would endeavor (by God's assistance) to take a more strict course hereafter."[13] The triumph of Dudley's strict discipline policy helped define the firm attitude of the General Court in the Hutchinson trial, in contrast to the leniency granted Roger Williams, an earlier dissenter.

Just as Henry Vane arrived, the General Court had finally issued a decree banishing from the colony the controversial hot-tempered thirty-two-year-old Reverend Roger Williams (c.1603-1683) of Salem and his supporters. For years Williams had been summoned periodically before the Court to answer the many charges levelled against him. Williams had advocated the separation of church and state insisting that magistrates had no power over conscience. He further claimed that the King had no right to grant charters to colonists to occupy land which rightfully belonged to the Native Americans. Although liberal in most views, Williams had taken a rigid stand against women who did not wear veils, and he refused to pray with any persons of his parish, including his own wife, who disagreed with him. Williams was banished on October 9, 1635, and left the colony in January of the following year for Rhode Island where he founded a colony that became a sanctuary for dissenting colonists. In accordance with his beliefs Williams purchased the land for Providence from the Narragansett Indians.

Two other arriving emigrants soon eroded further the tranquillity of the colony. The outspoken Reverend John Wheelright, Anne's brother-in-law, had finally managed to depart England after being silenced by Archbishop Laud. Wheelright and his wife Mary, enthusiastically welcomed by the Hutchinsons, soon gained membership in the Boston Church.

Also arriving in the colony were William Dyer, a milliner, and his wife Mary whom Anne had befriended in England. Mary, sympathetic with the Quaker cause, disregarded Anne's early warning that Quakers were not tolerated in the colony. Mary soon became one of Anne's chief supporters and another thorn in the side of colonial authorities. Before he knew her disrup-

tive capabilities, Winthrop called Mistress Dyer "a very proper and comely young woman."[14]

Disharmony Rocks the "City on a Hill."

After the birth of Anne's fifteenth child Zuriel, a son baptized on March 13, 1636, Anne was ready to resume her activities. She barely tolerated the preaching of John Wilson, recently returned from England, and she dared lead a group of women supporters out of church during one of Wilson's dull sermons. Wilson never forgot this affront.

Anne again conducted her house meetings and was delighted when even the dashing Henry Vane, who had defeated Winthrop for governor in May 1636, joined her home congregation. The number of people who crowded into her living room had increased phenomenally with more and more citizens of both sexes gathering to hear her speak. Some of the colony's wealthiest business men were her disciples.

With Anne's encouragement, her supporters circulated a petition to replace the irascible Wilson with Wheelwright as teacher and Cotton as the principal preacher. At the church meeting-house on Sunday, October 30, 1636, a public dispute followed the two-hour service. Winthrop, then reduced to the office of deputy governor, led a successful movement to retain Wilson and reject Wheelwright "whose spirit they knew not and one who seemed to dissent in judgment."[15] John Cotton straddled the fence. When the meeting ended, Wilson kept his position in the Boston Church, and Wheelwright was appointed to a new congregation at Mt. Wollaston (later Quincy), a safe ten miles from Boston.

During the winter months the colony suffered more religious and political discord. Following a clash with Winthrop, Governor Vane threatened to leave for England, but the General Court urged him to remain until the annual May election. At a conference of ministers and magistrates, Wilson made a harsh public speech laying blame for declining church membership on Mistress Hutchinson and her home meetings. Cotton moved to censure Wilson's charge, but the motion was rejected.

Soon after the conference, Anne was called before seven ministers to explain her statements that only Cotton and Wheelwright preached the true doctrines of the Covenant of Grace, while the others preached only the Covenant of Works. Anne now assumed she had three supporters facing her. When neither side wavered, Cotton in futility quickly terminated the meeting. The gulf between the two factions was widening.

In January 1637 on the general fast day, Wheelwright preached an inflammatory sermon at Boston that aroused more contention when he publicly supported his sister-in-law's position on the Covenant of Grace. Two months later the General Court rejected the petition supporting Wheelwright and found the minister guilty of sedition and contempt, the sentence to be delayed until after the May elections. They later meted out harsh punishment to those who had signed the petition.

To insure his victory as governor Winthrop had the voting moved to Newtown (later Cambridge) where he had strong support. At the heated May election Winthrop was again elected governor with Thomas Dudley as his deputy. In an attempt to tighten discipline in the colony and reduce nonconformity, the General Court passed an act to "keep out all such persons as might be dangerous to the commonwealth."[16] The magistrates would decide who was to be allowed into the colony. Anyone harboring a "dangerous" person would be fined.

Just after the annual election of 1637, the Puritans found themselves engaged for the first time in a serious military conflict. Since the early 1630s the growing colony had searched for additional land in the interior, and they had looked to the Connecticut Valley then occupied by the Pequot Indians. In 1633-34 a small pox epidemic took thousands of Indian lives and left their villages only partially inhabited and ready for occupation by the colonials. Winthrop rationalized, "If God were not pleased with our inheriting these parts, why did he drive out natives before us? and why dothe he still make roome for us, by deminishinge them as we increase."[17]

In accordance with the European "right of patent" giving a Christian monarch full authority over newly-discovered land providing the inhabitants were "heathen," the Massachusetts Bay Colony had from the first claimed rights to the land. When the Pequots challenged them and killed white colonists, troops were mobilized under Captains John Underhill and John Mason. The Pequot War was short-lived—the Pequots were no match for the Puritan militia with their firearms. Some 500 Pequot men, women, and children were killed, and captives were taken as slaves by colonists or sold in the West Indies. Other Indian tribes, fearful of the power of the whites, had assisted the militia.

During the Pequot conflict, all colonial men were "exercised in the use of armes."[18] When many male members of the Boston Church, including the Hutchinson men, refused to support the troops either financially or by bearing arms, Winthrop and the other magistrates were angered. Obviously, the Hutchinson woman was to blame.

In August 1637 after a sweltering summer, Governor Winthrop convened a synod of magistrates, clergy, and citizens at Newtown in an attempt to reconcile political and religious conflict. Before the session ended, the root of the conflict, Mistress Hutchinson, had been accused of harboring eighty-two blasphemous and false religious views and conducting "disorderly" assemblies of women. She would be summoned to appear before the General Court in November.

Before the trial Zuriel, the youngest Hutchinson child, developed spasms and died. Anne's enemies said the death was God's judgment. Soon after, Anne's friend, Mary Dyer, then five months pregnant, went into premature labor. At the onset it was apparent that this was not a normal delivery as the baby was in a difficult breech position. Midwives Anne Hutchinson and Jane Hawkins delivered a stillborn baby girl after great pain to the mother. The baby was badly deformed, "a monster" Winthrop wrote in his diary adding a graphic description.

In desperation Anne ran to John Cotton for advice. "Conceal it," he said. As had been the practice in England and with approval from Cotton, the two women buried the baby in a grave in the nearby woods assuming they were not noticed. Some five months later Winthrop was alerted to the tragedy, had the body exhumed and inspected. He had more evidence that the devil had taken control of Mary Dyer, Anne Hutchinson, and Jane Hawkins.

The Breeder and Nourisher of All These Distempers.

Winter came early and brutally that November in 1637 when the hearings were conducted by the General Court at Newtown. Anne had been summoned to appear "for Moving against Public Law and Order and the Tranquillity of the State."[19] The five-mile journey to Newtown took Anne and her husband's brother Edward one-half day, traveling first by foot to the northern end of the Boston peninsula, then by ferry across the Charles River to Charlestown, then again by foot over Indian trails west to Newtown. Edward carried a gun required by ordinance of every traveler who ventured farther than one mile from home as protection from wolves and unfriendly persons.

Despite the cold weather the unheated frame meeting-house with its crude wooden benches was jammed with spectators. At a table at the front sat the nine magistrates garbed in their greatcoats to ward off the drafts. They alone had foot-warmers, and Winthrop occupied the only chair with the added comfort of a pillow. Nearby were the deputies and the clergymen who were to be both prosecutors and witnesses against Mistress Hutchinson. Representing the Boston Church were John Cotton, who still hoped to support the defendant, and John Wilson, who was bent on revenge against the woman who had ridiculed him in his own church. Zechariah Symmes from Charlestown was there to witness against the woman he had encountered on the *Griffin*.

On the first day with Governor Winthrop presiding, the forty member General Court disfranchised, banished, and penalized those Hutchinson followers accused of seditious acts and signing the Wheelwright petition at the Boston Church. Only William Coddington, the wealthiest man in the colony, had enough prestige to be allowed to keep his seat in the Court. At dusk the Court adjourned.

In a stormy session the following day, the Reverend John Wheelwright, Anne's brother-in-law, was disfranchised and banished from the colony. Rather than suffer house arrest until spring, Wheelwright left the colony for New Hampshire during the winter.

Next, Edward Hutchinson, William's brother, was accused of disloyalty to the governor. When he protested, he was jailed, heavily finded, and later released when he apologized to the Court. Four other men, including William Dyer, Mary's husband, were disfranchised.

Then came the main business on the agenda—proceedings against Mistress Hutchinson, "the breeder and nourisher of all these distempers" who was "convented for traducing the ministers and their ministry in this country."[20] What transpired in the meeting-house that day was a travesty of justice that besmirched the career of John Winthrop and the reputation of the Massachusetts Bay Colony.

Anne Hutchinson, dressed in her mourning black, was called before the Court. She had been provided with no counsel, nor had she been advised beforehand of the charges against her. Governor Winthrop acted as both judge and prosecuting attorney. Most of the Hutchinson sympathizers had been disfranchised, so the Court was packed with hostile members. The interrogation and Anne's answers have been recorded both by Winthrop and by an anonymous person who appeared to be somewhat sympathetic to the defendant. Justice was not served as:

> . . . the accused, unprovided with counsel, was not only examined and cross-examined by the magistrates, her judges, but badgered, insulted and sneered at, and made to give evidence against herself. The witnesses in her behalf were browbeaten and silenced in careless disregard both of decency and a manly sense of fair play. Her few advocates among the members of the court were rudely rebuked, and listened to with an impatience which it was not attempted to conceal; while, throughout, the so-called trial was, in fact, no trial at all, but a mockery of justice rather,—a bare-faced inquisitorial proceeding.[21]

While her accusers sat, Anne, appearing to be pregnant again, was made to stand until "her countenance discovered some bodily infirmity,"[22] and a chair was brought.

Although her chief offense appeared to be her bold criticism of the Reverend Wilson and the other ministers who preached the Covenant of Works, Winthrop had to diplomatically skirt that embarrassing issue. He began with a general accusation charging that ". . . you have maintained a meeting and an assembly in your house that hath been condemned by the general assembly as a thing not tolerable nor comely in the sight of God nor fitting for your sex." He then threatened ". . . if you be in an erroneous way we may reduce you so you may become a profitable member here among us; otherwise if you be obstinate in your course that then the court may take such course that you may trouble us no further."[23]

In an angry exchange, Anne quickly refuted Winthrop's first charge. "It is lawful for me to do so as it is all your practices," she said. "Can you find a warrant for yourself and condemn me for the same thing?"[24] Winthrop dropped the issue.

The Governor next offered the argument that she had transgressed the Fifth Commandment, "Honor thy father and mother." He explained that in supporting the Wheelwright petition, though she herself did not sign it, she had dishonored "the fathers of the commonwealth" and so should be punished. To this Anne replied, "I do acknowledge no such thing; neither do I think that I ever put any dishonor upon you."[25]

Winthrop was not faring well. Hoping to be on firmer ground, he moved to the third charge. She had been holding meetings in her home and there had preached unlawfully to both men and women. Winthrop firmly believed that it was not right for a woman to "meddle in such things as are proper for men, whose minds are stronger."[26] Anne countered that all had come of their own free wills. She then drew upon a Biblical reference where Titus had instructed the elder women to teach the younger. After arguing the meaning of the passage, Winthrop adopted another strategy, one which would appeal to men in the Court and audience. He accused her of tempting women to forsake their duties as wives and mothers, causing many families to be neglected with consequent damage to the commonwealth. Anne denied the charges, and this exchange followed:

> GOVERNOR. Well, we see how it is. We must therefore put it away from you; or restrain you from maintaining this course.
>
> MRS H. If you have a rule for it from God's Word, you may.
>
> GOVERNOR. We are your judges, and not you ours. And we must compel you to it.[27]

During the preliminary questioning by Winthrop, the other magistrates and ministers had remained mute. But now it was time to move to the heart of the trial. Mistress Hutchinson "had publicly said that Mr. Cotton alone of the ministers preached a Covenant of Grace; the others, not having received the seal of the Spirit, were consequently not able ministers of the New Testament, and preached a Covenant of Works."[28] Anne declined to plead guilty to this charge.

This was the sensitive issue that brought the ministers, one after another, to their feet to witness for the prosecution. They claimed that Anne had enunciated that very position before them at the conference in December at Boston. Anne then accused the ministers of telling in public what she had told them in private, a breach of confidence, she said.

When the trial became mired in theological minutiae, Winthrop announced, "Mrs. Hutchinson, the court you see hath labored to bring you to acknowledge the error of your way so that you might be reduced. The time now grows late. We shall therefore give you a little more time to consider of it, and therefore desire that you attend the court again in the morning."[29] Anne went to her lodging to consult her notes and prepare for the next day.

A Woman Not Fit for Our Society.

The next morning when Anne appeared before the Court, she stated that in reviewing her notes she had found "things not to be as hath been alleged. Therefore," she said, "if [the ministers] accuse me, I desire it may be upon oath."[30] Another insult to the clergy! When Winthrop asked for an opinion from the spectators, a few of Anne's supporters spoke in favor of an oath, but their voices were quickly quashed. To move the matter along, Winthrop then declared he would give the oath if the ministers would consent.

Before the preachers were sworn and called to testify, two ineffective witnesses for the defense were called to give their knowledge of Anne's testimony before the clergy in Boston. Cotton, who had seated himself beside Anne, rose to his feet and with eloquent skill attempted to defend her and at the same time pacify the Court. After much wrangling with Cotton, Deputy Dudley came to the crucial point. "They affirm that Mrs. Hutchinson did say they were not able ministers of the New Testament." Cotton hedged, "I do not remember it." The prosecution seemed to be crumbling. Anne would have to be freed, or condemned on vague generalities.

As the Court pondered its dilemma, Anne, savoring her apparent victory, delivered herself "into the power of the Court, as guilty as that which all suspected her for, but were not furnished with proof sufficient to proceed against her."[31]

In a long speech she told of her many revelations from God and concluded by saying, "I fear none but the great Jehovah, which hath foretold me of these things, and I do verily believe that he will deliver me out of your hands." Then came the threat, "Therefore take heed how you proceed against me; for I know that for this you go about to do to me, God will ruin you and your posterity, and this whole State."[32]

Finally the Court had real ammunition! Mistress Hutchinson had condemned herself with her heretical confession of divine revelation and miraculous intervention, and had even dared to threaten the members of the Court. Heated arguments followed, and Cotton could no longer defend her. The Court then wrangled over what punishment to mete out—most of them favored strong measures. Only William Coddington, Anne's loyal friend, claimed, "Here is no law of God that she hath broken; nor any law of the country that she hath broken. Therefore she deserves no censure."[33] His support was futile.

When Winthrop called the question, the Court voted to imprison and banish her from the colony. Only Coddington and William Colburn from Boston voted against the decision, and another man abstained. Cotton, fearful for his own future in the colony, abandoned her and voted with the majority. The trial concluded with the following exchange:

> GOVERNOR WINTHROP. Mrs. Hutchinson, you hear the sentence of the Court. It is that you are banished from out our jurisdiction as being a woman not fit for our society. And you are to be imprisoned till the Court send you away.
>
> MRS. HUTCHINSON. I desire to know wherefore I am banished.
>
> GOVERNOR WINTHROP. Say no more. The Court knows wherefore, and is satisfied.[34]

The official sentence of the Colony of Massachusetts read as follows:

> Mrs. Hutchinson, (the wife of Mr. William Hutchinson,) being convented for traducing the ministers, and their ministry in this country, shee declared voluntarily her revelations for her ground, and that shee should bee delivred, and the Court ruined, with their posterity; and thereupon was banished, and the mean while was committed to Mr. Joseph Weld untill the Court shall dispose of her.[35]

House Arrest, Banishment, and Excommunication.

During the trial Anne Hutchinson and her followers had been branded as "Familists," but later were called "Antinomians," a derogatory label derived originally from the Greek "anti" (against) and "nomos" (law). Antinomianism was not unlike early schisms such as second century Montanism and Gnosticism, and it predated the Quaker movement. Martin Luther had applied the term to the beliefs of the German

Protestant minister, Johann Agricola, with whom he broke in 1536. Because Antinomians preached freedom from civil, moral, and church laws, they were often accused of allowing the "slothful sinner" to lead immoral lives. Furthermore, the Antinomians did not believe in the immortality of the soul. Although Anne denied she advocated total freedom from Christian laws, her critics were convinced that she was a practicing Antinomian.

As a warning to others who harbored similar beliefs, the General Court resolved to purge dangerous citizens from the colony. Winthrop was determined that nothing should destroy his vision of the "city on a hill," the citadel of God's chosen people. All dissenters were disfranchised and dismissed from office, and to thwart any attempts at armed resistance, the Court hastily ordered seventy-five Hutchinsonians to relinquish their firearms and ammunition. With no guns to protect livestock from predators or to kill game, many men soon recanted. The action precipitated an outcry against Winthrop at the Boston Church, but the Governor calmed the furor by a conciliatory speech claiming he had acted by God's direction in the best interests of the colony.

Anne spent the winter under house arrest at the home of Joseph Weld, a brother of the austere Reverend Thomas Weld, in Roxbury, a difficult two-mile journey from Boston. She was to have no visitors except family and clergymen who would visit her periodically hoping to straighten out her "twisted mind." Her husband was ordered to pay for her food and shelter. By leniency of the Court, she was granted time to arrange for the care of her seven children at home in Boston, and she could wait until spring to leave the colony.

During the severe winter of her house arrest at Roxbury, Anne, then nearing forty-seven, had few callers. Only her husband William, son Edward, and the local preachers were allowed to visit her. She became increasingly depressed, and her usually healthy body suffered from what appeared to be a menopausal pregnancy. Preoccupied with death and immortality, she searched her Bible for answers.

The ministers, fearful that she was still spreading her poison through the colony, wanted yet to deal with her "in a church way." They called a meeting at the Boston Church at 10:00 A.M. on the Thursday lecture day, March 15, 1638. In the congregation sat a few of her friends, subdued by threats of recriminations. She missed her husband William who had left the colony for Rhode Island where Roger Williams had helped him purchase land on which to build a house. When called to the front of the church, Anne, pale, drawn, and feeling quite alone, walked shakily down the aisle to face the grim-faced ministers. Governor Winthrop, Deputy Dudley, and Treasurer Richard Bellingham lent their official presence.

Elder Thomas Leverett, chief interrogator, read twenty-nine errors compiled by Thomas Weld and the other ministers. The inquisition continued for nine long hours, each clergyman in turn levelling abusive denunciations on her. At times they became hopelessly mired in theological questions. When asked to admit her errors, Anne refused. Only her eldest son Edward and son-in-law Thomas Savage spoke in her defense.

John Cotton, once Anne's idol and spiritual guide, rose to speak. He was intent on proving to his colleagues that he repudiated this woman and her heresies. He first unleashed a tirade against Edward and Thomas claiming that "you have proved vipers to eat through the very bowels of your mother to her ruin." He then cautioned the women of the congregation:

> Let not the good you have received from her make you to receive all for good that comes from her; for you see she is but a woman and many unsound and dangerous principles are held by her. . . . if you have drunk in with this good any evil or poison, make speed to vomit it up again and to repent of it and take care that you do not harden her in her way by pitying her, or confirming her in her opinions.[36]

Cotton then turned his wrath on Anne. Cushioning his denunciation first with compliments, he proceeded to condemn her libertine views that had led many poor souls to "filthy sin." He warned her not to defile "the hearts of young women with such unsound and dangerous principles."[37]

At 8:00 P.M. the interrogation was adjourned, to be continued one week later. Anne lodged with John Cotton where for seven days she was subjected to his constant pounding to admit her errors and avoid excommunication from the church.

When the hearing resumed on March 22, a subdued Anne Hutchinson read a recantation of her unsound opinions saying, "I spoke rashly and unadvisedly. I do not allow the slighting of ministers, nor of the Scriptures, nor anything

that is set up by God." Then she added, "It was never in my heart to slight any man, but only that man should be kept in his own place and not set in the room of God."[38]

Immediately the offended clergymen arose to denounce her as a heretic, an instrument of the devil, a woman who had not been humbled, the root of disorder. Cotton concluded, "I think we are bound upon this ground to remove her from us and not to retain her any longer, seeing she doth prevaricate in her words, as that her judgment is one thing and her expression is another."[39]

Reverend John Wilson delivered a triumphant final verdict:

> . . . in the name of the Church I do not only pronounce you worthy to be cast out, but I do cast you out and . . . deliver you up to Satan that you may learn no more to blaspheme, to seduce and to lie. Therefore, I command you in the name of this church as a leper to withdraw yourself out of the congregation; that as formerly you have despised and condemned the holy ordinances of God and turned your back on them, so you may now have no part in them nor benefit by them.[40]

Anne turned to face the congregation, and with revived strength and head held high, walked down the aisle. Her friend Mary Dyer rose from a bench, slipped her arm in Anne's, and walked boldly out beside her.

Freed From This Great and Sore Affliction.

After three and one-half unsettling years in the colony, Anne was ready to dismantle her house in Boston and leave Massachusetts. For six days she and her children traveled on foot through deep lingering April snow and by canoe over streams and rivers, before they arrived at Aquidneck in Rhode Island where William had built a crude cabin. It wasn't long before Winthrop's tentacles again ensnared them. The news of Mary Dyer's "monstrous" birth some five months earlier had leaked out. Winthrop wrote of his discovery to Roger Williams and told of the efforts of Anne Hutchinson and Jane Hawkins to "conceal" the body. Williams denounced the act.

In mid-summer, Anne herself in poor physical condition, suffered a painful miscarriage with severe bleeding. She was aided by John Clarke, a sympathetic local minister. When the news of her aborting a "hydatidiform mole," a mass or growth with some twenty-six lumps, the magistrates and clergy of Boston gloated. Now they had more concrete evidence of God's justice.

The heavy hand of the General Court had also descended on Jane Hawkins, who was banished from the colony, as were several other women accused of consorting with the devil. Witch trials were soon to become routine occurrences in New England.

At Aquidneck Anne established herself as a leader of a small group of excommunicants. However, her message had become more strident often bordering on a call for anarchy which few settlers in Narragansett Bay condoned.

In 1642 Anne's beloved and loyal husband William died leaving her crushed with grief. With her six youngest children, her son-in-law, and a few Rhode Island families, she moved to a lonely spot on Long Island Sound in Dutch territory. Her last home in Pelham Bay lay in an isolated spot miles from neighbors.

In the late summer of 1643 Anne and five of her children were killed by a band of Mohegans who were fighting to reclaim their hunting grounds from white settlers. Ten-year-old Susanna was taken captive. After four years the girl was freed by a payment of ransom, and she reluctantly returned to civilization. At age eighteen Susanna married a man from Boston and passed into obscurity.

The Boston authorities found great satisfaction in Anne's death. The Reverend Thomas Weld wrote back to England, "God's hand is the more apparently seen herein, to pick out this woeful woman, to make her and those belonging to her, an unheard of heavy example. . . . Thus the Lord heard our groans to heaven, and freed us from this great and sore affliction."[41]

Some of Anne's supporters fared no better than their leader. Mary Dyer and her husband had followed the Hutchinsons to Rhode Island where they advocated religious freedom. When Mary went back to England, she officially joined the outlawed Quakers. She then returned to Boston to challenge the death penalty imposed on Quakers in the colony. She was tried before the General Court and sentenced to hang in the Boston Commons. As the rope was placed around her neck, she was granted a reprieve. After a year of banishment, Mary returned to Boston, was again sentenced to hang. This time there was no reprieve. She refused to admit her errors and died on the gallows on June 1, 1660. At the present time bronze statues of both Mary

Dyer and Anne Hutchinson grace the east and west wings of the Massachusetts State House.

The aristocrat and one-time governor of Massachusetts, the young Henry Vane, had returned to England in August 1637 after his defeat by Winthrop. In England his reputation was besmirched with rumors that he was responsible for both Mary Dyer's and Anne Hutchinson's unfortunate pregnancies, and he was executed after being charged with complicity in the death of one of Charles I's ministers.

Many of Anne's followers joined the Quakers in Rhode Island and continued the fight against religious oppression. Anne's five surviving children settled in various locations in New England. Her eldest son Edward, a leading citizen of Boston, was killed on a peace mission to the Nipmuc Indians. John Wheelwright, Anne's brother-in-law, was reinstated in 1644 when he wrote letters to Boston renouncing his earlier beliefs.

Through the ensuing years most accounts of the Antinomian Controversy relying on the information recorded by Winthrop discredited Anne. In 1676 a sympathetic view was published anonymously, and in 1765 Anne's great-great grandson, Thomas Hutchinson, published a history of the colony in which he presented a more compassionate view of his ancestor. Two centuries later George Ellis of Boston wrote a scholarly biography chastising the Puritans and their beliefs. Not until the latter part of the twentieth century have other biographies, some of varying reliability, been written.

What is the legacy of Anne Hutchinson? Her advocacy of certain religious tenets will be questioned and debated, but at a time when most people believed as did Winthrop that "women's minds could not stand the strain of profound theological speculation,"[42] she had proved him wrong. She had a keen mind, a prodigious memory, a facile tongue, a nimble wit, and a dynamic personality. She stood her ground alone before a court of men who had prejudged her and conspired to "reduce" her to her proper place.

She had acquired her theological education through her own initiative, and had defended her views courageously against overwhelming opposition from educated authorities who maneuvered unjustly to discredit her. She had shaken single-handedly the very foundation and attitudes of the infant Massachusetts colony and had nearly toppled Winthrop's "city on a hill." The fathers of New England, fearful of her charismatic power as a female to corrupt gullible persons, will long be judged less noble for their abuse of a brilliant woman whose ideas and independence have spawned recent admirers. Anne Hutchinson was one of the first American women to question the appropriate status of women in the church and society. Had she been born three centuries later, she would have been hailed as a crusader for women's rights.

Notes

1 Selma R. Williams, *Divine Rebel* (New York: Holt, Rinehart and Winston, 1981), p. 12.

2 Ibid., p. 44.

3 Ibid., p. 67.

4 Roger Lundin and Mark A. Noll eds., *Voices from the Heart* (Grand Rapids, Michigan: William B. Eerdmans Publishing Company, 1987), pp. 3-6. Four previous quotations found here.

5 Deborah Crawford, *Four Women in a Violent Time* (New York: Crown Publishers Inc., 1970), pp. 87-88. Two previous quotations found here.

6 Williams, p. 81.

7 Crawford, p. 95.

8 Williams, p. 97.

9 Ibid., p. 99.

10 Ibid., pp. 95-96.

11 Ibid., p. 63.

12 Ibid., p. 99.

13 Ibid., p. 113.

14 Ibid., p. 63.

15 Ibid., p. 123.

16 Ibid., p. 130.

17 Alden T. Vaughan, *New England Frontier* (Boston: Little, Brown and Company, 1965), p. 104.

18 Ibid., p. 95.

19 Crawford, p. 109.

20 Charles Francis Adams, *The Antinomian Controversy* (New York: DaCapo Press, 1976), p. 121.

21 Ibid., p. 126.

22 Ibid.

23 Williams, p. 149.

24 Philip F. Gura, *A Glimpse of Sion's Glory* (Middletown, Connecticut: Wesleyan University Press, 1984), p. 258.

25 Adams, p. 127.

26 Emery Battis, *Saints and Sectaries* (Chapel Hill: The University of North Caroline Press, 1962), p. 120.

27 Adams, p. 128.

28 Ibid., p. 129.

29 Williams, pp. 156-57.

30 Ibid., p. 158.

31 Adams, pp. 136-37. The previous quotation found here.

32 Ibid., p. 140.

33 Ibid., p. 144.

34 Ibid., p. 146.

35 Ibid.

36 Williams, pp. 178-79.

37 Ibid., p. 180.

38 Ibid., p. 181.

39 Ibid., p. 183.

40 Ibid.

41 Ibid., pp. 194-95.

42 Edmund S. Morgan, *The Puritan Dilemma* (Boston: Little, Brown and Company, 1958), p. 135.

Chapter 7

Juana Inés de la Cruz

(1651 - 1695)

NUN, WRITER, AND INTELLECTUAL, KNOWN AS THE GREATEST LYRIC POET
OF COLONIAL MEXICO.

A YOUNG MEXICAN girl of six or seven begged her mother to allow her to leave her grandfather's country home and journey to Mexico City. The girl wanted to live with an aunt so she could attend the University to study the sciences. However, only males were allowed to enter that institution. The girl offered a solution—she would dress as a boy. When her mother firmly disapproved of the plan, the precocious youngster, eager to learn, turned to the books in her grandfather's library.

Juana Inés de Asbaje y Ramirez de Santillana was born November 12, 1651,[1] at the hacienda Nepantla near the mountain village of Chimalhuacan, a short distance southeast of Mexico City. It was the coldest season of the year in the highlands, and the candle-lit chamber in the adobe house was barely heated by the fire in the hearth.

The family soon moved to a nearby village, Amecameca, a picturesque town in the upland valley between the volcanoes of Iztaccihuatl (the White Lady) and Popocatepetl (the Smoky Mountain). Here Juana was baptized on December 2 and registered as a "daughter of the Church" because her parents were not married. Juana's father, Don Pedro Manuel de Asbaje y Vargas Machuca, was a Spanish adventurer who had emigrated from the Basque country in northern Spain to Mexico to seek his fortune. He and Juana's mother had three daughters who were able to claim legitimacy by Don Pedro's acknowledgment of his paternity. Juana knew little or nothing of her father, for he soon left the family for other adventures, or met with an unrecorded death.

Juana's maternal grandfather, Don Pedro Ramirez, an immigrant from Spain, owned a considerable amount of land in New Spain as Mexico was then called. He raised sheep, cattle, and mules on his estate at Nepantla, a considerably harder existence than had been his former life in Spain. But being an educated and cultured Spaniard, he had brought his books to the colonies where he kept a library of well-read and well-marked volumes. He died in 1655.

Don Pedro's daughter, Isabel Ramirez de Santillana, Juana's mother, had learned the necessary female lessons in sewing, cooking, and religion, but she was never taught to read. She could not even sign her last will and testament. But being an ambitious, capable woman, she resolved that her daughters, Josefa Maria, Juana, and Maria would be schooled in reading and writing. Little is known about Isabel's other three children fathered by Diego Ruiz Lozano, a Mexican farmer.

Kindled With the Desire to Read.

After Pedro de Asbaje abandoned his wife and family, Isabel managed the estate at Amecameca and raised her children. She sent her eldest daughter Josefa to a local primary school. Juana, then only three years old and "kindled with the desire to read," tagged along with her sister to school. The teacher gave the little girl lessons, and Juana later wrote, "I learned to read in so short a time that I already knew how when my mother learned of it." Juana had kept it secret "believing that they would whip me for having done it without permission."[2]

As a young girl Juana's appetite for learning was greater than her appetite for food. When she heard that cheese made one stupid, she abstained from eating it, because ". . . the desire to learn weighed more with me than that of eating, as overwhelming as the latter is in children."[3]

After her mother forbade her to masquerade as a boy to attend the University of Mexico City, Juana delved into her grandfather's books of poetry, science, history, and theology, many of them written in Latin and Portuguese. Isabel hired Martin de Olivas, an instructor in Latin, who declared after twenty lessons that Juana had learned everything he knew.

To hasten the learning of Latin, Juana inflicted "punishment for stupidity" on herself— she cut off her hair to the "length of four or six fingers," and if it grew back before she had conquered Latin, she vowed to cut it again. She said, ". . . it did not seem right . . . that my head should be clothed with hair when it was so naked of learning, which was the more desirable adornment."[4]

At some period during her formative years, Juana also learned to read Portuguese and later was able to read the works of Padre Antonio de Vieyra (1608-1697), the famous Jesuit from Portugal, whose basic tenets she disputed and recorded in her "Carta atenagórica" (The Athenagoric Letter). The publication of this letter caused the Jesuit fathers in New Spain to condemn the nun at the Convent of San Jeronimo who had the audacity to publicly disagree with the renowned Vieyra.

The Conquest of New Spain.

By the time Juana was born, Mexico, or New Spain, had been an established colony of Spain for over 100 years. After the conquest by Hernan Cortes (1485-1547), the country was ruled by the "peninsulares" (persons born in Spain), who were appointed to high government and church positions. The "creoles" (persons of Spanish ancestry born in the New World) were given the unimportant posts, and the "mestizos" (persons of mixed white and Indian blood) made up the laboring class. Indians had almost no rights of citizenship, and along with black slaves imported from Africa, worked the mines and did manual labor on the large estates.

Spanish rule prevailed in Mexico for three centuries from the conquest of Hernan Cortes in 1519 until 1821 when Mexican independence was finally accomplished and the last viceroy returned to the mother country. Spanish influence has continued to the present time. Juana, herself, was more Spanish than Mexican. She lived the greater part of her life in Mexico City, which, after its destruction by Cortes, had been rebuilt to resemble the opulent cities of Old Spain. The viceroy's court, where Juana was a lady-in-waiting during her impressionable teen years, was fashioned after the courts of Spain. The poetry Juana wrote in later years, Spanish in character, caused critics of the seventeenth and early eighteenth centuries to claim she "borrowed" heavily from Luis de Gongora y Argote, the great Spanish poet.

In the 1600's Spain, the strongest military and sea power in Europe, was in its golden century. The conquest of Mexico brought great wealth to the Spanish empire, and offered the conquerors opportunities to acquire land, status, and power. By the time Cortes and his conquistadors had claimed Mexico as a Spanish colony, he had taken Montezuma, the Aztec emperor, hostage and destroyed Tenochtitlan (Mexico City), the Aztec capital city. He had also conquered the native peoples and destroyed their culture, art, architecture, and religion.

As a reward for successful conquest, Cortes

was given vast lands at Cuernavaca thirty miles south of Mexico City. In 1522 Charles V (1500-1558) made him captain-general of the colony and bestowed on him the title of Marques del Valle. But the Emperor became suspicious of the ambitious conquistador and wanted to limit his power and influence. In 1528 Charles created an "audiencia," a royal court, with legislative and governing powers, and in 1535 Antonio de Mendoza, a Spanish nobleman, became the first viceroy to head the new government. When Juana lived at the court, the Marques de Mancera was the twenty-fifth viceroy to rule New Spain.

In Old Spain the church and state were one. Charles V reigned from 1519 to 1556 as the Holy Roman Emperor and also ruled as Charles I, King of Spain, from 1516 to 1556. Religion offered holy justification for conquest, and missionaries were soon sent to the colony to convert the natives. Although million of Indians were baptized, many still clung to their ancient religious ceremonies, frustrating the work of the missionaries who wanted to bring Christianity to the "heathens."

The role of the church went far beyond religion, reaching into all facets of colonial life. Franciscan, Dominican, Jesuit, and Augustinian clerics took over formal education beginning with the primary schools and extending through the institutions of higher learning. The National University of Mexico was founded by Emperor Charles V in 1551. Unfortunately, only upper class males living near large cities were given formal education—Indians and females were excluded. But the missionaries did teach trade skills, crafts, and new methods of agriculture, opened hospitals, and dispensed charity to the native people.

An Inquisition similar to that in Spain was formed in 1571 for the purpose of weeding out harmful influences and moral abuses that would damage the church. Although the authority of the Inquisition in New Spain never reached the level of that in the mother country, books were burned, libraries destroyed, and heretics punished. As she wrote secular literature and defied authority, Juana knew that she might be considered a target for such a purging.

During the century that followed the Spanish Conquest, struggles continued as the two cultures clashed over territory, resources, and religion. The gap between the rich and the poor widened. For a time Spanish aristocracy had complete rule in high government positions, but soon blood lines became mixed as Indian women married or bore children to Spanish men. Today the vast majority of Mexicans are "mestizos" of mixed ancestry.

I Became Religious.

During the early years of the reign of Charles II, King of Spain from 1665 to 1700, a new viceroy was sent to rule the colony. Antonio Sebastian de Toledo, the Marques de Mancera, was a well-educated, refined man who desired not only good government, fair laws, and beneficial public works, but was interested in promoting intellectual and cultural pursuits. His wife, the Marquesa Dona Lenor Carreto, had heard of a young Mexican girl of exceptional accomplishments and made inquiries.

Juana, then in her teens, had matured into a beautiful and intellectually precocious young woman. She had a lively imagination, an inquisitive mind, a quick sense of humor, and a passion for learning that caused her to yearn for opportunities other than those afforded in Amecameca and her grandfather's library. Her mother, recognizing Juana's restlessness, sent her to Mexico City to live with an aunt who had married a Spanish nobleman. The Marquesa invited Juana to live at the court as her lady-in-waiting and a companion to her eight-year-old daughter.

Juana was an instant favorite at the palace. She quickly adapted to the elegant, sophisticated life and was constantly alert to political and religious discussions going on around her. Visitors at the court were charmed by the unusual young girl, but some were skeptical when they heard tales of her genius.

To confirm the talents of his protege, the Marques summoned forty learned men—theologians, philosophers, poets, scientists, mathematicians, and historians—to examine Juana's proficiency in various subjects. The fifteen-year-old girl appeared before them and answered brilliantly the questions they put to her. The Marques bragged, ". . . just as a royal galleon would defend itself from smaller sloops which were attacking it, so did Juana Inés extricate herself from the questions, arguments, and rejoinders that all, each in his own field, propounded."[5]

The Marques and his wife were proud of their ward, but Juana remained humble. Years later she wrote, "Such a triumph left me with as little satisfaction in myself as if I had been able to work a small hemstitching more neatly than my teachers."[6]

While at court she wrote poems, most of them adolescent expressions of unrequited love, death, and bereavement. When her poems were published, some critics thought she wrote from experience, perhaps of a lover who had disappointed her or died. In her autobiography Juana never mentioned such an incident, and it could be assumed that such emotional verses could be easily penned by an imaginative, passionate young girl.

Juana soon found life at court to be frivolous and distasteful. She wrote in verse:

> with all the applause, I
> succeeded in loving no one,
> being loved by everyone.[7]

Juana also had concerns for her future. Women of her day had few choices—society offered no outlet in the professional world, and there were no other *respectable* occupations for single women. She must choose between marriage or a convent. Her confessor, the famous Jesuit Antonio Nunez de Miranda, also serving the Marques and Marquesa, feared for the temptations presented a beautiful young woman in court. He advised her to enter a convent.

Juana considered the advice of her confessor, but was frank to admit that at first she chose the religious life for pragmatic reasons—she did not want to marry, and she wanted to be able to study and learn. She later wrote in her autobiographical essay, "Respuesta a Sor Filotea" (Reply to Sor Filotea):

> I became religious because, although I knew the estate had things very repugnant to my temperament (I speak of accessories, not of forms), with its total denial of matrimony it was the most favorable I could choose as to the security which I desired of my salvation, to which I gave my chief attention, as being in the end the most important. And I subjugated all the impertinences of my spirit, which were the desire of living alone, of not wishing to have any compulsory occupation to hinder the freedom of my study, nor communal noise to impair the peaceful silence of my books.[8]

On August 14, 1667, on the Feast of the Assumption, Juana entered the Convent of San Jose of the Discalced Carmelites. She had never enjoyed vigorous health, and after three months of the austerity imposed by that order, she suffered a physical breakdown. Her physicians advised her to leave. In November of the same year, shortly after her sixteenth birthday, she withdrew from the convent and returned to the care of the Marquesa to regain her health.

During the next year-and-a-half while Juana recovered from her illness, she continued to write. One poem signed by Dona Juana de Asbaje (the only published work bearing that name) appeared in a publication honoring the completion of the splendid Cathedral of Mexico City which had been under construction for ninety-five years at the cost of 1,752,000 pesos. She also dedicated one poem to her protectoress, the Marquesa de Mancera.

On February 24, 1669, Juana signed her name to a document at the Convent of San Jeronimo. It stated: "I, Sor Juana Inés de la Cruz, legitimate daughter of Don Pedro de Asbaje y Vargas Machuca, and of Isabel Ramirez, . . . make my profession . . . to live and die all the time and space of my life in obedience, poverty, without anything of my own, chastity, and perpetual cloister . . ."[9]

She made her vows before the Vicar General, and her confessor paid for the celebration that was attended by a host of eminent guests from the clergy and nobility. A wealthy man from a distinguished family sponsored her and provided the dowry which her family could not afford. Padre Nunez rejoiced that Juana had chosen this path to a secure and godly future.

Sor Juana Inés de la Cruz, the name she chose when she took her vows, spent the remainder of her life with the Hieronymites at the Convent of San Jeronimo, an order founded by St. Jerome (c. 347-c. 420), who in his day was the spiritual adviser to a number of noblewomen, including the eminent St. Paula. Although Jerome's writings showed him to be a misogynist, he did believe in educating highborn women. The convents bearing his name did not discourage such pursuits.

The rules at San Jeronimo were considerably more relaxed than those in Spanish convents of the same order. All of the nuns held daily devotions and vespers and participated in the masses, feasts, and ceremonies of the church, but were afforded considerable freedom for social activities. Juana was often commissioned to write "villancicos," church carols, for special religious observances.

The convent was the educational and cultural center of the community. Often visiting clerics, nobility, and distinguished persons from different parts of the region and from abroad enjoyed comfortable lodging, enticing food, and living entertainment provided by the sisters. Juana wrote verses for singing and composed music for dancing.

Most of the nuns at San Jeronimo came with ample dowries from wealthy families. They were accustomed to living the good life with fine foods, servants, and generous allowances, all of which were allowed them at the convent. They also kept pets. Black and mulatto women waited upon them, sometimes numbering as many as five servants to one nun. Juana herself was given a slave as a gift from her mother.

The extravagance of life at the convent disturbed the provincial clerics and the Archbishop, who soon tightened the rules, restricted social activities, and forbade the keeping of animals. The women were reminded that they had taken vows of poverty when they entered.

I Studied All Things That God Created.

As Juana's reputation spread, she received distinguished visitors offering praises and gifts, seeking advice, and requesting her approval on their literary efforts. She corresponded with writers of the day and continued her friendship with the viceroys at court. Her intellect and her beauty, as shown in a portrait painted by Cabrera while she was a nun, attracted many visitors. The other sisters also sought out her company and counsel and sat at her feet to learn from her.

In spite of the routine of convent life and the interruptions from visitors and sisters, Juana found time to withdraw to her spacious cell to study and write. She delved into one subject after another, her insatiable appetite for knowledge never being satisfied. Her room became a laboratory where she studied astronomy and conducted scientific experiments. She purchased musical instruments which she learned to play, she composed, studied music theory, and wrote a book on harmony. She also painted, studied medicine, law, theology, architecture, and mathematics. It was said she had a library of 4,000 books, perhaps an exaggeration considering the number of volumes available in the New World even though a printing press had been set up in Mexico City in 1539.

Juana continued to write secular and religious verses, sonnets, love poems, satires, poems for friends and admirers, and verses to commemorate the death of an important person or to celebrate some event. She also wrote secular and religious plays for the theater.

But her popularity aroused resentment within the convent. A jealous Mother Superior ordered her to leave her books, cease her studies,

and quit writing poetry. For three months Juana obeyed. She closed her books, but could not turn off her active mind—instead she observed nature and the heavens, and composed poems in her sleep. She wrote, ". . . even though I did not study from books, I studied all things that God created—the whole of the universal machine serving me in place of books."[10] When she became seriously ill, the doctor reluctantly prescribed that she return to her books. She soon recovered.

As more words flowed from her prolific pen, so did ink from her critics. They claimed her verses were sentimental, artificial, affected, and were just copies of the great Spanish writers Gongora (1561-1627) and Calderon (1600-1681). Her defenders claimed she was a "true poet . . . [with] the key to the sentiments of the human heart." They prophesied that her works would live "as long as Spanish is spoken."[11]

Other criticisms arose from within the convent and among the clerics—she was spending too much time with secular things and forsaking the things of God. The censures from the inside hurt her the most. She wrote, ". . . those with good intentions, loving me, desiring my welfare, who belittle me by saying 'she affronts sacred ignorance by studying as she does; she will certainly fall from the great height she has reached.' "[12] Juana penned this verse:

Why, people, do you persecute me so?
In what do I offend, when but inclined
with worldly beauties to adorn my mind,
and not my mind on beauty to bestow?

I value not a treasure trove, not wealth;
the greater measure of content I find
in placing riches only in my mind,
than setting all my intellect on wealth.

And I esteem not beauty, for, when past
it is the spoils of age's cruelty;
nor faithless riches carefully amassed.

Far better nibble, so it seems to me,
at all life's vanities unto the last
than to consume my life in vanity.[13]

Although Juana Inés de la Cruz was the most celebrated member of her family, she kept close contact with her mother and sisters. Hardworking Isabel, her mother, managed a hacienda near Mexico City. Josefa Maria, her older sister, was abandoned by her husband, but fortunately she and her four children were taken in by a kind man who sheltered, fed, and clothed them. He adopted the children, gave them his name, educated them, and willed them his inheritance when he died. The younger sister Maria lived for a time with her mother, then married, had three children, was widowed, and died in 1691. Two of Juana's nieces entered the Convent of San Jeronimo. When Juana died, her brother-in-law and nephew wrote a eulogy.

The Reply to Sor Filotea.

The church was growing increasingly intolerant of this nun who chose to fill her mind with secular subjects and worldly things that were not of God. She was not attaining spiritual perfection as the "bride of Christ." The sacramental allegory, El divino Narcisco (The Divine Narcissus), which later was considered her masterpiece, and her participation in discussion of sacred topics did not prove that she was dedicating herself wholly to God. It might be a sham, and she must be watched. The inquisitors should be alerted!

The crisis came following a discussion of a fiery sermon given forty years earlier by the renowned Portuguese Jesuit, Antonio de Vieyra, in the Royal Chapel of Lisbon. The sermon had been published in a collection of Vieyra's works and had drawn the belated attention of Mexican scholars. In the sermon Vieyra had presented theological opinions that disagreed with those of St. Augustine, St. John Chrysostom, and St. Thomas of Aquinas.

Juana had read Vieyra's sermon and expressed her disagreement with several of its tenets. A superior, perhaps the Bishop of Puebla, who heard Juana's arguments suggested that she put them in writing. In her reply Juana indicated that she was writing in response to the orders given her. She addressed her letter to "My dear sir" and wrote, ". . . your command makes excusable an error that to other eyes might seem disproportionately presumptuous in a sex so discredited by all the world in the subject of letters."[14]

To rationalize her position, Juana asked the question—how did Vieyra dare contradict Augustine, Chrysostom, and Thomas without risking being contradicted himself? Furthermore, she said ". . . just as I was free to disagree with Vieyra, so others are free to disagree with my judgment."[15] Using Biblical references and logic, she defended her position and those taken by the three saints.

Without her knowledge the Bishop of Puebla, Don Manual Fernandez de Santa Cruz,

had the letter published under the title "Carta atenagórica." He added a brief letter of his own as an introduction and signed the name of a fictitious nun, Sor Filotea de la Cruz.

In a letter dated November 25, 1690, with its transparent disguise, the Bishop first praised Juana's brilliant exposition, then made suggestions to her. He wrote:

> I have seen your letter and admired your proofs and the clarity of your argument. Consequently I have had your letter printed. Now I should like to make some suggestions. You have a great talent and although I do not suggest you stop reading books, I do suggest you read more about Christ Our Lord. I do not agree with those who say that women should not be learned. St. Jerome certainly approved of their learning, and in spite of the fact that St. Paul said women should not preach, he did not say they should not learn. I suggest you continue your studies, but you ought to better the books you read, for knowledge should enlighten us and lead us toward salvation. Subordinate profane letters to sacred letters: you must study the latter more.[16]

The publication of Juana's letter stirred up controversy in the religious community. The incensed Jesuits called her a heretic, and much to Juana's sorrow, her confessor abandoned her. Other clerics, who respected her abilities and sincerity, defended her.

Although Juana herself was hurt by the criticism, she had fully expected to be rebuked in some manner for her impertinence. For three months she pondered her reply. She gathered courage from reading the life of St. Teresa of Avila, who had experienced similar difficulties with the hierarchy of the church.

On March 1, 1691, Juana made her reply in her autobiographical essay, the "Respuesta a Sor Filotea de la Cruz." She knew she was addressing none other than the Bishop himself, but with exceptional daring she attacked some of the issues he had raised that had offended her and all women who served the church.

In the "Respuesta" Juana wrote the story of her life, told of her passion for knowledge and her motivation for seeking the religious life in the convent. Then she launched into an argument for women's freedom to learn, to express opinions, and to write. She cited the examples of St. Catherine of Egypt, St. Paula, St. Teresa, and others. From the Bible she alluded to Deborah, Judith, and the Queen of Sheba.

She argued that St. Paul had been misunderstood when he said that women should be silent in the church. Juana wrote ". . . in the early Church women began to preach doctrine to one another in the temples, and this noise caused confusion while the apostles were preaching, so that the women were ordered to be silent. And the same thing happens today, namely that while the preacher is preaching, one should not pray out loud."[17] She further claimed that Paul referred only to women in the *pulpit*, and that everyone, men and women alike, if *incompetent*, should remain silent in church.

Juana cited statements by a Doctor Arce, a learned scholar who concluded in his *Bibliorum* that although ". . . teaching publicly from a University chair, or preaching from the pulpit, is not permissible for women . . . to study, write and teach privately not only is permissible, but most advantageous and useful."[18]

Juana closed her letter by indicating that most of her writing had been at the request of others and that she had never written anything specifically for publication, especially the "Carta atenagórica." She enclosed two of her devotional works printed anonymously for the Bishop to read.

Although Juana did not intend her reply, the "Respuesta," to be published, fortunately it did appear in print in 1700. "Carta atenegórica" and "Respuesta" have been hailed as Juana's best prose works. Not only is the "Respuesta" one of the most charming autobiographies written in the Spanish language, but it is looked on today as evidence of Juana's brilliant mind, her logical genius, and her understanding of theology. It establishes her as one of the earliest and most vocal advocates of women's rights.

Of What Use Is It to Know So Much?

The two years that followed were disturbing years for all of New Spain. Floods, pestilence, famine, and discord ravaged the colony. In 1692 an Indian uprising caused violence and destruction.

Despite the disturbances in the land and the controversy in the church, Juana continued to write for two more years. In 1692 the second volume of her *Poemas* was published in Seville, the first volume having been published in Madrid three years earlier. Included in the second volume was "El sueño" (The Dream), her longest poem of 975 verses, admittedly her favorite work written for her own pleasure. "El sueño," a fantasy poem, raised many questions among puzzled interpreters as they struggled to analyze its philosophical meaning. The third and last volume of her poems was published in 1700 after her death.

Also published in 1692 was *Los empeños de una casa* (The Trials of a Noble House), a three-act comedy presented originally at a festival in 1683. Interspersed between the three acts were poems dedicated to the Viceroy and his family. Both this and Juana's sacramental play, *El divino Narciso*, were written for seventeenth century audiences and would not be appreciated in modern theater.

In 1693 Juana closed her books forever, renounced her studies, and stopped writing. She gave away her entire library, keeping only three small prayerbooks. Money from the sale of her musical instruments and science equipment was given to the poor.

She renewed her vows, dedicated herself to God, and imposed such severe penance on herself that her spiritual director in concern for her health tried to restrain her. With the same intensity that she had sought knowledge, she now sought the things of the spirit. She said, "If we are to live such a little while, of what use is it to know so much?"[19]

In 1695 the dreaded plague struck Mexico City, and the contagion spread rapidly to the convent. Juana nursed her ill sisters without regard for her own welfare, cheered and comforted the dying. In her weakened condition she too contracted the disease. She received the last sacraments, and died serenely at 4:00 A.M. on April 17, 1695, at the age of forty-three.

The church bells tolled through the day as the entire city mourned her death. Crowds jammed the Church of San Jeronimo and overflowed into the street. Tributes and eulogies extolled her in both New and Old Spain.

Old records were discovered at the convent containing the Acts of Profession and Ratification, signed by Juana in her own blood. The last paragraph read:

> Immediately above will be noted the day, month and year of my death. I plead that, for the love of God and His purest Mother, my beloved Sisters in religion, those now living and those who have gone before, will recommend me to God, who have been the worst among them. I, the worst of the world—Juana Inés de la Cruz.[20]

The life and writings of Sor Juana have been analyzed and evaluated through succeeding centuries. A "black legend" has grown up around her, stemming from a series of books written between 1940 and 1952. The authors claimed that Juana was a clever woman who used the convent and religious life as a guise for her personal intellectual pursuits. They said she professed faith in God and wrote sacred works solely to avoid the wrath of the Inquisition and her superiors. In other words, she was a heretic and a fraud.

Another theory was expounded about Sor Juana—that she was a mystic such as St. Teresa of Avila and St. John of the Cross. An analysis of her more visionary poems and contemplative prose have led some authors to believe she wrote mystical literature.

Both theories have been generally discounted. A thorough reading of Juana's serious prose, in particular "Carta atenagórica" and "Respuesta," offers clear testimony of her religious convictions and her knowledge of Scriptures and theology. She could be called an anomaly in her day, but not a heretic. She was a woman who dared to use her brilliant mind in an era when most women were either ornamental or servile.

Neither does the label of "mystic" properly apply to Juana. Her life did not include the acts generally associated with mystics—visions, raptures, ecstasies, miracles, or locutions—and her writing does not have the characteristics usually found in mystical literature.[21]

Juana Inés de la Cruz's intellectual genius and her literary skill earned her a respected place in Spanish baroque literature. Among contemporaries her lyric poems won her the title of "The Tenth Muse of Mexico." She can be claimed by today's women as one of their earliest advocates. Diego Calleja, her first biographer, wrote in his *Vida de Sor Juana*, ". . . she was born into the world to justify the vanities of prodigiousness in nature."[22]

Notes

1   There are contradictory dates given for the year of Juana's birth—1648 and 1651. The most authentic sources indicate the date as 1651.

2   Juana Inés de la Cruz. *The Pathless Grove* (Prairie City, Illinois: Decker Press, 1950), p. 51.

3   Ibid.

4   Ibid., p. 53.

5   Carlos Gonzáles Pena, *History of Mexican Literature*, third edition (Dallas: Southern Methodist University Press, 1968), p. 112.

6   Fanchón Royer, *The Tenth Muse* (Paterson, New Jersey: St. Anthony Guild Press, 1952), p. 28.

7   Judith Thurman, *I Became Alone* (New York: Atheneum, 1975), p. 90.

8   Juana Inés de la Cruz, p. 53.

9   Ibid., pp. 3-4.

10   Royer, p. 75.

11   Ibid., p. 45.

12   Thurman, p. 93.

13   Ibid., p. 25.

14   Royer, p. 86.

15   Gerard Flynn, *Sor Juana Inés de la Cruz* (New York: Alfred A. Knopf, 1969), p. 108.

16   Ibid., p. 18.

17   Ibid., p. 23.

18   Rosemary Radford Ruether, and Rosemary Skinner Keller, *Women and Religion in America*, volume 2 (San Francisco: Harper & Row, 1983), p. 67.

19   Royer, p. 135.

20   Ibid., p. 137.

21   Flynn, pp. 13-14, 99-107.

22   Royer, p. 138.

Chapter 8

Kateri Tekakwitha
(1656 - 1680)

THE MOHAWK HOLY WOMAN CALLED BY HER PEOPLE "THE FAIREST FLOWER THAT EVER BLOOMED AMONG THE REDMEN."

"THE MOHAWKS are coming!" The warning struck terror in neighboring enemy tribes and European settlements along the eastern shore of North America. The Mohawks were reputed to be the fiercest, the cruelest, and the bravest Iroquoian Indians in the region around the St. Lawrence River.

Into this heritage was born Kateri Tekakwitha, known as the Lily of the Mohawks, the First Iroquois Virgin, the Glory of the Mohawks, the Holy Savage—names that attest to the esteem granted this young Indian woman during the last of her twenty-four years on earth and for centuries after her death. When she approached the age of eight, young Kateri had been given her formal name, Tekakwitha (Tegakouita, Tegawita, or Tega-Kouita),[1] Iroquois for "one who puts things in order" or "one who moves things out of her way." After her baptism in 1676 she added her first name, Kateri (Catherine or Katharine). The young girl stemmed from both Iroquois and Algonquin ancestry, her father being a Mohawk chieftain and her mother a Christian Algonquin.

The League of Five Nations.

In the seventeenth century the Iroquois nation controlled a large portion of the land stretching from the St. Lawrence River to the Georgian Bay of Lake Huron in Canada and the area west of the Hudson River to Lake Erie in present-day Ohio. These same lands were coveted by the Algonquins, bitter enemies of the Iroquois. The French, English, and Dutch fur-traders, eyeing the strategic waterways, competed for friendship with the Indians who inhabited the lands along the St. Lawrence and its tributaries. The Iroquois favored trading with the English and tolerated the Dutch who provided them with guns and liquor. They fought the French and the enemy Indian nations that furnished French traders with valuable furs.

The Iroquois were unified by their federal

organization, a forerunner of colonial and con-
stitutional government in the United States and
a prototype of the charter of the present-day
United Nations. The Iroquois had formed a
confederacy called the League of Five Nations,
including from east to west the Mohawks,
Oneidas, Onondagas, Cayugas, and Senecas.
Later they added the sixth nation when the
Tuscaroras from the Carolinas were forced
northward by the white settlers who took their
lands.

Though outnumbered by the Algonquins,
the Iroquois were a more unified nation. All
Iroquoians were joined linguistically allowing
them to communicate with each other. In most
cases their houses were built in similar fashion—
the communal longhouses where from six to ten
families shared one dwelling. Culturally, they
observed many of the same traditions and customs, generally tracing their ancestry through
their mothers.

Dates for the founding of the League vary
widely from 1000 to 1570. Deganawidah, a
Huron refugee, is credited with first introducing the idea that members of the Iroquois nation
could avoid bloody and divisive warfare by
forming a union based on brotherhood, equality,
and unity. Hiawatha, an Onondaga chief, traveled from tribe to tribe to negotiate the peace
envisioned by Deganawidah. The original constitution, the "Great Law of Peace," was probably written in pictographs on wampum belts
and translated into English around 1880. The
League was governed by male delegates from
each tribe who met annually at the capital settlement, the Castle of the Onondagas. Each tribe
was given one vote, and all decisions had to be
unanimous. The ideal was noble.[2]

The League influenced American colonial
leaders and the drafters of the United States
Constitution. Three years prior to proposing a
union of colonies at Albany in 1754 Benjamin
Franklin, a loyal friend of the Iroquois, shamed
his compatriots:

> It would be a very strange thing if Six Nations
> of Ignorant Savages should be capable of form-
> ing a Scheme for such an Union and be able to
> execute it in such a manner, as that it has sub-
> sisted Ages and appears indissoluble, and yet a
> like union should be impracticable for ten or a
> dozen English colonies.[3]

An Orphan Must Be Given Care.

Kateri was born in 1656 at Ossernenon, a
village on the south bank of the Mohawk River,
the site of present-day Auriesville, New York,
some thirty miles west of Albany. This was the
place where ten years earlier two French Jesuits,
Father Isaac Jogues and Brother Jean de la Lande,
had been brutally murdered by the Mohawks.
Their deaths ignited another round of bloody
encounters between the Iroquois, the French,
and the Hurons, who maintained friendship
with the French. The Jesuits were named North
American martyrs and saints by Pope Pius XI
in 1930.

Kateri was the daughter of Kenhoronkwa,
an Iroquois chieftain of the Mohawk clan, and
Kahenta, an Algonquin mother who had been
taken captive when Iroquois warriors raided
the Algonquin Mission of the Immaculate Conception at Three Rivers in Quebec. Kenhoronkwa, a high level chief, or "sachem," had taken
Kahenta as his wife, entitling her to full privileges in the tribe. Perhaps he found the docile
Algonquin woman more to his liking that the
more domineering women of his own tribe.

Some enemy captives did not fare as well.
The fortunate ones were assimilated into the
tribe to replace warriors who were killed in
battle; others were tortured or executed, or made
slaves.

Kateri's mother, remembering her religious
training and baptism at the Three Rivers Mission, continued to practice her Christian beliefs
in secret. She prayed that her two children would
be baptized, a wish not granted her before her
death.

In the fall of 1659 and early 1660 a small
pox epidemic brought in by the Europeans struck
the Mohawk villages, causing scores of men,
women, and children to die torturous deaths.
Kateri's entire family contracted the disease, and
her father, mother, and little brother died. Four-
year-old Kateri barely escaped death, but thereafter suffered from impaired eyesight and a pock-
marked face.

Father John Chauchetière, one of Kateri's
early biographers wrote:

> Her face, which was formerly pretty, became
> ugly; she almost lost her eyesight, and her eyes
> were so hurt by this disease that she could not
> bear a strong light. This obliged her to remain
> wrapped in her blanket, and favored her wish
> to remain unknown. She often thanked Our
> Lord for this favor, calling her affliction a bless-
> ing, for if she had been pretty she would have
> been more sought by the young men, and so
> might have abandoned herself to sin as did the
> other girls in the country of the Iroquois.[4]

Kateri was adopted by Iowerána (Onse-gongo), an elderly uncle and highly venerated chieftain. In the custom of the Iroquois to care for their aged and young, the childless uncle and Karitha, his wife, took the orphan Kateri and another girl named Ennita to live with them and the other families in the long-house. A young girl was an advantage to a Mohawk family because when she married, her husband moved into her house, bringing to the family an able-bodied hunter. Among Mohawk couples divorce was uncommon, although a man was allowed to move out of the longhouse whenever he wished. Polygamy was not widely practiced, thus establishing close-knit family units.

The Iroquois were a matriarchal society. Women were the backbone of the family, and all descendants were traced through their mothers. Females did the domestic work while males hunted big game, protected the settlement from enemies, fashioned weapons and tools, practiced the art of war and peace, and taught their sons manly skills. After marriage all possessions belonged to the women; men owned just their weapons and their bones. Women controlled the land, raised the crops, and conducted various ceremonies and festivals celebrating seasonal plantings and harvests. They prepared animal skins for clothing, sewed the garments, educated and cared for the children. Women were more respected in Iroquoian culture than in most European nations.

Matrons were given special authority. They had a leading voice in choosing tribal chieftains, and they could save a male captive from torture or death by adopting him into the family or by protesting the cruelties inflicted upon him. The French explorer and fur-trader Radisson was saved twice by a Mohawk woman.[5]

Unlike the Algonquins, who sought to eliminate their elderly as an encumbrance to their mobility, the Iroquois revered their aged, particularly their old women whose sage advice was respected in tribal councils. But veneration for the elderly and worship of the dead sometimes proved a handicap. When a Mohawk village was under siege by an enemy, escape to safety was delayed by having to evacuate their elders and move the bones of their ancestors.

Early Virginity, Chastity, and Purity.

It was the custom among the Iroquois for a seven or eight-year-old girl to be promised to a lad of the same age with the hope that when she reached adolescence, they would marry. When Kateri was eight, her aunts arranged such a betrothal with the parents of a young boy of the village. As with many child betrothals, this union did not materialize.

As Kateri grew older, she preferred to hide in the seclusion of the dark longhouse because she was embarrassed by her disfigured face. But her aunts insisted that she join the other eligible young girls who were decorated with necklaces, bracelets, rings, and beaded belts. They painted their faces, oiled and braided their hair to attract the young warriors of the village. Kateri reluctantly complied, but years later she inflicted harsh penance on herself in atonement for the sinful adornment she had displayed in her youth.

When Kateri reached adolescence, her aunts began to arrange an advantageous marriage for her. Kateri refused to consider all offers, angering her aunts and prompting them to trick her into wedlock. They arranged a nuptial agreement with the parents of a brave young hunter who was invited to their lodge. The eager young man, dressed in his finest buckskin clothes and bearing a gift of beaver pelts, entered and seated himself beside Kateri. After some conversation the aunts asked Kateri to offer the young suitor some sagamité, or porridge, as a pledge of honor. Kateri then realized that by doing so she was consenting to marry him. She arose abruptly, dashed from the lodge, and hid in the fields until the disappointed suitor left.

The embarrased aunts scolded Kateri for insulting their guest, disobeying their authority, and violating the tribal code of hospitality. They threatened and ridiculed her, but Kateri adamantly refused to consider marriage. The aunts finally gave up and decided to punish her by assigning her to the hardest and most menial tasks usually given to captive slaves. Kateri accepted the work cheerfully and without complaint. After the aunts were reprimanded by Iowerána for their harsh treatment, they relented and once again treated Kateri as a daughter. Those who promoted Kateri Tekakwitha's sainthood after her death cited her refusal to marry as evidence that God had led her to virginity and chastity at an early age.

As she matured, Kateri assumed her share of manual work expected of all Mohawk women. She gathered firewood from the forest, built the fires under the cooking stones, fetched water from the river or spring, worked the fields of corn, beans, and squash. To supplement the big game killed by the hunters, Kateri and the other women fished and hunted for small animals, scavenged the woods for berries and nuts. In the spring they collected the "sweet water" that dripped from the maples and boiled it into syrup. Kateri learned to cook a variety of cornmeal dishes to be served in wooden bowls.

Although Kateri worked in the fields with the other women, her injured eyes suffered in the bright sunlight. She preferred doing handwork in the seclusion of the dark longhouse where with nimble fingers she fashioned beautiful wampum belts, moccasins, leggings, and tobacco bags decorated with moose hair, quills, or shells. She was skilled at using colored dyes from native plants or the brilliant reds from the sturgeon that abounded in the river. She made bark cradles for the newborns, wove baskets from strips of split ash and sleeping mats of corn husks.

Father Pierre Cholenec, a Jesuit priest and early biographer, wrote of her:

> The child had a lovable disposition; she was sweet and as she grew in years she also grew visibly in goodness; all her inclinations tended to virtue. God, who wished her for Himself, early inspired her with love of work and solitude; it may be said that these two inclinations were the sources of the innocent life she led in the country of the Iroquois. She went out in public only when she had some purpose to accomplish; she was always at work in the lodge.... What was still more admirable in her was the natural horror she had of all that was against purity.[6]

Kateri found that life in the longhouse was not conducive to solitude, purity, or chastity. There was no privacy in the bark-covered lodge that housed from six to ten families numbering up to fifty people. The longhouses were barn-like dwellings from fifty to one-hundred feet in length, twenty-five feet in width, and up to twenty feet in height. Families lived in open compartments along the walls of the structure, with two to four families sharing the fire pits on the earthen floor in the center corridor. The only openings were the skin-covered entrances at either end of the longhouse and the holes in the roof to let out smoke. Lodges were always dark, drafty, smoky, and filled with strong smells from cooking pots, drying meats and hides, and body odors. Families slept on cornhusk pallets on platforms along the side walls where food, tools, weapons, and clothing were stored. Babies, diapered in dry moss, were tightly wrapped in buckskin blankets and tucked into cradle boards

that could be suspended from the support poles.

To find a private place for solitude and contemplation, Kateri often sought some secluded spot away from the village. One such sanctuary was the spring that bubbled nearby where she daily filled her bark bucket with drinking water. It became known later as "Tekakwitha's spring."

During long winter evenings Kateri joined the family around the longhouse fire to listen to the tales told by the hunters and warriors, who made long speeches and bragged of brave deeds and exploits. Here one generation taught the next the tribal legends and traditions.

Shamans, White Faces, and Black Robes.

After the small pox epidemic had ravaged Ossernenon, the tribe, fearful that the old site was contaminated, moved one mile west. At a settlement they called Ganáwage (Gandawagué), they rebuilt their longhouses enclosed by a log stockade to defend against enemy attack. The palisade was no protection from the well-armed French troops commissioned by Louis XIV, King of France.

In 1663 the French had claimed the area around Quebec as a province and named it "New France," but the belligerent Mohawks posed a threat to further expansion. In October 1666 the French under General de Tracy marched up the Mohawk River burning Iroquois settlements along the banks. When the army arrived at Ganáwage, the Indians fled in terror to the woods where from their hiding places they watched their village go up in flames. When the troops withdrew, Kateri and the others returned to find only the charred ruins of their village, the entire food supply destroyed, and the fields burned.

The Mohawks built a new settlement on the north side of the river, fourteen miles to the west near present-day Fonda, New York. Their fortified village with a double stockade stood high on a hill overlooking the Mohawk River. They named it Caughnawaga (Kagnawage), or "laughing waters."

After decades of hostilities with the French, the Mohawks finally conceded they were no match for the "White Faces" and their firearms. They dispatched emissaries to Quebec to arrange a peace treaty, and agreed to the terms imposed by the French, one of which was the safe entry of missionaries into Iroquois country. Thus began eighteen years of relative peace and the Christianizing of the Iroquois by the Jesuit "Black Robes."

In September 1667, Fathers Frémin, Pierron, and Bruyas journeyed down from Canada into Iroquois territory. At first the Mohawks received them with suspicion, fearing that an army must be following, but when the Jesuits showed they were unarmed and meant no malice, the Indians were less apprehensive.

When the Black Robes arrived at Caughnawaga, they were given a polite but cool welcome by Iowerána. He hated the French and the Christians, and they were both. The Huron and Algonquin converts, who had been captured and adopted into the tribe, rejoiced at being able finally to worship, go to Mass, and have their children baptized. The three priests were given lodging at Iowerána's longhouse, and Kateri was assigned the task of attending to them.

Father Cholenec recalled, "The modesty and sweetness with which she acquitted herself of this duty touched her new guests, while on her part she was struck with their affable manners, their regularity in prayer, and the other exercises into which they divided the day."[7] Kateri kept her thoughts and desires to herself.

After three busy days administering to the converts at Caughnawaga, the three Jesuits left to go on to other settlements. Although Father Pierron returned for periodic visits to conduct Mass and baptize, Kateri was not one of those requesting baptism. Without the continual guidance of a priest, some converts returned to their former beliefs, finding the concept of one Christian God hard to accept.

The Iroquois' beliefs were pantheistic, joining them spiritually with the gods, or "okis," that existed in nature—the gods of thunder, the sea, the sun, the moon, or animals and birds. Other god heroes were born in legends that personified good and evil, life and death. One of their most important gods was Areskoi, the war god, to whom they offered their own flagellations and tortures, and often sacrificed the lives of their captives. Before Father Isaac Jogues was tomahawked to death at Ossernenon, he suffered "holy tortures" offered up to Areskoi.[8]

The Iroquois believed in dreams and superstitions and relied on the supernatural powers of the medicine-men, or "shamans," the local purveyors of magic and scientific knowledge. The shamans could ensure a bountiful harvest, a successful hunt, or victory over an enemy; they could cure illnesses and cast out evil spirits. The medicine-men regarded the Black Robes with contempt and resented the priests' intrusion into their exclusive domain. The missionaries were well aware of the control and authority the shamans held in tribal life.

Religious ceremonies were governed by the "Keepers of the Faith," three men and three women of good standing in the tribe. Traditions and customs were strictly observed, and those who strayed sometimes killed themselves rather than suffer dishonor.

The Iroquois respected and venerated their ancestors to a degree unheard of in Christian cultures. When the Iroquois died, their souls were believed to depart immediately to the village in the sky or to the land of the spirits. Only the weak and the cowardly were condemned to eternal torment. The death of a sachem was observed with long ceremonies and speeches and elaborate gifts to the dead.

When a man died, his body, dressed in the best buckskins, was laid on a bark scaffold outside the village. Alongside him were his bow and arrows, his war club, and a leather bag of parched corn and dried meat for his long journey to the sky. Near a woman's body were placed her quill or bone sewing needles, an awl, her leather scraping tool, her burden basket, and a supply of dried food.

After several months the bodies of the dead were moved to a small bark house near the family longhouse where the bones of other ancestors were kept. One year after the person's death, the relatives celebrated the arrival of the deceased at the happy land in the sky.

It was customary for the Mohawks to move their village site about every ten years for sanitary and practical reasons, if they had not been forced by an enemy to move earlier. The bones of the dead were then carried in procession to the new location and placed in a common burying ground. This was a sacred place, and here the greatest celebration of all was held—the Festival of the Dead—with elaborate rituals, lengthy speeches, and lavish gifts to the departed. Ten-year-old Kateri would have watched such a ceremony when the bones of her mother, father, and brother were moved to the new burial ground at Caughnawaga in 1666.

When Father John Pierron returned to the village, he was plagued with difficulties. He was dismayed at the Mohawk's worship of Areskoi, their reliance on dreams and superstitions, their rituals for the dead, and the sacrifice of humans to the gods. Furthermore, he could not speak the language fluently. To help communicate the truths of the Christian religion, the priest, being somewhat an artist, resorted to painting pictures on linen to illustrate his message. The Mohawks were fascinated by this device.

Father Pierron also elicited the help of a famous Onondaga sachem, Garakontié, in an attempt to convert the Mohawks from their "pagan ways." Garakontié declared to the Indians, "What he has told thee, and what he teaches thee are important truths for thy welfare; they have entered into my heart."[9]

In 1670 Father Pierron moved to the Mission of St. Francis Xavier at La Prairie near Montreal where converts had begun to move. Their exodus from Caughnawaga met with strong opposition from Kateri's uncle and the other village chieftains.

After Father Pierron's departure, another Jesuit priest, Father Francis Boniface, arrived at the village. The new cleric took on the role of the village priest and erected a "wigwam of prayer" built in the shape and size of a longhouse. He named it St. Peter's Chapel.

At his first Christmas the priest planned an event that attracted the attention of the entire village. He decorated the tiny chapel with evergreen boughs, candles, and torches, and placed the image of the Baby Jesus on moss in a simple crib near the altar. A choir of seven and eight-year-olds sang the carols he had taught them. Baptized natives were admitted inside, but others, including Kateri, stood near the door in the snow straining to catch a glimpse of the unique celebration. Father Boniface recognized an opportunity and allowed the Christmas ceremonies to continue until Easter.

More conversions and baptisms followed. Marie Tsiaouentes, a Mohawk woman who had been baptized by Father Pierron, had become a zealous Christian missionary. Marie lived in a village to the west and occasionally visited Caughnawaga on her travels eastward to Dutch trading posts. Whenever she appeared in the village, she caused an uproar of opposition, but some listened and marvelled at her convictions and her courage to speak them.

Even more consternation was aroused by the conversion of Athasata, known as Kryn, the Great Mohawk, who in the past had been the bravest and most fearsome of all the great chiefs. Kryn had been baptized by Father Frémin at the St. Francis Mission. To the dismay of all, Kryn came to Caughnawaga, reconciled with the wife he had abandoned earlier, and preached loudly about the wonders he had witnessed at the La Prairie mission. When he went back to the mission, he took with him forty Mohawks

including Ennita and Onas, Kateri's adopted sister and brother-in-law. Father Boniface, fearing the wrath of the chiefs, also left the village but later returned to Caughnawaga where he stayed until his death in December 1674.

During his four years at Caughnawaga, Father Boniface translated the prayers of the Mass, the catechism, and hymns into the native language. He conducted prayer services morning and evening, trained a children's choir, and baptized converts.

Tekakwitha's uncle disliked the missionaries and their religious zeal, but he tolerated the services at the village chapel. He vehemently opposed the exodus of converts to the St. Francis Xavier Mission fearing that Caughnawaga would be greatly weakened and made helpless against enemy attack. Kateri was well aware of her uncle's rage, so for the time being she observed, listened, and reflected in silence on what she had heard from the missionaries.

A Lily in the Midst of Thorns.

After Father Boniface's death, a young thirty-five-year-old priest, Father Jacques de Lamberville, came to Caughnawaga. He had left his theological pursuits at Rouen, France, in 1674 to join his missionary brother in Canada. During most of his lifetime he worked tirelessly among the Iroquois, often with extreme difficulties.

In the spring of 1675, Father Lamberville arrived at the village knowing little of the Iroquois language. One year later he confessed, "Although I am not very well versed in the language of the Iroquois, with whom I have lived only a year, and consequently cannot labor for their conversion as much as I would like, God has nevertheless had pity on some of the savages who are under my charge."[10]

Soon after he arrived at Caughnawaga, Father Lamberville made his rounds of the village and stopped at the door of Kateri's lodge. The house should have been empty because it was summer and all the able-bodied were out in the fields working. It was not certain that the priest knew at whose house he stopped, or whether he entered by mistake, by impulse, or, as some chroniclers claimed, by God's guidance. But he lifted the leather flap, walked in, and discovered Kateri sitting inside in the dark nursing an injured foot.

The priest wrote of the visit:

I spoke to her of Christianity and I found her

so docile that I urged her to be instructed and to attend chapel, which she did with wonderful assiduity after she had been cured. When I found her so faithful I inquired as to her conduct in the cabin; all spoke well of her. In fact, I noticed that she had none of the vices of the girls her age; this encouraged me to instruct her regularly. Finally after having taught her her prayers, and seeing that she was resolved to live in a Christian manner, I gave her Baptism on Easter Day itself in the year 1676. Since that time I can say I have found nothing in her in which she would seem to have relaxed in the slightest degree from her first fervor. I regretted only that so pure a soul and one so disposed to receive the impress of the Holy Spirit should remain in a land subject to all sorts of vice, and where the mere effort to resist the attacks of the enemies of Christianity is no mean achievement.[11]

Iowerána, in a mellowing mood, did not forbid his niece's conversion if she promised to be discreet about outwardly displaying her new religion and if she would remain in his household at Caughnawaga. He was fond of her and did not want to lose her.

On Easter Sunday, 1676, the day of Kateri's baptism, the rough wooden walls of the small chapel were decorated with luxuriant animal pelts and festooned with garlands of wampum and necklaces. The earthern floor was covered with bearskins and buffalo hides, and a bower of newly-planted shrubs and trees led to the chapel entrance. Curious spectators, some Christian, some not, crowded inside to witness the rare event—the baptism of the twenty-year-old niece of one of their chiefs.

Kateri entered. With head bowed and covered by a blanket, she walked meekly to the altar where Father Lamberville performed the baptismal ceremony. He gave her a name common to many saints, Catherine or Katherine, Kateri in Iroquois. From then on she became known in the village as "the Christian," a name which at first was one of admiration and respect.

Father Chauchetière wrote:

Not only did Katharine practise her faith in such a manner that her confessor declared she never once relaxed from her original fervor, but her extraordinary virtue was remarked by everyone, as much by the heathens as the faithful. The Christians observed her exactitude in obeying the rules of life which the priest had prescribed: that is to say, to go every day to prayer morning and evening and every Sunday to assist at Mass, and (naming what she must avoid), nor to assist at the 'dream feasts,' nor

at dances, nor at other gatherings among the savages which were contrary to purity; nor yet at the liquor debauches of the heathens.[12]

Kateri practiced her Christian religion openly, faithfully following the priest's instructions. She attended Mass, prayed constantly, avoided tribal rituals and feasts, and refused to work in the fields on Sundays and holy days. But her holiness became an annoyance in the village, and "the Christian" soon became a name of derision and contempt. The people of the longhouse called her lazy when she didn't accompany them to the fields on Sundays, and they punished her by removing all the food from the lodge. Kateri simply made Sunday her fast day.

Persecutions increased. She was taunted as she went to the chapel, children hurled stones and spit at her, the members of her longhouse ostracized her and tried to force her to give up her rosary. Drunken warriors accosted her. One day a young Mohawk brave dashed into her cabin and threatened to kill her with his tomahawk if she tried to follow the other Christians to La Prairie.

Kateri calmly went on with her work, and the young man, embarrassed by his brashness and impressed by her courage, fled quickly.

Karitha, her aunt, had developed a special dislike of her niece and her show of piety. In a fit of jealousy she charged that Kateri had had an incestuous affair with Iowerána, her husband, while on a hunting expedition in the woods. When Kateri had addressed her uncle by his proper name instead of calling him "father," the customary salutation, the aunt seized this as evidence that there were improper relations going on between the two. She brought her accusations to Father Lamberville saying, "So Katharine whom you think so virtuous is after all a hypocrite who deceives you. Even in my presence she solicited my husband to sin."[13]

The priest, recognizing the aunt's evil intent, rebuked her severely for spreading slander and evil rumors. When the priest told Kateri of her aunt's accusations, Father Cholenec recorded:

Kateri told the missionary that this trial was nothing compared to the misery and suffering of our Saviour; that the purity of His life was always before her; and that this was one sin that she would never have to answer for on judgment day. She was, truly, as the Beloved One of the Psalm, a lily in the midst of thorns."[14]

The person most sympathetic to Kateri appeared to be her own uncle. He had not forbidden her to take instructions in the Christian faith, and he allowed her to be baptized. No doubt he hoped that life at Caughnawaga would not become so intolerable that she, too, would leave for the mission at La Prairie.

"The Christian" Has Fled.

Father Lamberville worried about Kateri's welfare as life had become unbearable for her following her baptism. She had often expressed the wish to go to the Mission of St. Francis Xavier at La Prairie to join her relatives Ennita and Onas who had told her about mission life and had offered to give her shelter.

During the fall of 1677 the opportunity arose. Louis Garonhiague, a respected chieftain of the Oneida tribe, commonly called Cendre Chaude, or Hot Ashes, was fired with missionary zeal after his conversion at the St. Francis Mission. Accompanied by Onas and a Huron convert, Hot Ashes arrived by canoe at Caughnawaga to preach his Christian message. While his two companions hid by the river, Hot Ashes entered the village and orated at length and with great passion to the Mohawks assembled in the house assigned him. He told of his depraved life before his conversion. "I never had a soul," he said. "I lived as if I were a beast. But now, I am acquainted with the Great Spirit, the true master of heaven and earth, and now I can call myself a man."[15]

Kateri listened intently to Hot Ashes as he described life at the mission. When he finished his long speech, Kateri ran to Father Lamberville and begged him to help her go to St. Francis with Hot Ashes. The priest agreed, and he and Hot Ashes planned how to manage Kateri's safe escape. Hot Ashes decided to send Kateri northward with his two companions, taking his space in the bark canoe, while he would continue his journey to other villages to the west. Fortunately, Kateri's uncle was away negotiating a treaty with the Dutch at Fort Orange.

Father Lamberville and Hot Ashes made hasty preparations, stocking the canoe with provisions and arms. The priest blessed Kateri and gave her a letter of introduction to Father Cholenec at La Prairie. In the early dawn Kateri crept from the lodge taking only her blanket so she would not be accused of stealing. She climbed into the hidden canoe, and they pushed off into the waters of the Hudson.

When the village awoke, they soon discovered that their Christian had fled. The angry village chiefs assumed she was on her way to the St. Francis Mission with Hot Ashes and immediately dispatched a messenger to Fort Orange to inform Kateri's uncle of her escape.

When he learned of Kateri's defection, Iowerána was furious. Armed with a gun and three charges, he set out hoping to intercept the runaway. At a bend in the Mohawk River he met a lone man coming toward him in a canoe. Not knowing whom he was looking for, he did not recognize Onas on his way to Fort Orange to buy provisions. When Onas returned to Kateri and the Huron who had remained hidden in the woods, they rejoiced at their narrow escape but knew they must proceed with caution.

Sometime later, while portaging, they decided to walk single file with Onas some distance at the rear with his gun ready to sound a shot if Iowerána should overtake them. When a man appeared on the trail, Onas discharged his gun into the air, then pretended to search for the game he had obviously missed. Kateri, hearing the shot, quickly hid in a thick clump of bushes, while the Huron sat down on the path and calmly lit his pipe. Iowerána, discouraged and weary, gave up the chase and returned to his childless home with a heavy heart.

The three runaways continued the rest of the trip with little difficulty. They paddled northward to Lake St. Sacrement (now Lake George), on to Lake Champlain and the Richelieu River. From the post at Fort Chambly they went inland through the autumnal forests fringing the St. Lawrence and arrived at the village of St. Francis Xavier at Sault St. Louis in October 1677. Kateri, then twenty-one, had followed the two hundred-mile route back to the mission where her mother had been captured.

This Whole Village Is a Veritable Monastery.

The Mission of St. Francis Xavier was first established in 1667 by the Jesuit priest, Father Raffeix, at La Prairie on the St. Lawrence opposite Montreal. The land had been deeded to the Jesuits twenty years earlier, but it could not be colonized safely until French troops had driven out the Iroquois. The first settlers were the French lured there from surrounding forts by Father Raffeix. A small chapel, the original St. Francis Xavier, was erected. Father Raffeix hoped to entice a few Indians to the mission for conversion.

An Oneida, Francis Tonsahoten, who had been baptized elsewhere twenty years earlier, and his saintly wife, Catherine Ganneaktena, came to La Prairie and settled near the chapel with five others of their tribe. Within three years twenty other families had joined them, making the mission more Indian than French.

The site of the mission proved to be a poor one. The land was unsuitable for raising corn, and the French traders, as was their custom, supplied the Indians with liquor to maintain good relations and keep the supply of furs flowing. Father Frémin, who succeeded Father Raffeix, managed to halt the supply of liquor at the mission, but just across the river at Montreal, spirits and immorality abounded.

Father Frémin sent a request to Count de Frontenac, Governor of New France, for another site on which to relocate. Frontenac looked on the Jesuits attempts to Christianize the Indians with skepticism. He was more interested in keeping the lucrative fur trade away from the Dutch and English, and he believed a liberal supply of liquor was a valuable tool of barter.

King Louis XIV intervened. He wrote to Frontenac:

> I have granted the Jesuit fathers the concession of land which they have asked of me, at a place called the 'Sault' near La Prairie de Madeleine for an establishment for the Indians. I agree to this request, because I feel that this settlement will be advantageous, not only to help convert the Indians and sustain them in the practice of the Christian religion, but it will, at the same time, serve to accustom them to the manner and mode of the French way of life.[16]

The new location, up the river three or four miles, proved successful for raising crops, for fortifying against enemies, and it was far enough away from Montreal to remove the temptation of liquor and vice. The settlement grew rapidly. Father Chauchetière wrote glowingly of the new site near the Sault rapids:

> We are in a very high and beautiful location, with a fine view, sixty leagues distant from Quebec, which is called "the Iroquois mission." It is the finest mission in Canada, and as regards piety and devotion, resembles one of the best churches in France. The river St. Lawrence here forms a lake two leagues wide; and the place where we are is so high that the waters of this great river fall here with a loud roar, and roll over many cascades, which frighten one to look at. The water foams as you see it do under a millwheel.[17]

The new mission became St. Francis Xavier of Sault St. Louis, known also by its Indian name Kahnawaké, or Caughnawaga, meaning "the neighborhood of the rapids." It prospered as an all Indian community, the only White Faces being those of the Jesuit priests. Father Frémin had learned from serving in all of the Five Nation villages that the native people should be allowed to retain the best of their traditions and speak their own language. The French authorities, however, thought otherwise—the Indians should be turned into Frenchmen. One colonial official complained:

> The Jesuit Fathers, to whom I have made a kind of a reproach, though civilly enough, of not having up to now given the attention, they should, to the polishing of the natures of the savages and to the cultivation of their manners, have promised me that they would work to change the barbarians in every respect, beginning by their language.[18]

Father Frémin, being fluent in the native tongue, disregarded the reproach and continued to speak to his flock in their own language. However, the Jesuits did try to change one Indian tradition, one they considered pagan—the burial rites. It was not until the death of Catherine Ganneaktena, the Oneida missionary, that the old customs were brought to a halt. When Catherine died in the spring of 1677, her husband refused to observe the usual elaborate rituals for the dead, allowing instead only a simple burial service. From then on, the former tribal ceremonies for the dead were not conducted at the mission.

At St. Francis the Indians governed themselves, choosing their own civil and religious leaders. As more people from different tribes were attracted to the mission, unity was preserved by allowing each tribe to choose its own leaders. The population increased rapidly, soon numbering from 120 to 150 families living in sixty longhouses.

A stockade enclosed the church and the crude homes of the missionaries. The longhouses were scattered at random outside the palisade. The priests, not wanting to be set apart from their flock, lived a simple life with no servants to cook their meals or launder their clothes.

The center of religious life was the chapel, a twenty-five-by-sixty-foot structure. Mass was celebrated three times daily, the last service being an instructional period for children to learn the catechism. The priests incorporated the native celebrations of planting and harvesting into the Mass, and encouraged the Iroquois to chant parts of the service in their native tongue. At times a children's choir sang. During the services the men sat on the earthen floor on one side, the women on the other. A chanter leading the prayers stood in the middle.

The Indians attended Mass regularly, going to the fields or out to hunt between services, returning to the chapel later in the day for prayer. After a visit to the mission, a bishop from Quebec wrote:

> In my first visit, the piety which I saw surpassed exceedingly the estimate I had formed from the reports sent me. Married couples are as devoted to God as are the unmarried. In fact, this whole village is a veritable monastery. They all carry on the practices of Christianity so well, and they are endeavoring so zealously to lead well-ordered lives, which lead to sanctification, that it would be difficult to criticize anything at all.[19]

We Have Sent You a Treasure.

When Kateri and her two escorts arrived at La Prairie in the autumn of 1677, she presented the letter of introduction from Father Lamberville to Father Cholenec, who had temporarily replaced Father Frémin as head of the mission. The message read:

> Katharine Tekakwitha is going to live at the Sault. Will you kindly undertake to direct her? You will soon know what a treasure we have sent you. Guard it well! May it profit in your hands, for the glory of God and the salvation of a soul that is certainly very dear to Him.[20]

Father Cholenec and his assistant, Father Chauchetière, read the letter of introduction with a bit of skepticism. They knew the reputation of the Mohawk village at Caughnawaga, having heard the tales carried to them by the converts who had fled the settlement. How could such a treasure possibly have been nurtured in such a sinful place? They were willing to bide their time, instruct her, counsel her, observe her, and, as with other native people, wait to see if conversion was real and not some temporary emotional experience.

Kateri lived with Ennita and Onas who cared for her until her death. In the same cabin lived the elderly widow, Anastasia Tegonhatsihongo, who had known Kateri's mother before her capture at La Prairie and had lived with Kateri's family at Ossernenon. She had cared for Kateri as a child. Because the old woman was a devout Christian, she was assigned to instruct

Kateri. A loving bond soon developed between the two with Kateri eager to learn all that Anastasia could teach her. It wasn't long before the pupil surpassed the instructor in piety. When Anastasia tried to convince Kateri that she should marry to avoid gossip and temptation, and secure her future welfare, Kateri, annoyed with Anastasia, announced emphatically that she had no intentions of ever marrying.

The priests watched Kateri closely, noting her progress. Even on the most bitter of winter days, she always appeared at the chapel just after the first bell rang at 4:00 A.M. She remained at the church in prayer through the first Mass at daybreak and the second Mass at sunrise an hour later. Because there was always work to be done, Kateri joined the others in the fields or at the lodge, but she left her labors whenever possible to return to the chapel for private devotions. She was back again for the evening prayer service, always being the last to leave. On Sundays and holy days she spent most of the day in church, going back to the lodge only for a bite of food.

Father Cholenec was pleased with her progress. He recorded:

> As she was noble and generous of heart and quick of spirit, and since, as far as we were able to discover, she possessed an insatiable desire to learn what was good, and an equal ardor to put into practice what we had once learned, her well-disposed soul caught fire, and, placing her own strength to the work, she began to practise the things she saw the others doing. She did them so well and with such noticeable progress that within less than a few weeks she distinguished herself among all the girls and women of the mission. She soon gained the esteem and admiration of everybody.[21]

Kateri pursued her religious life with extreme sincerity and dedication. She carried her rosary constantly, seeking God wherever she went—in church, in the woods, in the fields, in the lodge. To prepare herself for the confessions she made every Saturday night, she began to inflict punishment on her body in penance for her sins. In the woods she gathered willow switches and beat her shoulders until they bled.

Although it was the practice of the priests to delay Communion until they were sure the converts would not backslide, they found Kateri's conduct so exemplary and guileless that they had no reason to postpone her first Communion. When they announced to her that the event would take place at Christmas, she was ecstatic.

The entire village was honored that one of their own, and one so young, had proved to be worthy. They postponed their annual winter hunt to celebrate the occasion with her.

On Christmas Day, 1677, the people gathered in the chapel they had decorated with luxuriant furs and elaborate costumes and ornaments, just as had been done for Kateri's baptism at Caughnawaga. Kateri, in a simple buckskin dress, walked modestly with bowed head to the front of the St. Francis Church. She knelt at the crude altar rail and received for the first time the Sacrament of the Holy Eucharist.

Work for Perfection.

Just after Christmas the winter hunt began. For three or four months all able-bodied men and women moved to the forests where game and furs were abundant. Only the elderly remained back at the village with dwindling food and provisions.

The hunting party, equipped with snowshoes, guns, bows and arrows, sleeping mats, cooking utensils, clothing, and fur robes, quickly erected temporary lodges of logs and bark. Each lodge housed three or four families. The men, eager for the hunt, left to track down caribou, bear, fox, beaver, and porcupine, their most valuable game for food, clothing, tools, and pelts. The women enjoyed the winter hunts, regarding them as a vacation from the usual labors at the village and work in the fields. There were no aged ones to care for, fresh meat was plentiful, and firewood was all around them. They had free time to gossip, play games, or sew.

Although Kateri preferred staying back at the village where she could attend Mass, pray, and go to confession, she felt obligated to help Ennita and Onas replenish their food supply and gather furs and skins. But she knew what had happened on winter hunts at her former settlement: how men exchanged wives, how tribal inhibitions and restraints were put aside, how people gorged themselves on fresh meat. Reluctantly she accompanied the hunters to the woods.

The Jesuits, also aware of the enticements on the hunt, warned their converts of the temptations they would encounter. They devised bark calendars on which they had drawn symbols to mark Sundays and holy days, what prayers were to be said each day, what fasts and abstinences were to be observed. They gave the calendars to a catechist or a proven Christian in each family

group to lead morning and evening prayer services. One priest reported that the Indians returned to the settlement with clear consciences "without any matter for absolution, that is, without sin."[22]

At the winter camp Kateri was not satisfied with just morning and evening prayers in the cabins. She made the practice of arising long before the others, at what she thought to be the prayer hour at the mission. She waded through the deep snow to a spring hidden beneath a canopy of snow-laden pine branches. Here, in the silence of the woods, she prayed at her own private sanctuary before a cross she had carved on a tree trunk. Sometimes as a penance she walked barefoot through the snow and beat herself with willow wands. At the lodge at night she continued to pray long after the rest had gone to sleep.

Kateri stole prayer time from her meals and observed fast days on Wednesdays and Saturdays, the rest of the week eating just one meal a day. When the members of the lodge urged her to join them as they feasted on fresh venison, she complied, but secretly sprinkled ashes on her meat to make it less palatable.

During the day when the women gossiped and chattered, Kateri turned their conversation to stories of saints and martyrs. While they sewed and repaired clothing, Kateri encouraged them to sing the songs and chants they had learned at the mission.

Even though the women considered Kateri far above them in Christian sanctity, they watched her carefully for a slip or a sin that would prove otherwise. One morning one of the women of her lodge discovered her husband fast asleep on a pallet near Kateri. He had come home late the night before, weary from the long day's hunt. In the dark he had collapsed on a vacant mat near Kateri's, leading his wife to conclude that they had been intimate during the night. For a time the woman kept her suspicions to herself, but later when they were preparing to break camp and return to the village, she heard her husband ask Kateri, instead of herself, to help him mend his canoe. This confirmed the woman's suspicions. When the hunting party returned to the village, the wife reported the incident to one of the priests. The Father questioned Kateri and reminded her of her Christian vows. Kateri was deeply hurt when the priest appeared not to believe her denial of any wrongdoing, and she resolved to be even more rigorous in her pursuit of virtue. She vowed never again to go on a winter expedition.

The hunting party returned to the mission in time to celebrate Holy Week. After listening to the Good Friday sermon on Jesus Christ's suffering on the cross, Kateri, thinking herself unworthy of His sacrifice, decided she must increase her own tortures. From then on she inflicted harsher austerities on her body causing the priests to worry that she was going to extremes.

After spending Holy Week in meditation and prayer, Kateri received her second Communion on Easter Sunday and was given the special privilege of membership in the Confraternity of the Holy Family, a small group of older men and women who had proved their holiness and virtue. They served as models in the village, instructing beginners, visiting the sick, and praying for the people. It was unusual for Kateri to be so honored, being young, unmarried, and only seven or eight months in the village. Father Cholenec defended her right to be a member:

> . . . her virtue placed her above the rule for the ordinary people of the village, and they, moreover, far from being jealous, generally approved of her election. The members of the Holy Family especially showed their joy, looking upon Katharine as capable of sustaining of herself alone this saintly society by her good example. She was the only one who considered that she herself was unworthy, such humble ideas did she have of herself; but the more she thought of her unworthiness, the more she thought it a duty to work for her perfection, so as not to lower the fervor of the Confraternity, to which she gave a new renown by her own.[23]

Only Jesus Christ for Her Spouse.

Shortly after her second Communion Kateri met a young woman from the Oneida tribe named Marie Theresa Tegaigenta who had been baptized earlier by Father Bruyas in Iroquois country. She and her non-Christian husband were addicted to Dutch brandy, and Marie Theresa's reputation as an alcoholic had followed her to Kahnawaké. Earlier she had left the mission at La Prairie to go on a disastrous winter hunt that produced no game. As the hunting party faced starvation, Marie Theresa experienced cannibalism, the death of her ill husband, and fear for her own life and that of her small nephew. Faced with these trials, Marie Theresa vowed to God she would change her life if allowed to survive. Five starving Indians dragged themselves back to Montreal, Maria Theresa among them.

In the spring of 1678 when Kateri returned from the winter hunt, she and Maria Theresa became instant friends. They were inseparable: they worked together, talked together, prayed together, practiced their penances together.

On occasion the two traveled to Montreal to visit the Hospital and the Teaching Sisters of Marguerite Bourgeois. They were so impressed by the nuns at the hospital, they resolved to form an order of their own—the Iroquois Sisters. They invited a third woman to join them—Marie Skarichions, an older woman who at one time had been nursed by the nuns of Quebec. The three women decided to dress alike, live a life of austerity, and build a small convent on Heron Island in the St. Lawrence at the base of the rapids.

Kateri felt obliged to discuss their venture with one of the missionaries. The priest, restraining laughter at their naiveté, listened patiently to the proposal, then gently gave them many practical reasons why such an ill-advised plan would not work. Disappointed, they abandoned the idea, but Kateri and Marie Theresa vowed to live as nuns and practice celibacy and virginity privately.

Ennita and Onas, however, worried that time was elapsing and Kateri still had not married. There were several eligible young men who would consider it an honor to marry this saintly woman, and they would be a fine addition to the longhouse family. With the help of Anastasia and others of the longhouse, they confronted Kateri with their concerns. Who would care for her in the future? Was not marriage a safer existence than single life for a young woman? Was not wedlock the custom of the tribe? The arguments were many, but Kateri rejected them all. She promised not to be a burden to them, she would work, and her needs were meager. Kateri hurried to Father Cholenec in great distress. He questioned her motives for not marrying and advised her to think about it for at least three days. In a few minutes Kateri returned. Father Cholenec recorded, "She declared plainly that she had renounced marriage in order to have only Jesus Christ for her Spouse, and that she would consider herself happy to live in poverty and misery for His love."[24]

Father Cholenec, sensing Kateri's determination, promised, ". . . I would defend her against the others, and that neither I nor the other missionaries would ever abandon her or let her be in want of anything."[25]

The priest had to begin his defense of Kateri

immediately. No sooner had Kateri left his presence than Anastasia appeared to complain to him of Kateri's refusal to marry. Father Cholenec recorded:

> I answered her coldly that I was astonished that she wished to torment Katharine about a matter which deserved so much praise, and that she, who had been a Christian for such a long time, had not opened her eyes to the beauty and merit of such a saintly resolution; and that, far from objecting, if she had any faith, she should esteem Katharine all the more, and feel happy and honored herself because God had chosen a young girl from her cabin to raise the banner of virginity among the Indians, and to teach them this sublime virtue which makes men like angels.[26]

To his surprise Anastasia acknowledged her mistake and humbly withdrew her objections. The matter was not approached again. The people of the village recognized that Kateri was an unusual person to be allowed unusual privileges.

On the Feast of the Annunciation, March 23, 1679, Kateri took Communion and made her vows of perpetual virginity. She knelt motionless at the altar for several hours. She had attained her wish to become a bride of Christ and a daughter of the Virgin Mary.

Father Cholenec recalled:

> After her heroic sacrifice had been made, she no longer seemed of this world; her conversation was of heaven alone, her soul already tasted of its sweetness, while she mortified her body by her new austerities, which, joined to her intense striving to be constantly united to God, finally exhausted her forces, so that she fell dangerously ill the same summer and narrowly escaped death.[27]

Outwardly Kateri appeared no different from any other Iroquois maiden in her simple buckskin dress, a blue blanket pulled low over her face, her hair in two braids down her back, but after she took her vows of virginity and chastity, her penances and austerities singled her out from the others. She and Marie Theresa whipped each other with thorny branches until they drew blood and put burning coals between their toes. Kateri slept on a mat strewn with sharp thorns and made a daily practice of walking through snow up to her waist while saying her rosary.

The people of the village admired her dedication to holiness and her courage to withstand pain. Bodily torture was not foreign to them—to be able to suffer without flinching was a mark of heroism for both men and women. But Father Cholenec regarded some of the practices as excessive. He wrote:

> They [women] even went to such extremes that when it came to our knowledge we were obliged to moderate their zeal. Besides the ordinary instruments of mortification which they employed, they had a thousand new inventions to inflict suffering upon themselves.[28]

Along with her increased penance, Kateri also intensified her prayer life. Father Cholenec observed:

> Every day she was seen to pass whole hours at the foot of the altar, immovable, as if transported beyond herself. Her eyes often explained the sentiments of her breast by the abundance of tears she shed, and in these tears she found so great delight that she was, as it were, insensible to the most severe cold of winter. Often seeing her benumbed with cold, I have sent her to the cabin to warm herself. She obeyed immediately, but the moment after returned to the church, and continued there in long communion with Jesus Christ.[29]

One day when Kateri was cutting down a tree for firewood, a branch caught her as it fell, knocking her to the ground unconscious. Her companions feared she was dead, but a little later she revived. Her first words were, "Oh Jesus, I thank Thee for having rescued me from danger."[30] She believed that God had saved her life so she could prove her love for Him with more penance for her earlier sins. From then on she added new austerities to her frail body, extreme measures that weakened her physical strength and hastened her early death.

Her Life Itself Is a Miracle.

During the winter of 1680 Kateri did not go on the annual hunt. She had developed severe headaches accompanied by a stomach disorder that caused retching and fever. She spent most of the winter months on her fur mat in the longhouse. As her physical strength diminished, Father Cholenec observed, ". . . [her] soul acquired new strength in proportion as her body decayed. The nearer she approached the end of her days, the more clearly she shone forth in all those virtues which she had practised with so much edification."[31]

As she lay ill in the lodge, there were few

hands to nurse her, all the able-bodied being out on the hunt. The old woman attending her could only leave a bowl of sagamité and some water to drink near her bed. When Father Chauchetière, second in command at the mission, began to visit her, she delighted in listening to the priest tell stories of Jesus and talk of God's goodness. To cheer her, he gathered a group of children at her bedside to hear her explain the pictures he had drawn for them. After her death the children cherished the remembrance of her words.

With the spring thaw came the return of the hunting parties. As Holy Week began, the missionaries encouraged the people to visit Kateri, hear her joyous testimony, and witness her Christian devotion. It was customary for the Iroquois to give special honor to the words of the dying.

On Tuesday of Holy Week, Kateri, too weak to be brought to the chapel, was given the Blessed Sacrament in the longhouse. Knowing she did not have long to live, Kateri asked her dear friend, Maria Theresa, to find her a better garment in which to die. Maria Theresa lovingly dressed Kateri in one of her own new buckskin dresses and covered her with a blanket.

The following morning Kateri received the Sacrament of the Anointing. By afternoon she was unable to utter "Jesus" and "Mary," two names that had been on her lips constantly. At 3:00 P.M. on April 17, 1680, she died peacefully in her sleep. She had earlier predicted the time of her death. She was just twenty-four years old.

Those who gathered at her bedside reported that her face shone with a radiance clearly visible in the dim light of the longhouse. They gasped in wonder as the pockmarks on her face disappeared, and she became indescribably beautiful. They kissed her hands, tore fragments from her dress as treasures, and rejoiced in her death. Father Cholenec wrote:

> . . . the entire village [was] moved by her virtue and deeply impressed by her sanctity, especially as a few hours later I eulogized her at evening prayers and made known to the Indians the treasure they had possessed and lost before they came to know her. Her virginal body was buried the following day at three o'clock in the afternoon, not with sorrow, but with the public joy which was inspired in the entire village by her holy life; a joy increased by having in Katharine a powerful advocate near God, and in her precious remains, which they have always venerated, the support, the bulwark, and the guiding spirit of the mission.[32]

On Holy Thursday Kateri was buried in a shallow grave on a slight elevation near the river, a spot she had designated earlier as her final resting place. A large cross was erected above her grave. People from neighboring settlements came to pray, to invoke her intercession, and to carry away handfuls of earth from the grave which later were credited with effecting numerous cures and miracles. Kateri's passing inspired passionate religious fervor at the St. Francis Mission. For years after her death, people told of her visitations, hearing her voice, and witnessing miracles attributed to her intercession. After a request from Kateri in a dream, Father Chauchetière painted a crude portrait of her from memory, the only picture in existence made by a contemporary who had seen her.

When the land around the mission was no longer productive, St. Francis was moved to a new site farther upstream also called Kahnawaké, or Caughnawaga. What remained of Kateri's body, after worshippers had removed many fragments as relics, was moved to the new site and buried in a sealed tomb at the St. Francis Xavier Church.

The Jesuits now in charge of Kateri's remains hope to see the day when she will be canonized. The missionaries who knew her best, Fathers Lamberville, Cholenec, and Chauchetière, left a complete record of her life written after her death. This and other documents and testimonies were introduced for her beatification in 1939. In 1943 she was declared venerable by Pope Pius XII and in 1980 was beatified by Pope John Paul II at St. Peter's Basilica in Rome.

Today thousands of pilgrims visit the three shrines that honor her. Her birthplace, Ossernenon, is at the National Shrine of the North American Martyrs at Auriesville, New York; Caughnawaga, where she spent ten years of her life, is located at the Tekakwitha Friary at Fonda, New York; Kahnawaké, the Canadian Caughnawaga, where she lived for her last four years, is at the site of the St. Francis Xavier Mission, Province of Quebec, Canada.[33]

On the doors of St. Patrick's Cathedral on Fifth Avenue in New York City, Kateri Tekakwitha is immortalized in bronze with saints and other honored ones. The sculptor, John Angel, chose figures from many nationalities and ethnic groups to portray the universality of the church.

At this writing efforts for Kateri Tekakwitha's canonization are still in progress. More evidence of miracles and healings due to her intercession must be documented before she can be named a saint of the church. Although recognized by her people as "the fairest flower that ever bloomed," the real wonder is that this young Mohawk maiden, who could not read or write, has by her exemplary life become the very symbol of saintliness. She arose above the poverty, misfortune, hostility, and illness dealt her during her short twenty-four years on earth to become a timeless example of dedication, faith, and virtue. Considering the culture in which she was raised, she was all the more remarkable. As Pope Pius stated, "Her life itself is a miracle."[34]

Notes

1. There are numerous variations in the spelling of names and places in reports on Kateri Tekakwitha, e.g. the *Index of the Documents Relating to the Colonial History of the State of New York* lists seventeen different spellings of the place name Caughnawaga. Some are phonetic translations from the Iroquois language, others are French or English adaptations. The names used in this chapter are the ones most commonly found in the references cited. To distinguish the New York Caughnawaga from the Canadian village of the same name, the settlement at the St. Francis Mission is here referred to by its other name Kahnawaké.

2. Bruce E. Johansen, *Forgotten Founders* (Ofipswich, Massachusetts: Gambit Inc. Publishers, 1982), pp. 22-23.

3. Ibid., pp. 56, 66.

4. *The Positio of the Historical Section of the Sacred Congregation of Rites on the Introduction of the Cause for Beatification and Canonization and on the Virtues of the Servant of God Katharine Tekakwitha, the Lily of the Mohawks* (New York: Fordham University Press, 1940), Document VIII, p. 120.

5. Daniel Sargent, *Catherine Tekakwitha* (New York: Longmans, 1936), p. 43.

6. *The Positio*, Document X, pp. 242-43.

7. Ibid., Document XII, p. 345.

8. Sargent, pp. 59-61.

9. Ibid., pp. 168-69.

10. Ibid., p. 175.

11. *The Positio*, Document III, p. 79.

12. Ibid., Document VIII, p. 138.

13. Ibid., Document XII, p. 352.

14. Edward Lecompte, *The Glory of the Mohawks* (Milwaukee: Bruce Publishing Co., 1944), p. 47.

15. Ibid., p. 51.

16. Ibid., p. 63.

17. *The Positio*, Document II, p. 71.

18. Sargent, p. 188.

19. Lecompte, p. 65.

20. *The Positio*, Document I, p. 69.

21. Ibid., Document X, p. 251.

22. Lecompte, p. 75.

23. *The Positio*, Document X, p. 264.

24. Ibid., p. 279.

25. Ibid.

26. Ibid., p. 280.

27. Ibid., p. 289.

28. Ibid., Document XII, p. 369.

29. Ibid., p. 372.

30. Ibid., Document X, p. 266.

31. Ibid., Document XII, p. 371.

32. Ibid., Document X, p. 303.

33. Thomas J. Coffey, *Kateri Tekakwitha* (Auriesville, N.Y.: Tekakwitha League, 1956), pp. 31-32.

34. Ibid., p. 31.

Chapter 9

Susanna Annesley Wesley
(1669 - 1742)

THE MOTHER OF JOHN AND CHARLES WESLEY, ALSO KNOWN AS THE
"MOTHER OF METHODISM."

JOHN WESLEY, the father of Methodism, wrote, "From the time I was six or seven years old, if any one spoke to me concerning marrying, I used to say, I thought I never should, 'Because I should never find such a woman as my father had.' "[1] John Wesley, though he did marry, never did find such a woman as his mother, Susanna Annesley Wesley.

Would Susanna Wesley be remembered today if it had not been for her two famous sons, John, the preacher, and Charles, the hymnist?

Or, would John and Charles have achieved their place in the history of the Protestant Church if it had not been for the early training they received from their mother? These questions will remain unanswered.

Susanna Wesley, a daughter of Puritanism and Anglicanism, has been called the "mother of Methodism," and the name "Methodist" is said to have stemmed from her *methods* of educating her children. She was an important link in the development of the Protestant tradition.

The Annesley Family.

Susanna was the twenty-fifth and last child of Dr. Samuel Annesley (1620-1696), well-known Puritan cleric in London. He was known as the "St. Paul of the Nonconformists."[2]

Annesley was a strikingly handsome man, tall, dignified, and fired with a pastoral zeal and spirit which exceeded his intellectual abilities. He was a loving, compassionate father to his large brood of children. At Susanna's baptism Dr. Thomas Manton, who conducted the ceremony, was asked how many children Annesley had. Manton answered that he "believed it was two dozen or a quarter of a hundred."[3] Not all of the quarter of a hundred have been accounted for, many children not living beyond infancy, as was the case in most large-familied English homes in the seventeenth century. John Dunton, Annesley's son-in-law, observed that his father-in-law had "produced much fruit for Heaven!"[4]

Annesley's first wife, Mary, bore him a son, Samuel, in 1645. She died one year later, and the child followed her in four years. In 1652 Dr. Annesley married Susanna's mother whose name is unknown except that she was the daughter of John White, a Puritan lawyer. Their first-born son, also named Samuel, lived to become a wealthy trader for the East India Company. He died from unknown causes—illness, accident, or foul-play. Another son, Benjamin, followed his father into the ministry and became the executor of Annesley's will.

Most of the Annesley children were girls, but only five were identified by name: Judith, a handsome, strong-minded, pious woman; Anne, a beauty and a wit who married a wealthy spouse; Elizabeth, who married John Dunton, an eccentric printer and bookseller; Sarah and three others who reached womanhood and married; last, Susanna, said to be slim, tall, pretty, and the most serious of the daughters. Susanna and Elizabeth, who resembled each other, were especially close.

At the time of Susanna's birth, Dr. Annesley was the clergyman at Little St. Helen's, a Puritan meeting-house on London's Bishopgate Street. The Declaration of Indulgence of 1672 had eliminated the danger of legal prosecution for Dissenters, or Nonconformists, so they could safely hold organized meetings. Annesley served St. Helen's until his death in 1696.

Susanna descended from distinguished ancestors. Her father, the nephew of the Earl of Anglesey, traced his lineage back to William the Conqueror. At the age of twenty-four Samuel Annesley earned a Master's degree from Oxford, two years later he became a Doctor of Civil Laws. After ordination and a short assignment as chaplain on His Majesty's warship, the *Globe*, he was assigned to his first parish at Cliffe in Kent. Though the parishioners resented his puritanical ways, Annesley labored tirelessly to save their souls while earning a good living of 300 pounds a year.

In seventeenth-century England, politics and religion were inseparable. The clergy argued over the right of the king to reign with divine authority as an absolute monarch. Nonconformists disagreed with the established church and splintered away into dissenting factions. At one occasion during the controversy, Dr. Annesley preached a probing and disturbing sermon to the House of Commons criticizing King Charles I whose reign spawned flagrant corruption and debauchery. After the King was

beheaded and Prince Charles was sent into exile, Oliver Cromwell was declared the Lord Protector. Annesley denounced the execution and criticized Cromwell for his intolerance of non-Anglican Protestants. He called Cromwell "the arrantest hypocrite the Church of Christ was ever pestered with."[5] The outspoken Annesley was constantly in hot water with all factions.

When Prince Charles returned from exile in 1660, England again crowned a monarch. After he took the throne, Charles II called together a commission to resolve the differences between the Anglicans and the Nonconformists. But the bishops of the church were unrelenting, and the Act of Uniformity of 1662 mandated compliance from all Nonconformists or expulsion from Anglican parishes. On August 24, 1662, Samuel Annesley and 2,000 other clergymen walked away from their pulpits to uncertain futures.

Little is known of Dr. Annesley until 1672 when he established his Puritan meeting-house at Little St. Helen's. Being a generous man, he gave away much of his inheritance and salary to needy Dissenters. When he died, he had little to leave his children. To Susanna, his favorite child, be bequeathed his manuscripts and valuable papers.

After her birth on January 20, 1669, details of Susanna's early childhood are scarce. As she matured, she grew fond of her well-bred, cheerful father and learned early the importance of religion in the home. The Annesley family gathered daily for prayer, Bible reading, and Christian instruction.

Susanna's father also believed that both his sons and daughters should be educated. Because girls were not admitted to the universities, Annesley, and perhaps his wife, taught his daughters himself. Susanna was a prolific reader favoring religious books to secular ones. She also learned French, and some biographers claim she knew Greek and Latin.

Despite the emphasis on religion, the Annesley home was not joyless. There were games and amusements at the proper times, and one can be sure that a houseful of spirited daughters found time for pleasures. Susanna, however, even as a child, practiced self-discipline. In a letter to her son John in later years, she wrote, "I will tell you what rule I observed ... when I was young and too much addicted to childish diversions, which was this: never to spend more time in any matter of mere recreation in one day than I spent in private religious duties."[6]

The bustling Annesley household was open at all times to Nonconformists who came to discuss religion with the Doctor. After listening intently to the debates and arguments, Susanna drew her own conclusions. When she was only thirteen, she announced to her father that she was returning to the Church of England. In letters written later she explained her reasons: she had become disenchanted with the Nonconformists and their free form of religion; she favored the Anglican's ordered structure of worship; she approved of their moderation and Christian community.

Dr. Annesley could have been bitter that his own daughter chose to return to the church that had expelled him and caused him such suffering, but he respected Susanna's decision, and the close personal relationship between them was not broken. She remained his favorite child.

In 1682 Susanna's sister Elizabeth married John Dunton, Dr. Annesley officiating. Among the guests attending the reception at the Annesley home was Samuel Wesley, a poor theological student in training for the Nonconformist ministry at the Rev. Edward Veal's Academy at Stepney. Samuel Wesley had struck up a friendship with Dunton, the printer, who eagerly sought authors wanting to be published. Wesley, a student of religion, also fashioned himself to be somewhat of a poet and writer and thought Dunton would be useful. At the wedding Wesley presented the bride and groom with an "Epithalamium," or poem, he had composed in their honor. It was an unpolished work, but Susanna's attention was drawn to this young man probably for the first time. She was then only thirteen.

The Wesley Family.

Samuel Wesley (1662-1735) came from a long line of gentlemen and scholars, including a number of Nonconformist preachers who established early the Wesley tradition of igniting ecclesiastical fires within the established church. Samuel's father, John Wesley (first known as Westley), had been recognized at Oxford for his proficiency in Oriental studies. Although not an ordained minister, the elder John Wesley earned a meager living by serving as a sometime rector at Winterbourn Whitchurch at Dorset. It was here his son Samuel was born on December 17, 1662.

When the Bishop of Bristol questioned his right to conduct services without ordination, John Wesley ignored the Bishop and continued to preach. John and his father, Bartholomew Westley (Samuel's grandfather), were among the 2,000 clerics who were ejected from the Anglican Church after refusing to acquiesce to the Act of Uniformity. The elder John Wesley then became a traveling evangelist just as his grandson and namesake, young John Wesley, was to do some eighty years later. Four times John Wesley Sr. was imprisoned and tormented. He died at the age of forty-two, leaving his wife with little money to raise and educate her two sons.

With financial help from friends, Samuel's mother was able to send him to Veal's Academy in London. The other son, Matthew, was educated as an apothecary and surgeon, later setting up a profitable practice in London. After two years at Veal's, Samuel transferred to Charles Morton's Academy, another Nonconformist institution. But Samuel soon began to find fault with the doctrines espoused by the Dissenters. In 1683 at the age of twenty-one he decided to join the Church of England and seek enrollment at its hallowed seat of learning, Oxford. Was it mere coincidence that at about this same time, thirteen-year-old Susanna was also leaving the Nonconformist movement to join the Anglicans?

One early autumn morning in 1684 Samuel slipped out of the house without waking his mother and with only forty-five shillings in his pocket and a knapsack on his back set out on foot for Oxford. He enrolled at Exeter College as a "pauper scholaris," the poorest of the poor. By frugal living, tutoring other students, and writing lampoons, satires, and a book of novelty poems, *The Maggots*, or *Poems on Several Subjects Never Before Handled*, for John Dunton, Wesley managed to stay at Oxford until June 1688 when he earned his Bachelor of Arts degree.

In August of the same year Samuel was ordained a deacon and given a temporary assignment as curate of St. Botolph, Aldersgate, in London. He was passionately in love, and disregarding his sorry financial state, he proposed to Susanna. Dr. Annesley did not oppose the wedding even though Samuel also had returned to the Anglican Church. At least Samuel and Susanna agreed on religious matters, and Samuel had steered Susanna away from Socinianism, a sixteenth and seventeenth century heretical movement that denied the divinity of Christ and disavowed the Trinity.

Susanna and Samuel were married in the parish church of St. Marylebone on November 12, 1688. Susanna was nineteen, Samuel was twenty-six. Samuel, in need of money, accepted an appointment as naval chaplain on a man-of-war, which earned him a salary of seventy pounds. He left his pregnant wife with her family and went to sea for six miserable months. In November 1689 just before their first anniversary, he returned to Susanna.

Religion did not pose a barrier between them, but another difficulty arose immediately and plagued them for most of their married life. They had a constant battle against poverty, and money-management posed an ever-present problem. Samuel was a scholar, a writer, and by his own admission he paid little attention to practical affairs. Susanna, on the other hand, was a disciplined, thrifty woman who through their entire married life worried about keeping her family clothed and fed. The newlyweds rented "mean lodgings" in Holborn, London, and with Samuel's meager salary as a curate at Newington Butts in Surrey supplemented by extra income as a hack-writer and proofreader, they remained debt free during the first two years of married life.

Samuel had joined John Dunton and a few other writers in publishing *The Athenian Gazette*, a weekly penny paper, that promised to answer all questions of the "modern day" on any subject. The most sought-after advice was on love and marriage. Each writer was assigned a particular field of expertise—Samuel's was religion, church history, poetry, and philosophy. In the course of the paper's existence, from 1691 to 1696, it gained considerable popularity and attracted contributions from such distinguished writers as Daniel Defoe and Jonathan Swift.

A Mean Cot at South Ormsby.

In February 1690 baby Samuel, the first of nineteen children, was born. Susanna had a painful delivery and later wrote that because the child was born with such "deep affliction of body and mind,"[7] he was her most-favored child.

A few months later the Wesleys moved to the small village of South Ormsby, about ten miles from Horncastle, county of Lincolnshire in northeastern England. The Marquis of Normanby, a wealthy gentleman and patron of the church, had given Samuel charge of the parish of St. Leonard. South Ormsby was a pleasant enough village of some thirty-six houses and 260 inhabitants. The ancient church stood atop a rise overlooking the parsonage which Wesley described as a "mean cot composed of reeds and clay."[8]

For Susanna, then twenty-two and born to a respectable life of relative comfort in London, the move to South Ormsby was a shock. She was not to see her beloved London again for forty years. Samuel earned a salary of only fifty pounds a year, a sum not befitting a man of his education. His writing brought in little tangible income although he hoped that "The Life of Our Blessed Lord and Saviour Jesus Christ," a long and labored heroic poem dedicated to Queen Mary, would ingratiate himself profitably with the "Beauteous Queen." The work was believed to have prompted Queen Mary to confer on Samuel the appointment to his next parish at Epworth where he moved two years after the Queen's death.

The Wesleys stayed at South Ormsby for seven years, all the time trying to bridge the cultural gap between themselves and their parishioners. While Samuel took charge of his flock and his literary pursuits, Susanna was busy bearing children. Six babies were born during their stay at Ormsby. Samuel complained, "one child at least per annum, and my wife sick for half that time."[9]

Their first daughter named Susanna arrived in 1691 during their first year at South Ormsby. Little Susanna lived less than two years. One year later came Emilia, who lived to be seventy-nine years of age. In 1694 the twins, Annesley and Jedediah, arrived. They died in infancy. Another daughter, also named Susanna, but known in the family as Sukey, appeared in 1695. She lived to be sixty-nine. The next arrival in 1696 was Mary, who, after a fall in early childhood, suffered a deformity for the rest of her thirty-eight years.

Samuel Wesley, a forthright pious man, did not flinch from denouncing evil whenever he encountered it. When he discovered sin in his own home, he acted without hesitancy. Lord Castleton, then renting the Marquis's residence, kept a mistress at the Hall. This woman grew quite attached to the pretty Mrs. Wesley and often visited the parsonage. One day when Samuel found the lady sitting comfortably at his very fireside, his temper flared and he "took her by the hand and very fairly handed her out."[10] Later young John Wesley wrote, perhaps erroneously, that his father's tenure at Ormsby was quickly terminated by the irate Marquis. This appeared to be a wrong conclusion because Wesley still continued as the Marquis's chaplain and received the nobleman's donations some years later when there were more financial difficulties.

Samuel Wesley acquired his next position at Epworth as a gift from the Crown. As they were about to leave South Ormsby, Susanna received news that her father, Dr. Annesley, had died in December 1696 after five months of illness. As he requested, Annesley was buried beside his wife in London. Susanna grieved the loss of her beloved father, but through the rest of her life she felt his presence in communion with her.

Trials at Epworth.

In early 1697 the Wesleys packed their belongings, bundled up their four children, and made the wearisome journey from South Ormsby to Epworth on the other side of Lincoln county. Their coach jolted over rutted roads and rough fields to the ferries that brought them to their new home.

Epworth was the capital of what had become known as the Isle of Axholme, an area enclosed by four rivers which in the past had flooded the region. An expensive and controversial drainage project had transformed most of the land into fertile loam pastures and fields suitable for growing hemp and flax, but the area remained accessible only by remote ferries crossing the rivers.

The old church of St. Andrew's stood on a promontory overlooking the town where about 2,000 inhabitants lived. The parsonage, larger than the Ormsby house, was a three-storied structure of timber and plaster covered with straw thatch. The house with its seven rooms—"a kitchinge, a hall, a parlour, a buttery, and three upper rooms and some others for common use"[11] stood on three acres of cultivated parish land along with a large barn, a dove cote, and a hemp kiln.

In all respects Epworth was an improvement over South Ormsby, and the position paid 200 pounds a year, if the parson could collect tithe money from the parishioners. But Samuel had to borrow heavily to finance the move across Lincolnshire, pay the legal fees required for securing his new title, purchase furniture for the larger house, buy equipment and animals for the farming he intended to do, and rebuild the run-down buildings. The Wesleys began their new position with debts equal to a year's salary, not counting the heavy interest to be paid in the future on the loans.

And there were more babies. Shortly after they arrived at Epworth, another daughter, Mehetabel, or Hetty, arrived, and before Susanna could regain her strength, another was on the way. Hetty lived to be fifty-three, but the next six children, including one unnamed set of twins, all died as infants. These children, as the others, were delivered by midwives, who could practice with no more than a small payment and a promise to the bishop not to substitute babies, abort, use sorcery, or overcharge. There were no anesthetics and little sanitation.

At the time of Hetty's birth, Susanna's elder sister Elizabeth died after what appeared to be an ideal marriage to John Dunton. During their fifteen years together, John declared, an angry look had never passed between them. Their correspondence brimmed with love and sentimentality. Six months after Elizabeth's death, Dunton remarried, and Wesley's contact with his publisher was ended.

There were not only financial difficulties at Epworth, but the Wesleys soon discovered they were at odds with the citizens of the town. The Wesleys were cultured intellectuals of noble heritage, while the Epworth people were crude uneducated fenland folk isolated from the outside world. Their "manners were coarse and vicious" and "fights were their favorite diversions."[12] They resented Wesley's heavy-handed attempts to improve their morals and correct their waywardness. Their parson had a sharp tongue and a hot temper and was not always tactful, patient, or understanding. As time went on, the citizens found vengeful ways to harass the family. They ridiculed Samuel's awkward attempts to farm and burned his flax crop; they stabbed his cows so they "all dried up;" they chopped off one leg of the family dog; and they pried off the hinges of the parsonage doors.

The men of Epworth also disliked Wesley's politics, his loyalty to the Tory royalists, and his High Church affiliation. Matters came to a head in a local election in 1705. Samuel backed two Tory candidates instead of the Whig candidates supported by most of the Epworth folk. While the rector was away voting at Lincoln (women, of course, did not vote), Susanna and the children were disturbed all night by pounding, shouting, and the firing of pistols. At the time Susanna was recovering from the birth of another baby who was being cared for by a nurse across the street. When the ruckus finally stopped, it was very late. The weary nurse went into a deep sleep, rolled over on the baby, and smothered it. Frantically, she ran to the rectory with the child, handed it to a servant who brought the dead child to its mother. Samuel reported that his wife "composed herself as well as she could, and that day got it buried."[13]

More difficulties followed. One irate parishioner, to whom Wesley owed a debt of thirty pounds, demanded immediate payment. When the parson could not pay the man on the spot, Samuel was arrested and locked in the debtor's prison at Lincoln Castle. Although Susanna had only ten shillings to feed her family, she sent her rings to her husband to pay his debt. Gallantly, he returned the rings to her, but as was his custom, he sent a desperate appeal to Archbishop Sharpe for money to aid Susanna. When the Archbishop met Mrs. Wesley, he inquired if she had ever really wanted bread. She answered, "I will freely own to your Grace that, strictly speaking, I never did want bread. But then I had so much care to get it before it was eat, and to pay for it after, as has often made it very unpleasant to me. And, I think, to have bread on such terms is the next degree of wretchedness to having none at all."[14]

The Archbishop gave her a "handsome sum," but her husband remained in prison for three months until his clerical and political friends made arrangements for payment of his debt. While at Lincoln Castle, Wesley preached to the other prisoners, saying he hoped to do more good in his prison parish than with the flock at Epworth.

As the difficulties with the Epworth citizens worsened, Wesley's friends tried to convince him to leave the parish. But the preacher was no quitter. He said, "I may yet do good there and 'tis like a coward to desert my post because the enemy fire thick about me. . . . They have only wounded me yet, and I believe, can't kill me."[15]

The rector, unlike his wife, found ways to remove himself periodically from the frustrations of parish discord, financial obligations, household annoyances, and child-rearing. He retreated to his third-floor study where without disturbance he produced quantities of verse and prose. In appraising his brother-in-law's talents, John Dunton once commented, "Mr. Wesley had an early inclination to Poetry, but he usually wrote too fast to write well. Two hundred couplets a day are too many by two-thirds to be well-furnished with all the beauties and graces of that art."[16]

But Samuel Wesley was not dissuaded by criticism—he continued to write, dedicating his compositions to members of the royal family with an eye to gaining their attention and favor. His writing did achieve some success, but did little to help pay the bills. In a letter to the Archbishop of York in 1702, he rationalized his poverty: "He that's born to be a poet must, I am afraid, live and die so [in poverty]."[17]

The rector found other ways to escape the pressures at Epworth. He accepted a three-year term as Proctor in Convocation for the Lincoln Diocese, an appointment which cost him fifty pounds a year, a sum he could ill afford. But the office had appealing personal compensation for Samuel—he could travel to London, the literary and cultural center of England, for several months each year, and while there he could further his career as a writer and dine at the coffee houses with well-positioned ecclesiastics and literary persons who might be of benefit to him. No doubt Samuel also welcomed the reprieve from the contentious parishioners at Epworth, the turmoil of a house full of children, the constant worry of debt, and the labors of farming. These duties he gladly turned over to Susanna whom he readily conceded could manage domestic affairs better than he.

Susanna meanwhile was confined to the Epworth rectory. She had no contacts outside her home, no friends, no social life, and no outside stimulation, even during those rare periods when she was not either in or out of pregnancy. Uncomplaining, she tackled the job of running the household and the farm, and assumed the task of teaching her children.

Susanna, the Born Teacher.

By 1709 there were five more children at the parsonage to be fed, clothed, and educated. There was Anne, born in 1702, and John, or Jacky as he was called, born one year later. The last three children were Martha, or Patty, born in 1706, followed by Charles in 1707, and Kezziah, or Kezzy, born in 1709.

At that time early childhood education was usually provided by a tutor if the parents could afford one. When of age, the sons were singled out for formal training at academies and universities to prepare them for successful careers. The daughters were given instruction in practical matters and social graces that would make them good wives and mothers. If girls were taught to read, it was usually only what was sufficient for everyday life. Shelbourne, a prominent statesman, expressed the mentality of the day. "Women," he said, "are domestic animals and should never be taught to go from home."[18] Susanna resolved that her daughters would not be taught to sew before they learned to read.

But even Susanna agreed that their sons should be given the best education possible. Before the boys went off to school, they had been taught the fundamentals by Susanna and introduced to classical languages and other academic subjects by Samuel. The girls all received their education in their mother's "school" with advanced work from their father if he thought them capable of learning.

All her life Susanna corresponded at length with her children, especially with her son John with whom she discussed weighty religious matters, offered advice on courses of action, and related personal family matters. When John asked his mother to share her method of educating children, she reluctantly wrote a long letter dated July 24, 1732 which delineated her philosophy and outlined the household routine she had developed.

Mrs. Wesley believed in beginning early. At age one, they were "taught to fear the rod and to cry softly" so that "the crying of children was rarely heard in the house." At mealtimes the chidren ate only what was on their plates, never asked for more, and dared not request snacks between meals. After prayers and supper, the maid washed them, beginning with the youngest. The children were all in bed by 8:00 o'clock.

On shaping the young child's character, Susanna was firm. She wrote, "In order to form the minds of children, the first thing to be done is to conquer their will and bring them to an obedient temper." She said that parents who indulge and spoil their children were really being cruel to them. When children misbehaved, they must be punished, but "a great many childish follies and inadvertencies may be passed by." On manners and courtesy Susanna insisted that the children always treat the servants with respect, and they must never be rude to anyone. Although she allowed time for play, even cards, there was never to be loud noise or talking in the home.

Susanna listed several rules that she made for the household. To prevent a child from lying, she insisted that if a child confessed and made amends, he or she should not be beaten. Her husband disagreed with this rule, insisting that a child should be whipped for any disobedience. Stanley also opposed her rule that: "No child should be ever chid or beat twice for the same

fault, and that if they amended they should never be upbraided with it afterwards." In regard to individual rights, Susanna insisted that no child should "invade the property of another in the smallest matter" and "promises must be strictly observed."

Not all of Susanna's rules were negative. She reinforced good behavior claiming that "every signal act of obedience, especially when it crossed upon their own inclinations, should be always commended, and frequently rewarded according to the merits of the case," and "if ever any child performed an act of obedience, or did anything with an intention to please, though the performance was not well, yet the obedience and intention should be kindly accepted, and the child with sweetness directed how to do better for the future."[19]

The spiritual development of the children was of utmost importance. Susanna taught them to say the Lord's Prayer as soon as they could speak, and as they grew older, they joined with the family in devotions, reading the Scriptures, and singing hymns. The Sabbath was strictly respected, and profanity was not allowed at any time. When the children were older, their mother set aside a special time each week to guide and nurture each child individually. She wrote, "On Monday, I talk with Molly; on Tuesday, with Hetty; Wednesday, with Nancy; Thursday, with Jacky; Friday, with Patty; Saturday with Charles; and with Emily and Sukey together, on Sunday."[20] In later years her son John had precious memories of his Thursdays alone with his mother.

Formal education began at the age of five when each child was taught the alphabet, usually in one day. This was followed by learning to read and spell words from the creation story in Genesis. When the child had learned one verse perfectly, he or she was allowed to go on to the next verse.

The school day was six hours in length, from 9:00 o'clock to noon and from 2:00 to 5:00 in the afternoon. Susanna taught them grammar, history, mathematics, geography, and religion. When her husband was home, he helped with the classics and more advanced subjects. At times the older children were assigned to teach the younger ones. No child could leave the classroom during the study hours except for pressing personal needs.

While teaching her many children, each with varied talents and capabilities, Susanna had infinite patience. As her husband watched her repeat and repeat a certain item to one child, he commented, "I wonder at your patience, you have told that child twenty times that same thing." Susanna replied, "If I had satisfied myself by mentioning it only nineteen times, I should have lost all labour. It was the twentieth time that crowned it."[21]

By modern standards Susanna's methods seemed harsh and inhumane. But measured against eighteenth century education and child-rearing where abuse of children was common and disciplinary floggings were the norm, her methods appeared moderate and purposeful. She coupled strictness and control with liberal doses of love, individual attention, and high expectations for each child. She warned herself:

> Never correct your children to satisfy your passions, but out of a sense of your duty to reclaim them from their errors, and to preserve your authority. And then be exceeding careful to let the measure of correction, be proportionable to the fault. Make great allowances for the weakness of their reason, and immaturity of their judgements.[22]

The success of Susanna's system was evidenced by the high-spirited, intelligent children that came from the Wesley home. Her influence over them was powerful and enduring, and in adulthood they did not complain about rigid rules and heavy-handed discipline. Rather, her three sons, John in particular, continued to seek her advice on personal problems, spiritual matters, and theological questions.

Susanna's busy life as a wife, and teacher often left her yearning for time for herself. She wrote:

> Were I permitted to choose a state of Life, or positively to ask of God anything in this world, I would humbly choose and beg that I might be placed in such a Station, wherein I might have daily bread with moderate care without so much hurry and distraction; and that I might have more leisure to retire from the world, without injuring my [?husband] or Children.[23]

Later she was able to retreat from family activities three times a day for periods of quiet where she meditated, reflected, and recorded her thoughts in her religious journal. Here she enunciated her own theology and philosophy which she often expounded further in letters to her sons.

Just as Susanna set rules for her children, so she also defined parameters for herself in accordance with her well-tuned conscience. At one time she vowed never to "drink above two Glasses of any strong Liquor at one time."[24] Even though her husband absolved her from strictly observing the pledge, she kept her resolution and so advised her acquaintances to "prevent temptation."

You Did Not Say "Amen."

When Susanna Annesley Wesley was born, Charles II, a Roman Catholic, was King of England, Scotland, and Ireland. His reign was marked by political and religious controversy that saw the rise of anti-Catholic feeling in England. In a battle over the throne in 1681, Charles dissolved Parliament and declared himself an absolute monarch. When he died, his brother James succeeded to the throne because Charles had fathered only illegitimate children by various mistresses, leaving no direct heirs.

James II's reign from 1685 to 1688 saw the rise of two great political parties: the Whigs, who favored limiting royal authority and increasing parliamentary power; and the Tories, who sought to maintain rule of the king and defeat parliamentary reform.

By 1689 the Prince of Orange had with little opposition wrested the throne from James, who escaped to France. The Prince mounted the throne as William III and ruled jointly from 1689 to 1702 with his wife Queen Mary II. William and Mary were astute politicians and during their reign England witnessed the bloodless "Glorious Revolution" and a decisive victory for Parliament.

Political discord entered the Wesley home. Samuel, a loyal Tory, had accepted William III as the lawful sovereign, while Susanna, a Jacobite, favored the deposed James of the Stuart line. She considered William a usurper.

The clash came following prayers one morning in 1702. According to John Wesley's "Journal," his father as usual ended with a prayer for the king. Angrily, he asked Susanna, "Why did you not say *amen* this morning to the prayer for the king?" Susanna answered, "Because I do not believe the Prince of Orange to be king." Samuel replied, "If that be the case, you and I must part; for if we have two kings, we must have two beds."

John reported that his mother was "inflexible" and his father "went immediately to his study; and, after spending some time with himself, set out for London" to attend Convocation where he "remained without visiting his own house for the remainder of the year."[25]

On March 7, 1702, Susanna wrote a more graphic account of the incident to Lady Yarborough, a friend: "He immediately kneeled down and imprecated the divine Vengeance upon himself and all his posterity if ever he touched me more or came into a bed with me before I had begged God's pardon and his, for not saying Amen to the prayer for the Kg. (sic)"

Susanna lamented her conflict between loyalty to her husband or to her conscience. She wrote to her friend, "I am inexpressibly miserable, for I can see no possibility of reconciling these differences, though I would submit to anything in the world to oblige him to live in the house with me."[26]

The day after she wrote the letter, King William died, but his death did not heal the breach between them. On March 15 she again wrote to her friend, "I am persuaded nothing but an omnipotent power can move him. . . . He is for London at Easter where he designs to try if he can get a Chaplain's place in a Man of War."

Whether Samuel's threat to go off to sea was sincere or just a ploy to manipulate his wife was not apparent. Susanna rationalized, "I'm more easy in the thoughts of parting because I think we are not likely to live happily together."[27]

It took a personal disaster to bring them back together. A fire destroyed two-thirds of their house, but fortunately the library and its books were saved. Samuel and Susanna reunited and began the costly task of rebuilding. One year later on June 17, 1703, the child of their reconciliation was born—none other than John Wesley.

The "amen" dispute showed that both Samuel and Susanna were indeed strong-willed, independent persons. Susanna remained loyal to her husband, often writing to the children of his godliness, devotion, and piety. For his part, Samuel was acutely aware of his wife's competence, courage, and saintliness.

The Brand Plucked from the Burning.

Susanna and Samuel rebuilt the old house, piling up more debt. Just before the birth of Kezzy, their last child, the house again caught fire one night in 1709. Hetty, asleep in a small room under the eaves, awoke when sparks fell on her. She ran to her father's room to awaken him. Someone in the street shouted, "Fire!"

Samuel in his nightshirt aroused the rest of the family. The fire spread quickly forcing some to evacuate through the windows. Susanna,

confined to her bed expecting another child, was partially burned as she ran through the flames to the front door and collapsed outside in the garden. When Samuel counted his children, one was missing—John was still in the burning house. His cries could be heard from the upstairs room. Samuel made attempts to re-enter the burning house, but flames drove him back. Neighbors then spotted little John's face at the window. One man climbed on the shoulders of another and pulled the boy to safety just before the roof collapsed.

Samuel led the family and neighbors in prayer. "Let the house go," he said, "I am rich enough."[28] The rectory was completely destroyed as were all their belongings, books, manuscripts, and papers Susanna had inherited from her father. Samuel's lifelong *Dissertation on the Book of Job* was lost, and he had to begin again. Stoically, Susanna wrote in her prayerbook of John, "I do intend to be more particularly careful of the soul of this child, that thou hast so mercifully provided for, than ever I have been."[29] John Wesley often referred to himself as "the brand plucked from the burning."[30] Kezzy was born just weeks after the fire.

Much to Susanna's distress, the children had to be sent to stay with relatives, friends, and villagers for a year while the rectory was being rebuilt. When the children were again gathered under her wing in the new house, Susanna complained that they had learned uncouth manners and bad habits. It took considerable time and patience to get them back on track.

Samuel secured financial aid from the Ecclesiastical Commissioners to rebuild the house, this time of substantial brick, but it took many years before the home was furnished and the family had respectable clothes to wear. For nearly 250 years the house remained the Rectory of the Epworth Parish of St. Andrews. In 1954 the World Methodist Council purchased it, restored it to its original condition, and opened it to the public.

The Kitchen Ministry.

When the new rectory was completed, Samuel Wesley set out for London to represent his diocese at the Convocation. Before he left, he arranged for a curate, the Rev. Inman, to tend the Epworth parish during his absence. Inman's Sunday sermons were not popular with the parishioners or with Susanna, for he hammered on one theme—the responsibility to pay one's debts. Susanna assumed the message was meant for her husband, but she bore the insult in silence. However, she resolved to do something to improve parish worship.

It was a modest beginning. She gathered her family together in the kitchen for Sunday evening devotions, psalm singing, and short sermons which she found in her husband's library. When the servants, neighbors, and friends begged to attend, the kitchen parish grew to over 200. Susanna dutifully reported the meetings to her husband in London. Inman also reported them to the rector with complaints that more people attended Susanna's kitchen meetings than attended church Sunday morning.

Samuel's reply came promptly and bluntly. Because it was unsuitable for a woman to give the sermons, Susanna should find a man to read them. Susanna answered that there was no man in the parish who was able to read the words. Samuel then ordered her to stop the meetings. To this Susanna responded:

> I am a woman, so I am also a mistress of a large family. And though the superior charge of the souls contained in it lies upon you, as head of the family, and as their minister, yet in your absence I cannot but look upon every soul you leave under my care as a talent committed to me under a trust, by the great Lord of all the families of heaven and earth.[31]

In another letter she wrote of the success of the evening meetings:

> Our meeting has wonderfully conciliated the minds of this people toward us, so that now we live in the greatest amity imaginable, and, what is still better, they are very much reformed in their behaviour on the Lord's Day, and those who used to be playing in the streets now come to hear a good sermon read. . . . Some families who seldom went to church, now go constantly, and one person who had not been there for seven years is now prevailed upon to go with the rest.[32]

Susanna clinched her argument with the challenge:

> If you do, after all, think fit to dissolve this assembly, do not tell me that you desire me to do it, for that will not satisfy my conscience; but send me your positive command, in such full and express terms as may absolve me from all guilt and punishment for neglecting this opportunity of doing good.[33]

Samuel did not send a positive command to dissolve the assembly, so Susanna continued

her kitchen ministry. When Samuel returned from London, he found that much good will had invaded the parish. He continued the evening services in the church, and after hearing the Rev. Inman preach another sermon on the duty of men to pay their debts, Wesley, too, was convinced of the curate's inadequacies.

While her husband was gone, Susanna had not only triumphed as a minister, but she had nursed her five children through a smallpox epidemic with no resulting deaths or disfigurements.

Old Jeffrey.

Ghosts and apparitions are for haunted houses and people of a superstitious nature, not for church parsonages and rational, reasonable folk. But the new house at Epworth had a ghost.

In early December 1716 extraordinary noises of unknown origin were heard from all quarters of the house. At various times Mrs. Wesley heard them, as did her husband, daughters, and servants. Even the family dog cowered in fear when he heard them. The ghost, affectionately named "Old Jeffrey" by Emilia, appeared to family members in various forms and with odd sounds. At times he was a man in a long nightgown, a headless badger, or a small rabbit. At other times he was not seen but only heard to groan, knock, saw wood, tap, rattle doors and windows, and even violently shake the house. He was especially noisy when Mr. Wesley prayed for the king, leading them to conclude that Jeffrey was no Tory. He sometimes gently tapped on the beds of the daughters when it was time to sleep. Old Jeffrey was particularly fond of annoying nineteen-year-old Hetty during her sleep.

Old Jeffrey was a regular visitor for about two months, but came back for occasional hauntings until March 1717. The entire family wrote of the strange apparition to Samuel Jr., John, and Charles, who were away from home. John, in particular, was curious about the ghost and in his letters made numerous inquiries about Jeffrey's appearances. Rational explanations cannot account for Old Jeffrey. Was he a poltergeist or an omen? Was he a diabolic force or a supernatural spirit? The legend of Old Jeffrey remains a fascinating and incomplete chapter of the Wesley story.

The Wesley Sons.

If Susanna, the consummate mother, at the

end of her life had been asked to assess her greatest contribution to the world, she probably would have answered, "It is my children." Her life revolved around her sons and daughters, their welfare, education, and religious training. Susanna's story would not be complete without relating something of her children, her prime accomplishment.

Samuel Jr., their eldest son, born in 1690 in London, was a worry to his parents during his early years. By age five, he still had not spoken a word. One day when he had disappeared, his mother hunted through the house and garden for him, calling as she went. From a hiding place under a table came a clear child's voice, "Here am I, Mother!" From then on young Samuel was as voluable as the other children. Nine years later, when Samuel Jr. went away to school, Susanna addressed him, "You, my son—you who was once the son of my extremest sorrow, in your birth and in your infancy, who is now the son of my tenderest love, my friend, in whom is my inexpressible delight, my future hope of happiness in this world."[34]

At age fourteen young Samuel was sent to the distinguished Westminster School in London where he became an outstanding scholar. He moved on to Christ Church College at Oxford where in a short time he received his Master's degree. Then began his life in the academic world as an educator, scholar, poet, and hymn-writer. He moved in the best circles in London, but kept correspondence flowing with his parents at Epworth. He sent money home to help finance the Oxford education of John and Charles and became the adviser for his sisters, often disapproving of their suitors. When Hetty was in disgrace, he pleaded with his parents to forgive her.

In 1715 Samuel Jr. married Phillis Berry, the daughter of a minister, who bore a number of children, only two living to maturity. His son, Samuel III, died before his sixteenth birthday, but his daughter, Phil, became a favorite of her uncle Charles Wesley.

As a loyal Tory and High Churchman, Samuel Jr. disapproved of the involvement of John and Charles in the Methodist movement. The family learned of Samuel's sudden death in Devon after his burial. The inscription on his gravestone at Tiverton reads:

An excellent preacher:
But whose best sermon
Was the constant example of an edifying life.[35]

When Samuel Jr. died, his mother was seventy and in poor health. She missed her "Son Wesley" deeply. Shortly after his death she wrote to Charles, "Your brother was exceeding dear to me in this life, and perhaps I have erred in loving him too well. I once thought it impossible to bear his loss, but none know what they can bear till they have tried."[36]

Because the lives of John and Charles have been covered so comprehensively, it is appropriate here to write only a brief summation as members of the Wesley family.

John, or Jack as he was known in the family, was born in June, 1703. John was his mother's child. He inherited Susanna's logical, sensible mind, and practical nature. He was a serious, thoughtful child, who even when very young, weighed all sides of a question before making a decision. His father made the wry observation, "I think our Jack would not attend to the most pressing necessities of nature unless he could give a reason for it."[37]

At age eleven John was sent to the Charterhouse School, a famous preparatory institution in London. At seventeen he enrolled in Christ Church College at Oxford. In 1726 he received his Master's degree from Oxford, after which he launched his lifelong career as preacher, writer, and evangelist. Throughout his lifetime he corresponded frequently with his mother.

John was a methodical man. On his mother's recommendation he kept a journal in which he detailed his activities and thoughts and assessed his spiritual life. For a brief period he kept a daily diary written in his own cryptic shorthand which gave an hour-by-hour account of how he spent his time. The diary was not decoded until well into the twentieth century.

For two years, from 1736 to 1738, John and his brother Charles went on a missionary journey to America to the colony of Georgia founded by James Oglethorpe. It was John's hope to minister to the Native Americans, but he found himself dealing instead with a strange assortment of savory and unsavory colonists. After a calamitous love affair with eighteen-year-old Sophy Hopkey and a threat of a lawsuit, he quickly departed America and returned to England, a disillusioned, but wiser, man.

Some biographers claim that the Georgia experience brought John to a "remarkable transformation of character" from a "self-sufficient, arrogant young priest into the subsequent reviver of the church."[38] After Georgia, John had what has become known as his "Aldersgate experience," a religious awakening that inspired him to lead the Methodist revival in England. While attending a meeting at the Aldersgate Street Society, he heard Martin Luther's preface to the Epistle to the Romans and was so touched he wrote, "I felt my heart strangely warmed. I felt I did trust in Christ, Christ alone for salvation; and an assurance was given me that He had taken away my sins, even mine, and saved me from the law of sin and death."[39]

Nine years after the death of his mother, John, then forty-eight, married Mrs. Mary Vazeille, a widow with four children, who had nursed him when he was ill. It was an unfortunate choice. After twenty unhappy years together, his wife left him never to return. John was never to find "such a woman as his father had."

John Wesley died on March 2, 1791, at the age of eighty-seven. He was buried in London's City Road Churchyard which lay across from the Bunhill's Cemetery where his mother was buried. The brief words inscribed on the marble monument were:

> John Wesley
> Born, A.D. 1703
> Died A.D. 1791[40]

Charles, the Wesley's youngest living son, was born prematurely at Epworth in March 1707. He was said to be his father's favorite son and in many ways resembled Samuel Wesley, being quick-tempered and impulsive. At eight he was sent to the Westminster School in London where he was supported and counselled by his older brother Samuel. In family tradition, he, too, went to Oxford where he graduated from Christ Church College in 1730 with a Bachelor's degree, later earning a Master's degree.

Charles, as John, was short of stature, but of sturdier build. He was a friendly outgoing young man, not as seriously religious as John, though at Oxford he did organize the Holy Club, nicknamed "The Methodists," a society of young religious zealots whose creed was based on a regimen of self-discipline and service. Later John took over the leadership of the Holy Club whose members administered to the sick, the needy, and the imprisoned.

John and Charles were very close, each complementing the other. John was the deeper thinker, the preacher who stirred people's souls with his dynamic personality and deep convictions. Charles's sermons were spontaneous outbursts of passion and emotion. Charles's specialty was music. He loved to sing and wrote over 6,500 hymns, many of them still in hymnals of all denominations.

Charles and John did not always agree. While John saw the Methodist movement as an entity detached from the Church of England, Charles was a true Anglican and Royalist. Although Charles joined John as an itinerant preacher in "field ministry," Charles believed the movement should take place within the established church. Both brothers suffered hostilities and ridicule from many sources.

Charles, as did John, married late in life, but he was more circumspect in his choice. He and Sally Gwynne, nineteen years his junior, had a happy marriage in spite of the early death of six of their nine children. When Charles moved from Bristol to London, he preached in the City Road Chapel, John's Methodist parish. He died in March 1788 at age eighty after several years of disability. He was buried in the parish cemetery in Marylebone, London.

While John was largely responsible for enunciating Methodist theology, Charles was the one who carried the message to people of many faiths through his well-known and beloved hymns—"Jesus Lover of My Soul," "Hark the Herald Angels Sing," "Christ the Lord is Risen Today," and others.

The Wesley Daughters.

Samuel Wesley Sr., was determined that his three sons get the best possible education. He got his wish—all three graduated from Oxford and went on to distinguished careers. But there was no such opportunity for his seven daughters. Girls were supposed to marry, even without their consent, and the more advantageous the match, the better. There was no family planning, so marriage meant babies, many and often.

Fathers were "lords of the manor," and Samuel Wesley was a typical eighteenth-century father. Susanna called him "my master Sir." But Susanna was determined that her daughters, too, should be given an education, if not at Oxford, then at home.

Emilia, the eldest surviving daughter, born in South Ormsby in 1692, was the mainstay of the family. She was intelligent, handsome, and outspoken. Following the disastrous fire at Epworth she took care of her mother and Baby Kezzy, and later nursed her father at the end of his life.

Her brother John commented that Emilia, or Emily, had been taught so well at home that she could read Milton better than any other person he knew. Emily worked as a governess at Lincoln, then taught at a boarding school in London. Later she opened her own school in Gainsborough with financial help from John. Emilia loved her mother and brothers dearly, but was often critical of her father. In letters she confided her innermost thoughts to John and often complained of her father's mismanagement of money.

Emilia had two passionate, but disappointing, love affairs before marrying Robert Harper, an unlicensed druggist who absconded with her savings and left her with a dying infant. Emilia's last years were spent in London at the Foundry where she helped further Methodism. After suffering a loss of memory she died in 1771 at age seventy-nine.

Susanna, or Sukey, the second surviving daughter, was born at South Ormsby in 1695. She was a beautiful, intelligent woman, who for a time lived in London with her two uncles, Matthew Wesley and Samuel Annesley.

Sukey made a hasty marriage to a Lincolnshire man, Richard Ellison, who was known as "a gentleman of good family, who had a respectable establishment."[41] However, Mrs. Wesley found him to be a coarse fellow who was a "little inferior to the apostate angels in wickedness."[42]

Ellison's treatment of Sukey was cruel and humiliating. After a fire destroyed their home, the couple never lived together again. While Richard tried to locate Sukey to entice her back to Lincolnshire, she hid at the homes of her four children in London. Richard even issued a false notice of his death hoping to get his wife to return. When she found him healthy and alive, Sukey returned to London never again to see Lincolnshire.

Ellison lost his property, moved to London, and with the help of John became associated with the Methodist movement. Susanna Ellison spent the last years of her life with her children and died in London in December 1764 at the age of sixty-nine "in full assurance of faith." Her last words were, "Jesus is here! Heaven is love!"[43]

The third daughter, **Mary**, called Molly, was born in South Ormsby in 1696. When just an infant she was injured, probably being dropped by a careless nurse. For the rest of her life she suffered a disability which caused her great agony. She wrote to her brother Charles, "I have been the ridicule of mankind and the reproach of my family."[44] But Mary was unusually attractive, loving, and sweet-tempered.

At age thirty-eight romance entered her life in the person of John Whitelamb, an impoverished young man who helped Samuel Wesley Sr. with his writing. For a time John lived at the Wesley home, where he was tutored in classics and foreign languages by Mr. Wesley. After John finished Oxford, Wesley Sr. appointed him as curate, or assistant, at Epworth.

The Wesleys gave their approval when John Whitelamb proposed to Molly. The wedding took place in January 1734. Instead of a dowry for Mary, which he could not afford, Samuel Wesley gave Whitelamb charge of his parish at Wroot. The newlyweds were poor, but happy. Unfortunately their bliss was terminated in less than a year when Mary and her newborn infant died in childbirth. They were buried in the same grave.

Mehetabel, or Hetty, the fourth daughter, was born in Epworth in 1697. Of all the daughters, hers is the story most often recorded in detail because of the personal tragedy that haunted her life.

Not only was Hetty beautiful, but she was considered the wit and genius of the family. Her father was proud of his remarkable daughter who could read the New Testament in Greek at age eight. But Hetty was also independent, and when she came of age, she challenged her parents' authority and rebelled at their restrictions.

Hetty had many suitors, most of them meeting with her father's disapproval. In 1725 while working as a governess at the town of Kelstein, she became infatuated with a young lawyer, but her father refused to consent to their marriage. Hetty became pregnant and returned home, a disgrace to herself and her parents. As Hawthorne's Hester Prynne, she had committed the unpardonable sin and was to pay the consequences. Hetty's sister Mary and her brother John tried to intervene with their father, but Samuel Sr. rejected his daughter the rest of his life.

Hetty, in defiance, resolved to marry the first man who proposed. Her parents didn't dispute her decision and thought it best that she marry anyone who appeared on the scene, the sooner the better. Unfortunately that man happened to be William Wright, an illiterate plumber, far less intelligent and refined than Hetty. They were married in October 1725 at Louth. The Louth parish register recorded the baptism of "Mehetabel d. of William Wrightt" on February 18, 1726. The child was buried in December of that year.[45]

Hetty was extremely unhappy in her ill-suited marriage, but she made every effort to please her husband. Soon William began to drink, ignored his business, and ran up debts. To compound Hetty's tragedy, in the course of a few years she bore four children all of whom died in infancy.

As Hetty longed for reconciliation with her parents, she wrote letters to her father telling of her unhappiness and begging for his forgiveness and understanding. Samuel Wesley wrote back that her penitence was feigned, that her troubles flowed from her own sin, and that she was probably to blame for her unhappy marriage to her "honest husband."

Except for the kindnesses of her brothers and sisters and her Uncle Matthew Wesley, Hetty suffered alone. Even her mother seemed to abandon her, perhaps not daring to countermand her husband's authority.

After the death of her father and her sister Mary, Hetty moved to London to live with John and her mother, who had finally forgiven her. Her uncle introduced her to London's famous literary figures who inspired her to write and publish some poems.

After the death of her mother in 1742, Hetty lived her last years as an invalid. Death came on March 21, 1750, at the age of fifty-three. In life she was forsaken, and so in death. She was buried in an unknown grave with only her brother Charles in attendance.

Little is known of **Anne**, or Nancy, the fifth daughter, born in Epworth in 1702. When she was seven, her father saved her from the Epworth fire. In about 1725 she married John Lambert, an Epworth land surveyor, who appeared to be a suitable husband until he found a ready drinking partner in Hetty's errant husband, William Wright. The couple had at least one son, named John, who apparently died in his youth.

Anne and her husband moved to London where their home was always open to the family. Anne spent time with her mother before Susanna died, but subsequently there was no further information about her.

After all the difficulties with the older daughters, **Martha**, or Patty, the sixth daughter born in May, 1706, must have been a welcome reprieve. She was sweet-tempered, loving, of a serious disposition, and everyone's favorite child. She was her mother's dearest daughter, her brother John's preferred sister, and her Uncle Matthew's chosen niece.

Martha had several love affairs, all terminated by her father. While staying with her indulgent Uncle Matthew in London, Martha met and became secretly engaged to Westley Hall, a supposedly pious clergyman. But when Hall accompanied John Wesley on a visit to Epworth, he met Martha's youngest sister, Keziah, or Kezzy, and promptly fell in love with her. The Wesleys approved of him as a suitor for Kezzy, but when he returned to London, Hall resumed his romance with Martha. Hetty and her parents were irate with Martha for stealing Kezzy's beau, until Martha explained the circumstances. A few months after her father's death, Martha and Westley Hall were married. Uncle Matthew gave them a generous wedding gift and added Martha to his will.

All went well in the marriage for the first few years at their residence in Fisherton, near Salisbury. Martha gave birth to ten children, but only one survived infancy. The boy, John, died of smallpox at age fourteen.

After a time Westley Hall's true nature emerged. He adopted one religion after another, seduced Martha's seamstress, and left town when the seamstress bore his child. Martha found her a midwife and took care of the infant as her own. For a while Hall returned to Martha, but was so cruel to his son John that Martha's brothers removed the boy from his care.

Westley Hall abandoned Martha to go to the West Indies with his mistress but returned to London after the woman died. All-forgiving Martha nursed him until his death in 1776.

During Hall's absence Martha had begun to lead a life of her own. She became friendly with the great Samuel Johnson and was introduced to London's intellectuals, though she always remained a quiet, reserved person.

Martha died in July 1791 only four months after her brother John. At age eighty-five she had outlived the entire Wesley family. Fittingly Martha, who had wholeheartedly embraced Methodism, was buried beside her favorite brother John at the City Road Chapel Cemetery.

The saga of the Wesley children ends with **Keziah**, or **Kezzy**, the seventh and last daughter. She was born in March 1709 just after the Epworth fire. While a baby, her parents were so occupied rebuilding the house and recovering from the fire that Kezzy was given little attention. As she grew older, Kezzy, not known for her beauty or her intellect, was often in the shadow of her more outgoing and illustrious sisters. For all of her life, she suffered from poor health and an inferiority complex.

For a time Kezzy worked in her sister Emilia's boarding school, but poverty drove her back to Epworth where she was alone with her aging parents. It was here that she met Wesley Hall, Martha's betrothed. Hall courted Kezzy, proposed to her, and gained Susanna and Samuel's blessing to marry her. Kezzy was crushed when he returned to London to marry her sister Martha. Celibacy was going to be Kezzy's lot.

Charles and Kezzy, just two years apart in age, were particularly close, just as John and Martha had been. Before Kezzy died in 1741 at age thirty-two, Charles had converted her into a true Methodist, and he rejoiced that his "sister Kezzy died in the Lord Jesus."[46]

Susanna, the mother of ten living children, must have suffered with each misfortune that befell her large family. The complex relationships that existed within the Wesley family— parents to children, sibling to sibling, husbands to wives—obviously molded the personalities and behavior of each individual. Susanna was the constant that endured for them all.

As He Lived, So He Died.

In 1724 Samuel Wesley willingly added the parish of Wroot to his duties at Epworth. For a time the family lived in the run-down rectory at Wroot, a desolate village in a swamp often accessible only by boat. But the position brought in an additional annual income of fifty pounds.

Emilia returned home to Wroot after the closing of the London boarding school where she taught. In a letter to John, she complained of her father's capacity to pile up "infinite debts" despite the added income and the adequate food supply available at Wroot. She also wrote of her own dissatisfaction at home "without three things, money, liberty, and clothes," but added, "while my mother lives I am inclined to stay with her; she is so very good to me, and has so little comfort in the world besides, that I think it barbarous to abandon her."[47]

In the forty years at Epworth and Wroot, Susanna made only one trip back to her birthplace, London. She read an announcement that her brother Samuel Annesley was returning from India, and she eagerly traveled to London to meet him. The ship docked, but her brother was not aboard and was never heard from again.

His disappearance was never solved, and Susanna never received the thousand pounds he had promised her.

Poverty and adversity still plagued the Wesleys despite the additional income from Wroot and from Samuel's pen. The extra salary was soon eaten up hiring a curate to care for the second parish. In 1725 Samuel suffered a slight stroke which paralyzed his right hand. With customary determination he put his left hand "to school . . . to learn to write, in order to help its lame brother."[48]

Despite the tragedies of their daughters' many unfortunate marriages, there was one happy event to celebrate. In 1726 son John had become a Fellow at Oxford, a position that offered prestige, a yearly salary, freedom to pursue his own studies, opportunities to earn extra money as a tutor, free lodging, and other benefits. John retained his Fellow position for twenty-six years until his ill-conceived marriage in 1751. For a time John returned home to help his father with the Wroot and Epworth parishes. This was one of Susanna's happiest times as she and John spent hours together discussing personal and religious matters and reading together.

During the trauma of child-bearing and child-rearing coupled with periodic confinements to her bed, Susanna revitalized her spiritual life by spending an hour early in the morning and another in the evening in private meditation. Later she added another solitary period at noon. She also began to write long letters to her children, and recorded daily meditations and prayers. Fortunately her religious journal and many letters have been preserved. Her prayers show her deep commitment to the Creator, her reverence for nature, and her devotion to living and sharing a godly life. She prayed, "Help me, Lord, to remember that religion is not to be confined to the church or closet, not exercised only in prayer and meditation, but that everywhere I am in Thy presence. So may my every word and action have a moral content."[49]

In 1774 her son John reminisced, "For many years my mother was employed in abundance of temporal business. Yet she never suffered anything to break in upon her stated hours of retirement, which she sacredly observed from the age of 17 or 18 to 72."[50]

While on a trip in 1731 Samuel Wesley was thrown from his wagon as his horses galloped out of control. He was badly bruised and never completely recovered from the injuries. He still continued to preach, but as he felt age and infirmities creeping on, he tried to convince one of his three sons to take over the Epworth parish. Although John did return as a curate for a time, none of the sons wanted to assume a permanent position as their father's successor. After Mary's untimely death, her husband, John Whitelamb, left his curate's position at Wroot to return to Epworth to help Samuel Wesley complete the *Dissertation on the Book of Job*, a work that had consumed Samuel's attention for twenty-five years. Samuel hoped this monumental treatise would finally bring him recognition and fortune. He made a trip to London, his final visit, to promote the book, but he never saw it in print. His son, Samuel Jr., completed the work and had it published. Unfortunately, the weighty *Dissertation*, written in Latin, met with little success, and Queen Caroline, to whom it was dedicated, paid little attention to it when John offered her a copy.

Before drawing his last breath, Samuel gave final admonitions to Emilia, Kezzy, John, and Charles gathered at his bedside. Susanna, distraught and infirm, could not stay in the sickroom without fainting. Samuel Wesley died peacefully on April 25, 1735, at the age of seventy-two. As was his wish, he was buried "very frugally, very decently" in the graveyard at Epworth. His epitaph began with the words, "Here lieth all that was mortal of Samuel Wesley," and ended with, "as he lived so he died in the true Catholic Faith."[51] He had served Epworth for nearly forty years.

The Soul Was Set at Liberty.

After Samuel Wesley's death, Susanna left Epworth to live with her children. John settled his father's debts and sold everything of value.

In October 1735 John and Charles began their two-year missionary venture to Ogelethorpe's Georgia colony in America. When they returned, John had his Aldersgate experience and began to draw large crowds to hear his impassioned preaching. He established the headquarters for the Methodist movement at the Foundry, an old London munitions factory practically in ruins. It was rebuilt to provide a chapel, a library, a free school, a free dispensary, living quarters for workers, and apartments for himself and his mother.

In spite of Susanna's failing health, these were happy years. She had her family close by. She advised her sons, promoted the Methodist movement, and taught classes for women at the Foundry, laying the groundwork for the women's movement in the Methodist Church.

On July 23, 1742, at the age of seventy-three, Susanna died with all of her living children, except Charles, at her bedside. John recorded the last hours:

> She was in her last conflict; unable to speak but, I believe, quite sensible. Her look was calm and serene, and her eyes fixed upward, while we commended her soul to God. From three to four the silver cord was loosing and the wheel breaking at the cistern; and then without any struggle, or sign, or groan, the soul was set at liberty. We stood around the bed and fulfilled her last request uttered a little before she lost her speech: 'Children, as soon as I am released, sing a psalm of praise to God.'[52]

Susanna was buried on Sunday, August 1, in the Dissenters' Cemetery at Bunhill Fields just opposite the City Road Chapel. At graveside John preached one of his most stirring sermons to a large assemblage. Susanna was laid to rest with other Puritan notables—John Bunyan, John Owen, Isaac Watts, and Susanna's own sister, Elizabeth.

Though Susanna Wesley's greatest contribution to the world may have been her two sons who dramatically changed Protestantism, she herself was a connecting link between three major traditions—Puritanism, Anglicanism, and Methodism. Without the advantage of a formal education she had developed an understanding of theology and religion that earned the respect of her Oxford-educated sons. John and Charles regarded their self-taught mother as their theological mentor. She had read widely from the philosophers, theologians, and historians, and was acquainted with such diverse writings as John Locke's dissertations on reason and Teresa of Avila's mystic revelations. During the quiet periods of meditation and reflection, she formulated her own personal convictions which she recorded in her religious journal.

At times Susanna in despair would write, "Lord, I am Nothing! I have Nothing! I can do Nothing!"[53] At other times she drew great strength from her well-honed conscience, her sense of reason, and her deep religious experience.

Susanna Wesley was not the stereotypical eighteenth-century woman. She dared confront her husband when he proved unreasonable or overbearing, and, as did Katherine von Bora Luther, she managed the household efficiently despite her spouse's financial incompetence. She raised her children with infinite patience and with great regard for their personal welfare. She was practical and had an abundance of common-sense, yet at the same time she nurtured her inner spiritual life and set down on paper her many profound thoughts and observations.

Susanna was a woman of great determination, resolute faith, and unflagging devotion to her family and religion. She made her own mark and left her imprint on the Methodist Church. But, would she have been remembered had it not been for her two famous sons? Her chief biographer, Adam Clarke, believed she would. Clarke wrote, "Many daughters have done virtuously, but Susanna Wesley has excelled them all."[54]

Notes

1 Richard P. Heitzenrater, *The Elusive Mr. Wesley*, vol. I (Nashville: Abingdon Press, 1984), p. 181.

2 Frank Baker, "Salute to Susanna," *Methodist History*, vol. 7, no. 3, April 1969, p. 3.

3 John A. Newton, *Susanna Wesley and the Puritan Tradition in Methodism* (London: The Epworth Press, 1968), p. 44.

4 Ibid., p. 43.

5 Rebecca Lamar Harmon, *Susanna, Mother of the Wesleys* (Nashville: Abingdon Press, 1968), p. 25.

6 Newton, p. 55.

7 Rita F. Snowden, *Such a Woman* (Nashville: The Upper Room, 1962), p. 9.

8 Eliza Clarke, *Susanna Wesley* (London: W. H. Allen & Co., 1890), p. 17.

9 Newton, p. 69.

10 Harmon, p. 43.

11 Clarke, p. 22.

12 Harmon, p. 16.

13 Clarke, p. 52.

14 Ibid., pp. 56-57.

15 Maldwyn Edwards, *Family Circle* (London: The Epworth Press, 1949), p. 20.

16 Newton, p. 73.

17 Ibid., p. 71.

18 Frederick E. Maser, *Susanna Wesley* (Lake Junaluska, North Carolina: Association of Methodist Historical Societies, no date), p. 19.

19 Clarke, pp. 30-36. The eight prior quotations are found here.

20 Newton, p. 122.

21 Snowden, p. 27.

22 Newton, pp. 113-14.

23 Charles Wallace, "Susanna Wesley's Spirituality: The Freedom of a Christian Woman," *Methodist History*, vol. 22, no. 3, April 1984, p. 158.

24 Ibid., p. 162.

25 Newton, pp. 87-88.

26 Ibid., p. 89.

27 Ibid., p. 90.

28 Harmon, p. 53.

29 Heitzenrater, pp. 41-42.

30 Harmon, p. 53.

31 Clarke, p. 103.

32 Ibid., pp. 107-108.

33 Ibid., p. 109.

34 Snowden, p. 12.

35 Harmon, p. 150.

36 Newton, p. 175.

37 Willie Snow Ethridge, *Strange Fires* (New York: Vanguard Press Inc., 1971), p. 23.

38 Ibid., p. 245.

39 Ibid., p. 247.

40 Harmon, p. 141.

41 Franklin Wilder, *Father of the Wesleys* (New York: Exposition Press, 1971), p. 150.

42 Harmon, p. 108.

43 Wilder, p. 151.

44 Ibid., p. 152.

45 Harmon, p. 123.

46 Wilder, p. 164.

47 Harmon, p. 87.

48 Ibid., p. 88.

49 W. L. Doughty, ed. *The Prayers of Susanna Wesley* (London: The Epworth Press, 1956), p. 15.

50 Ibid., p. 9.

51 Edwards, p. 15.

52 Snowden, pp. 53-54.

53 Wallace, p. 169.

54 Maser, p. 31.

Chapter 10

Ann Lee
(1736 - 1784)

FOUNDER OF THE UNITED SOCIETY OF BELIEVERS IN CHRIST'S SECOND APPEARING, COMMONLY KNOWN AS THE SHAKERS.

'Tis the gift to be simple, 'tis the gift to be free,
'Tis the gift to come down where we ought to be, and
When we find ourselves in the place that's right
'Twill be in the valley of love and delight.

"Simple Gifts," a Shaker hymn

THE LIFE OF Ann Lee, founder of the American Shaker movement, was far from the utopian "valley of love and delight" extolled in the

Shaker hymn. The wonder of her life is that Ann, an illiterate, uneducated woman born to a life of poverty, hard work, ridicule, imprisonment, and persecution should establish a sect remembered for its humanity, godliness, charity, and brotherly love. Today the Shakers, all but extinct, are respected for their quality of character, their cultural and artistic contributions, their thrift and industry, and their religious devotion.

The Industrial Revolution of the mid-eighteenth century had wrought great social and economic changes in the cities of King George II's Great Britain. Droves of country folk swarmed to the cities in search of better wages and improved living conditions. Instead they found meager pay, long hours, and squalid rat-infested slums where disease and infant mortality were rampant. Young children supplied the cheapest labor for unskilled jobs and were often beaten when they fell asleep or fainted from heat or hunger.

England's Manchester with its burgeoning mechanized textile industry was such a city. Here Ann Lees (later changed to Lee) from the age of eight toiled fourteen hours a day in a cotton mill preparing thread for the looms, cutting velvet, and trimming hatter's fur. Neither she nor her five brothers or two sisters had ever been to school, so none were able to read or write.

Ann, the second in the family, was born on the "last day of February," believed to have been

February 29 because 1736 was a leap year. Her father, John Lee, was a poor, but respectable and industrious blacksmith. Ann's mother, whose name was never recorded, was known as a religious woman who reared her eight children with strict piety. She died, probably in childbirth, when Ann was still young.

The family lived on Toad Lane, a dirty narrow street, in one of the slum districts near the Manchester Cathedral where Ann's baptismal date was entered on June 1, 1742. Ann, a sensitive, emotional girl "not addicted to play," escaped from the squalor of everyday life into her own fantasy world. She was said to have experienced divine manifestations from early childhood. She frequently brooded about the evils of society, often weeping through the night over the sins of the world. Especially loathsome to her, even at an early age, were the lusts of the flesh, possibly acquired from seeing her mother so often in painful child-birth.

Shaker testimonials written in 1816 stated:

> It is remarkable that, in early youth, she had a great abhorrence of the fleshly co-habitation of the sexes; and so great was her sense of its impurity, that she often admonished her mother against it; which coming to her father's ears, he threatened and actually attempted to whip her; upon which she threw herself into her mother's arms and clung round her to escape his strokes.[1]

Ann found little inspiration in the Anglican service at the Cathedral. She longed for more fire than was in the rigid formality of the Church of England. But jails were full of people who dared dissent from the official religion of the country, so she learned to be discreet, at least at the onset of her conversion.

Her family offered Ann little support in her pursuit of holiness. She testified that one of her brothers became so enraged by her singing that he beat her over the head until the stick, the size of a broom handle, broke. She said God had warded off his blows so she "felt no harm from his strokes; but he was out of breath, like one who had been running a race."[2] If the beating did occur, it may have caused the fracture found on her skull when her remains were moved in 1835.[3]

At age twenty Ann worked as a cook in a public infirmary, an institution that also took in mental patients. This may account for the rumors that she was once "confined to a madhouse."[4]

Quitting the Marriage Bed.

Religious unrest marked the first half of the eighteenth century in England. John Wesley had left the Church of England to form the Methodist Church; George Whitefield, English revivalist, had transported Calvinist Methodism to America igniting the "Great Awakening" in settlements from New England to Georgia. The Religious Society of Friends, commonly known as the Quakers, had from the middle of the seventeenth century preached pacifism, abolition of slavery, equality for men and women, and freedom from the rigid ceremonies of sacramental worship. Among the common people there was a movement away from orthodox religions.

A small band of French Prophets, or Camisards, a radical sect of Calvinists, who after exile from southern France, sought to recruit converts and find freedom to worship in England after the passage of the British Toleration Act of 1706. But in England, as in France, their fanatical beliefs and their claims that they could predict the Second Coming of Christ, or the millennium, brought them ridicule and at times persecution. Divine voices inspired them to move in frenzied abandon while speaking in strange tongues. The French sarcastically called them "Les Trembleurs," or "the Shakers," a name that in time became acceptable.

Former Quakers James Wardley, a Manchester tailor, and his wife Jane had organized the Society of Shaking Quakers, a group similar to the French Prophets. Their beliefs were apocalyptic and millennial, and they voiced strong opposition to the established churches. Jane Wardley, known as Mother Jane, was the leading spirit. Here Ann Lee found herself. She joined the Shaking Quakers in 1758, drawn to the sect by their religious passion and burning indignation against sin. By age twenty-two Ann was convinced that men and women who had sexual relations, even though married, were sinning against God. Her convictions were put to the test four years later.

Ann's father, concerned for his daughter's future, arranged for her to marry his apprentice, Abraham Standerin (later changed to Stanley). The wedding was held in the Manchester Cathedral where Ann was still listed as a member. The banns of marriage published in the church indicated that on Januay 5, 1762, Abraham Standerin, blacksmith, married Ann Lees, spinster. At the bottom of the document the bride and groom both signed "X's," evidence of their illiteracy.[5]

One can only imagine the state of Ann's married life with Abraham, "a kindly man, who loved his beef and beer, his chimney corner and seat in the village tavern."[6] The couple settled at the Lee household where four children were born to them during the next four years. Three died in infancy. The last child, Elizabeth, was born after a difficult forceps delivery which brought Ann close to death. This child died in early childhood.

The years of toil in the textile mills, the unsanitary conditions in the slums, the unwanted marriage, the birth of children in quick succession followed by their deaths, left Ann in a state of physical and mental collapse. Testimonials indicated that for six months Ann suffered:

> . . . watchings, fastings, tears and incessant cries to God . . . day and night, for deliverance from the very nature of sin. And under the most severe tribulation of mind, and the most violent temptations and buffetings of the enemy, she was often in such extreme agony of soul as caused the blood to perspire through the pores of her skin. . . . By such deep mortification and sufferings, her flesh wasted away till she became a mere skeleton. . . . Her earthly tabernacle was so reduced that she was as weak as an infant.[7]

Ann was convinced that her illness and the death of her children was her punishment for carnal sexual acts. In desperation she sought the counsel of Mother Jane Wardley, her mentor, who offered this advice, "James and I lodge together but we do not touch each other any more than two babes. You may return and do likewise."[8]

Ann acted on Jane's advice. She recalled later:

> I went to bed with my husband; but could not sleep, seemingly, any more than if I had been in a bed of embers. I quitted the bed in great tribulation, and continued laboring and crying to God, for the space of twelve days and nights, to know how the creation was falled, and how the restoration should take place.[9]

Abraham was furious at Ann's "quitting" his bed. When he could achieve nothing by arguing with his wife, he strode over to the cathedral to complain to the Anglican priests. They listened sympathetically, then summoned Ann and confronted her with St. Paul's admonition to women from Colossians 3:18:

"Wives, submit yourselves unto your husbands, as it is fit in the Lord." Their words did not alter Ann's resolve to sin no more in the conjugal bed.

Surprisingly, Abraham reconciled himself to his celibate role, and was converted, though reluctantly, by his zealous wife. Other members of her family—her father, her younger brother William, her sister Elizabeth, and her niece Nancy—joined the Shaking Quakers. Some townspeople, a few of wealth and position, also were drawn into the fold.

Contemptuously Disturbing the Congregation.

When Ann regained her health, she threw herself wholeheartedly into the emotional meetings led by Mother Jane Wardley, a passionate preacher who could inflame her listeners. Mother Jane's message was simple: "Repent, confess your sins, amend your lives!"

In eighteenth century England a bona fide woman preacher was unheard of except among the Quakers, who had since 1670 given women roles of leadership. The orthodox churches kept women *quiet*, their position buttressed by St. Paul's admonition, "Let your women keep silence in the churches: for it is not permitted unto them to speak. . . . And if they will learn anything, let them ask their husbands at home: for it is a shame for women to speak in the church."[10]

Encouraged by the Wardleys, Ann poured out her affirmation of faith and confession of sins in public. She said later, "I labored to remember the time when and the place where I committed them. And when I had confessed them, I cried to God to know if my confession was accepted; and by crying to God continually I traveled out of my loss.[11]

Hostility increased. The officials and citizens of Manchester viewed the small band of Shakers to be disruptive and dangerous. Their frenzied meetings, at times continuing through the night, disturbed the neighbors and aroused resentment and suspicion. Members of the little flock were often arrested, fined, and if they could not pay the fines, were thrown in jail.

One day an angry mob burst into the John Lee home where the group was worshipping, singing, and dancing. They seized Ann, dragged her to the street, abused her, and hurried her off to prison where she was confined for several weeks with her father.

In 1770, while in a house of correction for

"profaning the Sabbath," two revelations came to Ann through "astonishing visions and divine manifestations."[12] God was revealed to her as both male and female, father and mother, and as she meditated, she became one with Jesus Christ. The second revelation convinced her that sexual desire had caused the fall of Adam and Eve and was the root of all suffering and evil in the world. No human relationship should be allowed to come between a soul and God, and, as did Catherine of Siena and Teresa of Avila, she believed that true unity with Jesus Christ could occur only through self-denial and celibacy. In later years Ann called the prison revelations her spiritual birthday.

Upon her release from jail Ann became more vehement in her public exhortations, particularly preaching against sins of the flesh. As her listeners became more attentive to her words, so did political and ecclesiastical opponents. During the summer and fall of 1772 the Manchester constable recorded his expenses for apprehending and jailing "Ann Lees" and other Shakers at six different occasions.

In May 1773 the magistrate of Manchester reported that Ann had spent two days in jail for "disturbing the Congregation in the old Church." Two months later she was imprisoned again. The Manchester *Mercury* published the following account:

> Saturday last ended the Quarter Sessions, when John Townley, John Jackson, Betty Lees, and Ann Lees (Shakers) for going into Christ Church, in Manchester, and there willfully and contemptuously, in the time of the Divine service, disturbing the congregation then assembled at morning prayers in the said church, were severally fined [in pounds] 20 each.[13]

A twenty-pound fine at that time was exorbitant. Ann was unable to pay it, so was again hustled off to the Manchester House of Correction, this time put in solitary confinement for several weeks. During her imprisonment, she had another vision. Jesus Christ appeared to her, entered her spirit, and commissioned her to preach the gospel. "I feel the blood of Christ running through my soul and body," she said. "I feel him present with me, as sensibly as I feel my hands together. . . . It is not I that speak. It is Christ who dwells in me."[14]

A testimonial confirming Ann's revelation noted:

> . . . a light shown upon her, and the Lord Jesus had stood before her in the cell, and become

one with her in form and spirit. . . . when Ann Lee came out of prison, the little church of six or seven persons to whom she told her story, had raised her to the rank of Mother. . . . Christ had come again; not in His pomp and power, as the world expected Him, but in the flesh of a factory girl, who could neither read nor write.[15]

When Ann was released from prison, she immediately revealed her vision to the Wardleys and the other members. They marvelled at her radiance and were convinced they had witnessed the Second Appearing of the Spirit of Christ in the form of a woman, or "Ann the Word." She assumed leadership of the group as their Mother in Christ and was known thereafter as Mother Ann.

To disbelievers, Ann's elevation to what appeared to be a female Christ was blasphemous, but to her followers it was a fulfillment of divine prophecy. They espoused an androgynous theology claiming that God had come first as the male Jesus, and again as the female Mother Ann. More recent Believers clarified their convictions:

> Ann Lee herself is not an 'incarnation' of Christ. The reality of Christ is indeed experienced in her, but also equally in each and every one united in Christ. She is a spiritual Mother because she ministered this indivisible Christlife given to her, giving Christlife to others.[16]

In the latter part of the nineteenth century Aurelia Mace, a devout Shaker, explained their creed: "To us God is Father and Mother and has been from the beginning. Jesus was an inspired man. Ann Lee was an inspired woman. Inasmuch as Jesus became the Christ, so may all be in possession of the same spirit."[17]

In 1872 another Shaker wrote that Mother Ann's vision was "not a second appearing of Christ, but a *Second Revelation* of the Gospel first revealed by Jesus, the Christ; and that revelation was made through a woman. . . ."[18]

We Shall All Arrive Safe to America.

After imprisonment and stonings, there was a period of relative calm for the small band of Believers. The constable recorded no more offenses and fines. Perhaps Ann and her followers had become more prudent in conducting their public displays, or perhaps their thoughts were turning elsewhere. They were disappointed that their numbers had not increased significantly in England, and they had little hope of escaping for long the oppressive scrutiny of the Anglican Church and the civil authorities. The future in the homeland appeared bleak.

At this propitious time the Reverend George Whitefield returned to England from his fifth revival mission in America. He came to Manchester, preached fiery sermons, and recounted with great passion what wonderful opportunities were offered believers of all faiths in the New World. The colonists, he claimed, were even willing to go to war against the British for their religious freedom. Mother Ann listened with rapt attention. She did not approve of war—the Shakers were pacifists—but the colonies might allow her the freedom to establish her millenial church there without opposition and persecution.

One Saturday evening as the Shakers were on a twenty-mile walk to a church meeting, they rested by the roadside to "eat some vituals." James Whittaker, a devout young weaver, said:

> While I was sitting there I saw a vision of America; and I saw a large tree, every leaf of which shone with such brightness as made it appear like a burning torch, representing the Church of Christ which will yet be established in this land. After my company had refreshed themselves, they travelled on, and led me a considerable distance before my vision ceased.[19]

Whittaker believed he was destined to help Mother Ann plant the tree of faith in the New World. The visionary tree later became a Shaker symbol.

In 1774 Mother Ann, too, had a vision of going to New England where she would be welcomed in a place prepared especially for the Believers. Others also received signs that God intended them to sail for America to establish their new religion. After they decided to follow God's command, they sang and danced until morning.

Anxious to leave, they made hasty plans for their departure. Mother Ann assigned John Hocknell, a well-to-do textile merchant, to arrange their passage. Nine members decided to risk the hazardous ocean voyage. They said farewell to Manchester, journeyed to the port of Liverpool where Hocknell had arranged and paid for the cheapest passage available on the *Mariah*, a leaky vessel that had been condemned as being unfit for sea travel. Captain Smith of New York was the skipper. Hocknell reported

the condition of the ship to Mother Ann. Undaunted, she retorted, "God would not condemn it when we were in it."[20] On May 19, 1774, they set sail for the promised land.

Accompanying Mother Ann were three members of her own family: her recalcitrant husband, Abraham Stanley, who soon "fell away;" her brother William, a spirited young man who had served in the Royal Cavalry; and her niece Nancy Lee. The other five were: John Hocknell, the only man of means in the group; Hocknell's son Richard, who later married Nancy Lee and abandoned the group; James Whittaker, the young man who had the vision and later became Ann's successor; James Shepherd, who had witnessed Ann's marriage to Abraham; and Mary Partington, wife or sister of John Partington, who later joined the movement in America.[21] The Wardleys and other members of the original group decided to remain in England where nothing more was recorded of them.

The voyage was rough and long. As soon as the *Mariah* hit the high seas, Mother Ann organized daily religious services on deck with singing, dancing, praying, preaching, and shouting. At first the sailors looked on the antics with good humor, but when Mother Ann proclaimed the crewmen to be wicked and sinful, they protested. Captain Smith ordered the Shakers to stop their worship immediately. Mother Ann ignored the command saying she took orders only from God. When the services continued, the enraged Captain threatened to lock them up, and if they still persisted, throw them overboard.

Shaker testimonies claimed that God intervened. A violent storm arose, and the ship began to leak when a plank in the hold broke loose. Water poured in faster than the crew could pump it out. The Captain "turned pale as a corpse," but Mother Ann assured him, "Captain, be of good cheer. There shall not a hair of our heads perish. We shall all arrive safe to America. I just now saw two bright angels of God standing by the mast, through whom I received this promise."[22]

Mother Ann and her companions joined the sailors at the pumps. Soon a huge wave struck the ship forcing the loose plank back into place. The *Mariah* was saved! Divine intervention, the Shakers claimed. The rest of the voyage was uneventful, and Captain Smith did not interfere with their worship again.

After almost three months at sea, the *Mariah*

sailed into New York harbor. On a warm Sunday afternoon, August 6, 1774, the nine passengers stepped onto American soil. New York seemed inviting, a world apart from dreary Manchester. Mother Ann knew that among New York's 20,000 inhabitants they would find a place to lodge.

She confidently led her band up Broad Way, turned the corner into what was then Queen Street. They came to a stop before a house where a woman sat cooling herself on the front steps. Mother Ann called to the woman, addressing her by name. "I am commissioned of the Almighty God to preach the everlasting Gospel to America," she said, "and an Angel commanded me to come to this house, and to make a home for me and my people."[23]

Whatever the surprised woman on the steps replied was not recorded, but the Cunninghams did take in the travelers temporarily until they found employment. Ann and Abraham stayed on with the family for over a year, Ann doing menial tasks, Abraham assisting his landlord as a blacksmith. Mother Ann longed to gather her flock together in one place, but they had scattered and were earning such meager wages that none could afford to buy any property. When they did meet, Ann assured them that God would reward them for their faithfulness and endurance.

The winter of 1775 proved to be especially difficult for Mother Ann. She and her husband were no longer able to stay with the Cunninghams, perhaps because of Abraham's heavy drinking and his violent outbursts when his wife refused to sleep with him. When Abraham became severely ill, Ann nursed him day and night until he regained his health. He then "began to associate with the wicked at public houses, and soon lost all sense and feeling of religion, and began to oppose Mother Ann's testimony in a very ungodly manner, and urged her to renounce it, and live in sexual cohabitation, like the rest of the world."[24]

When Ann refused, Abraham threatened to bring a "lewd woman" into the house to satisfy his needs. Mother Ann had no intention of sinning in bed, so Abraham left and went off with the other woman. Whether Ann and Abraham's unsuitable marriage of thirteen years was dissolved officially was never known. Mother Ann, penniless, ill, and dejected, lived alone in a barren unheated room with "a cold stone for a seat, and her only morsel a cruse of vinegar."[25]

Put Your Hands to Work and Your Hearts to God.

A buoyant and resilient person, Mother Ann soon recovered. She and her flock planned their next move.

New York was not a city for British citizens, even pacifists, to feel secure. Colonial patriotism was running high after the skirmishes at Lexington and Concord. In June 1775 the British army achieved a more decisive, but costly, victory at the Battle of Bunker Hill in Boston. The colonists' hatred for the British led to increasing acts of violence against the Loyalists, or Tories.

It was time for Mother Ann and her followers, who opposed war of any kind, to find a safer and more hospitable place to establish their American Millennial Church. John Hocknell again came to the rescue. He had found a promising piece of land that lay in the wilderness about eight miles northwest of Albany in Watervliet township. The Indians called it "Niskeyuna," or "where the water flows."

To secure enough money to lease the land, Hocknell, then seventy years old, sailed to England, sold his property, and returned to America with his profits, his wife Hannah, and his friend John Partington. In the meantime, James Whittaker and William Lee had cleared land at Niskeyuna and erected a crude log cabin to house the group.

Mother Ann and her flock left war-torn New York City sometime in the spring of 1776. It took them three days to travel on a sloop up the Hudson River from New York to Albany. They were happy to be leaving for a place of their own, no matter what were to be the future hardships. They departed just in time. In angry response to the colonial Declaration of Independence adopted on July 4, 1776, General Howe marched his British troops into New York City while his brother, Lord Howe, sailed his frigates to the mouth of the Hudson River to divide the colonies.

Niskeyuna offered the Shakers their first chance to practice communal living. The *sisters* were assigned to quarters on the first floor, the *brothers* climbed to an attic loft above. Husbands and wives did not sleep together.

The first months at Niskeyuna tested the mettle of even the most devout Believers. The food supply was short, but insects and snakes from the numerous swamps were in abundance. Illness struck often, and there was the back-breaking work of draining marshes, felling trees, tilling land, planting crops, and erecting buildings. As Mother Ann labored alongside the others, she admonished them to put their hands to work and their hearts to God. This became her oft-repeated watchword.

The closest neighbors were the Mahican Indians, known for their hatred of the Mohawks and the white settlers who occupied their land. One day Mother Ann decided to pay them a call. The Indians were no doubt astonished to see this plain, short, stocky, white woman with the sharp blue eyes, engaging smile, and dignified manner, sit down with them to smoke the peace pipe. The Mahicans called her the "Good Woman" and thereafter brought gifts of food to the hard-pressed colony. The Indians also taught their white neighbors the skills of wilderness survival—how to raise corn, tap maples for syrup, weave baskets, make herbal medicines, trap animals for food, and fish through the ice.

The Shakers welcomed the attention of the Mahicans, but as time went on, the Believers became discouraged when their church attracted no new members to their wilderness settlement. Mother Ann constantly propped up sagging spirits with her cheerful message. "O my dear children," she urged, "hold fast, and be not discouraged. God has not sent us into this land in vain; but he has sent us to bring the gospel to this nation, who are deeply lost in sin; and there are great numbers who will embrace it, and the time draws nigh."[26]

Mother Ann believed that a strict regimen of hard work was tonic for depression, but she also knew that their souls needed revitalizing. She prescribed daily and sometimes hourly intervals for worship. Every evening she conducted prayer sessions, where the Believers could shed their weariness and despondency in exalted singing and dancing. Unlike the Puritans who forbade "sinful song and dance," the Shakers regarded these expressions of jubilation as gifts from God. They chanted, shouted, sang, and gyrated in dances that later became formal rhythmic step-dances and group movements where men and women marched forward and back in separate lines, circling, twirling, bending, but never touching.

Mother Ann had organized her American colony under the established Shaker belief in Christ's Second Coming, confession of sins, and celibacy. In accordance with her new visions, Ann advocated there should be no privately owned property, no bearing of arms, and no inequality of men and women.

She preached the benefits of leading the simple life. There should be no indulgence in showy clothing or furnishings, no waste of food or resources. She insisted on cleanliness and orderliness. "There is no dirt in heaven," she said. Members should be humble, charitable to the poor and needy, kind to each other, and respectful of all people. She admonished her flock to be strong of character and frugal. "Do all your work," she said, "as though you had a thousand years to live, and as you would if you knew you must die tomorrow."[27] Mother Ann's philosophy of living the simple life became the standard for all the Shaker settlements that flourished following her death.

After three years of hardship and discouragement at Niskeyuna, even Mother Ann succumbed to spells of depression when she cried out, "O that the fishes of the sea, and the fowls of the air and all things that live and breathe, yea, all the trees of the forest and grass of the fields would pray to God for me."[28] But her spirits revived when in her visions she saw great throngs of converts coming to Niskeyuna. To be prepared, she advised her followers to lay up a large store of supplies.

A Large Sacrifice, But Great Rewards.

In 1779 in the two border towns of New Lebanon, New York, and Hancock, Massachusetts, there flourished a New Light Baptist revivalist movement led by the Reverend Joseph Meacham, forty-two, a fiery lay preacher from Connecticut, and the Reverend Samuel Johnson, a former Presbyterian minister at New Lebanon. After a time their revivalism lost its appeal for a number of members. When two disenchanted men visited Niskeyuna, they were received warmly, given immediate assurance of salvation, and to their astonishment met a remarkable female leader who appeared to be the realization of the Second Coming.

The men hurried back to New Lebanon to tell Meacham and Johnson of their discovery. The ministers were skeptical—how could this female in the backwoods be the embodiment of the spirit of Christ and the preacher of the Millenium? Meacham dispatched Calvin Harlow, one of his most reliable friends, to Niskeyuna to challenge Mother Ann's credibility and ask specific questions designed to expose her as a fraud. When Harlow confronted Mother Ann, he quoted St. Paul's words forbidding women to speak in church and chastised her saying,

"... you not only speak, but seem to be an Elder in your Church. How do you reconcile this with the Apostle's doctrine?"[29]

Mother Ann answered with a parable likening the authority given her to the structure existing in the family. She reasoned:

> The man is the first, and the woman the second in the government of the family. He is the father and she the mother; and all the children, both male and female, must be subject to the parents; and the woman being second, must be subject to her husband, who is the first; but when the man is gone, the right of government belongs to the woman: So is the family of Christ.[30]

Apparently Harlow was convinced. A few weeks after he had reported to Meacham, the Reverend, himself, accompanied by two brethren traveled to Niskeyuna to see for themselves.

When they arrived, they were greeted cordially and fed. Then Meacham directed sharp interrogations to young James Whittaker whom Mother Ann had wisely appointed to be her spokesperson. Whittaker, despite his youth and lack of formal education, answered Meacham's questions directly and convincingly. He asserted the Shaker philosophy—it was possible for humans to live perfect lives free from sin, thereby attaining eternal rewards here on earth.

Meacham challenged, "Are *you* perfect? Do *you* live without sin?" Whittaker replied without hesitation, "The Power of God does enable souls to cease from sin; and we have received that power. We have actually left off committing sin, and we live in daily obedience to the will of God."[31]

Mother Ann could no longer hold her silence. She apprised the visitors of the Shaker requirements for attaining true godliness: celibacy, total self-denial, confession of sins, work, worship, prayer, and simple living that forsook all worldliness. The sacrifice was large, she said, but the reward, true unity with God, was great.

Meacham was convinced. He became Mother Ann's first American convert, whom she called her "first-born son." From then on he worked tirelessly to bring in others, the first being his own wife, children, father, and relatives. He later became the first American leader of the movement.

Soon the throngs of converts envisioned by Mother Ann began to appear. There were people from all walks of life—some common folk, some distinguished individuals. The Reverend Samuel Johnson, the Presbyterian minister and Yale graduate, came with his wife Elizabeth. George Darrow, a wealthy farmer, joined. Couples came, willing to give up married cohabitation. Children were especially welcome because there would be no increase in the fold except by conversion or adoption.

Women were drawn to the sect for apparent reasons—they could escape undesirable marriages forced upon them, and there would be no painful child-bearing. They were accepted as equals to the men, a status not afforded them in other faiths and in society.

Curious people flocked to Niskeyuna to inquire of this strange wilderness phenomenon and to see the female whose disciples called her "an angel of glory" and "a glorious inhabitant of the heavenly world, singing praises to God."[32] Even to skeptical eyes, Ann had a solemnity about her that "inspired confidence and commanded respect. . . . she appeared to possess a degree of dignified beauty and heavenly love, which they had never before discovered among mortals."[33] Unfortunately Mother Ann's physical likeness was never captured on canvas by an artist because such self-adulation was forbidden.

On May 10, 1780, a meteorological event, no doubt a solar eclipse which has been historically documented, hastened the Shaker cause. With no clouds in the sky, the sun disappeared and caused a "dark day." Issacher Bates, a Revolutionary War fifer, who later joined the Shakers, described it:

> That day was as dark as night—no work could be done in any house, without a candle! and the night following was as dark accordingly, although there was a well grown Moon. . . . The people were out wringing their hands, and howling, 'the day of judgment is come!'—for darkness covered the whole face of the land of New England!

> And what next!—Right on the back of this—On came the Shakers! and that made it darker yet—for they testified, that an end was come on them; and proved it, by their life of seperation (sic) from the course of this world; and by the wicked persecutions they endured, from this adulterous generation.[34]

The panic of the dark day signalling the Millennium, the rumors of the strange woman at Niskeyuna, and the stories of the wild antics of the converts began to worry citizens and officials in neighboring villages. "Witchcraft!" they cried.

The "Grand Actress" in Prison.

In other parts of New England, the war was raging and colonists were fearful of British spies in their midst. The Shakers, being English, were viewed with suspicion. In early July 1780 Albany patriots attacked David Darrow, a New Lebanon farmer, and Joseph Meacham as they drove sheep to Niskeyuna to ease the food shortage. The two men were accused of supplying food to the British troops stationed along the Hudson River. The sheep were divided up among the attackers, and Darrow and Meacham were thrown into jail at the Old Fort at Albany.

A short time later the Albany commissioners issued a warrant for the arrest of Mother Ann, William Lee, Mary Partington, and several others. All were brought to Albany, questioned about their loyalty to the American cause, and ordered to take an oath of allegiance. When they refused saying that all wars were evil and they would not bear arms, they were thrown into jail. The charge was treason!

Mother Ann, the "grand actress" as she was mockingly called, was sent south to a Poughkeepsie jail for a possible exchange with the British for an American prisoner. Mary Partington, who had been released from the Albany jail, accompanied her, and Mary Hocknell joined them later. Both women administered to their leader during her imprisonment.

James Boyd, an influential sympathizer, managed to secure the release of Mother Ann to his custody. At Boyd's private home Mother Ann used every opportunity to recruit converts and conduct services, arousing anger in the neighborhood.

The irate patriots, disguised as Indians, surrounded the Boyd house, tried to throw bags of gunpowder through the window into the fireplace. When that failed, they attempted unsuccessfully to throw powder down the chimney. To maintain order, the Poughkeepsie officials sent Mother Ann back to the jailhouse.

Meanwhile at Albany the other prisoners were judged "infatuated," but harmless. They were released one by one to the care of various relatives who vouched for them and posted bond of 200 pounds each. Mother Ann, however, was kept in prison at Poughkeepsie, still considered a religious fanatic and a danger to the American cause.

When William Lee and James Whittaker were released from jail, they made several unsuccessful attempts to secure Mother Ann's freedom. As a last resort Whittaker went directly to George Clinton, the illustrious Governor of New York. On bended knee and with great passion, Whittaker related the plight of Mother Ann's imprisonment and begged the Governor to order her release. Clinton claimed no knowledge of the affair, and being a firm believer in religious freedom and embarrassed by her long incarceration, ordered Mother Ann's immediate release. In early December James Whittaker and William Lee posted the 200 pound bond and vouched "for her good Behaviour and not saying or consenting to any Matters or Things inconsistent with the Peace and safety of this the United States."[35] After her five month imprisonment, Mother Ann and her companions returned to a joyful celebration at Niskeyuna.

Ann Lee, Satan in Disguise.

News of Mother Ann's imprisonment traveled fast. Those colonists, who themselves had come to America to escape religious persecution, claimed she had been wrongly-treated. The followers at Niskeyuna were outraged at this miscarriage of justice in a country that was fighting for freedom and personal rights. But Mother Ann chided them, "You can never enter into the Kingdom of God with hardness against anyone, for God is love, and if you love God you will love one another."[36]

Curious visitors journeyed to Niskeyuna (or Watervliet) to see this woman who had been wronged and to learn of her strange religion. Each caller was greeted warmly at the new frame building that served as a residence and meetinghouse. If they wished, they could participate in the ecstatic worship service. Some guests found themselves hypnotized by the wild enthusiasm; others were repulsed. A Baptist minister from Pittsfield, Massachusetts wrote:

> When they meet together for their worship, they fall a-groaning and trembling, and every one acts alone for himself; one will fall prostrate on the floor, another on his knees and his head in his hands. . . . Some will be singing, each one his own tune; some without words, in an Indian tune, some sing jig tunes, some tunes of their own making, in an unknown mutter, which they call new tongues; some will be dancing, and others stand laughing, heartily and loudly; others will be drumming on the floor with their feet, as though a pair of drum-sticks were beating a ruff on a drum-head; others will be agonizing, as though they were in great pain; others

jumping up and down; others fluttering over somebody, and talking to them; others will be shooing and hissing evil spirits out of the house, . . . [making] a perfect bedlam; this they call the worship of God.[37]

Within the Shaker community there were those who became disenchanted, finding the experience too demanding, too extreme, or too sexually restrictive. Some withdrew from the sect peacefully; others hurled vitriolic accusations. One of the latter was the Reverend Valentine Rathbun, a Baptist minister from Connecticut, who had become incensed by the Shaker antics and beliefs. In a scurrilous pamphlet entitled "Some Brief Hints on a Religious Scheme Taught and Propagated by a Number of Europeans Living in a Place Called Nisquenia, in the State of New York" Rathbun wrote, "Shakerism is a religion of bluff and its adherents are fanatics." He then described the jumping, groaning, singing, and talking in tongues. He accused Shaker women of dancing naked in the woods pretending to be angels. He further wrote, "I am convinced the spirit which prevails over this new scheme is the spirit of witchcraft! . . . Ann Lee is Satan in the guise of a sweet angel of light."[38]

Mary Hocknell answered Rathbun's charges of naked dancing. She explained that in hot weather men and women often removed *some* of their warm clothing as they moved about.

Years after Mother Ann's death, a disillusioned Shaker, Mary Marshall Dyer, sued the United Society of Believers for the loss of her husband, children, and property. In inflammatory publications she charged that the Shakers were obsessed with sex, and she accused the founder, Mother Ann, with sadism, prostitution, and drunkenness. Dyer further claimed that Mother Ann tortured and abused children. Dyer's charges were judged to be unfounded, and she lost the case.

Over the years the bizarre nature of Shaker religious observances have been documented, analyzed, and scrutinized by authorities of Shaker culture. During her lifetime Mother Ann remained charitable toward the skeptics who viewed her as a fanatic. She insisted that one should always counter hate with love.

Spread the Word.

By the spring of 1781 requests for "laboring and witnessing" poured into Niskeyuna. Mother Ann decided that the time was ripe to take her message out of the wilderness to the settlements in New England.

She chose her brother William Lee, Elder James Whittaker, John Farington, James Shepherd, Samuel Fitch, Margaret Leeland, and Mary Partington to accompany her on what promised to be a two-year mission. On May 31, 1781, Mother Ann, then forty-five years old, set out on horseback with her seven companions.

After a day's journey, they stopped at a small village in the Berkshires near the Massachusetts border. A few Shaker families had already settled there, and they offered their houses as meeting places. But soon opposition arose. A suspicious preacher led his parishioners to a home meeting intending to disrupt it. Elder Whittaker interceded, and violence was avoided.

The missionaries moved on to Enfield, Connecticut, to the home of David Meacham, brother of Joseph Meacham. Here they were accused of spreading witchcraft. Next they traveled northward to Harvard, Massachusetts, a hamlet twenty-five miles northwest of Boston. Mother Ann hoped to establish a community in what appeared to be a peaceful rural setting. Despite strong opposition they were able to purchase Square House, so named because of its flat roof. The house had once belonged to the Reverend Shadrack Ireland, a New Light Baptist preacher, who claimed to be immortal. When Ireland died and failed to rise on the third day, his disillusioned disciples joined the Shakers. However, Ireland's "ghost" haunted Square House until Mother Ann exorcised and banished his spirit from the place.

No sooner were they settled at Square House than rumors spread that the Shakers had come with a large supply of firearms. Rathbun's pamphlet had circulated widely and was inflaming the citizens. Area clergymen organized to stamp out this dangerous fanaticism. A town committee was formed "to remove the people called Shaking Quakers who are collected in this town." Accompanied by the town militia, they marched to Square House to bring their charges. Elder James Whittaker requested permission to speak:

> I understand that you have heard that we have weapons of war here, and are apprehensive that we are enemies of the country; we are harmless, inoffensive people; we do not want to injure any man either in person or property; we want no man's silver or gold, but only their souls to God; this is all we want of anyone; but if you believe those reports, you may have free liberty

to search the house, or barn, or any of these surrounding buildings.[39]

Some of the protesters were satisfied and left; others stayed for further argument. Whittaker then used the opportunity to speak to them of religious matters. A few listened and were moved to convert.

For two years Square House was the center of Mother Ann's activities. She met with scores of men and women who traveled to Harvard to learn of the new religion. People with maladies came and hoped she would cure them. During this period Mother Ann and her party often traveled from Harvard to nearby villages to preach and proselytize. Curious crowds gathered at the meetings, but not everyone was ready to hear a female preach to them on the evils of sex and lusts of the flesh. Some even suggested that she was not a woman at all, but a man parading as one.

In December 1782 at Petersham, Massachusetts, a "company of lewd fellows" plotted to kidnap Mother Ann to find out if she really was a woman. Testimonies given in 1816 tell a lurid story:

> They immediately seized her by the feet, and inhumanly dragged her, feet foremost, out of the house, and threw her into a sleigh, with as little ceremony as they would the dead carcase (sic) of a beast, and drove off, committing at the same, acts of inhumanity and indecency which even savages would be ashamed of.
>
> In the struggle . . . [she] had her clothes torn in a shameful manner. Their preference was to find out whether she was a woman or not.
>
> Father William, feeling great concern for Mother's safety, . . . and David Hammond, followed the sleigh. He told the ruffians that she was his sister, and he would follow her; and attempting to hold on by the hind part of the sleigh, they gave him many blows with the butts of their sleigh-whips. He and David, however, followed to the aforementioned tavern. Elder James, being badly wounded, was not able to follow them.[40]

When Father William and David Hammond arrived at the tavern, they protested the unlawful behavior of the drunken hoodlums. Mother Ann was released as soon as David promised not to prosecute them. As William and David brought her back to safety, she sang for joy to be once again with her children. It was reported that disaster and ill fortune later plagued the "ruffians" who had persecuted her.

Other atrocities followed. At Harvard a mob surrounded Square House, dragged the praying Shakers to the street, and drove them like cattle to Lancaster ten miles away. On the road James Shepherd was brutally beaten and another Shaker, Abijah Worster, was tied to a sycamore tree and horsewhipped. Mother Ann was away from Harvard so escaped this brutality, but she suffered other trials as she and her friends traveled to towns in Massachusetts and Connecticut. She returned to Harvard the first part of May 1783.

In June when the Shakers were again set upon, James Whittaker was lashed so severely that his back was "all in a gore of blood, and his flesh bruised to jelly."[41] Wiliam Lee was also harshly beaten. Both men suffered from the blows the rest of their lives. A stone slab marked the place where Whittaker was beaten. The inscription read: "On this spot a Shaker was whiped [sic] by a mob for religious views in 1783."[42]

The Good Woman Is Come!

In July 1783 Mother Ann and her friends left inhospitable Harvard to journey home to Niskeyuna. The trip back was not entirely peaceful. At Lebanon, just across the border into New York, Mother Ann was seized and brought to court again. As the judge looked on, the constable struck her across the breast causing an injury she carried until her death. After her friends posted bond, the judge released her, but did nothing to prevent a crowd from barring her mount into her carriage. Her friends again rescued her, and the group proceeded on its way.

At the Albany ferry she was welcomed by the friendly Mahicans who cried, "The Good Woman is come!" It was quite different from the greeting given her by some Christian New Englanders. The party arrived at Niskeyuna at 11:00 P.M. on September 4, 1783, a day after the peace treaty was signed ending the American Revolution. They had been gone two years and four months.

Though she never regained her robust health, Mother Ann continued her work at Niskeyuna, preaching and receiving visitors. By this time her reputation had spread through much of New England, even to reach the ears of the Frenchman General Marquis de LaFayette. The General, long interested in mysticism, went to Niskeyuna to inquire of this strange religion and its female leader. LaFayette and

Mother Ann had little in common, but they held some similar beliefs—freedom of expression and worship, abolition of slavery, and equality of the sexes. But LaFayette was a man of war who fought for his convictions; Mother Ann was a woman of peace who sought change through love and worship.

On July 21, 1784, one year after the return to Niskeyuna, Mother Ann's brother William, then forty-four, died. He had been a robust young man, but the physical abuse he suffered while traveling had shortened his life. Mother Ann grieved over the loss of her beloved sibling who had been a faithful and devout disciple.

After her travels to New England, Mother Ann's health failed, and she had premonitions of her own death. "Brother William is gone," she said, "and it will soon be said of me that I am gone, too."[43] She used her final days to advise, encourage, and direct the future of her children.

Mother Ann, forty-eight, died on September 8, 1784, between midnight and one o'clock in the morning, less than two months after her brother's death. Before she died, she had a vision. "I see Brother William, coming in a golden chariot to take me home," she said. John Hocknell had a similar vision. He reported that "when the breath left her body he saw in vision a golden chariot, drawn by four white horses which received and wafted her soul out of his sight."[44]

On September 9 *The Albany Gazette* published Mother Ann's obituary. It read: "Departed this life, at Nisquenia, Sept. 7, Mrs. Lee, known by the appelation [sic] of the Elect *Lady* or *Mother of Zion*, and head of that people called Shakers. Her funeral is to be attended this day."[45]

In Shaker tradition her followers celebrated Mother Ann's departure, not to death, but to glory where she was one with Christ. Brother Abijah Worster built her a simple wooden coffin "devoid of decoration," and Brother Eleazer Rand helped dig her grave. She was buried in the Shaker cemetery in a shady grove near a stream. A plain marble tombstone bore the inscription:

MOTHER
ANN LEE
BORN IN MANCHESTER
ENGLAND.
FEB. 29, 1736.
DIED IN WATERVLIET N.Y.
SEPT. 8, 1784.[46]

After Mother Ann.

Mother Ann's death was a shock to many followers. Some had believed her to be immortal, that her ministry would never end. When she died, they were disillusioned.

Young James Whittaker, then only thirty-three, was formally installed as the new leader. He was a gifted preacher and a dynamic mover who was determined to keep alive the spirit of Mother Ann. However, James Shepherd and John Partington refused to serve under him because they considered him too fanatical and demanding.

For almost three years Father Whittaker worked tirelessly to strengthen the scattered Shaker communities. In October 1785 the New Lebanon Shakers built the first structure to be used specifically as a meeting-house. Here Whittaker served as the principal preacher for a year. He then took to the roads to visit the New England settlements following a regimen so strenuous that his health, already weakened by earlier brutalities, failed. He died in July 1787 at the age of thirty-six.

Leadership then passed to forty-six-year-old Joseph Meacham, the skeptic who had come to Niskeyuna full of doubts about the female leader. Mother Ann called Meacham, "the wisest man that has been born of a woman for six hundred years."[47]

One of Father Joseph's first acts was to elevate Lucy Wright, twenty-eight, a remarkable matron, to female leadership. Mother Ann, upon meeting Lucy for the first time, had commented, "We must save Lucy, if we can, for, if we save her, it will be equal to saving a nation."[48]

Father Joseph and Mother Lucy are credited with giving structure and organization to the Shaker communal societies. Father Joseph, also suffering from earlier tortures, fell ill and died in August 1796. Mother Lucy became the supreme head and carried on alone for the next twenty-five years. During this time new communities were found, membership increased, and religious education became an important part of Shaker life. Mother Lucy died in 1821. She had fulfilled Mother Ann's assessment of her outstanding abilities.

New Shaker communities were established in New York, the New England states, Ohio, Kentucky, and Indiana. Shaker membership reached its peak between 1830 and 1850 under the leadership of Elder Frederick Evans when some 6,000 members owned collectively over

100,000 acres of land in nineteen communities and ten missions. By 1909 membership had fallen to 1,000; by 1930 only 100 members remained. In 1988 only two elderly Shaker sisters still lived at Canterbury, New Hampshire, and a few at Sabbathday Lake, Maine. Some Shaker villages have been preserved as historic landmarks and tourist attractions.

The decline of Shakerism can be attributed to a number of social and economic factors. Because the Shakers could increase their membership only through conversion of adults and adoption of children, theirs was a society destined to decrease in numbers. In later years they suffered from weakened leadership and financial mismanagement. The Shaker philosophy of communal living and sharing the fruits of one's labors did not have popular appeal. Sacrifice for one's convictions was not attractive, nor was giving up marital relations and bearing children. In addition many Americans preferred the exciting opportunities in the West or financial success in the East to life in the seclusion of a remote community. Women were becoming increasingly independent, no longer looking for shelter and protection.

Ironically, the United Society of Believers, noted for frugality, simplicity, and religious dedications, gained acceptance through their material successes. Recognition came because of their industry, their excellence, ingenuity, craftsmanship, orderliness, artistry, and creativity. Today they are credited with numerous inventions; their architecture and furniture are models of simplicity and efficiency; their songs have inspired choral and orchestral compositions; they have made important contributions to American folk art; their textiles and weavings have long been admired.

Undeniably Mother Ann was a controversial figure with her messianic proclamations and her obsession with lusts of the flesh. To make a reasonably accurate summation of her life, one must strike a balance somewhere between the hostile denouncements of her detractors and the effusive testimonials of her defenders. Mother Ann left no records of her own—the story of her life and the words she spoke were preserved by her followers some thirty-five years after her death.

Although Mother Ann was a charismatic woman who demonstrated her convictions in a revolutionary manner that aroused much resentment and skepticism, her philosophy has affected secular society to the present time. She founded a creative religious community whose culture and theology is still admired and studied today. She and the early Quakers were among the first to advocate conscientious objection to war. Despite the indignities heaped upon her during her lifetime, she elevated the status of women in general. Mother Ann preached that men and women were equal in God's sight at a time when females were totally subordinate to males. She could be called a precursor of the feminist movement in America.

How did this poor illiterate woman from Toad Lane in Manchester, England, manage to draw so much hostility and adulation during her lifetime and after her death? How could she remain forgiving and resolute despite the hatred and opposition that plagued her? The answer appears to be that Ann Lee was a spirit-filled woman acting on what she considered divine authority. She was infused with a calling from God, and she obeyed the call regardless of the consequences. Though her life had been one of poverty, adversity, and misfortune, her faith remained unshaken to the end.

After Mother Ann's death, the Shakers experienced many changes, but their fundamental beliefs remained true to those of the founder. Mother Ann had a noble dream of a new Eden where love would reign. An old Shaker hymn preserves her dream:

> Love, love, is a blessing
> It is worth possessing.
> Mother's love is precious and pure,
> So I will labor for love, love, love,
> Mother's love will always endure.

Notes

1   Flo Morse, *The Shakers and the World's People* (New York: Dodd, Mead & Company, 1980), p. 11.

2   Ibid., p. 18.

3   Edward R. Horgan, *The Shaker Holy Land* (Harvard, Massachusetts: The Harvard Common Press, 1982), p. 200.

4   Edward Deming Andrews, *The People Called Shakers* (New York: Dover Publications, 1963), p. 5.

5   Morse, p. 12.

6   Ibid., p. 11.

7   Ibid., p. 13.

8   Ibid.

9   Ibid.

10 I Corinthians 14: 34, 35.

11 Nardi Campion, *Ann the Word* (Boston: Little, Brown & Co., 1976), p. 23.

12 Stephen A. Marini, *Radical Sects of Revolutionary New England* (Cambridge, Massachusetts: Harvard University Press, 1982), p. 76.

13 Horgan, p. 11.

14 Marini, p. 76.

15 Morse, pp. 14-15.

16 Robley Whitson, ed. *Shakers, Two Centuries of Spiritual Reflection* (New York: Paulist Press, 1983), p. 43.

17 Campion, p. 43.

18 Morse, p. 15.

19 Morse, pp. 19-20.

20 Doris Faber, *The Perfect Life* (New York: Farrar, Straus & Giroux, 1974), p. 26.

21 Henri Desroche, *The American Shakers from Neo-Christianity to Presocialism* (Amherst, Massachusetts: University of Massachusetts Press, 1955), pp. 49-50.

22 Campion, p. 54.

23 Morse, p. 21.

24 Ibid.

25 Campion, p. 62.

26 Andrews, p. 17.

24 Ibid., p. 24.

28 Campion, p. 80.

29 Horgan, p. 15.

30 Ibid.

31 Campion, p. 88.

32 Morse, p. 23.

33 Horgan, p. 16.

34 Morse, p. 22. The date of the *dark day*, May 19, 1780, given in this reference appears to be wrong. Most sources stated the date to be May 10, 1780.

35 Andrews, p. 34.

36 Campion, p. 117.

37 Faber, p. 47.

38 Campion, pp. 120-22.

39 Horgan, p. 26.

40 Morse, p. 28.

41 Horgan, p. 35.

42 Ibid., p. 41.

43 Ibid., p. 36.

44 Ibid.

45 Ibid.

46 Campion, p. 175.

47 Andrews, p. 55.

48 Morse, p. 61.

Chapter 11

Narcissa Prentiss Whitman

(1808 - 1847)

A MISSIONARY TO THE CAYUSE INDIANS IN OLD OREGON AND ONE OF THE
FIRST WHITE WOMEN TO CROSS THE ROCKIES ON THE OVERLAND ROUTE.

AT THE LITTLE Presbyterian Church in Angelica, New York, a rare event followed a congregational meeting held on Thursday evening,
February 18, 1836. The first order of business
was the installation of three elders, one of them
the Honorable Judge Stephen Prentiss, leading
citizen of the town. Next, a letter was read re-
leasing the Judge's daughter Narcissa to go to a
mission somewhere "beyond the Rocky Mountains." Following a communion service came
the ceremony the congregation anticipated.

Narcissa Whitman, almost twenty-eight,
calm and composed, walked to the altar. She
wore her best black bombazine dress of silk twill.
No wedding veil hid her glowing golden hair.
In the pews sat her approving family, all dressed
in black. Beside her stood Dr. Marcus Whitman,
thirty-four, tall, muscular, and tanned from his
recent exploratory expedition to the Rocky
Mountains. As Narcissa repeated the marriage
vows, she not only promised to be a faithful and
loving wife to the doctor, but renounced her
civilized life in New York in exchange for an
unknown future of service to the Indians somewhere on the far side of the continent. She assumed she would never see her beloved family
and friends again.

Brother Hull preached a sermon, one which
Narcissa often read and meditated upon during
the lonely hours in the far west "until the truth
of it burns upon my heart and cheers my soul
with its blessed promise."[1] The congregation
then sang a closing hymn, "Yes, My Native Land!
I Love Thee," a sentimental song commonly
used in farewell services for departing missionaries. The congregation began to sing the hymn
but became so wet-eyed and choked with emotion they could not continue. Only Narcissa's
unwavering soprano "as sweet and musical as
a chime of bells" finished the final verse:

> In the deserts let me labor,
> On the mountains let me tell,
> How he died—the blessed Saviour—

To redeem a world from Hell!
Let me hasten, let me hasten,
Far in heathen lands to dwell.[2]

The following day the bridal couple finished their packing, said their farewells to family and friends in Angelica, and began the first
leg of their journey into the unknown. They
traveled first by sleigh to Ithaca and Rushville,
New York, stopping occasionally to make
speeches and say goodbyes. Then they began
their way across Pennsylvania. On March 15 at
Pittsburgh they booked passage on the steamboat *Siam* which sailed down the Ohio River
at about thirteen miles an hour to the thriving
river town of Cincinnati. There they met the
Rev. Henry Spalding and his wife Eliza, their
comrade missionaries. The two couples then
boarded the *Junius* to sail to Chester, Illinois.
After a layover to avoid traveling on Sunday,
which was against their religion, they took the
Majestic up the Mississippi arriving at St. Louis
on March 29.

Searching for the "Book of Heaven."

In the summer of 1831 four Indians (three
Nez Perces and one Flathead) came to St. Louis
from west of the Rockies with Lucien Fontenelle's American Fur Company caravan. They
were searching for the white man's "Book of
Heaven" and wanted to see General William
Clark (1770-1838).

Clark, formerly of the Lewis and Clark Expedition, was a devout Episcopalian and then
superintendent of Indian affairs in St. Louis.
He listened to the Indians' pleas, talked to them
about the Christian religion, and reported the
visit to William Walker, agent from the Wyan-
dotte Indian reservation in Ohio.

Two of the four Indians died in St. Louis.
The other two, No-Horns-on-His-Head and
Rabbit-Skin-Leggings, began their homeward
journey in the spring of 1832. As they traveled
by steamboat west to the mouth of the Yellow-
stone River, they met George Catlin, the famed
artist of Indian portraits who later painted them
in the beautiful dresses given them earlier by
the friendly Dakotas.[3] Only Rabbit-Skin-Leggings lived to admit to his tribe that he had failed
to bring back the Book of Heaven. He never
knew what were the fruits of his trip to St. Louis.

Some time later Walker wrote to his friend,
Gabriel Disosway, a New York merchant who
had an interest in the Methodist Missionary

Society, telling him of the Indians' visit. The
letter soon found its way to New York City where
on March 1, 1833, it was published in *The Christian Advocate and Journal*. Citizens read that the
"red savages" of the Rocky Mountains were crying for missionaries to teach them the Word
and the Way. More articles appeared in religious
journals throughout the states and in Europe.
Preachers cried from their pulpits, "Can we ig-
nore the heathen who come knocking at our
very doors?" Immediately the message, coupled
with frontier romantics, stirred the hearts and
emotions of Christians and ignited the missionary torch.

The Methodist Church lost no time in re-
sponding to the appeal. Dr. Wilbur Fisk, an
influential Methodist and president of Wesleyan
University in Middleton, Connecticut, began to
solicit funds. In July 1833 the Methodist Missionary Society appointed the Rev. Jason Lee as "missionary to the Flathead Indians."

After an exhaustive overland journey with
a fur brigade, Lee and his companions arrived
at Fort Vancouver on the Columbia River on
September 15, 1834. Lee did not locate his mission in the isolated Flathead mountain country,
but chose instead a pleasant location at French
Prairie on the Willamette River.

Lee's appointment paved the way for more
Protestant missions to be sent to Old Oregon.
Dr. Samuel Parker, who had served both Congregational and Presbyterian churches, read the
articles in *The Christian Advocate* and volunteered to go "beyond the Rocky Mountains to
establish a mission among the Flathead Indians,
or some other tribe."[4]

Parker applied to the American Board of
Commissioners for Foreign Missions, the first
foreign missionary board in the United States
established first in 1810 by the Congregation-
alists, joined later by the Presbyterians. "Foreign
missions" included service to any non-English
speaking people.

At first Samuel Parker's request was rejected because he was considered too old at age
fifty-four, and he had a wife and three children
to consider. Besides, the American Board was
reluctant to appear to be competing in the mission field with the Methodists, an unnecessary
concern considering the vastness of Old Oregon.
When Samuel offered to raise his own funds
and find recruits, the Board reconsidered.

Parker went on a speaking tour through
small villages and towns to promote mission
work and raise money. At Wheeler, New York,

a young doctor, Marcus Whitman, heard Parker's impassioned request for volunteers and decided to offer himself. Parker then brought his message to Amity, New York. Among those gathered in the log schoolhouse was Narcissa Prentiss, daughter of a distinguished judge. Narcissa had long dreamed of being a missionary and asked Parker, "Is there a place for an unmarried female in my Lord's vineyard?"[5]

When Parker posed the question to the American Board, he received a reply from its secretary, "I don't think we have missions among the Indians where unmarried females are valuable just now."[6] While Marcus Whitman was soon approved by the Board to assist Samuel Parker on an exploratory trip to the Rockies, Narcissa's rejection led her to further decisions.

Early Consecration to Missionary Work.

Narcissa Prentiss was born in Prattsburg, New York, on March 14, 1808, a year which found Thomas Jefferson in the Presidency, seventeen states in the Union and about six and a half million people in the country. During her lifetime eight other presidents served in office, and before she died, twelve more states had joined the Union and about fifteen million more citizens had been added to the population.

The first Prentiss home soon proved too small for the growing family that eventually numbered nine children. In the larger house built by her father, Narcissa, the third child and the oldest daughter, often cared for her two younger brothers and four younger sisters. She was particularly close to her sisters Jane and Harriet.

Stephen Prentiss, Narcissa's father, came from five generations of New Englanders, all descendants of Henry Prentice (later changed to Prentiss), who emigrated from England some time before 1640. After Stephen Prentiss, a sturdy heavy-set man, married Clarissa Ward, they moved to Prattsburg in Steuben County in western New York. Here Prentiss farmed, operated a sawmill and a gristmill, did carpentry, and ran a distillery until he closed it fearing the temptations it offered his sons. For a time he served as Probate Judge earning him the honored title of Judge Prentiss.

Although not as religious as his wife, Stephen Prentiss joined the Presbyterian Church where he directed the choir. For a time he left the Presbyterians to join the Methodists who looked more kindly on his affiliation with the Freemasons, but soon he rejoined his family at the Presbyterian Church.

Narcissa's mother, Clarissa, came from Puritan stock. She was a serious woman never "given to laughter" which she considered especially inappropriate on Sundays. Her queenly demeanor, sterling Christian character, intelligence, and gifted conversation brought her great respect in the church and community. Narcissa inherited many of her mother's qualities, but unlike her mother, Narcissa developed a zest for life and a robust sense of humor.

From birth Narcissa was a child of the church. When she was four months old, she was baptized at the Prattsburg Church, and through her early life she listened patiently to lengthy Sunday sermons. At age eleven she made a public confession at a revival meeting. Five years later at another service she dedicated herself to missionary work.

Narcissa was particularly fond of reading to her mother from weighty tomes perhaps borrowed from the pastor. She also loved to sing with a soprano voice that rang clear and strong in the church choir. Years later her singing charmed the Cayuse Indians at the mission at Waiilatpu. She wrote, "I was not aware that singing was a qualification of so much importance to a missionary."[7]

Narcissa's girlhood was filled with many happy hours. Young people and visiting clergy often gathered at her home causing her mother to complain of all the company. Family activities revolved around the church, and Narcissa was always willing to sing, serve, and witness.

The Franklin Academy in Prattsburg, opened in 1824 as an all-male school, had become coeducational three years later due in part to the influence of Judge Prentiss, a trustee of the school. His daughter, Narcissa, was one of the twenty-eight women enrolled during the first term at the Academy. During her second term she met Henry Harmon Spalding, then twenty-eight, who had tried to live down his illegitimate birth and his unstable and abusive boyhood. Narcissa, in sympathy for Henry and his unfortunate background, befriended him and helped him with his spiritual problems and academic limitations. During the course of their association, Henry fell in love with his vivacious tutor and dared to propose that together they should bring God to the heathen. Narcissa refused him, a rejection that Henry, a bitter loser, never forgave or forgot.

In spite of a promise to Judge Prentiss that

he would hold no animosity toward Narcissa in their missionary venture, Spalding's resentment of Narcissa was often evident as he traveled west and opened missions in Old Oregon with the Whitmans. In October 1840 Narcissa wrote to her father from the mission, "The man who came with us is one who never ought to have come. My dear husband has suffered more from him in consequence of his wicked jealousy, and his great pique toward me, than can be known in this world."[8]

After Narcissa completed her work at the Franklin Academy, she attended Mrs. Emma Willard's prestigious Female Seminary at Troy, New York, an institution specializing in teacher training. She then taught school for several years, and her pupils recalled that she had been an inspiring teacher. But school teaching was not what she had in mind for her life, not when there were mission fields calling. Unfortunately single females were not wanted, so she was forced to find another way. Enter Marcus Whitman.

A Doctor on Horseback.

By birth Marcus Whitman (1802-1847) had inherited the right ancestry to prepare him for a life of dedication and adventure. Born in Rushville, New York, the third child of Beza and Alice Whitman, he was a seventh generation descendant of John Whitman who sometime before 1638 had emigrated from England to John Winthrop's Massachusetts Bay Colony. All of John Whitman's progeny were moral, stable characters with honorable trades and professions. The Whitmans had strong church inclinations, and most harbored anti-British sentiments. Somewhere in the distant past Marcus Whitman and Abraham Lincoln could claim the same lineage.

In 1799 Beza Whitman (1773-1810), Marcus' father, and his wife Alice had moved with their first son Augustus to Canandaigua, a frontier settlement in the Finger Lakes area in western New York. After the death of their second son, they moved to Rushville, New York, where they settled in a crude log cabin. Here their third son Marcus was born on September 4, 1802. While an infant, Marcus barely escaped death when a log rolled from the fireplace and ignited his cradle. His mother, who had stepped into her husband's tiny shoe shop nearby, rushed back just in time to save the sleeping baby. Later there were three more children born to Beza and Alice.

Beza Whitman, a paradigm of industry, soon built a large frame house that provided space for his tanning and shoemaking business and allowed him to open a tavern. He also acquired forty acres of land costing $450, a substantial amount at that time. But Beza didn't have many years to enjoy his success. He died in April 1810 at the age of thirty-seven.

Alice Green (1777-1857), Marcus' mother, also a descendant from a long line of New England stock, had married Beza Whitman in March 1797. Alice was a determined woman, though not particularly religious, a state that worried Marcus during his entire lifetime. Industry was her religion, and laziness was a cardinal sin.

When Beza died, Alice could not support her five children, all under the age of twelve. Marcus, just turned eight, was sent to live with his Uncle Freedom Whitman and his wife Sally in Massachusetts. Also in the household was Grandfather Samuel Whitman, an austere widower with one blind eye. Freedom and Samuel, both pious Baptists, gave Marcus "constant religious instruction and care."

When he was thirteen, Marcus returned for the first time to Rushville where he found his mother married to Calvin Loomis, who had carried on Beza Whitman's enterprises. There were three half-brothers with whom Marcus developed little contact.

For the next five years Marcus lived in Plainfield, Massachusetts, with Colonel John Packard. Here he attended the school of the Reverend Moses Hallock, the local Congregational minister, along with schoolmate William Cullen Bryant. Whitman recalled later that he had learned "the english Branches, together with some knowledge of Lattin (sic) and a little of Greek."[9] More enduring than his instruction in Latin and Greek was his religious training. From Pastor Hallock, Uncle Freedom, Grandfather Samuel, his Sunday School teacher, and the Congregational Church he learned strict lessons in piety, sin, and salvation. Sunday was a holy day to be observed by attending church and abstaining from all frivolous activities such as playing games, running, skipping, or even laughing. These attitudes became firmly implanted in Marcus' character and future.

In 1820 after Marcus had experienced a conversion, he decided to become a minister, although the expense of four years in college and three years in a seminary seemed financially impossible. While at Rushville helping his stepfather run the business, his family persuaded him that a medical career would be more practical and attainable.

An aspiring medical student was required to train first with a practicing doctor, known as "riding with the doctor." This Marcus did for about two years with Dr. Ira Bryant, a Rushville physician. In the fall of 1825 he entered the Fairfield College of Physicians and Surgeons where after a sixteen-week session he earned a county license to practice medicine. For four years he practiced at various locations in New York and Canada, but the urge to become a minister still nagged at him. However, after studying theology for a short time, he decided it would be imprudent at age twenty-eight to change careers. This brought him back to the Fairfield Medical College for another sixteen weeks to earn his M.D. degree and the official title of Doctor.

Dr. Whitman opened a practice in the little village of Wheeler, New York, but most of his doctoring took him on horseback to patients miles away in the country. His medical instruments were primitive, sanitation was minimal, and treatment was reduced to prescribing a few drugs, mainly calomel, a purgative made of chlorine and mercury. The only pain-killer for surgery, amputations, or tooth extractions was a shot of whiskey or brandy, or strong-armed assistants to hold down the patient. A doctor's earnings were nominal—twenty-five cents for an office call, ten cents for a tooth extraction, two to five dollars to deliver a baby.

Although he was a rough-mannered man lacking a polished bedside manner, Dr. Whitman earned the respect and love of the community. While practicing medicine, he also labored in the Lord's Presbyterian vineyard. Sometime during this period he had become acquainted with the Prentiss family of Amity.

When Marcus heard Samuel Parker's appeal for missionaries, he had already applied to the American Board to go as a medical missionary to the Indians, but had been rejected because of an "affliction of the spleen." After listening to Parker and with restored health, he reapplied and was accepted as Parker's companion for the exploratory mission to the west. They were given no salary—just the necessary travel and living expenses.

Marcus had learned that Narcissa Prentiss also wanted to go west as a missionary, an intriguing bit of news for a thirty-three-year-old bachelor eager for a companion in the mission field. In February he visited Amity, proposed to her, and was accepted. Their engagement was a contract borne of convenience and expedience—marriage would have to wait until Marcus could be sure that women could safely cross the Rockies. Love would come later.

On February 23, 1835, the exhilarated doctor left Amity with anticipation of a bride and adventures in the west. Narcissa, unhappy at the delay but hopeful for the future, made a formal application to the Board as a missionary. The letters of recommendation accompanying the application informed the Board that she would now qualify as she intended to marry Dr. Whitman. She was accepted and had only to wait for Marcus' return to claim her.

Women Can Cross the Mountains.

It soon became evident that Whitman and Parker were incompatible traveling companions. The two were opposite in temperament, manners, and conduct. Marcus was earthy, carelessly-groomed, overly-generous, and casual, while Samuel Parker was thrifty, refined, prim, and fastidious. Throughout the trip they often had disagreements. Only their aversion to sin and dedication to their mission united them. For the entire trip Parker, dressed in his beaver hat and dress suit, remained aloof and uninvolved, while Whitman tended to the many disagreeable jobs that needed to be done.

On May 14, 1835, they left Liberty (Independence), Missouri, near present-day Kansas City, with a caravan of the American Fur Company under Lucien Fontenelle, a hard-driving Frenchman who tolerated no pampering of the two pious men in his charge. The mountain men in the brigade delighted in taunting the missionaries and ridiculing their distaste for whiskey and sin.

When they reached Bellevue, 200 miles from Liberty, several men including Fontenelle came down with cholera, a plague which had run rampant in the east in 1832 and had reappeared during the following two years. The men had probably consumed contaminated water on the trip. Whitman recognized the symptoms, and for three weeks the caravan was laid up while Marcus isolated and treated the ill men as best he could. Three men died, but to those who recovered, Dr. Whitman became a hero.

From Fort Laramie in the Black Hills they proceeded under the command of Thomas Fitzpatrick, a famous mountain guide. They crossed the mountains at South Pass, and two days beyond the Continental Divide they stopped at Green River for the rendezvous of trappers, traders, and Indians. It was August 12, and they were two months behind schedule.

The two missionaries were not prepared for the debauchery at Green River—gambling, drinking, shooting, brawling, and carousing accompanied by vigorous trading of horses, cattle, furs, whiskey, and supplies. While there, Marcus successfully removed a stone arrowhead imbedded for three years in the back of Jim Bridger, the famous mountain man. Thereafter they became fast friends. Soon other trappers and Indians came to the doctor to have more lead shots and arrowheads removed. Whitman's reputation was greatly enhanced.

While at Green River, the two missionaries agreed to separate, but promised to meet at the rendezvous the following year so Parker could guide the returning missionaries to their destination. Parker, then fifty-seven, continued on to Walla Walla with Nez Perce Indian guides, while Whitman eagerly returned to the east to claim his bride. He took with him two young Nez Perce lads renamed Richard and John whom he intended to show off, educate, and Christianize. They would be useful as interpreters on his return trip west. Whitman and Parker never met again as they planned.

At the end of August Marcus and the boys left Green River with the Fitzpatrick caravan. In early December Whitman appeared in Angelica, New York, where the Prentiss family had moved. During Marcus' nine month absence, he had sent letters back to Narcissa, but he had much more to tell his eager wife-to-be. He saw no reason why women and wagons could not cross the mountains, and he suggested they begin their adventure together as soon as possible if she so wished. Narcissa did so wish, and the two were married on February 18, 1836.

The Search for Companions.

When Whitman returned from the west, he had many pressing duties to attend to before marrying Narcissa. It was important that they join the caravan in the spring of 1836 for if they missed it, they would have to wait a whole year for another brigade. There were long reports to be made to the Board about his exploratory trip as well as arrangements for transportation and supplies for the next journey. But his most urgent task was to find another couple to accompany them, a recommendation of the American Board.

By this time the missionary zeal kindled by the visit of the four Indians to St. Louis had cooled. Candidates soon realized the difficulties and uncertainties of serving isolated Indian tribes, and most missionaries preferred to go abroad to more settled and glamorous stations. Whitman unsuccessfully explored all possibilities—there remained only Henry Harmon Spalding, the suitor Narcissa had rejected, and his wife Eliza. Henry had finished his pastoral training at the Lane Theological Seminary in Cincinnati and had married Eliza Hart, a deeply religious and well-educated woman.

Henry and Eliza had earlier accepted an appointment to the Osage Indians near present-day Emporia, Kansas, but were detained when Eliza gave birth to a stillborn baby girl. When Marcus suggested going to Old Oregon, Henry and Eliza were willing to change their plans if Eliza's health permitted. Narcissa appeared not to resent the remark Henry had made in public, "I do not want to go into the same mission with Narcissa Prentiss as I question her judgment."[10]

However, the secretary of the Board had some reservations about Spalding. He said, ". . . I have some doubt whether his temperament will fit him for intercourse with the traders and travellers in that region." He did add kinder words, "As to labouriousness, self-denial, energy and perseverance, I presume few men are better qualified than he."[11]

In spite of Eliza's poor health and the Board's reluctance to appoint the Spaldings, the two couples were finally on their way. They agreed to meet in Cincinnati to begin their journey west together.

Marcus had promised to return the two Nez Perce boys to their fathers during the summer of 1836, so they, too, would be in the caravan. While in the east, Richard and John had stayed with various families and had learned some English, a great help to the missionaries when later they had to communicate with the Nez Perce Indians. The boys were an attraction in the east, and observers chuckled when they saw the frightened boys run to hide whenever they saw men with guns. Guns to them meant death.

Off to the Benighted Tribes of the West.

At Cincinnati Narcissa and Eliza met for the first time. Although opposites in appearance and demeanor, they became instant friends. Narcissa's robust vigor and exuberant buoyancy contrasted markedly with Eliza's frail health and shy reserved manner. They no doubt discussed artist Catlin's warning to Eliza's husband that "he would not attempt to take a white female into that country. . . . because the enthusiastic desire to see a white woman . . . may terminate in unrestrained passion, consequently in her ruin. . . ." Furthermore, Catlin said, "the fatigues of the journey . . . will destroy them,"[12] but both women had infinite faith that God would protect them. Narcissa packed her black wedding dress and some colorful print dresses thinking they would please the traders and Indians.

When the two couples arrived at St. Louis, a homesick Narcissa was disappointed to find no letters from her family waiting for her. She wrote in her diary, "Why have they not written, seeing it is the very last, last time they will have to cheer my heart with intelligence from home, home, sweet home, and the friends I love." She added, "But I am not sad."[13]

Marcus, however, did find mail including an official document from the United States government giving him and Spalding permission to travel through Indian country with protection from the United States Army and the Indian agents. Also came a letter from David Greene, Secretary of the American Board, with sage advice on how to conduct themselves with the traders and agents. Greene wrote:

> Let your conduct be unblameable, exemplary & free from the appearance of evil. Do not feel it necessary to be the forward reprover of everything wrong among this class of persons, remembering that your business is almost exclusively with the Indians. While you are strict & uncompromising as to yr. own principles & conduct, do not be harsh & dictatorial to others. Do them good & be kind to all as you have opportunity. Let Christian love shine brightly in all that you do.[14]

Greene also admonished them to be strict in their observance of the Sabbath as an example to the traders and the Indians, and he warned them to avoid secular and political involvements. He concluded with, "May . . . yr. mission be as life from the dead to the benighted tribes of the remote west."[15]

At St. Louis the two couples boarded the steamer *Chariton* for a 300-mile journey up the Missouri River to the frontier town of Liberty. Aboard the boat Marcus and Narcissa enjoyed a delayed honeymoon whenever Spalding did not demand their presence for devotions, Bible-reading, and prayer. Narcissa continued to re-cord the events in her personal diary, a suggestion made by her mother in Angelica. Fortunately the diary and her letters have been preserved and published.

For three weeks at Liberty, Marcus and Henry bargained with traders for animals, equipment, guns, ammunition, food, and a heavy wagon to carry their supplies. Narcissa and Eliza shopped for Mackinaw blankets, tinware, iron spoons, and knives in sheaths for each to carry on a belt ready for immediate use. They were acutely aware of Marcus' warning that supplies must be kept to a minimum. They also stitched together a cone-shaped tent of oiled bed-ticking large enough to shelter eight to ten people.

When purchases were completed, Marcus was shocked to discover he had spent $3,063.96, over one-third of that amount going for twelve horses, six mules, and seventeen head of cattle, four of which were milk cows.

Whitman and Spalding welcomed the addition of William Gray, a carpenter and mechanic, who had been accepted by the board with reservations. Although the testimonials for Gray said he was a "skillful mechanic," he was reported to be a "slow scholar" with "slender literary acquisitions" who had "confidence in his own abilities *to a fault.*"[16] Unfortunately Gray caused problems later at the mission.

At Liberty the party divided. Spalding, Gray, and the hired men who had been added to the party, left on April 27, to take the animals and supply wagons overland along the west bank of the Missouri to Council Bluffs. Whitman and the women planned to board the American Fur Company vessel *Diana* going up the Missouri, but the boat failed to stop for them.

To catch the Spalding-Gray party, Marcus hired a team and a wagon, and on May 3 they set out across the prairie toward Fort Leavenworth. They had a rude initiation into life on the plains as they slept outdoors with no tent and managed with few supplies. Though exhausted and sore from riding side-saddle, Narcissa grew steadily hardened to the discomforts, but each day found Eliza growing weaker as she bumped along in the rough wagon. Marcus was concerned for her welfare on the arduous trip that lay ahead.

On May 14 the two mission parties finally met near the Otoe Agency on the south bank of the Platte River about thirty miles west of the Missouri, but they learned to their dismay that the fur trade caravan was four days ahead of them. They dared not enter the hostile Indian territory farther west without the protection of the brigade. Marcus rode ahead on a fast horse, overtook Fitzpatrick, and begged him to hold up the caravan until the missionaries arrived. Fitzpatrick refused. He had his timetable, and every day lost was a risk to the entire expedition. When Marcus returned to his party, he urged them to proceed with all haste. If they could not catch Fitzpatrick's caravan, they would have to abandon the mission project for another year.

Just ahead lay the swollen Platte river to be forded with the animals and the cumbersome wagons loaded with heavy supplies. When one wagon broke, they lightened their load by giving some of their weighty baggage, including some of Spalding's theological books, to their guides. But the favorite Dearborn, or the "bride's wagon," and Narcissa's cherished trunk was to reach Oregon if at all possible.

During the three day crossing of the Platte, Narcissa wrote, "Husband became so completely exhausted with swimming the river on Thursday, the 19th, that it was with difficulty that he made the shore the last time. Mr. Spalding was sick, our two hired men good for nothing."[17]

Weary as Marcus was from crossing the Platte, he soon recovered his strength. One night on the vast plains he and Narcissa bedded down on their India rubber cloths and Mackinaw blankets. Apart from the prying eyes and ears of the rest of the company, they no doubt talked of their plans if they should fail to catch Fitzpatrick's caravan, and they must have discussed privately Henry Spalding's renewed hostility toward Narcissa, Eliza's failing health, and William Gray's growing arrogance and complicity. And on that May night under the stars they enjoyed a rare occasion for intimacy. Alice Clarissa Whitman was then conceived. Baby Alice Clarissa, born on March 14, 1837, in the Waiilatpu mission, was the first child born of white American parents in Old Oregon.

The missionaries pressed on through long days even traveling on Sundays, though with guilty consciences. After crossing the Elkhorn and Loup rivers, they finally caught up with the caravan in the middle of the night on May 26. With thankful hearts they settled in for a short sleep.

Never So Contented or Happy.

At daybreak the missionaries awoke to the commotion and din of the caravan breaking camp. The mountain men and Indians stared in disbelief as two white women emerged from the ticking tent. The men had some apprehensions. Would they have to mind their manners and watch their coarse language around these "holy" women? Could the women stand the rigors of the expedition?

The assembled caravan stretched over the dry plains as far as eye could see. In the lead was Fitzpatrick, followed by the pack animals loaded with supplies, next came the wagons heavy with trading goods and provisions each pulled by six mules and tended by seventy men. At the rear, eating the dust, were the missionaries and their detail. The fur caravan could travel up to twenty miles a day, and only at night did the missionaries catch them.

In a letter to her sister Harriet and brother Edward, Narcissa described the day's routine:

> In the morning as soon as the day breaks the first that we hear is the words—"Arise! Arise!"—then the mules set up such a noise as you have never heard, which puts the whole camp in motion. We encamp in a large ring, baggage and men, tents and wagons on the outside, and all the animals except the cows, which are fastened to pickets, within the circle. This arrangement is to accommodate the guard, who stands regularly every night and day, also when we are in motion, to protect our animals from the approach of Indians, who would steal them.... We are ready to start usually at six, travel till eleven, encamp, rest and feed, and start again about two; travel until six, or before, if we come to a good tavern, then encamp for the night.[18]

The caravan carried only enough food to last until they reached buffalo country where they could rely on fresh buffalo meat and dried "jerk" to carry along. Food was cooked and bread baked over an open fire fueled first by scarce wood, later by an ample supply of dried buffalo chips. Narcissa wrote:

> Our table is the ground, our table-cloth is an India-rubber cloth used when it rains as a cloak; our dishes are made of tin—basins for teacups, iron spoons and plates, each of us, and several pans for milk and to put our meat in when we wish to set it on the table.... Let me assure you of this, we relish our food none the less for sitting on the ground while eating.[19]

Enroute, the brigade passed through Pawnee villages. Narcissa found the Pawnees to be "noble" people with dignity "bespeaking an immortal existence within." She wrote, "We, especially, were visited by them both at noon and at night; we ladies were such a curiosity to them. They would come and stand around our tent, peep in, and grin in their astonishment to see such looking objects."[20]

Narcissa's letters reveal little of the unpleasantness of prairie travel—she revelled in the experiences and bore discomforts with good humor. She and "husband" developed a special love and respect prompting her to write, "I never was so contented and happy before, neither have I enjoyed such health for years."[21]

On June 2 the brigade entered buffalo country, and to everyone's delight they were able to indulge in the delicacies of fresh buffalo tongue, steaks, and ribs. Some meat was dried for later use, but most of the carcass was left on the plains for predators or to decay. Marcus displayed a remarkable talent for preparing the meat in many ways. Narcissa wrote:

> We have meat and tea in the morn, and tea and meat at noon. All our variety consists of the different ways of cooking. I relish it well and it agrees with me. My health is excellent. So long as I have buffalo meat I do not wish anything else. Sister Spaulding is affected by it considerably—has been quite sick.[22]

Traveling with the caravan were Captain James Stewart, a Scotch nobleman, and two other adventurers. When Narcissa learned of Stewart, she invited the three men and Fitzpatrick to a tea party in Stewart's honor. She brewed the tea in a basin over the buffalo chip fire. As they sat on the ground, she served them tea and scarce sugar in their own tin cups. Spalding and Gray expressed their disapproval of such frivolity.

On June 13 the brigade reached Fort Laramie where for eight days they rested, washed clothes, ate food other than buffalo meat, sat on chairs at tables for their meals, and held an outdoor Sunday service at which Spalding preached an appropriate sermon on the prodigal son. Ahead of them lay the mountains, which required the cargo to be lightened. Fitzpatrick loaded all his gear on the pack mules and horses, leaving the wagons behind at Laramie. Except for the light Dearborn wagon the missionaries shifted their essentials to the pack animals. Eliza, with improved health, joined Narcissa on horseback.

On July 4, 1836, the caravan reached South Pass where Narcissa and Eliza made history as the first white women to cross the Continental Divide. They had opened Old Oregon to women.

Welcome to the Rendezvous.

As the caravan neared the Green River rendezvous, a boisterous party of shaggy mountain men and bedecked Indians galloped out to meet them. Among the greeters was Joseph Meek, twenty-six, one of the west's most dashing and reckless trappers. He had heard that there were two white women in the caravan, and he wanted to be the first to welcome them. He was fond of women, particularly the Indian wives of other trappers, a penchant that often caused him great difficulty with irate husbands.

Firing wild shots into the air, Meek wheeled his horse up to the missionaries, doffed his hat to the two women, and gave them a sweeping welcome. Meek was particularly taken by the golden-haired one sitting tall on her horse. On following days at Green River Joe Meek often visited Narcissa and escorted her about. He even professed that he had once been a Methodist and a Bible-reader.

On July 6 when the caravan entered Green River, they were greeted by several hundred Nez Perce, Flathead, and Cayuse Indians, and numerous trappers and traders who eagerly awaited supplies, mail, and the important "firewater" to quench their thirst and to barter, watered-down, with the Indians for priceless furs.

Curious Indian women in their best doeskin dresses crowded about Narcissa and Eliza, and the Indian men put on dazzling displays of horsemanship, dances, and mock battles. Even the rough mountain men polished up their manners, moderated their drinking, and toned down their wild antics in deference to the two white women. Some of the men got doses of religion from Spalding and asked for Bibles. Narcissa was fascinated by the craggy mountain men and their ridiculous attempts at civility and mannerliness. Eliza, often confined to her tent, began to learn the Nez Perce language at which she later became fluent. Richard and John, the two Nez Perce boys who had returned from the east with Whitman, eagerly showed off their ability to talk a bit of "Boston" to admiring family and friends. But the Cayuses and Nez Perces disputed over which tribe would claim the missionaries.

Marcus Whitman was disappointed to learn that his early partner, Samuel Parker, was not at Green River to meet him, advise and guide the party to the far west as they had planned the year before. Instead Whitman found a letter from Parker giving just a few tips on locating a mission and indicating plans to return east by boat.

Captain Fitzpatrick, having reached his destination, was returning east with mules loaded down with bales of valuable furs. Fortunately the missionaries were able to join a Hudson's Bay party under John McLeod and Thomas McKay to continue west through what was still the roughest part of the journey. Despite the Britishers warning to lighten the loads for what lay ahead, Whitman and Spalding refused to leave behind the favorite Dearborn wagon.

Patience to Endure It.

On July 18 the Hudson's Bay brigade, the missionaries, and about 200 Nez Perce and Cayuse Indians left the rendezvous at Green River. Their final destination was Fort Walla Walla, but before them lay the treacherous Snake River which cut a winding course through deep canyons of volcanic rock, and the Wasatch and Blue Mountains with some of the wildest country of the west. To make travel even more strenuous, the caravan had to adjust to the Indians' schedule with no mid-day stops for rest and food.

Enroute to Fort Hall, twelve miles from present-day Pocatello, Idaho, their journey became progressively more difficult. On July 25 Narcissa wrote, "Very mountainous. Paths winding on the sides of steep mountains. In some places the path is so narrow as scarcely to afford room for the animals to place his foot. One after the other, we pass along with cautious steps."[23]

Despite constant trouble with the Dearborn wagon at creek crossings and over mountain trails, Whitman and Spalding stubbornly refused to abandon it. When an axle broke, Narcissa hoped to see the last of the Dearborn, but had to admit, "Our rejoycing (sic) was in vain however for they are making a cart of the hind wheels this afternoon and lashing the forward wheels on it, intending to take it through in some shape or other. They are so resolute and untiring in their efforts they will probably succeed."[24]

Along with traversing rugged mountain terrain, the missionaries had to subsist on an unpalatable diet of "jerk." Narcissa wrote, "We have plenty of dry Buffalo meat which we purchased of the Indians, & dry it is for me. I can scarcely eat it, it appears so filthy, but it will keep us alive, & we ought to be thankful for it." She

hastened to add, "Do not think I regret coming. No; far from it. I would not go back for a world. I am contented & happy notwithstanding I get very hungry & weary. Have six weeks steady journying before us. Will the Lord give me patience to endure it."[25]

After crossing a desert in 100 degree heat, they arrived at the crude log palisade of Fort Hall on the south bank of the Snake River. Two days later when they left the fort, most of the Indians parted from the company to take a longer route away from hostile Blackfeet territory. Only Richard and John and a few other Indians remained with the caravan to drive the cattle.

In the swamps beyond Fort Hall swarms of mosquitos drove both humans and animals wild. Along the Snake River the terrain again changed to desert with more oppressive heat. At the Glenns Ferry crossing of the Snake River, Whitman again struggled with the cart when it capsized in the water soaking all their belongings.

On August 19 they reached Fort Boise, or Snake Fort, the pride of Thomas McKay. Here for three days they rested, washed clothes, and ate refreshing meals. Whitman finally had to face the reality that his broken-down horses could not pull the broken-down cart through the Blue Mountains ahead. Reluctantly he left behind the cart and its saturated cargo. McLeod gallantly loaded Narcissa's precious little trunk on one of his pack animals.

After leaving Fort Boise they again forded the Snake River. The women had the luxury of riding in a rush and willow canoe towed by Indians on horseback, while the men, horses, mules, and cattle waded or swam across.

McLeod, anxious to get to Walla Walla, pushed on ahead with the Whitmans and Gray while the Spaldings and the Indians followed behind with the cattle. Narcissa delighted in the spectacular mountain scenery and the natural beauty of the Grande Ronde valley, but the mountains became less beautiful as she faced crossing them. Narcissa wrote, "Before noon we began to descend one of the most terrible mountains for steepness & length I have yet seen. I[t] was like winding stairs in its decent (sic) & in some places almost perpendicular.... We no sooner gained the foot on this mountain, when another more steep & dreadful was before us."[26]

At sundown McLeod led them to a high vantage point overlooking the Columbia River valley. To the west some 200 miles away glowed the cones of Mount Hood and Mount St. Helens in the last rays of the setting sun. Narcissa wrote, "The beauty of this extensive valley contras[ted] well with the rolling mountains behind us, & at this hour of twilight, was enchanting & quite diverted my mind from the fatigue under which I was laboring."[27]

That night they camped beside the Walla Walla River eight miles from the fort. Excited and thankful, they arrived the next day at the square stockade of Fort Walla Walla. It was September 1, and they were six months and 2,500 miles from home. Two days later the Spalding party and the cattle arrived. Eliza's health was greatly improved, some thought due to the climate.

Pierre Pambrun, the French-Canadian in charge of the fort, and his Cree wife were hospitable hosts. The missionaries revelled in a variety of foods—meats, fresh fish, and fruit and vegetables raised in the forty gardens. Well-fed domestic animals and fowl roamed the fort yards.

The missionaries soon realized that they could accomplish nothing at Walla Walla until the Indians arrived back from their summer hunting camps. They decided to take the 300-mile trip down the Columbia to Fort Vancouver, the metropolis of the area, to get supplies. Pambrun provided them with a company bateau, a heavy-duty canoe capable of carrying heavy cargo. For six days the oarsmen rowed on placid waters, portaged around The Dalles and the Cascades, and expertly shot the lesser chutes. At night they camped on shore and ate the fresh salmon prepared by Pambrun's cook.

On the morning of September 12 they arrived at Fort Vancouver. Anchored in the harbor were two British ships and high above the great palisade waved the Hudson's Bay Company flag, "the old Lady of the North."

Fort Vancouver, a Wilderness Paradise.

The weary travelers were not prepared for Fort Vancouver, the citadel of the Northwest, and its inhabitants. Among the men greeting them was a tall white-haired gentleman, Dr. John McLoughlin, the Chief Factor of the fort. The Factor, fifty-two, had left his profession as a physician for a more exciting life as a trader and through shrewdness, superior intellect, and determination had become the lord of all British trade in old Oregon. Although the British opposed American expansion into their territory, they considered the coming of the missionaries

a benefit in improving the life of the Indians. Little did they realize that the successful arrival of the missionaries on the overland route would pave the way for waves of American emigrants to follow.

McLoughlin and Margaret, his Swiss-Cree wife, extended every courtesy to the Whitmans and the Spaldings, but excluded the outraged Gray from the fort's amenities. The two missionary couples were guests in the factor's beautifully-furnished house, treated to sumptuous four-course meals served on English china, and taken on tours of the extensive gardens, orchards, and grain fields surrounding the fort. They visited the dairy, the grist-mill, and the animal farms. Narcissa made extensive entries in her journal noting useful bits of information for the future. She even saved seeds from the fruit and vegetables she ate at each meal and welcomed the offer of sprouts from the fort nursery. She shopped for household utensils, cloth for sheets, bedding, and gifts for Richard and John in the amply-supplied fort storehouse, and she gathered feathers from wild fowl to make herself a feather-bed.

Narcissa and Margaret McLoughlin became close friends, often taking horseback rides together on sight-seeing jaunts. They had little to do with the two English women who had come from London by boat.

But a few things bothered the Whitmans. They were surprised to learn that the Reverend Herbert Beaver, a pompous and "unchristian" Anglican who had just arrived with his wife from England, was assigned to become the fort chaplain. And they had heard that Dr. McLoughlin, a baptized but fallen-away Catholic, was expecting the arrival of a Roman Catholic priest to administer to the many French Canadian Catholics and Indians at the fort. There would be competition for souls in Old Oregon.

Narcissa wrote in her journal of another annoyance. As she described the wonderful food they were offered, she noted, "But there is one article on the table I have not yet mentioned & of which I never partake, That is wine. The gentlemen frequently drink toasts to each other but never give us the opportunity of refusing for they know we belong to the tetotal Society. We have many talks about drinking wine, but no one joins our society."[28]

Although the missionaries enjoyed the luxuries and hospitality at the fort, they were anxious to begin their mission work before the onset of the rainy season. They finally agreed that Whitman, Spalding, and Gray should go upriver with the supplies and equipment purchased from the fort, find suitable locations for their missions, begin to build shelters, and return for their wives in four or five weeks. It was mutually decided that they would establish separate missions, a wise move in view of their frequent quarrels and disagreements and Spalding's obvious dislike of Narcissa.

While the men were gone, Dr. McLoughlin asked Narcissa and Eliza to help teach the fifty mixed-blood children in the fort school. Chaplain Beaver made loud protests to the factor about the two women intruding into his domain, but McLoughlin insisted that the women continue their instruction. Narcissa also tutored the factor's daughter Maria, wrote letters, and made copies of her diary to send back east on the ship soon expected at the fort.

On October 18 Spalding returned to Vancouver to fetch the two women. He had come down the Columbia on the Hudson's Bay express that once a year traveled overland and by water to the fort from Montreal with supplies, personnel, and mail. McLoughlin tried to convince the women that they should stay at the fort for the winter where Narcissa, then five months pregnant, would have better care than at the wilderness mission. But Narcissa and Eliza were anxious to join their husbands and begin the work they had come to do.

In two weeks they were on their way upstream in the two heavily-loaded bateaus that McLoughlin provided. Unfortunately the rains had begun, and their ten-day trip up the Columbia was miserable. During the day the women managed to keep dry under oilcloth, and at night Narcissa was able to sleep on her new featherbed in a dry tent.

When they arrived at Fort Walla Walla, Narcissa was disappointed that Marcus was not there to greet her. He and Gray had stayed at Waiilatpu to work on a shelter. A few days later all five of the original missionary party were reunited at the fort, and on Sunday they worshipped together.

Waiilatpu, the Place of the Rye Grass.

While Narcissa and Eliza were waiting at Fort Vancouver, their husbands tried to find suitable locations for their missions. Whitman chose to locate at Waiilatpu, twenty-five miles east of Fort Walla Walla and seven miles west of present-day Walla Walla. Here there were 300 acres of fertile ground lying between the Walla Walla River and its tributary Mill Creek. Along the banks grew cottonwood and birch, and in the distance to the southeast lay the Blue Mountains. The land was covered with waves of tall rye grass from which it was given its Indian name of Waiilatpu, or "the place of the rye grass."

The Whitmans would work among the Cayuse Indians, a dwindling tribe numbering about three or four-hundred. Unfortunately Marcus chose not to heed a Nez Perce chief's warning that the Cayuses had "difficulties with the white man."

The Spaldings settled 120 miles northeast of Walla Walla at Lapwai, "the place of butterflies," about twelve miles from present-day Lewiston, Idaho. They were to serve the large Nez Perce tribe numbering from three to four-thousand. Their chief, Tackensuatis, nicknamed Rotten Belly, welcomed the missionaries warmly and offered them every assistance, quite unlike the Cayuses who thought it a disgrace to work for the Whitmans. When the Spaldings reached Lapwai, they lived in an Indian tepee until Gray could help them build a log cabin.

While Marcus worked on the house at Waiilatpu, Narcissa stayed at Fort Walla Walla as a guest of the Pambruns. Here she tutored Pambrun's daughter Maria in English. Finally on December 9 her husband came to the fort to escort his bride of almost one year to her first home. Narcissa wrote to her mother of the crude unfinished house made of split logs and adobe bricks:

> We arrived here on the tenth—distance, twenty-five miles from Walla Walla. Found a house reared and the lean-to enclosed, a good chimney and fireplace, and the floor laid. No windows or door except blankets. My heart truly leaped for joy as I alighted from my horse, entered and seated myself before a pleasant fire (for it was now night). It occurred to me that my dear parents had made a similar beginning, and perhaps a more difficult one than ours.[29]

Their first winter of 1836-37 was unusually cold and snowy. Because the Indians were gone on their winter hunt, mission work could not begin, so Marcus worked to make the cabin more comfortable. He replaced the blankets at the openings with real windows and doors, built two chairs, and nailed a crude wooden platform to the wall for Narcissa's featherbed. Pambrun donated a table and a heating stove. Narcissa bragged about having a barrel in which to pound her laundry, but she longed some day to prepare meals on an iron cookstove instead of at the fireplace.

Food was scarce. They ate horse meat purchased from the Indians, and bought flour and other staples from the fort. Only milk was in good supply from their own cows.

In March as soon as possible Marcus hitched his oxen to the plow to break ground for the gardens. He planted potatoes, corn, peas, and other vegetables, and after a time was rewarded with a bountiful harvest. It was his hope to teach the Cayuses how to plow and plant so they would not have to leave camp to hunt for food.

A Treasure Is Born.

On March 14, 1837, Narcissa's twenty-ninth birthday, little Alice Clarissa was born. For a time Mrs. Pambrun came from the fort to help, and with Marcus' expert care, Narcissa successfully delivered a healthy ten-pound daughter. Marcus though "excessively pressed with care and labor," tended the baby, washed diapers, and cooked the meals. Narcissa praised her "affectionate husband, who, as a physician and nurse, exceeds all I ever knew."[30] The Pambrun's daughter, Maria, and another Indian girl soon arrived to assist with the housework.

An ecstatic Narcissa rejoiced in the birth of her "treasure invaluable." Because there was no cradle for the child, Narcissa enjoyed holding the baby on her lap. Despite Marcus' attempts to keep them at a distance, the excited Cayuses paraded to the Whitman house to touch and gaze at the white child they proudly called a Cayuse "te-mi," or Cayuse girl. Narcissa wrote of her daughter to her family, "Her whole appearance is so new to them. Her complexion, her size and dress, etc., all excite a deal of wonder; for they never raise a child here except they are lashed tight to a board, and the girls' heads undergo the flattening process."[31]

Although the spring of 1837 was one of Narcissa's happiest times with her newborn to care for, she worried about her husband's health. The hard winter had taken its toll, and to their disappointment William Gray, who had ambitions to establish a mission of his own, had left. Dependable workers were hard to find. Responsibilities weighed heavily upon Marcus, and the old pain returned that had bothered him earlier.

During his eleven-year stay at Waiilatpu, Whitman, the only doctor in the area, was often called upon to deliver the babies of the missionaries living miles distant. Sometime in the fall of 1837 Whitman received a message from Henry Spalding calling him to Lapwai to deliver Eliza's baby. Marcus put a caretaker in charge of the animals, boarded up the windows of the house, locked the doors, and with Narcissa, eight-month old Alice Clarissa, and a Hawaiian helper he started out on the 120-mile trip to Lapwai. Narcissa riding sidesaddle managed to hold the baby in front of her. The five-day trip was strenuous with rain and snow and little dry wood for campfires. Enroute they had to change the baby's diapers out in the snow, tent at night in the cold, cross the Snake River, and climb over snowy elevations.

On November 12 they arrived at Lapwai and after three days Marcus delivered Mrs. Spalding's baby girl, named Eliza after her mother. While Marcus cared for the weakened mother, Spalding baptized both daughters, and served communion. After being gone one month the Whitmans returned home to find everything at Waiilatpu in good order.

During the first two years of her baby's life, Narcissa wrote numerous letters home about Alice Clarissa. In concern for her daughter's development she wrote:

> Situated as I am, I know not how I shall succeed in training her as I ought. So many Indians and children are constantly in and about our house, and recently I discover her much inclined to imitate and talk with them, or they with her. It makes them very much pleased to think she is going to speak their language so readily. They appear to love her much.[32]

In a long letter to her sister Jane, Narcissa wrote:

> . . . you cannot know how much of a comfort our little daughter, Alice Clarissa, is to her father and mother. O, how many melancholy hours she has saved me, while living here alone so long, especially when her father is gone for many days together. . . . She is now eighteen months old, very large and remarkably healthy. She is a great talker. Causes her mother many steps and much anxiety. She is just beginning to sing with us in our family worship.[33]

Earlier Narcissa had written about her precocious daughter, "My Clarissa is my own little companion from day to day, and dear daughter."[34] She requested that the family send flannel dresses, shoes, and other clothing for Alice. A month later she asked that they add Alice's name, the date and place of her birth to the Prentiss family Bible.

On Sunday morning, June 23, 1839, the Whitmans conducted a worship service for the Indians. Alice Clarissa, then two years and three months old, sang with them in her clear child's voice her favorite hymn "Rock of Ages." That afternoon Marcus and Narcissa sat down to read, an opportunity rarely afforded them. Alice was outdoors playing. After a time Narcissa, realizing she had not heard her daughter's usual chatter, inquired if anyone had seen her. A young girl staying with the Whitmans searched but could not find her, and a Hawaiian boy reported that he had found two cups by the Walla Walla River. To her horror Narcissa recalled that earlier Alice had taken two cups from the table to get some water.

The frantic parents ran up and down the river bank calling Alice's name. Others joined in the search, but the little girl was nowhere to be found. An old Cayuse Indian chief, later said to be Umtippe who caused the Whitmans much trouble, waded into the river, swam underwater, and pulled up the lifeless body. Whitman tried in vain to restore her breathing, but it was too late. When the bereaved Narcissa wrote to her mother she was able to say:

> Her spirit had been called to rise to worlds before unknown, and I could only say, 'Lord, it is right; it is right; she is not mine, but thine; she has only been lent to me for a little season, and now, dearest Saviour, thou hast the best right to her; Thy will be done, not mine.' I cannot wish her back in this world of sin and pain; her tender spirit was of too delicate material to remain here longer and be subject to the ills of this cruel and unfriendly world. Jesus' love for her was greater than mine. He saw it necessary for our good and in mercy to her to take her to Himself.[35]

The Whitmans sent a messenger post-haste to the Spaldings at Lapwai who arrived at Waiilatpu on Thursday, June 26. Narcissa made a shroud perhaps from her black wedding dress, while Marcus built a small coffin and dug a grave near the mission. Spalding preached the funeral sermon using a somber text from II Kings 4:26—"Is it well with the child?" Sometime later Whitman enclosed the grave site with a white picket fence.

Because of the slowness of the mail, Narcissa's family at Angelica received the joyful letters telling of Alice Clarissa along with the one telling of her death. A year later the flannel dresses and shoes arrived at the mission with an assurance from the family that Alice Clarissa's name had been entered in their Bible.

The Whitmans mourned their loss, and for months Narcissa's letters conveyed her sadness and loneliness. To salve the loss Narcissa began to take in homeless and mistreated children, at one time having eleven in her care. In her brood was Helen Mar Meek, the two-year-old daughter of the dashing trapper Joe Meek who had taken such a fancy to Narcissa on the overland journey. When his wife deserted him, Meek sent his daughter to the Whitmans to raise and educate. Helen proved to be a fretful, stubborn youngster. Another little girl arrived when the famous mountain man Jim Bridger sent his daughter Mary Ann to the mission to be cared for and trained. Mary Ann was of a milder, more obedient disposition. Later a two-year-old boy, abandoned by his mixed-blood parents, was left on the mission doorstep. Narcissa also took in this forsaken waif and named him David Malin. He was a lovable lad who became a favorite at the mission. With the three "adopted" children as permanent members of the family, the void left by her daughter's death was partially filled.

Difficult Beginnings at Waiilatpu.

At the outset of mission work there were many hurdles to overcome. In the spring of 1837 the Cayuses returned from their winter hunt at Grande Ronde and settled in their camp about three miles from the mission. One of the first problems for the missionaries was that of communicating with the Indians who had adopted the Nez Perce language. The Whitmans were disappointed that Richard, whom Marcus had taken east, did not interpret for them as they had hoped, and old Chief Umtippe expected to be paid for any assistance he gave. The Spaldings at Lapwai were more successful with the Nez Perces. Eliza had learned the language quickly and soon translated songs and lessons for her husband to print out later on the small press he had acquired.

Chief Umtippe, nicknamed Cut Lip, proved an annoyance until his death. Narcissa wrote a bitter letter about him:

> The old Chief Umtippe has been a savage creature in his day. His heart is still the same, full of all manner of hypocrisy, deceit and guile. He is a mortal beggar as all Indians are. If you ask a favour of him, sometimes it is granted or not, just as he feels; if granted it must be well

paid for. A few days ago he took it into his head to require pay for teaching us the language & forbade his people from coming & talking with us for fear we should learn a few words from them.[36]

Occasionally Umtippe reminded the Whitmans that the land they occupied belonged to him, and he had not been paid for it as Samuel Parker had promised two years before, nor had he received payment for the horses Jason Lee had received. Whitman reminded Umtippe that the missionaries were there because the Cayuses had requested them to come.

When Umtippe's wife became seriously ill, the chief called Whitman to cure her. But treating sick Indians was risky. "Umtippe got in a rage about his wife," Narcissa wrote, "and told my husband, while she was under his care, that if his wife died that night he should kill him. The contest has been sharp between him and the Indians, and husband was nearly sick with the excitement and care of them."[37] Fortunately Umtippe dismissed Whitman and called for a "te-wat," or medicine man, from Walla Walla to drive out the evil spirits. Presumably the chief's wife lived, because the te-wat was not killed to avenge her death. Later when the chief himself got sick, he again called Whitman. Marcus prayed ardently for the recovery of Umtippe and the other Cayuses he treated.

Sometime during the winter of 1840-41 when the old chief realized he was about to die, Narcissa wrote that he was a changed man. "Never can a person manifest a greater change. That selfish, wicked, cunning and troublesome old chief, now so still and quiet, so attentive to the truth, and grateful for favors now given! Surely nought but the spirit of God has done this."[38]

Another irritation soon arose when the curious Cayuses trailed in and out of Narcissa's kitchen at any hour of the day. Later, in the larger house, Marcus designated one room only as "the Indian room," a move that insulted and infuriated the natives.

Although the first relations with the Indians were not pleasant, as time went on, the situation improved. There were hopeful signs—the Cayuses did not steal, drink, or go naked, and the missionaries found them to be strict in attending worship, gathering daily at dawn and again in the evening and once on Sundays. However it was difficult to explain to the adults the important tenets of a Calvinistic doctrine, the concept of one God, and the lessons of sin and redemption in the Bible. Narcissa was more successful with the black-eyed children who were eager to learn and fond of singing hymns.

A Dispute Over Old Oregon.

By 1837 a controversy had arisen between Great Britain and the United States over the location of the northern boundary in Old Oregon. The British wanted a boundary that followed the Columbia River, while the Americans insisted on the 49th parallel which would give them Puget Sound with its navigational advantage. Both countries were hoping to settle the dispute by promoting colonization of the territory instead of going to war. The United States government, then under President Jackson followed by President Tyler, could see the benefits of encouraging the work of the missionaries as forerunners of emigration. The Reverend Jason Lee, the missionary who established the first Methodist mission at Willamette in 1834, was an important link in the west.

The Waiilatpu mission, located at a strategic juncture of trails and waterways, became a stopping point for travelers from both east and west. Agents of the Hudson's Bay Company often made courtesy calls, and missionaries from other locations came to visit. Trappers and traders left their children to be educated at the mission school. Later, caravans of settlers found the mission a welcome place to rest, eat, and recover from strenuous cross-country travels. The Whitmans were obliged to provide shelter, food, clothing, and medical care while carrying on their mission responsibilities.

One visitor proved to be particularly important. On an April day in 1838 the Reverend Jason Lee stopped to see the Whitmans. He was on his way east to solicit funds from the Methodist Society for his Willamette mission and to make an appeal for more workers. But more important was a task which involved the government in Washington. He carried with him a signed document from citizens in the Willamette Valley requesting that the United States take "formal and speedy possession" of Old Oregon and extend protection and enforcement of laws to American citizens. Lee was convinced that the United States must not delay in colonizing Oregon if they expected to wrest control from the Hudson's Bay Company and the British.

Lee told Whitman of his plans, then proceeded to the Lapwai mission to visit Spalding. When Lee returned, Spalding accompanied him bearing an eloquent letter he had written to David Greene, Secretary of the American Board in Boston. He first wrote something of the mission work, then made a startling request for no less than 220 adult workers (thirty ordained missionaries, thirty farmers, thirty teachers, ten physicians, etc.). Added to this was a long list of supplies and equipment needed. The Whitmans added more items: machinery, furniture, household items, dishes, clothing, books and teaching materials—even 2,000 gun-flints and 100 dozen scalping knives. The list was endless. Spalding and Whitman both signed the letter and sent it on with Lee. The Presbyterians were not to be outdone by the Methodists.

A year later when Greene received the letter in Boston, he was shocked at the demands. His answer was diplomatic, but firm. He said the Board would do as much as possible, but he added, "your expectations are too high for the means of the Board or for the spirit of a Christian community. . . . Or for the good of the cause of Christ in your region."[39]

When Whitman and Spalding received Greene's letter after another year had passed, they were not surprised. In the meantime they had received an earlier letter from Greene advising them that because of the financial panic of 1837, of which the missionaries were unaware, the allotment for each mission would have to be reduced to $500 a year.

Jason Lee, however, was surprisingly successful in the east. He received a total of $40,000 from the Methodist Board with which he was able to charter the sailing ship *Lausanne* to carry all the supplies and persons he requested around the Cape and north to the mouth of the Columbia River. The exorbitant sum given Lee drew sharp criticism from some Methodists. But surprising information came to light in 1846 when the boundary dispute with Great Britain was settled at the 49th parallel. It then became public knowledge that the United States government had subsidized the Methodist mission from a secret fund in order to colonize Old Oregon.

A Strange Company of Missionaries.

The Whitmans and Spaldings heard from the American Board the welcome news that "reinforcements" were on their way west. In August 1838 nine weary travelers came across the Blue Mountains with the Hudson's Bay brigade. There were four married couples, three of whom were clergymen, and one bachelor. William Gray,

who had originally come with the Whitman's as a mechanic and carpenter, was their leader. He had assumed the title of "doctor" after attending a few lectures at the Fairfield College of Physicians and Surgeons, the same institution where Whitman had taken his medical training. Gray and his new bride had visions of starting another mission somewhere in Old Oregon. During the journey west disharmony and dissatisfaction had developed because of Gray's incompetence, arrogance, and harshness. Mary Walker, one of the wives, wrote, "We have a strange company of Missionaries. Scarcely one who is not intolerable on some account."[40]

After the initial welcomes, the nine settled into the cramped quarters with the Whitmans whose household already numbered thirteen people. Personality conflicts and antagonisms soon arose among both the men and the women. The new arrivals began to complain of Narcissa's ill-temper, their lack of privacy, and their diet of horse meat. Narcissa, exhausted from the extra work of feeding nine more mouths, found some of the visitors' habits to be disagreeable. The men drank wine, chewed tobacco, and spit into her fireplace. In a letter to her sister Jane she criticized the lack of piety of "particularly the two Revs.":

> They think it not good to have too many meetings, too many prayers, and that it is wrong and unseemly for a woman to pray where there are men, and plead the necessity for wine, tobacco, etc. and now how do you think I have lived with *such folks right in my kitchen for the whole winter.*[41]

A few difficulties were resolved when the six men, including Spalding who had come from Lapwai, decided to form the Oregon Mission organization. They made decisions concerning the locations of the recruits, how best to deal with the Indians, and how to distribute the supplies that arrived. The women, excluded by the men, formed their own society, the Columbia Maternal Association, the first women's club organized west of the Rockies.

During the winter of 1838-39 it appeared that the "reinforcements" brought more dissension than help to mission work. Eavesdropping Indians were skeptical about the white missionaries who quarreled with each other while they preached brotherly love. By summer the nine new missionaries had settled temporarily at various places. William Gray resumed his work as carpenter and helped Whitman build a larger house.

One development unified the Protestants. In November 1838 two Jesuit priests arrived at Fort Vancouver to establish a church among the many French-Canadian Catholics and begin mission work with the Indians. The energetic priests, subsidized by the Hudson's Bay Company, coaxed Factor McLoughlin back into the fold and began to seek converts. They were highly visible in their distinctive "black robes," and the Indians were delighted with their picture lessons. The Protestants had found a mutual adversary to unite them. Narcissa wrote:

> A Catholic priest has recently been at Walla Walla and held meetings with the Indians and used their influence to draw all the people away from us. Some they have forbidden to visit us again, and fill all of their minds with distraction about truths we teach, and their own doctrine; say we ought to have baptized them long ago, etc., etc. The conflict has begun—what trials await us we know not. We never had greater encouragement about the Indians than at the present time. Could they be left unmolested until their minds should become settled upon the great truths they have been permitted to hear about—our hope and trust is in the Lord— we desire not to be moved by all the opposition of earth and hell combined, but to stay our souls upon Him, and to labor faithfully and diligently and leave the event with Him.[42]

A Bountiful Harvest and a New House.

The American Board, constantly pressed for money, hoped the Oregon missions, once established, would be partly self-supporting. Therefore the missionaries had to spend much of their time and energy raising crops and livestock to sell and barter for labor and goods. Despite primitive equipment and limited help, Whitman harvested a bumper crop in 1838. Asa Smith, one of the troublesome newcomers, helped Marcus gather his wheat, corn, potatoes, turnips, melons, and vegetables from the seventeen acres of cultivated land. Because there was no wagon to bring in the produce, Indian women carried bags of vegetables from the fields on their backs, and the oxen hauled in corn piled on branches.

Work continued on the new house situated farther from the river than the original house which had periodically flooded. The new T-shaped building, also made of "dobie" bricks and hand-sawed pine boards from trees that grew some twenty miles away in the foothills of the mountains, gradually took shape. The roof of split timbers laid over with sod was more or less leak proof.

The first section to be built contained the "Indian room" which served as the school and the church. In the attic above were sleeping quarters. Throughout the years other rooms were added, but the house was never completely finished. After three and one-half years of living in the crowded adobe hut with its lean-to, Narcissa was eager to move into the new house where there was more space, warmth, and privacy.

The crops were bountiful, the new house was progressing in spurts, a gristmill had been built to grind flour, and the Indians were learning to plant gardens of their own. Forty to fifty children were reading from the Nez Perce primer that Eliza Spalding had written, and Sunday services, often held outside, were well attended in the summer. Things seemed to be going well.

But the unending work was taking its toll on the Whitmans. In addition to supervising the farm work and the building, Marcus still rode hundreds of miles in all sorts of weather to answer sick calls. He also distributed mission supplies that arrived periodically, led the Sunday services, and taught some of the children's classes. His work was never-ending, and his health was failing. Narcissa, once a handsome vibrant woman, had aged markedly during the first years at the mission. Her eyesight was failing, and she suffered from kidney trouble and a weak heart. Although her letters usually reflected the better side of things, the joy of serving in the mission field was being ground down by disharmony, overwork, and disappointments.

Narcissa's Year Alone.

After the new missionaries had been in Old Oregon for a time, they began to send letters to Secretary Greene of the American Board in Boston complaining about Henry Spalding and recommending that he be recalled. Greene was also aware of Parker's cricitism of Whitman's expenditures. The Secretary was disturbed, particularly because Spalding's and Whitman's reports indicated that the missions were progressing well. After consulting his committee, Greene drafted a letter to the missioners, dated February 25, 1842. He wrote first of his "heaviness of heart," then listed the resolutions passed by the committees. The missionaries were to close the Waiilatpu and Lapwai missions; Spalding, Smith, and Gray were to return to the United

States; and the Whitmans were to move to the Tshimakain mission to work among the Spokane Indians.

Although the missionaries were stunned by Greene's order, the men of the Oregon Mission organization had already come together to discuss and resolve their differences. It was a heated meeting. Because of the delay in the mail Secretary Greene was not advised of this action until it was too late to rescind the action of the American Board.

The Oregon Mission group gathered again in September to discuss Greene's letter and decide what to do next. No one was surprised when William Gray resigned from mission work. It was Whitman's proposal that shocked everyone—he offered to leave for the east to urge the Board to withdraw their resolutions. It became evident later that he had other plans in mind as well. It was autumn, a dangerous time to be crossing the mountains, but Whitman assured the others that if he left immediately he could catch the spring brigade back. He would also find someone to care for the Waiilatpu mission during his absence. Reluctantly the men accepted Whitman's proposal.

Narcissa was in complete agreement with her husband's decision to go east. Before he left, he received promises from Archibald McKinlay, then in charge of Fort Walla Walla, to look after Narcissa. Tiloukaikt, a Cayuse chief, assured Whitman that his wife and property would be protected.

Asa Lovejoy, a thirty-four-year-old attorney who had just arrived in Oregon in 1842, accompanied Whitman. With two Cayuse ponies, several heavily-loaded pack mules, one Indian man, and Alice Clarissa's dog Trapper, they started toward the Blue Mountains on the first leg of their journey. Narcissa was left alone at the mission with her adopted children.

After Narcissa watched Marcus and his companions disappear along the trail, she realized that it would be a whole year before she would see her husband again. She discovered that he had left behind his comb, pencil, journal, and compass, and she had forgotten to remind him to buy her a pair of spectacles. She was the only white person at the mission, and she felt alone and vulnerable.

Three days after Marcus had left, Narcissa had a terrifying experience. Late at night she was awakened when she heard someone open her bedroom door. She rushed from her bed to hold the door shut, but the intruder was stronger.

The man ran away when she screamed for John, the Hawaiian boy who slept in another room. The next day Narcissa wrote of the encounter to her husband, "I fastened the door, lit a candle and went to bed trembling and cold, but could not rest until I had called John to bring his bed and sleep in the kitchen . . . had the ruffian persisted I do not know what I should have done."[43]

The following day Narcissa sent word of the intrusion to McKinlay at Fort Walla Walla, who ordered trader Tom McKay to move her to the fort as soon as possible. Evidence pointed to the intruder being none other than Tamsucky, or Feathercap, the Cayuse chief second in command. When questioned, Tamsucky professed his innocence and assured Narcissa there would not be any more such incidents. On Sunday Narcissa tried to carry on with church services as usual.

Too ill to ride a horse, Narcissa was moved to Fort Walla Walla on a trundlebed in a wagon. The cold room and damp bedding at the fort did nothing to help her recover. She wrote a lonely letter to Marcus hoping he'd receive it somewhere on the trail east:

> Almost three long weeks have passed since we exchanged the parting kiss, and many, very many, long weeks are yet to come before we shall be permitted, if ever in this world, to greet each other again. . . . I follow you night and day, and shall through the whole journey, in my imagination and prayers.[44]

At the end of October Narcissa and her two adopted daughters, Mary Ann Bridger and Helen Mar Meek, moved to the home of Methodist missionaries located at The Dalles on the Columbia. Although they gave her as much care as possible, her health did not improve. A pathetic letter to her parents indicated a different Narcissa from the buoyant woman who had first come to Oregon. She wrote:

> My health is very poor; this increases the trial, because, in consequence I have too many gloomy and depressing hours, and evil forebodings, in which I have not strength of mind to rise above. . . . My eyes are almost gone, my poor health affects them materially and writing is very injurious to me. I can neither read, write or sew without spectacles, and most of the time, and sometimes with them, I suffer considerable pain.[45]

Meanwhile William Geiger, an acquaintance of Narcissa, was taking care of the mission. But an angry Indian, thought to be Tamsucky's son, set fire to the gristmill, destroying 200 bushels of wheat and corn, flour, and lumber.

The incidents at Waiilatpu drew the attention of Dr. Elijah White, a pompous man who had been appointed the first United States Indian agent in Oregon, a move that disturbed both the Indians and the British. White, believing he had the authority to protect American citizens, arrived at Waiilatpu with a small contingent of men armed with rifles and "plenty of ammunition." He had arbitrarily drawn up a set of eleven "rules" to set things in order among the "savages." After several futile attempts, White's rules were finally accepted at a council meeting by the Nez Perces, the Walla Wallas, and the Cayuses. White returned to Willamette Valley pleased with his accomplishments, but the Indians were growing increasingly more restless and suspicious of their white brothers.

In early June Narcissa left Waiilatpu for Fort Vancouver where for two months she rested and was treated for an ovarian tumor. For the rest of the summer she stayed with friends at nearby missions.

While Narcissa was struggling with illness and loneliness, Marcus was suffering great adversities on his hastily-planned trip east. Because of fierce storms and an Indian uprising, he and Lovejoy were forced to turn southward through "Spanish country" toward Taos and Santa Fe, adding another 1,000 miles to their trip. After severe blizzards and extreme cold, they arrived at Taos in mid-December suffering from frost bite and near starvation. It wasn't until the end of March that Marcus arrived in the east.

In Washington D.C. he called on President Tyler to whom he recommended that the government establish supply depots across the continent to help emigrants going west and to speed up mail deliveries. Marcus' visit to Washington fueled rumors that his motives for going east were not solely to preserve Christian missions. Later the legend flourished that Whitman was responsible for opening the great Northwest for United States emigration.

After Washington he moved to New York, then on to Boston to the offices of the American Board. There the reception was cool. Secretary Greene was not overjoyed to meet this rugged bearded man who had left his post without permission. The treasurer of the Board gave Whitman money to buy presentable clothes.

The next day Marcus appeared properly dressed. He pleaded the cause of the missions and persuaded the Board to revoke their former resolutions. They agreed to allow Waiilatpu to continue and Spalding to remain at Lapwai "on trial." In a formal report to the Board, Whitman wrote enthusiastically about mission work, but warned of the "influx of Papist missionaries" in the territory. He asked for five to ten laymen to assist with the manual work, a request the Board rejected. Without appearing to promote the settling of Old Oregon, Whitman urged the Board to heed their responsibility to the increasing number of emigrants moving west.

Marcus had just a few days left to visit the relatives who regarded him as a hero. When his thirteen-year-old nephew, Perrin Whitman, begged to go west with Uncle Marcus, his father reluctantly consented. In the middle of May they left Liberty with the largest company of emigrants thus far.

Before Marcus reached his western destination, he was delayed when a messenger intercepted his return with an urgent call to go to Lapwai to treat the Spaldings who were ill from scarlet fever. He also made a call to deliver a baby at another mission. In the meantime, a disappointed Narcissa waited at The Dalles for his return. Not until late October were they finally reunited.

Narcissa wrote to her father, "It was a joyful and happy meeting and caused our hearts to overflow with love and gratitude to the Author of all our mercies, for permitting us to see each other's faces again in the flesh."[46]

Westward the Wagons.

Narcissa's delight at meeting "husband" was soon dulled by the stark reality of Waiilatpu. Memories of the midnight invader haunted her as she listened to drums and shouts drifting in from the Cayuse camp. In addition she found the mission house crowded with emigrants who had arrived in the fall of 1843 with the same company as Marcus and Perrin. Numbering 1,000 people, it was the largest party to date to cross the mountains.

After buying supplies and food from Marcus, most of the early travelers went on to Willamette Valley. Later, the sick, the helpless, and the indigent straggled in to stay for the winter. The Whitmans had to provide them with all necessities as well as medical care. Despite a shortage of food Narcissa had to feed forty mouths, the chief fare being potatoes, cornmeal, some milk, and cakes baked from wheat burned at the mill. Marcus, himself suffering from a tumor on his foot, cared for the sick, delivered babies, rebuilt the gristmill, and added another room to the house. Fortunately some of the emigrants were skilled tradesmen who could help him, and the women relieved Narcissa of some of her duties of cooking, sewing, washing, and supervising children. At times young men stayed for a time to teach the children.

The Indians watched the ever-increasing wagon trains with dismay and apprehension. Although a few of the enterprising Cayuses profited from trading one fresh horse for five or six wornout animals that would soon recover when put out to pasture, most of the Indians were suspicious and resentful of the whites. The United States government was offering one square mile, or 640 acres, of free land in Oregon to any man over eighteen years of age.

The seven Sager children, who had been orphaned on the trail when both their father and mother died, came with a wagon train numbering over 1,500 people that arrived in the fall of 1844. The oldest was John, fourteen years; followed by Francis, twelve; Catherine, ten; Elizabeth, six; Matilda, four; Louise, three; and five-month old Henrietta who was born enroute. Narcissa promptly washed and fed the dirty, hungry youngsters. For a time the Whitmans doubted they could add seven more children to their family, but finally agreed to adopt them all. The five older children were put in school and given duties about the house and farm. After adjusting to Narcissa's firm discipline, the Sager children were able to call the Whitmans "mother" and "father." Francis, rebelling at the strictness of the school teacher, ran away to join a family going to the Willamette Valley but soon returned to remain at the mission until tragedy struck. As adults the Sager girls wrote detailed and appreciative reminiscenses of their foster parents and their life at the mission.

An emigrant train of over 450 wagons arrived in the fall of 1845. About 100 wagons headed to California while most of the others took a cut-off to the Willamette Valley that bypassed Waiilatpu. This proved a disastrous route that exacted a heavy toll on animals and people. When fewer emigrants bought food from Marcus, he complained of losing profits, but Narcissa was pleased to be able to offer better fare at her table. She and Marcus had improved health, more help, increased livestock, and a repaired gristmill. Andrew Rodgers, a young teacher who was popular with his fourteen students, delighted Narcissa by playing his violin and singing with her. Although Narcissa complained that she didn't get enough letters from home and she had not yet convinced her sister Jane and brother Edward that they should come to Oregon, it seemed for a time that mission life was better. It was, however, the quiet before the storm.

The Massacre.

Hopes for improved relations with the Indians were short-lived. Tomahas, a Cayuse subchief, and Young Chief, a youthful man with much influence in the tribe, confronted Whitman with a series of accusations. Young Chief claimed that the whites had killed his nephew and another young man, and that Whitman was poisoning his people and spreading disease. Marcus recalled earlier accusations when the Indians ate the poisoned meat he had put out for the wolves that were killing his sheep. And he remembered being held responsible when William Gray had put a strong emetic which induced vomiting, into watermelons to keep the Indians from stealing them.

The winter of 1846-47 was extremely severe causing a heavy loss of mission livestock. The Cayuses, suffering from cold and hunger, held Whitman responsible for the loss of their horses and cattle.

In the summer of 1847 an epidemic of measles and dysentery swept through the eastern states, and emigrants coming west in the fall brought the disease with them. Many white children and adults in the mission were afflicted, but only one child died. But when the contagion spread to the Indian camp, it decimated the tribe, some said by half. Whitman, unable to stop the spread of the disease, offered medicines as best he could, only to have his weak feverish patients use their fatal Cayuse treatment of sitting in the sweat lodge before a quick jump in the icy waters of a stream. As their people died, the chiefs were sure that Whitman was using poison and "bad magic" on them.

Unfortunately Whitman did not heed the warnings to leave the mission during the summer and fall of 1847. Spalding suspected serious trouble and warned Whitman of the impending danger. At the mission, friendly Indians had heard the grumblings of the militant chiefs and urged the doctor to leave. But Marcus could not abandon those presently at the mission, and there were too many to move elsewhere. Nor did he want to arm the men and risk starting a shooting war that would turn the entire tribe against all Americans. Besides, he was a man of peace. So he chose to remain for the time being, but he planned to offer the mission to the Catholics who were making inroads into the territory. The Cayuse problem would then be off his shoulders, and the Catholics would be responsible for whatever happened.

Whitman acted on his plan quickly. He and Spalding left Waiilatpu during the night on Saturday, November 27. They rode twenty-five miles to a newly-established Catholic mission where they met with the priests. In the morning Whitman received another ominous warning about Joe Lewis, a mixed-blood troublemaker who had been inciting the Indians with lies and rumors about him. Whitman met briefly with Father Brouillet, invited the priest to visit him at Waiilatpu, and hastily left for home. As Spalding and Whitman said goodbye, past antagonisms were forgotten. Little did they know that they would never meet again.

Whitman arrived at Waiilatpu about 10:00 P.M. Sunday evening. Narcissa was in bed and the two Sager boys were watching over their sister Louise and Helen Mar Meek who were both seriously ill with measles. After waking his wife, Marcus sent the two boys to bed saying he would watch the sick girls. In hushed voice he told Narcissa of the latest developments, sent her back to bed, and continued his sick watch.

The events of the next two days were recorded by the survivors at various dates and with differing details, but the sequence is generally as follows:

The next morning, Monday, November 29, the mission was shrouded in a wet cold fog. Narcissa did not appear for breakfast as usual. When Whitman asked Nicholas Finley, a troublemaker of mixed-blood who lived in a lodge nearby, if he knew anything of a plot brewing, Finley innocently replied, "I should know doctor; you have nothing to fear; there is no danger."[47] Whitman did not suspect that the conspirators had met at Finley's own lodge to lay their plans.

Unaware of the danger the men of the mission went about their usual tasks. Francis Sager prepared to butcher an animal; Saunders, the teacher, was back in the classroom again after cancelling school the week before when too many pupils were sick. At 11:00 A.M. Whitman conducted a burial service in the cemetery for three Indian children, victims of the measle epidemic. They were thought to be Chief Tiloukaikt's offspring. There were just a few Indians at the burial, but more than the usual number loitered around the mission yard.

After noon lunch the work resumed. Narcissa, red-eyed and drawn, prepared to bathe the Sager girls in the sitting room while Marcus read. At about 2:00 P.M. came a knock on the door. Indians had entered the kitchen seeking medicine from the doctor. After Whitman went to the kitchen with the medicine, Narcissa bolted the door behind him.

Soon angry voices were heard followed by a gun shot. Mary Ann Bridger, then eleven years old, who had been in the kitchen washing dishes, escaped through a window, ran outside to the sitting room door, and burst into the room screaming, "The Indians are killing Father and John."[48] Paralyzed with fright she told the grim details.

While Whitman had talked to Tiloukaikt, Tomahas had struck him on the head twice from behind with his tomahawk. In a desperate effort to escape, the injured doctor pulled himself to the door and fell to the floor. The Indians in the yard drew the guns and tomahawks they had concealed under their blankets and began to shoot the men at work. One Indian lashed Whitman's face until it was no longer recognizable, then fired a shot into his neck.

Back in the kitchen John Sager, who had been preparing twine to make brooms, drew a pistol, fired and wounded two men, but was quickly felled by a shot in the neck that bled profusely. He had presence of mind to press a scarf into the wound to stop the bleeding. The Indians ran from the kitchen to join the massacre outside. Marcus and John lay on the floor, alive but fatally wounded.

Narcissa and three other women rushed to the wounded doctor, dragged him into the sitting room and lifted him to a settee where Narcissa tried to stop the bleeding from his neck wound. When she asked him a few questions, he struggled to answer before slipping into unconsciousness.

Andrew Rodgers, the former teacher, and another man, both wounded, burst into the sitting room. After more gun shots outside, Narcissa looked out the window in the upper part of the door and saw Joe Lewis in the yard. She cried out to him, "Is it you, Joe, who are doing this?"[49] Just then she was shot in the left breast and fell to the floor. Clutching her wound she struggled to her feet and forgetting herself thought only of saving the children. She ushered everyone, including the sick girls, up the stairs to the attic bedroom. There a dozen terrified people huddled together expecting the worst.

Meanwhile Josiah Osborn, one of Whitman's workers, hid himself, his wife and three children under the floor boards in the Indian room. Saunders, the teacher, was shot as he ran from the schoolroom. Francis Sager pushed his sister Matilda, and the other children into the loft above the classroom. Ten-year-old Eliza Spalding, who had been sent by her parents to the Whitmans for schooling, was there with the others. Joe Lewis soon discovered their hiding place and ordered them to line up in the yard to be shot. One Indian stopped the execution, but Joe Lewis, who for some reason hated Francis Sager, shot the boy.

When the Indians came back to search the house, they discovered those hiding in the attic room. By promising not to harm them, Chief Tamsucky lured Narcissa and the others downstairs. He then ordered Joe Lewis and the wounded Rodgers to carry Mrs. Whitman outside on a settee. No sooner were they out the door than the Indians opened fire and sprayed Narcissa and Rodgers with a volley of shots. Death for Narcissa was instantaneous, but Rodgers lingered for several hours. In one last hateful act, an Indian rolled Narcissa's body into a muddy ditch and lashed her face.

The Osborn family hiding under the floor heard the groans of Whitman and Rodgers before the two men died that evening. During the night the Osborns crept from their hiding place and began a torturous twenty-five-mile struggle to reach Fort Walla Walla and shelter.

Some forty survivors including the children sought sanctuary at the emigrant house, formerly the home of William Gray. The five Sager girls were there, but they had lost their two brothers and a second pair of parents.

Monday's slaughter left nine dead—one woman, six men, and two boys. Four more men were killed on following days, making a total of thirteen. Another man drowned later as he carried the news of the massacre to Willamette Valley.

Following the massacre the Indians looted the mission, taking clothing, household items, and valuables, and destroying the rest. Joe Lewis gleefully ransacked Narcissa's special trunk that had come from the east with her.

On Wednesday morning Father Brouillet learned of the massacre when he arrived at Waiilatpu to visit Whitman. At the cemetery the washed bodies covered with sheets were lowered one by one into a shallow grave dug by one of the survivors. Father Brouillet read the Roman Catholic burial service in Latin, an ironic twist at the funeral of the devout Presbyterians. Through the night wolves clawed through the thin layer of earth and dug up the bodies. The remains were reburied later.

The Spaldings barely escaped a similar fate and were overjoyed to learn that their daughter Eliza had survived at Waiilatpu. Whitman's nephew Perrin had left the mission earlier to go to The Dalles. Louise Sager and Helen Mar Meek soon died from the measles.

For one month after the massacre, forty-seven survivors were held hostage to insure against retaliation by the Americans. A few chiefs voted to shoot them all, but Tiloukaikt ruled otherwise. The captives were well fed from the ample supplies Marcus had stored. Eliza Spalding, the only one who knew the Indian language, became their interpreter. However, before the captives were rescued, three women were taken by the Indians as wives, and at least three others were raped.

The massacre had been plotted by only about fourteen Cayuses largely from Tiloukaikt's band. Most of the tribe had not participated in the conspiracy, and they feared there would be reprisals against them all. Some wept openly at the sight of the mangled bodies.

When word spread of the massacre and the restraining of the hostages, difficult questions loomed. Who could negotiate for the safe release of the captives? How could the murderers be apprehended and punished without starting an all-out war? And how could the angry Americans be stopped from retaliating against all Indians?

After attempts by the Catholic priests failed to secure the release of the hostages, Peter Skene Ogden of the Hudson's Bay Company at Fort Vancouver arrived at Fort Walla Walla to negotiate with the Indians. The Cayuses respected Ogden and were well aware that the Hudson's Bay Company supplied them with guns, ammunition, and provisions in exchange for furs and horses. Ogden could not guarantee that there would be no retaliation by the Americans, but he did offer a ransom of "fifty blankets, fifty shirts, ten guns, ten fathoms of tobacco, ten handkerchiefs, and one hundred balls and powder."[50] All of the hostages were to be released including Lorinda Bewley, the woman Five Crows had taken as a wife and was reluctant to give up. Although some of the militant chiefs objected, the prisoners were released from the mission on

December 29, one month after the massacre, and were on their way to Fort Walla Walla. In the meantime Ogden had paid another ransom to the Nez Perces for the safe journey of the Spaldings to the fort.

Sixty-seven people left with Ogden for Fort Vancouver in three loaded bateaus. Only David Malin, the Whitman's adopted boy, then eight or nine years old, was left behind standing alone on the shore crying bitterly when no one would assume care for him. David was not heard from again. The party of missionaries arrived at Fort Vancouver, then were sent on to Portland.

Blot Them from the Face of the Earth.

The Massacre at Waiilatpu triggered the start of what became known as the Cayuse War. An editorial in the *Oregon Spectator* on January 20, 1848, reflected the outrage of the Americans:

> Let the Cayuse be pursued with unremitting hatred and hostility, until their life blood has atoned for their infamous deeds; let them be hunted as beasts of prey; let their name and race be blotted from the face of the earth, and the places that once knew them, know them no more forever.[51]

Troops of Oregon Volunteers and militia from the Provisional Government of Oregon were mobilized to apprehend the murderers and prevent a coalition of all the Indian tribes of the upper Columbia. Skirmishes followed with casualties on both sides. When the troops arrived at Waiilatpu, they found the mission buildings burned and fragments of unearthed bodies strewn about. The remains were again reburied.

The military set up headquarters at Waiilatpu and renamed it Fort Waters. From there expeditions went out on their man-hunts. The troops also committed grave atrocities against innocent natives and stole hundreds of Indian horses and cattle that turned the friendly Cayuses against them. A peace council brought together representatives of the Walla Wallas, Nez Perces, and a few Cayuses, but pursuit of the elusive five who had been identified as the murderers continued for months until they supposedly "voluntarily surrendered" for the welfare of the entire tribe.

In the early summer of 1850 the trial of the five Cayuse captives began in Oregon City. Spectators crowded the courtroom. After a grand jury hearing and two days of testimony, the jury pronounced all five guilty. The judge sentenced them to be hanged on Monday, June 3, 1850. The five included: Tiloukaikt, who supposedly struck Marcus Whitman; Tomahas, who confessed to shooting the doctor; Ishishkaiskais (called Frank Escaloom), who was said to have shot Narcissa; Clokamas, who assisted in killing Francis Sager; and Kiamasumpkin, who was believed to be innocent.

Following the hanging some army personnel and officials claimed that all five were innocent and had sacrificed themselves for the survival of the tribe. It was believed that the real offenders, ten in number, had already been killed by either the troops or by the Cayuses themselves. Eye-witnesses later corroborated the complicity of the first four, but Kiamasumpkin's participation was never verified.

The massacre had far-reaching effects. Relationships became markedly more strained between Indians and whites, British and Americans, and Catholics and Protestants. In August 1848 President Polk signed the Oregon Bill which made Old Oregon a territory of the United States. The Cayuse Indians had lost their war, their land, and their identity as a people, and the British were moved north of the 49th parallel.

The Whitman massacre brought Protestant mission work in Oregon to a sudden halt. The buildings at Waiilatpu were burned by angry Cayuses, the fruit trees chopped down, and the cultivated land soon returned to fields of rye grass. In 1897 a granite shaft was erected atop a high hill overlooking the mission grounds. In the distance to the southeast lay the hazy Blue Mountains. At the present time on the grounds below, a marble slab covers the remains of the massacre victims in "the great grave." Nearby a small tombstone marks the grave of Alice Clarissa Whitman. In the 1940's archeologists uncovered the foundations of the mission buildings and marked them with cement blocks. All of these can be seen at the Whitman Mission National Historic Site seven miles west of present-day Walla Walla, Washington.

Adapted to a Different Destiny.

In April 1848 Henry Spalding sent a lengthy detailed account of the death of the Whitmans to Narcissa's parents. His letter evinced none of the ill-will he had harbored toward Narcissa, but he spared no details of the brutality of the massacre and the days of captivity of the hostages. He also told of the narrow escape of his own family. His report differs in some respects from other accounts.

When Jane Prentiss, Narcissa's sister, learned of the massacre, she wrote to the Reverend Henry Perkins, the Methodist missionary with whom Narcissa had stayed while Marcus was on his trip east. Jane inquired why her sister and Marcus had been killed when they had done so much good among the Indians. Two years later Perkins, who knew nothing of the Whitman's early days at Waiilatpu, wrote a frank appraisal of their unsuitability for mission work. He criticized Marcus for his independent spirit, his lack of identification with the natives, and his aid to the white emigrants to the detriment of the Cayuses. Of Narcissa he wrote:

> Mrs. Whitman was not adapted to savage but *civilized* life. She would have done honor to her sex in a polished & exalted sphere, but never in the low drudgery of Indian toil. The natives esteemed her as proud, haughty, as *far above them*. No doubt she really seemed so. It was her *misfortune*, not her *fault*. She was adapted to a different destiny. She wanted something exalted—communion with *mind*. She longed for society, *refined society*. She was intellectually & by association fitted to do good only in such a sphere. She should have been differently situated. . . . She was not a *missionary* but a *woman*, an American highly gifted, polished American lady. And such she died.[52]

Although Perkins' harsh assessment of the Whitmans had measures of truth, he did not take into account the effect of the measles epidemic on the Cayuses. Nor did he know the zeal with which the missionaries had first applied themselves to make the mission a success and their unflagging dedication to their cause. As Jane reread Narcissa's letters, she could readily trace the transformation of her sister during the eleven years at Waiilatpu. Narcissa had changed —she had been devastated by the loss of her only child and had grown weary, ill, and lonely. However, she did not lose her concern for the Indians. In her last letter to her parents on August 23, 1847, Narcissa wrote:

> The poor Indians are amazed at the overwhelming numbers of Americans coming into the country. They seem not to know what to make of it. Very many of the principal ones are dying, and some have been killed by other Indians, in going south into the region of California. The remaining ones seem attached to us, and cling to us the closer; cultivate their farms quite extensively, and do not wish to see any Sniapus

(Americans) settle among them here. . . . They would be willing to have more missionaries stop and those devoted to their good. They expect that eventually this country will be settled by them, but they wish to see the Willamette filled up first.[53]

The original goal of the Whitmans and the American Board was to evangelize the Cayuse Indians. In this respect their mission was a failure. The Whitmans could not bridge the cultural gap with these nomadic people, communicate fluently with them, or convert them to a foreign religion. Also working to defeat them were the internal struggles with the other Presbyterian missionaries, particularly with the Spaldings, and the strained relations with the American Board which from their remote Boston offices criticized the Whitmans for their non-religious activities and the expenses incurred for equipment and supplies. The Catholic-Protestant discord led the Indians to be distrustful and confused by the religion of all whites.

The success of the Presbyterian ministry to the Indians in Old Oregon was minimal if one looked at just the converts on the record books, another disappointment to the Board. During the eleven years from 1836 to 1847, Spalding had baptized only twenty-one Indians—twenty were Nez Perces, only one was a Cayuse (Five Crows from Waiilatpu). This was in stark contrast to the Catholic priests who registered hundreds of baptisms. An explanation lay largely in the attitude of the missionaries toward baptism. The Catholics looked on the sacrament as the *first* step to conversion, while the Presbyterians regarded it as a reward *after* achieving a certain level of religious instruction.

Marcus Whitman never regarded himself as an evangelist, and he could not conduct the pastoral duties of an ordained minister as could Spalding. Marcus was first and foremost a doctor. As the westward expansion escalated, the Whitmans believed their duties also included administering physically and spiritually to the emigrants.

Narcissa, a product of a religious upbringing in civilized New York state, was, as Perkins suggested, a misplaced person. Although she worked tirelessly at Waiilatpu, she was not prepared to bridge the vast gulf between herself and the Cayuses. Her greatest satisfaction lay in her work with the Indian children, but even there she drew the curtain between the Cayuse youngsters who came to the mission school and her own daughter and the adopted children she had taken into her home. She taught in the same manner she had been trained as a child, stressing the value of prayer, the Bible as the Word of God, and the danger of sin, all foreign concepts to her Indian pupils. Her beautiful singing voice was her most successful tool.

Narcissa loved orderliness, industry, cleanliness, and beauty. She was not prepared for the earthiness and apathy of the Indians. In later years she realized her failures, and her letters reflected her fear of losing her religious fervor and piety. But even to the end she insisted that she had made the right choice for her life. Her last letter to her sister again urged Jane and Edward to come west to join them.

As Perkins noted, Narcissa in some respects had failed as a *missionary*, but she did not fail as a *woman*. At age twenty-eight she had set her course, and she followed it with zest and vitality until she became worn down from the realities of mission work. Hers was the rare courage manifested by the women who forsook civilized life for the unknown frontier. She was brave enough to be the first woman to pursue an adventure reserved just for men. The commitment, faith, and sincerity with which she assumed her role as a missionary, a wife, a mother, and a Christian cannot be questioned. She followed her dream which unfortunately ended in tragedy.

Notes

1   Clifford M. Drury. *Marcus and Narcissa Whitman and the Opening of Old Oregon*, vol. I (Glendale, California: The Arthur H. Clark Company, 1973), p. 161.

2   Ibid., p. 162.

3   Catlin's pictures of the two Nez Perces are in the Smithsonian Institution, numbers 207 & 208.

4   Drury. vol. I, p. 54. Letter from Parker to the American Board, April 10, 1833.

5   Ibid., p. 109.

6   Ibid., p. 110. Letter from Greene to Parker, December 24, 1834.

7   Ibid., p. 105. Letter from Narcissa to her mother, March 30, 1847.

8   Ibid., p. 107. Letter dated October 10, 1840.

9   Nard Jones. *The Great Command* (Boston: Little Brown and Company, 1959), p. 22.

10   Drury. vol. I, pp. 155-6.

11   Ibid., p. 149. Letter from Greene to Whitman, January 22, 1835.

12   Ibid., p. 166. Letter from Spalding to American Board, March 2, 1836.

13   Ibid., p. 167.

14   Ibid., p. 169. Letter from Greene to Whitman, March 4, 1836.

15   Ibid., p. 170. From the letter above.

16   Ibid., p. 174. Testimonial from the Rev. Pettibone to the American Board.

17   Narcissa Whitman. *The Letters of Narcissa Whitman* (Fairfield, Washington: Ye Galleon Press, 1986), p. 20. From a letter to her family written on June 27, 1836. All quotations from Narcissa's journal and letters are printed as she wrote them, in some cases with misspelled words and faulty punctuation due probably to the haste and frequency with which she wrote.

18   Ibid., p. 16. Letter written on June 3, 1836.

19   Ibid. From Letter above.

20   Ibid., p. 21. From letter above.

21   Ibid., p. 16. Letter written on June 3, 1836.

22   Ibid., p. 21. Letter written on June 27, 1836.

23   Narcissa Prentiss Whitman. *My Journal, 1836,* (Fairfield, Washington: Ye Galleon Press, 1982), p. 16. Written on July 25, 1836.

24   Ibid., pp. 17-18. Written on July 28, 1836.

25   Ibid., p. 17. Written on July 27, 1836.

26   Ibid., p. 36. Written on August 29, 1836.

27   Ibid. From journal above.

28   Ibid., pp. 55-56. Written on September 23, 1836.

29   Whitman. *The Letters of Narcissa Whitman*, p. 46. Letters written on December 26, 1836.

30   Ibid., p. 47. Letter written to family on March 30, 1837.

31   Ibid. Although the custom of flattening the heads of infants was generally dying out, Narcissa had noted that some of the Cayuses still practiced it, hence the name Flatheads originated.

32   Ibid., p. 62. Letter written on September 18, 1838.

33   Ibid., p. 61. From letter above.

34   Ibid., p. 58. Letter written on April 11, 1838.

35   Ibid. pp. 85-86. Letter written on October 9, 1839.

36   Drury. *Marcus and Narcissa Whitman*, vol. I, p. 244. Letter written on January 2, 1837.

37   Ibid., p. 251. Letter written on May 3, 1837.

38   Ibid., p. 264. Letter written on May 10, 1837.

39   Jones., p. 175.

40 Drury. *Marcus and Narcissa Whitman*, vol. I, p. 315. Letter written on May 27, 1838.

41 Ibid., pp. 333-34. Letter written on March 23, 1839.

42 Whitman. *The Letters of Narcissa Whitman*, p. 89. Letter written on October 9, 1839.

43 Drury. *Marcus and Narcissa Whitman*, vol. II, p. 14. Letter written on October 7, 1843.

44 Ibid., pp. 16-17. Letter written on October 22, 1843.

45 Ibid., p. 18. Letter written on February 7, 1844.

46 Ibid., p. 35. Letter written on April 12, 1844.

47 Ibid., p. 223.

48 Clifford Drury. *First White Women Over the Rockies*, vol. I (Glendale, California: The Arthur H. Clark Company, 1963), p. 165.

49 Ibid.

50 Drury. *Marcus and Narcissa Whitman*, vol. II, p. 289. Different ransom amounts are cited in Thompson's *Whitman Mission National Historic Site*, p. 72.

51 *Idaho Yesterdays*, Spring/Summer Issue, 1987. Vol. 31, Nos. 1-2. "The Cayuse Indian War" by Terence O'Donnell, p. 59.

52 Drury. *Marcus and Narcissa Whitman*, vol. II, p. 394.

53 Whitman. *The Letters of Narcissa Whitman*, p. 225.

Chapter 12

Sojourner Truth
(c.1797 - 1883)

A BLACK SLAVE WHO BECAME AN OUTSPOKEN ABOLITIONIST, ITINERANT PREACHER, AND ADVOCATE FOR AFRICAN AMERICANS AND WOMEN'S RIGHTS.

"IF I AM eighty-three years old, I only count my age from the time that I was emancipated. Then I began to live. God is a-fulfilling, and my lost time that I lost being a slave was made up."[1] So spoke the illiterate ex-slave Sojourner Truth as she related her life story.

Isabella, or Belle as she was first called, never knew the exact date of her birth. When she was born, her parents knew nothing of writing or the calendar so they could not record the event. Their Dutch owner, Colonel Johannes Harden-

bergh, did not bother to write down the birth date of another baby born to one of his fourteen slaves. Belle was thought to have been born sometime in the year of 1797, twenty-one years after the adoption of the Declaration of Independence. She was the next to the youngest child of several born to her mother Elizabeth, usually called Mau-Mau Bett, and her father James, known as Baumfree.

Colonel Hardenbergh owned one of the largest farms in Ulster County in the Hudson Valley some eighty miles north of New York City. After the American Revolution, states north of Maryland and Delaware had abolished slavery with the exception of New York and New Jersey. Here gentlemen farmers such as Hardenbergh kept slaves so he and his family could enjoy the good life. But New York slave-owners feared that it was only a matter of time before the anti-slavery militants would prevail and force them to free or dispose of their black "chattel." The influential aristocrat, John Jay (1745-1829), had proposed that the first New York constitution adopted in 1777 include an antislavery clause. True to his convictions, Jay purchased slaves, trained them to earn a living, and gave them their freedom.

Jay, who later became the first Chief Justice of the United States, made several unsuccessful attempts to outlaw slavery before legislation was finally passed in 1785. It then became illegal to bring slaves to the state of New York to sell, or to transport slaves to owners in other states. This law also allowed an owner to free his slaves who were under fifty years of age by issuing a certificate of manumission, or freedom, without posting the bond previously necessary to insure that the slaves would not become public dependents. Slaves over fifty could be freed if the owner accepted responsibility for their support in the event they became indigent or incapable of providing for themselves. The law was not strictly enforced, and some slave-owners gave their sick and elderly slaves their freedom to avoid supporting them.

In 1799 a law was passed allowing female slaves born thereafter to gain their freedom after serving their masters without pay until age twenty-five. Male slaves were required to work until they were twenty-eight. After bills were introduced repeatedly in the state legislature, New York finally abolished slavery in 1827 for all slaves over twenty-eight years of age.

When Belle was just a baby, Colonel Hardenbergh died, and his son Charles inherited the slaves along with the other "property." Charles moved to nearby Hurley, a short distance to the north. In his large comfortable house, the master could look out on the creek and wooded meadows, while his slaves strained their eyes to see by the light that filtered through narrow slits high on the wall of their damp cellar room. They slept on straw piled on top of loose planks covering the muddy ground. At night they were kept warm by burning pine knots in the fireplace.

Belle knew her father only as a bent, rheumatic old man whose remaining days were numbered. Baumfree, whose Dutch name meant "straight as a tree," had once been a tall muscular man who pleased his master by his hard work. Belle's mother Mau-Mau Bett was Baumfree's third wife, the first two having been sold to other owners. Mau-Mau worked long hours in the Hardenbergh kitchen, which left little time for her two remaining children, Belle and Peter. At one time there had been ten or eleven other children, but the others had died or had been sold.

Belle's fondest memories from her dismal childhood were of her mother's rich husky voice as she sang the songs of Africa and told the sad stories of her lost children. Mau-Mau, imbued with a firm faith in a God somewhere in the sky, made sure that Peter and Belle could recite the Lord's Prayer in their Low Dutch idiom. God would look after them, she said, and send them kind masters if they only asked. To insure their success as "good slaves," Mau-Mau preached the importance of obeying their white masters.

When Belle was about nine, Master Charles became seriously ill and died. The slaves feared what would happen to them. One week after Charles's death, a notice was posted in the nearby town of Kingston: "the slaves, horses, and other cattle of Charles Hardenbergh, deceased"[2] would be auctioned off on the following Tuesday. When she reached adulthood and became a freed woman, Belle (then Sojourner Truth) captivated audiences with her story:

> As I told you, when I was sold, my master died, and we was going to have a auction. We was all brought up to be sold. My mother, my father was very old, my brother younger than myself, and my mother took my hand. There opened a canopy of heaven, and she sat down and I and my brother sat down by her, and she says, 'Look up to the moon and stars that shine upon your father and upon your mother when your're (sic) sold far away, and upon your brothers and sisters, that is sold away,' for there was a great number of us, and was all sold away before my remembrance. I asked her who had made the moon and the stars, and she says, 'God,' and says I, Where is God? 'Oh!' says she, 'child, he sits in the sky, and he hears you when you ask him when you are away from us to make your master and mistress good, and he will do it.[3]

The Hardenbergh heirs found an expedient solution to the problem of Belle's aging parents. They gave Baumfree and Mau-Mau their freedom and thereby released themselves of the responsibility and expense of caring for slaves no longer useful. As a token of their good will, the owners allowed the two slaves to continue to live in the cellar, but there would be no support for them. But Isabella and Peter, young and healthy, would be marketable.

Why Won't You Help Me?

As the auctioneer chanted his sing-song litany, Isabella stood on the auction block trying to be brave. Although she could not understand what was said, she soon surmised that the man who came forward with money would be her new master. He had purchased her, along with some sheep, for the sum of $100. She and the sheep soon trudged down the dusty road behind John Neely, a Yankee from Massachusetts. Neely, a new resident who had just opened a store at Twaalfskill, thought it would be of benefit to own at least one slave to prove to prospective New York customers that he did not disapprove of slavery.

But John Neely's wife was not pleased that her husband had spent good money on this thin, gangly girl with the blue-black skin, a slave who didn't speak or understand a word of English. Life with the Neelys was harsh. Belle could not understand her mistress's instructions and often was beaten for her mistakes. In the bitter winter she froze in her one shabby summer dress, worn-out shoes, and second-hand shawl. Belle said:

> When we were sold, I did what my mother told me; I said, O God, my mother told me if I asked you to make my master and mistress good, you'd do it, and they didn't get good. [Laughter.] Why, says I, God, maybe you can't do it. Kill them. [Laughter and applause.] I didn't think he could make them good. That was the idea I had. After I made such wishes my conscience burned me. Then I would say, O God, don't be mad. My master makes me wicked; and I often thought how people can do such abominable wicked things and their conscience not burn them. Now I only made wishes. I used to tell God this—I would say, 'Now, God, if I was you, and you was me [laughter], and you wanted any help I'd help you;—why don't you help me?[4]

For two years Belle prayed that she would be sent to another master. When Martin Schryver, an innkeeper and fisherman, appeared at the Neely's door with an offer to buy her for $105, Belle was sure her prayers were answered. Schryver and his wife were simple jovial Dutch folk who treated her well. She was expected to do farm work, haul fish, and run errands, an outdoor life she relished. There was time to just "browse around" and sing her mother's songs when no one was listening.

After a year and a half with the Schryvers, a tall gentleman stopped at the tavern, noticed the strong-limbed black girl who towered over most everyone. The man liked her erect bearing, her purposeful stride, and her large-featured face. On the spot he offered to buy her for $300 (then 70 pounds), a sum the Schryvers could not refuse. So Belle, then about thirteen, was off to live with the John J. Dumonts of New Paltz. Here she made her home for sixteen years until she gained her freedom.

White Man's Pet.

In 1810 Belle joined the ten slaves on the Dumont farm. Her main duty was to help Mrs. Dumont in the kitchen and when necessary apply her hand to field work. Dumont grew to be very fond of Belle and praised her good work. He boasted, "That wench is better to me than a man.

She'll do a good family's wash in the night, and by morning she'll be ready to go into the field, where she'll do as much raking and binding as my best field hand."[5]

But Mrs. Dumont did not share her husband's opinion because she felt uncomfortable with the lanky black girl who could not understand directions. In her crisp icy manner Mrs. Dumont often complained of Belle's clumsiness and ineptitude, while she praised Kate, the white indentured servant who had been sent to work for them from the county poorhouse.

Belle tried in every way to please her mistress, but things always seemed to get worse. When the Dumont family wanted boiled potatoes for breakfast, it was Belle's duty to prepare them. For three consecutive days the morning potatoes appeared gray and dirty, and Belle was blamed. Mrs. Dumont smugly pointed this out to her husband who scolded the puzzled Belle. With the help of Dumont's sympathetic daughter Gertrude, the two girls discovered that Kate had sprinkled ashes on the potatoes just before they were served, knowing full well that Belle would be blamed.

More than anything Belle feared incurring the displeasure of her master. As Mau-Mau had taught her, she tried by every means possible to be an obedient slave. When Dumont praised her, it spurred her on to greater efforts, and she became obsessed with gaining her master's approval. The other slaves noticed that she often worked until she was ready to drop, and they resented her because it made them appear lazy by comparison. "White man's pet," they ridiculed. But Belle ignored their taunts and kept her dreams and ambitions to herself. Something within her was stirring. She supposed that her white master must be God with omniscient powers to look into her very soul.

For years Belle had not seen her parents, and she had not been able to rejoice with them in their "freedom." She longed to see Mau-Mau again, listen to her wisdom, and hear her rich mellow voice. While Belle had been working for the Neelys, the Schryvers, and the Dumonts, her parents had been living in the Hardenbergh's cellar. Freedom to them was no blessing—they were ill, hungry, and had no means of support.

When she was about sixteen, Belle was allowed to visit her parents in Hurley, but she was too late to see her beloved mother alive. Mau-Mau had died suddenly from a "fit of palsy," and old Baumfree was left helpless and alone. Belle could do little to console her distraught father.

Baumfree was placed in the care of Mau-Mau's brother and his wife, but they too were old and soon died. Later Baumfree's frozen starved body was found in an isolated run-down shack. At the funeral Belle walked to the slave burial ground beside the black pine coffin the Hardenberghs had donated as a reward for Baumfree's years of slave labor. The Hardenberghs also gave the mourners a jug of their best corn whiskey to cheer them.

After her parents' death Belle's loneliness became unbearable. The other slaves distrusted her and accused her of being the white master's spy. Whenever possible, Belle retreated to a small island in a nearby stream where she built a hiding place of willow branches. Here she spoke aloud to God—perhaps Mau-Mau's God sitting in the sky would listen. Belle made promises, she begged, she bargained, but God gave her no answers. She said later, "Well, you see I was in want, and I felt that there was no help. I know what it is to be taken in the barn and tied up and blood drawn out of your bare back, and I tell you it would make you think about God." Then she would plead to God, "Now why won't you help me?"[6]

A Broken Promise.

Every spring the New York Dutch observed the arrival of Pinxster (or Pinkster), known as Whitsuntide or Pentecost. The slaves from surrounding farms were allowed to leave their work for a week-long celebration. It was an event all slaves waited for during the year. Belle watched their towering leader, Prince Gerald, a mighty black man bedecked with ribbons, a flashy decorated hat, and an old military jacket, as he beat the drums for the Congo dances, working up a frenzy of rhythm for dancing and chanting. For seven days and nights the slaves forgot their troubles, and in wild abandon they chanted, clapped, and whirled, and stopped only to eat, drink, and catch a bit of sleep. For one week there were no masters or slaves, no beatings, no harsh words, no heavy labor—just abandonment to the pounding beat of the drums and the rhythm of the dance. Pinxster was a therapeutic week for the slaves, and in time became almost exclusively a black celebration with curious white spectators just looking on.

At one such Pinxster celebration Belle met Robert, property of slave-owner Catlin, a neighbor of the Dumonts. Unlike most men, Robert was even taller than the six-foot Belle. They be-

came instant friends, and Robert made clandestine visits to Belle's hiding place on the island. When Catlin discovered Robert's trysts with Belle, he forbade his slave to continue seeing her. Robert's owner worried that if they should marry and have children, the offspring would belong to the Dumonts. One day when Robert visited Belle, Catlin followed him and ordered him beaten. When Dumont protested that no slave would be beaten on his property, Robert was dragged back to the Catlin farm and there was severely lashed. Although he suffered from the harsh beating, Robert continued to work. Soon he was ordered to marry one of Catlin's slaves, but died shortly, a broken and distressed man.

Seeing that Belle was of age to breed children, Dumont arranged for her to marry Thomas, an older slave whose stooped back showed scars from the lashings he had received as he attempted to follow his second wife when she was sold. After hiding for a month, he had been found by the slave-hunters, beaten, and returned to the Dumonts. Belle soon gave birth to her first child, Diana, followed shortly by Peter, Elizabeth, and Sophia. It was believed she bore at least five children.

The slaves in New York State waited anxiously for July 4, 1827, Freedom Day, when those who fulfilled the requirements of age and years of labor would be freed. Belle began to prepare for that glorious day. But she was jolted back to reality when Dumont informed her that he was selling "the services" of her four-year-old son Peter to Solomon Gedney, a neighbor who fancied the small boy. When Belle protested and cited the law, Dumont said he was not actually selling Peter, but was only selling his services. He promised that Peter would be well-cared for, have a fine home, and never would be sold as a slave. Belle watched as her young son was taken away.

With a tinge of conscience and in a burst of generosity, Dumont promised to free Belle in one year because of her loyalty and hard work. She would get her freedom on the next celebration of Pinxster. Belle believed him, and even though she had cut her hand severely on a scythe, she continued to wash clothes and work in the fields, disregarding the infected wound that refused to heal.

The Pinxster celebration arrived and passed, and there was no word from Dumont about Belle's freedom. Boldly she reminded him of his earlier promise, a pledge Dumont conveniently revoked saying that she had not done the necessary work during the past year because of her injured hand. He consoled her with a promise that in just one more year she would be free. Belle's disillusionment and anger were deep, and her faith in her white master was shattered. He was not God and was just as dishonest as other mortal white men. That night she made a plan— she would *take* her freedom.

After the summer work was completed, Belle packed a bandana with a little clothing, some summer sausage, and bread. She gathered up her baby Sophia and stole away as the dawn was just breaking. She left her husband Tom and the other children at the Dumonts for the time being—she would collect the children later.

She first went to the home of Levi Rowe, a Quaker who lived nearby, a kindly man who had spoken the unforgettable words to her earlier, "It is not right thee should be a slave. God does not want it."[7] She found Rowe seriously ill, but he directed her to another Quaker family down the road. When Belle and her baby appeared at the door of the Isaac Van Wagenen house, she was invited inside, fed, and promised shelter and work. But a pounding on the door interrupted them. An angry Dumont appeared demanding the return of his runaway slave and her child. Belle faced him squarely, and for the first time she dared defy him. She reminded him that she had not run away, but was claiming the freedom he had promised her, and she was keeping her child.

The quiet voice of Van Wagenen interrupted the confrontation. Although as a Quaker he did not believe in buying or selling people, he offered to pay Dumont $20 for Belle's services for one year, and $5 for the child. Dumont shrugged, took the money and left. Belle thanked her new benefactor, grabbed the broom, and began to work.

Render Unto Them Double.

Life with the Van Wagenens was placid and even comfortable for Belle and little Sophia. Belle helped with the housework, tended the small garden, the cow, and the chickens while the Van Wagenens ran a small neighborhood store. But she missed her children, the sight of other black faces, and the companionship about the fire in the Dumont's slave kitchen. For a time she considered giving up her freedom and returning voluntarily to Dumonts, but the notion soon vanished when she learned that Solomon Gedney had sold her son Peter to his daughter

Eliza and her husband Solomon Fowler. The Fowlers had taken Peter with them to Alabama. Belle felt betrayed and confused. She was determined to get Peter back, but she had yet to devise a plan.

Because the law of 1785 prohibited the transporting of slaves across state lines, Belle reasoned Dr. Gedney should be held responsible for allowing Peter to be moved out of New York. In her view, white folks must also live by the laws they, themselves, had made.

In the meantime Freedom Day had arrived in New York on July 4, 1827. In accordance with the law passed in 1817, Belle would then be legally free. But her children, who had by law been born free, were required to work out their years as unpaid servants before attaining their freedom. The event was not heralded in the newspapers, and no public ceremonies were held, but the slaves celebrated in private. Freedom was a reality, but the future for freed slaves was uncertain and even dangerous. The Van Wagenens held a private observance for Belle, and gave little Sophia her freedom although she could have worked for them without pay until age twenty-five. The Quakers paid Belle a small wage for her work and wrote out the paper of manumission.

Belle courageously stormed back to the Dumonts at New Paltz and demanded the return of her son. Mrs. Dumont ridiculed her for being so upset about such an "inconsequential matter." Belle then accosted Mrs. Gedney, the mother of Eliza Fowler, Peter's mistress in Alabama. Mrs. Gedney surveyed the awkward black woman with disdain and laughed at her demands and accusations.

Frustrated and not knowing what to do, Belle again turned to the Quakers who directed her to the Kingston County Courthouse where she hoped to find justice. Belle knew nothing of courts, lawyers, or legal procedures, so she endured much ridicule and faced many roadblocks. Finally she secured a writ for the constable of New Paltz to serve on Solomon Gedney ordering him to get her son back. Belle hurried on foot fifteen miles back to New Paltz. During the months of waiting while Gedney traveled to Alabama to get Peter, Belle worked for various white folks at Kingston. When he returned with Peter, Gedney refused to release the boy to Belle. The helpful Quakers again directed the distraught mother to a young lawyer who was willing to risk taking the case of a poor black woman against a powerful white landowner. The

Quakers gave her money to pay the attorney's fee.

When the two opposing parties appeared in the judge's chambers at Kingston, Peter, upon seeing his mother, clutched Gedney's legs and pleaded not to be taken away. Belle was crushed as the little boy refused to recognize her as his mother. The judge noticed Peter's terrified glances toward Gedney and saw scars and welts on the boy's face. When asked about the injuries, the boy answered that a horse had kicked him, and he had run into a carriage. The judge was suspicious and ordered Peter returned to his rightful owner, his mother.

When Belle was alone with her son, she pulled off his shirt and found on his back the scars of the many beatings he had suffered at the hand of Solomon Fowler in Alabama. Peter admitted that he had been threatened with more whippings if he made the wrong answers before the judge. In anger Belle prayed, "Oh Lord, render unto them double."[8]

Later Belle learned that Fowler had brutally murdered his own wife Eliza. Guilt surged through Belle. "Oh, God," she sobbed, "I did not mean quite so much."[9]

Belle's victory in a court of law was widely acclaimed by the opponents of slavery. But the slave-owners were fearful for future developments.

New York City and Freedom.

Belle soon realized that with her new-found freedom came new responsibilities. She could not help Tom, her aging husband, who since being freed by the Dumonts had wandered aimlessly from one place to another trying to find work and a place to sleep. He became a ward at the county poorhouse where he soon died. Neither could Belle support Peter or the growing Sophia. The Dumonts were willing to take Sophia back to live with her two sisters, and Peter was hired to raise and lower the locks for the barges that plied the waters of Rondout Creek. When Belle visited her children at the Dumonts, she noticed that there were fewer black faces among the workers. Many freed slaves were leaving the farms hoping for work in the bustling area around the new Erie Canal that had just opened in 1825. Those that remained were now to be paid a wage for their work.

One summer evening when Belle was walking past a church, she heard lusty voices and songs bursting from the open windows. She heard a familiar name, "Jesus," repeated over and over, a name she had often called upon for help and consolation. It was a white folks' church, and she didn't know if she would be welcome. She entered hesitantly. To her surprise, the Methodists accepted her. Later Belle recalled her religious conversion saying:

> Truly I don't know but God has helped me. But I got no good master until the last time I was sold, and then I found one and his name was Jesus. Oh, I tell you, didn't I find a good master when I used to feel so bad, when I used to say, O God, how can I live? I'm sorely oppressed both within and without. When God gave me that master he healed all the wounds up. My soul rejoiced.[10]

Belle soon met a schoolteacher, a Miss Geer, who convinced her that she should go to New York City, a place that offered better pay for domestics and a chance for Peter to go to school. Miss Geer even offered to pay for Peter's tuition. Belle's dreams for Peter would be realized, but what of her three daughters? Perhaps if she worked hard and saved her money, she could some day buy a small house and bring her girls to live with her when they would be free. After tearful farewells, Belle, Peter, and Miss Geer set sail on a small sloop down the Hudson River to the big city.

In 1829 New York City was becoming a metropolis. The opening of the Erie Canal had brought sailing vessels and steamboats of all descriptions with various cargoes and passengers to the growing port city. With increasing industry and trade came streets congested with horse-drawn carriages, wagons, omnibuses, and vendors' carts. Masses of immigrants and freed slaves flocked to the city to find employment. If they did find work, most of the unskilled laborers were paid poor wages and could afford nothing better than filthy tenement houses in the slums. White workers were angered by the black men who competed with them for jobs.

Peter lived in a boarding house, and with Miss Geer's help he enrolled in a school where he was to learn navigational skills as well as reading and writing. Belle found domestic work with the Whiting family. There she did what she had done all her life—scrubbing, washing, and cooking, but this time she was paid a wage for her efforts. She carefully put aside her money in hopes of some day buying her own home.

One Sunday Belle, dressed in her best apparel, appeared at the door of the largest Methodist Church in New York City, carrying with her a letter of introduction from the Ulster County Methodist Church. The elder at the door scrutinized her and asked her to return in the afternoon when the "coloreds" had their service. Belle was insulted and angry. She joined the Zion African Church, an exclusively black congregation, where she soon became known as the tall woman who gave eloquent prayers and sang stirring hymns. At Zion she met her sister Sophia and brother Michael who as children had been sold away from Baumfree and Mau-Mau Bett by the Hardenberghs. The siblings had been separated some thirty years.

During the first two years in New York City, Belle became involved with street ministry in the tenement district. However, she soon became disillusioned with the futility of trying to bring religion to the poor whose pressing needs were work, food, clothing, and liveable homes. Belle was ashamed that many of New York's freed or fugitive slaves, now living in close proximity, had banded together to harrass the white population with theft and arson.

Belle then met two religious zealots—Elijah Pierson, who claimed to be John the Baptist, and Matthias, who passed himself off as Jesus Christ. The two men set up a communal society just outside New York City called "The Kingdom." Members were to live together, contribute all their savings to the cause, and work cooperatively for the good of the commune. When Belle was invited to join, she left her other job, gave all her savings to the two men, and moved to the community house. Here she again found herself doing the menial tasks which no one else wanted, and now there was no pay. Dissension soon developed between the two founders over control of the commune, and in 1834 "The Kingdom" collapsed. Again Bell was disillusioned by religious pretenders.

Just as she was about to leave "The Kingdom" and return to her former employer, Pierson died suddenly and mysteriously. Matthias and Belle were accused of poisoning him. A court trial dragged on for months, and sensational accounts ran in the newspapers. With no concrete evidence against Matthias and Belle, the judge finally ruled that Pierson had died from ingesting an overdose of unripe blackberries.

But the trouble was not over for Belle. An unethical and opportunistic newsman decided to exploit the case by writing a book that immediately attracted wide attention. He accused

Belle of being a black witch who had plotted Pierson's death and had destroyed the "ideal" commune. The book was a sensation. Belle, no stranger to court cases, was helped by another news reporter, Gilbert Vale, who wrote a book telling Belle's story. He gathered testimonials from all of Belle's former owners and employers, including John Dumont. Everyone vouched for her honesty and good character. Vale also helped Belle sue the writer of the first book for slander. Again, she won the case and was awarded $125. Belle had lost all her savings and furniture to Pierson and Matthias but had emerged a more wary and confident individual.

Back in New York City with the Whitings, Belle faced another problem. Her son Peter had been expelled from school and was constantly getting into trouble with the law. He had fallen in with a group of older boys who exerted strong influence on him and led him into petty thefts and misdemeanors that often ended in jail.

Belle, fearing that Peter was headed for more serious trouble, urged him to become a seaman, a life she realized was little better than slavery. In August 1839 Peter reluctantly joined a whaling crew and left for the sea. Belle never saw her son again, but she did receive five letters from him. She dictated replies to her son, but Peter never received her letters.

Meant to Do Greater Things.

To Belle New York became a city of sin and decadence, a den of money-changers where the rich robbed the poor, and the poor robbed each other. Here the hopes of immigrants and freed slaves were crushed as they lived with poverty, hunger, discrimination, and inhumane treatment. Some of her people, though free, faced an existence worse than slavery. Those who had escaped or bought their freedom feared being kidnapped by slave-hunters who were paid a good price to bring them back to the South in chains. Belle concluded, "There is no brotherly love here." She, herself, had nothing to show for over forty years of strenuous labor but the scars on her back, two wrinkled gnarled hands, graying hair, an aching body, and a tortured soul. She asked:

> Why do I remain here, tied down, a slave to work, accomplishing nothing, moving from one worry to another, getting nowhere? What has been holding me to this one spot, praying and preaching, working and slaving, and making no headway? I am meant to do greater things than

these I am doing. I feel it in me. . . . Lord, what wilt thou have me to do?[11]

As in the past, Belle received the answer direct from God. "I hear a voice telling me to travel east," she said, "to tell them about the Lord Jesus. . . . There must be persons out there who will hear me . . . persons who will love me and care for me. . . . I must go."[12]

Belle wasted no time in answering God's call. The next morning without any hesitation, she gathered into a pillow-case some clothing, bread, cheese, and twenty-five cents, and announced to her astonished mistress that she was going away. Mrs. Whiting thought she was out of her mind and asked, "Where are you going?" Belle replied, "The Lord has directed me to go East, and leave the city at once."[13] With that she bade the Whitings farewell and on June 1, 1843, she turned her face to the sun and headed down to the ferry. There she paid her fare east to Brooklyn. For the first time she felt truly free— from now on she would be only God's slave. She was not worried about the future for she was sure God would provide her simple needs of a little food and a place to sleep.

As Belle walked the roadways waiting for more directions from God, she believed she heard a voice telling her to find a new name. Since her birth she had been just Isabella, or Belle, attached to whatever was the last name of her immediate owner. Now she needed a new identity to fit the new person she was becoming. As she strode along the dusty road, the name came to her—she was a traveler, a wanderer, a sojourner. That was it! "Sojourner" would be her new name. But she needed another name too. She prayed, "Oh, God, give me a name with a handle to it." A voice came, and she said, "And my heart leaped for joy—Sojourner Truth. 'Why,' said I, 'thank you, God. That is a good name. Thou art my last master and thy name is Truth, so shall Truth be my abiding name until I die.'"[14]

As she made her way across Long Island, Sojourner soon discovered that when she sought shelter and food at the palatial homes of the rich, the doors were often slammed in her face. But when she approached a run-down shack, the poor inside often shared with her what little they had. When she found no house, she would drop down for the night on straw in a barn or a shed. Often she stopped to work for lodging and food but never accepted much pay for her labors.

She turned her direction northward into Connecticut where she became acquainted with outdoor camp meetings. For several days families would come together to hear any preacher who needed a platform and an audience. Tents and hastily-built shacks dotted the nearby fields. Sojourner was often granted permission to tell her own story and speak of her Lord. Listeners were soon captivated by this towering ebony-faced woman with the deep booming voice who spoke in her unusual accent and sang songs in a rich contralto voice. As her reputation spread, crowds began to gather just to hear her speak and sing.

Not all of Sojourner's listeners were receptive to her message. It bothered the white preachers and their followers that a black woman, obviously an unlearned, unschooled individual, should be preaching the word of God, condemning sin, and inciting emotional outbursts. At times there were violent arguments, but Sojourner, a battle-scarred warrior from other frays, could usually talk down her adversaries. She was fearless and rarely lost her dignity or self-control. Her sharp mind and wit could turn many a hostile combatant into a defender, but she had learned to be cautious of sooth-sayers and false prophets.

While she was in Connecticut, Sojourner dictated a letter to her three daughters she assumed were still living at the Dumont's farm in New York. She learned later that only Diana still worked for Dumont; the other two daughters, now grown, had married and moved away from New Paltz. Sojourner could no longer hope that someday her family would be united in their own home. Besides, she was now a wanderer, a sojourner without need of an earthly home.

Forever Unfit to Be a Slave.

As Sojourner tramped through Connecticut and into Massachusetts, her heavy men's shoes seemed to weigh more with each passing day. She hoped to find some place where she could put down her roots for a time. She found such a residence in Florence, Massachusetts, a town about 100 miles west of Boston. Here a newly organized cooperative community, the Northampton Association of Education and Industry, founded by George Benson and Samuel Hill, brought together educated men and women who dreamed of establishing a utopia dedicated to freedom and equality.

The members planned to support themselves by breeding silkworms and manufacturing silk cloth to sell. Seventy or eighty men, women, and children shared crowded living quarters with heavy machinery and looms, and the daily routine was anything but utopian. The members were accustomed to Harvard classrooms, academic and professional pursuits, and genteel life styles rather than repairing broken-down machines, cooking large kettles of food, and laundering bundles of clothes. Sojourner soon adjusted to the crowded, noisy quarters and offered her services with the washing. The Association paid to buy her metal-rimmed spectacles so her failing eyes could see what she was ironing.

Everyone was eager to work, share, and express opinions. Unlike "The Kingdom," religion was not important at Northampton. Members were of various religious persuasions, and some had no religion at all, a state that bothered Sojourner. What mattered to most members was equality regardless of sex, race, or religion.

There was only one other black face in the group—David Ruggles, a former editor of an antislavery newspaper, a doctor, and an active participant in the illegal underground New York Vigilance Committee which had helped fugitive slaves escape to New England or Canada. At one time Ruggles had helped Frederick Douglass in his flight from a Maryland slave-owner. Ruggles, blinded in a fight with slave-hunters, was a respected and well-liked man at Northampton.

Children in the commune were given a liberal education where they learned the rudiments and even the classics from scholarly teachers. They also shared the many duties with the adults. The children loved to read, and Sojourner often gathered them around her to read the Bible to her. She longed to know what the Bible actually said, and unlike the adults who added their own embellishments, the children would read the exact words and would repeat them as often as she wanted to hear them. Sojourner's brilliant memory soaked up the Bible passages like a sponge, and she quickly could quote Scriptures verbatim.

Soon after Sojourner arrived at Northampton, she attended a camp meeting in town. About 100 young hoodlums descended upon the gathering with clubs and torches, threatening to set the tent on fire. The audience froze, the preacher trembled and sent for the constable. Sojourner, the only black in the crowd, fearing she would be the first target, hid behind a trunk. But something within her raised the courage of "three hearts." She strode outside the tent, pushed her way through the unruly mob, and

stationed herself on a small mound nearby. Then in the moonlight she lifted her powerful voice in her favorite song, "It was early in the morning. . . ." For a time the ruffians circled about her, then stopped in puzzlement when she demanded why they had accosted her with sticks when she was doing them no harm. A voice from the mob called out that they did not intend to hurt her, but just wanted to hear her sing.[15] Others picked up the cry, "Sing to us." Sojourner ordered them to move back, and asked if they would go away peacefully if she sang one more hymn. When they promised to leave, she sang one more song. The young men ran off confounded by this female giant who showed no fear. The camp worshippers were amazed and unharmed.

During the three years that Sojourner stayed at the commune, she was introduced to the large issues that had been tearing the nation apart for decades. She learned about abolition, women's suffrage, and the temperance movement from activists who often visited the residence. She met Wendell Phillips (1811-84), the outspoken Boston abolitionist who was called "abolition's golden trumpet." William Lloyd Garrison (1805-79), the fiery editor of the controversial Boston newspaper The Liberator, spoke to them of his contempt for the Constitution that condoned and protected such wicked atrocities as slavery.[16]

Sojourner listened to the words of the bearded, heavy-set Frederick Douglass (c.1817-95), who so eloquently told of his escape from slavery in Maryland. He had become one of the most influential black advocates of the antislavery movement, and he had the ability to inspire and lift the spirits. Douglass spoke of knowledge and the ability to read the Bible as the pathway from slavery to freedom.[17] Sojourner had never before heard such words of wisdom from one of her own race. Although she couldn't read the Bible, Sojourner hoped that some day she would be as resolute and bold in her convictions as Douglass.

The Northampton experiment ended when the founders, Benson and Hill, assumed individual control over the business operations. Benson arranged to care for the homeless members and hired Sojourner to do his domestic work. Some time later Samuel Hill gave Sojourner a cottage in return for a promissory note of $300 to be paid back with interest in a year. On April 18, 1850, she signed the mortgage papers with an "X."

Sojourner's Narrative.

Slave stories of atrocities in the South flooded the book stores in the North. Frederick Douglass wrote his autobiography, the *Narrative of the Life of Frederick Douglass*. Upon its publication he became a hunted man and had to leave for England. There his English friends raised money to purchase his manumission papers.

Prompted by the passage of the Fugitive Slave Law of 1850, Harriet Beecher Stowe (1811-96) wrote *Uncle Tom's Cabin*. It first ran as a serial in an abolitionist paper, *The National Era*, in 1851-52. It was published as a two-volume book in Boston in 1852. *Uncle Tom's Cabin* crystallized antislavery sentiments in the North and drew condemnation in the South. The entire first printing of 5,000 was snapped up the first week, and during the first year 300,000 copies were sold. In England one-and-a-half million pirated editions were sold. Despite the volume of sales, Stowe realized little profit from the book. When meeting the famous author, Lincoln exclaimed, "So this is the little lady who made this big war.[18] The book was later turned into a drama by G. L. Aiken and was translated into several foreign languages.

Olive Gilbert, a religious New England woman, realizing the demand for books on slavery, became interested in writing Sojourner's story as a slave in New York. By telling of slave conditions that also existed in the North, she hoped to shake the sanctimonious northerners from their complacency and hypocrisy. Sojourner approved the idea and dictated her story to her author friend. Gilbert recorded Sojourner's life story as it was told to her, often with names written phonetically and misspelled, and dates sometimes in error. Gilbert added details from Sojourner's letters, testimonials from friends, and stories of other slaves. Nowhere in the book did Olive Gilbert claim authorship—she wanted Sojourner to have all the profits and the credits.

William Lloyd Garrison arranged to have the book printed, and it first appeared in 1850 as the *Narrative of Sojourner Truth, a Northern Slave*. It was an unassuming little book with a thin brown cover, 130 pages, and a picture of Sojourner as the frontispiece (Sojourner said this was the only page she could read). The first edition covered Sojourner's life up to 1849 when she left Northampton to assume her itinerant ministry. A second edition in 1853 carried the original text and a preface by Harriet Beecher Stowe stating that "her [Sojourner's] object in

the sale of this little work is to secure a home for her old age, and the kind-hearted cannot do better than to assist her in this effort."[19]

In 1875 Frances Titus, a friend and traveling companion from Battle Creek, Michigan, paid to publish another edition with a preface by William Lloyd Garrison and 200 additional pages called the *Book of Life* taken from material in Sojourner's scrapbook. Altogether there were six editions of the *Narrative*. The final edition was published in 1884, one year after Sojourner died.

When Sojourner's autobiography first appeared, William Lloyd Garrison publicized it in *The Liberator*, but book sellers were hesitant to stock it for fear of embarrassing the northerners who piously opposed slavery in the South. This true story of slavery in New York would be inflammatory and arouse criticism. Sojourner decided that she would peddle the book herself to pay for the printing and earn money to pay her mortgage. With new causes to support she longed to be out on the road again to preach the "truth" as she now saw it, and she could sell her books wherever people gathered to listen. Later she earned money by selling pictures of herself and words of a song she had written.

Before setting out on her journeys, she made a trip back to the Dumont farm to visit her ailing daughter Diana. She found Diana had improved, and Dumont, now white-haired and aging, had come to believe that slavery was wrong. Later Dumont left for the West.

A System to Destroy.

The year that Sojourner's autobiography was published, the infamous Fugitive Slave Law of 1850 ushered in a decade of turbulent politics in America. The earlier law of 1793 had dealt with the extradition of runaway-slaves, and the Missouri Compromise of 1820 had admitted Missouri to the Union as a slave state and Maine as a free state. The Compromise also allowed slavery to exist in the rest of the Louisiana Purchase south of Missouri. The 1850 Fugitive Slave Law, signed by President Fillmore and supported by some northern legislators as a compromise bill to keep the South from seceding from the Union, spelled out strong measures for dealing with fugitive slaves. The law inflamed the abolitionists and spread despair and panic among the black population in the North. As many as 50,000 blacks had found sanctuary north of the Mason-Dixon line that separated

Pennsylvania from Maryland.

Fugitives or those suspected of having escaped could be arrested and turned over to a claimant with nothing more than a sworn testimony of ownership. For captured slaves or freed blacks taken illegally, there was no jury trial or chance to testify. The law was retroactive and applied to slaves who had escaped in the past. Anyone helping a slave escape was fined $1,000 and was liable for six months imprisonment, so sympathetic white persons hesitated to assist, shelter, or feed runaways. Commissioners who ruled in favor of slave-owners were paid a double fee, and law officers were offered bounties for each runaway slave captured. This led to fugitive and freed blacks alike being kidnapped when an accuser could be bribed to make a false claim of ownership.

The passage of the Fugitive Slave Law led to increased militancy by the abolitionists who claimed that the law made a mockery of justice. Armed clashes developed, and loud voices were raised in protest. Frederick Douglass said, "Under this law the oaths of any two villains (the capturer and the claimant) are sufficient to confine a free man to slavery for life."[20]

William Lloyd Garrison, who hoped to arouse northerners to action without violence, declared, "I have a system to destroy, and I have no time to waste."[21] Garrison held that slavery was a moral and a Christian issue that could be eliminated without violence if enough consciences were pricked. He made many enemies with his bold editorials in The Liberator that advocated "No Union with Slaveholders," a call for the North to secede from the South. As he lectured, Garrison was mobbed in Boston, Harrisburg, and other cities. Garrison and Douglass later parted company when Douglass advocated using political means to accomplish the abolition of slavery. Later Douglass concluded that violence might be the only recourse to gain emancipation.

The Fugitive Slave Law galvanized antislavery sentiments among many leading citizens in the North. Major poets and authors lent their voices to the cause. Ralph Waldo Emerson (1803-82), one of William Lloyd Garrison's loyal defenders, wrote, "This filthy enactment . . . I will not obey it, by God!"[22] John Greenleaf Whittier (1807-92), the Quaker poet and reformer, wrote bold antislavery pamphlets such as "Justice and Expedience." He was mobbed for participating in unpopular national antislavery conventions. William Cullen Bryant (1794-1878), poet and essayist, defended human rights and advocated the abolition of slavery in his New York Evening Post.

Women, too, were not silent or inactive. Although the antislavery movement was the most pressing issue at the time, women saw the connection between freedom for the slaves, woman suffrage, human rights, improved working conditions for workers, and temperance. Often these issues were addressed simultaneously.

Along with Harriet Beecher Stowe, other women of great ability joined the movement. Lucretia Mott (1793-1880), a Quaker feminist, reformer, teacher, and lecturer, aided fugitive slaves and organized the Philadelphia Female Anti-Slavery Society. With Elizabeth Cady Stanton (1815-1902) Mott organized the first Woman's Rights Convention in the United States at Seneca Falls, New York, in 1848. Stanton became intimately associated with Susan B. Anthony (1820-1906) in the woman's suffrage movement and the temperance association.

Sarah Grimké (1792-1873) and her sister Angelina Grimké (1805-79) left their aristocratic slave-holding family in Charleston, South Carolina, and moved north in 1832. There they became activists in the cause of abolitionism and women's rights. Amy Kirby Post (1802-89) ran the Rochester, New York, terminal of the Underground Railroad and was among the first to open women's rights conventions in New York and Massachusetts. She also advocated temperance and improved working conditions for the poor. Julia Ward Howe (1819-1910) assisted her husband in editing the Boston Commonwealth, an abolitionist paper, and lectured on emancipation and woman suffrage. She helped found a world peace organization. Her chief fame came when she wrote the words for "The Battle Hymn of the Republic" in 1861 after watching the Union troops march off to battle.

No woman was as fearless and undaunted as Harriet Tubman (c.1823-1913), a runaway slave from Maryland, who became one of the most successful "conductors" in the Underground Railroad. Often armed with a loaded pistol to keep frightened runaways from returning to their masters, Tubman single-handedly made nineteen trips to escort over 300 slaves to freedom. After the passing of the Fugitive Slave Law, she privately brought eleven fugitive slaves all the way north to Canada. There she stayed for a time to help them find food, shelter, and employment before returning to the South for another group. Tubman became such an irritant to slave-owners that they posted a reward of $40,000 for her capture. Tubman said, "I nebber run my train off de track, and I nebber lost a passenger."[23] During the Civil War she helped the Union forces in coastal South Carolina as a nurse, laundress, and spy.

Such were the individuals that Sojourner Truth was about to meet in the next stage of her life. Soon she would join them.

I've Come to Hear What I Have to Say.

Sojourner found herself in a new world where complex and explosive issues often precipitated discord. At the first convention of the American Anti-Slavery Society formed in Philadelphia in 1833, females were not seated or asked to sign the convention documents. Women, feeling slighted, then formed their own Female Anti-Slavery Societies in Boston and New York. Other splinter groups formed when the leaders differed on methods to achieve their goals. But by 1840 membership in the parent organization, including both men and women, had grown to 250,000 with fifteen state organizations and 2,000 local chapters.

Garrison and his followers still believed that emancipation would come through moral persuasion and passive resistance. The Garrisonians also believed that women were almost as oppressed as slaves, and they condemned the churches for taking a stand in favor of slavery and against women's rights. Garrison's opponents believed that political action and even violence were necessary to abolish slavery. They generally refused to support women's issues. Abolitionist newspapers expounded both points of view with passion.

The melding of women's rights with the antislavery movement clouded the issue for many males. At the first Woman's Rights Convention at Seneca Falls, New York, in 1848, Frederick Douglass was the only man present who supported a resolution for the legal enfranchisement of women.

In October 1850 Sojourner attended for the first time a Woman's Rights Convention in Worcester, Massachusetts. Douglass, Garrison, and Phillips were there to support the women's cause, but the pro-slavery forces had rallied behind their male leaders who ridiculed the women's efforts. One clergyman threatened to evict from his church any member who attended the meeting. Newspapers sarcastically labelled the assembly the "Hen Convention."

As Sojourner listened to women delegates present their resolutions and argue their points of view, she was confused. She couldn't understand why all the talk, with no action. When she was asked to speak, she made a blunt observation. "Sisters," she said, "I aren't clear what you be after. If women want any rights more than they got, why don't they just take them and not be talking about it?"[24]

Sojourner soon joined the lecture circuit, and over the years she traveled thousands of miles, many on foot, through New York, New Jersey, and the Midwestern states. She lugged her heavy carpetbag with books to sell wherever she went. In 1850 she joined the Britisher, George Thompson, who had helped emancipate the slaves of the British West Indies. Thompson, a popular abolitionist, did not mind sharing the stage with Sojourner who related her own story in a folksy style with wit and humor. At times she would capture the attention of the audience with a clever opening remark. "Children," she would say, "I've come here like the rest of you to hear what I have to say."[25]

In 1851 when Sojourner, Thompson, and others traveled through western New York, the former slave would tell her white listeners, "I'm against slavery because I want to keep white folks who hold slaves from getting sent to hell."[26] At times, overflowing with God's love, she admitted, "I used to hate the white people so, and I tell you when the love came in me I had so much love I didn't know what to love. Then the white people came, and I thought that love was too good for them. Then I said, Yea, God, I'll love everybody and the white people too. Ever since that, that love has continued and kept me among the white people."[27]

While in Andover, Massachusetts, Sojourner stayed for a time with Harriet Beecher Stowe. The famous author recorded her impressions of the woman with "that silent and subtle power" who displayed an "unconscious superiority" mixed with a "solemn twinkle of humor. . . . [and] a gloomy sort of drollery which impressed one strangely." Stowe observed, "I cannot but think that Sojourner with the same culture might have spoken words as eloquent and undying as the African St. Augustine or Tertullian. How grand and queenly a woman she might have been, with her wonderful physical vigor, her great heaving sea of emotion, her power of spiritual conception, her quick penetration, and her boundless energy!"[28]

Not all audiences were receptive and respectful. When racists yelled barbed epithets at her, Sojourner usually could shame them with sharp retorts and ridicule. But at times nothing could dissuade the "nigger-haters" from shouting and hurling insults that drowned out her words.

Ain't I a Woman?

In 1851 Sojourner headed west. In Akron, Ohio, she decided to attend another Woman's Rights Convention. Uninvited, she walked into the church. When she couldn't find a seat, she strode to the front and seated herself on the pulpit steps. The women organizers feared the worst. They did not want their cause to become confused with abolition, and surely the appearance of the famous Sojourner Truth meant only one thing—she would turn the talk to the explosive issue of slavery. Members whispered to Mrs. Frances Gage, who presided over the meeting, that under no circumstance should the unwelcome black woman be allowed to speak.

Throughout the first day of the convention Sojourner sat on the pulpit steps, silent, but listening and digesting what she heard from the opposition, mainly clergymen, who contemptuously pointed out the inferiority of women as supported by the Bible and the life of Jesus Christ. Sojourner held her tongue until the second day when her rage boiled over. She arose, marched to the platform, and asked to address the crowd. Hisses and catcalls greeted her, but Mrs. Gage called for silence and granted her permission to speak.

All eyes were riveted on the tall gaunt woman in the plain Quaker dress. Sojourner gazed for a moment at the hushed audience, then began to speak. She delivered one of her most famous speeches which fortunately was recorded in its original idiom. In the following excerpt the dialect has been dropped:

> Well, children, where there is so much racket there must be something out of kilter. I think that 'twixt the negroes of the South and the women at the North, all talking about rights, the white men will be in a fix pretty soon. . . .
>
> That man over there says women need to be helped into carriages, and lifted over ditches, and to have the best place everywhere. Nobody ever helps me into carriages, or over mud-puddles, or gives me any best place! And ain't I a woman? Look at me! Look at my arm! I have

ploughed, and planted, and gathered into barns, and no man could head me! And ain't I a woman? I could work as much and eat as much as a man—when I could get it—and bear the lash as well! And ain't I a woman? I have borne thirteen children [no doubt an error], and seen them most all sold off to slavery, and when I cried out with my mother's grief, none but Jesus heard me! And ain't I a woman?

> . . . . If my cup won't hold but a pint, and yours holds a quart, wouldn't you be mean not to let me have my little half-measure full?
>
> . . . . Then that little man in black there, he says women can't have as much rights as men, because Christ wasn't a woman! Where did your Christ come from? Where did your Christ come from? From God and a woman! Man had nothing to do with Him. . . .
>
> If the first woman God ever made [Eve] was strong enough to turn the world upside down all alone, these women together ought to be able to turn it back, and get it right side up again! And now they are asking to do it, the men better let them.[29]

When she concluded, the dissenting clergymen sat silent while the women thundered their approval. In a few well-chosen words Sojourner had refuted the age-old myths of the inferiority of the black race and women. Frances Gage wrote, "I have never in my life seen anything like the magical influence that subdued the mobbish spirit of the day and turned the jibes and sneers of an excited crowd into notes of respect and admiration."[30]

For a time Sojourner joined the temperance movement, but a friend advised her to give up her own bad habit of smoking a pipe before she could in good conscience chastise the imbibers of liquor. Her friend challenged, "The Bible tells us that 'no unclean thing can enter the Kingdom of Heaven,' Now what can be more filthy than the breath of a smoker?" Sojourner shot back, "Yes, child, but when I goes to Heaven I spects to leave my breff behind me."[31] She eventually gave up the habit which she had acquired in her slave days. Her friends called it an act of heroism.

Forces Gathering.

The South was a powder keg on the brink of explosion. Slaves had become more militant and were threatening to revolt against their owners. Nat Turner (1800-31), a deeply religious black slave, thought himself to be divinely appointed to free his people from bondage. In 1831 in Southampton County, Virginia, Turner led a small band of slaves in a rebellion against the white masters. The slaves ravaged the neighborhood and killed about sixty whites including the family of John Travis, Turner's owner. The revolt was soon crushed, and some twenty slaves, including Turner, were hanged. About 100 innocent blacks were killed. After the insurrection, fear gripped the South, and more stringent slave laws were enacted. William Lloyd Garrison, however, praised Turner as a hero and wrote numerous articles about him in *The Liberator*. In retaliation several southern cities levied fines or jail sentences on persons who circulated Garrison's paper.

Passions were further aroused by the Dred Scott Decision of 1857. Dred Scott (c.1795-1858), a Missouri slave, had been taken by his master into Illinois, a free state, and to Fort Snelling in free Wisconsin Territory (now in Minnesota). When Scott returned to Missouri, he sued his master's widow for freedom for himself, his wife and two children on the grounds that he had been a resident of a free state and territory. When the case reached the Supreme Court, the justices denied Scott his freedom. The northerners were incensed by the decision.

Two years later John Brown (1800-59), a radical northern abolitionist, rented a farm near Harpers Ferry, Virginia (now West Virginia), gathered a force of twenty-one armed men, stormed and captured the United States arsenal at Harpers Ferry. The following day United States marines under Colonel Robert E. Lee captured Brown and killed ten of his men. Brown was convicted of treason and on December 2, 1859, was hanged at Charles Town. Ralph Waldo Emerson said the martyr Brown made the gallows "as glorious as a cross." Union troops later rallied to the song "John Brown's body lies a-mouldering in the grave; His soul goes marching on."

The United States was being catapulted closer to the Civil War. At a protest meeting of abolitionists in Boston, Sojourner listened to Frederick Douglass, the main speaker, arouse the antislavery audience. Douglass had become convinced of the futility of nonviolence, and he aimed to whip his listeners into action. As Douglass listed the struggles of the slaves, the abuses, the violence, and the lack of justice from the government, he believed that slavery could only be destroyed by bloodshed. In his autobiography Douglass wrote:

. . . I was suddenly and sharply interrupted by my good old friend Sojourner Truth with the question, 'Frederick, is God dead?' 'No,' I answered, 'and because God is not dead slavery can only end in blood.' My quaint old sister was of the Garrison school of non-resistants, and was shocked at my sanguinary doctrine, but she too became an advocate of the sword, when the war for the maintenance of the Union was declared.[32]

By the mid-1850s the antislavery conflict had reached the Midwest. In 1854 after bitter debate, Congress had passed the Kansas-Nebraska Act that partially repealed the Missouri Compromise. Settlers in the Kansas and Nebraska territories were to determine for themselves whether they would be slave or free. The Act proposed by Stephen A. Douglas and supported by President Pierce and the South, drew opposition from the North and the new Republican Party. Contemptuously called "squatters sovereignty," it stirred up strong dissension among the settlers and caused terrorism at the polls.

During these unsettling times, Sojourner decided to carry her message westward. In Michigan she found that antislavery sentiments ran high even though the black population of the state was low. In Battle Creek she discovered that even the Quaker mayor operated a station for the Underground Railroad. Sojourner felt comfortable in Battle Creek and stayed there for a time before returning in the fall of 1857 to Northampton, Massachusetts, to lecture, collect more books, and sell her house for about $750.

Upon returning to Michigan she purchased a small cabin in Harmonia, a small spiritualist community six miles west of Battle Creek. During the next three years her three daughters and two grandsons came westward to Harmonia. Sojourner's younger grandson, Sammy Banks, became one of her favorites and accompanied her on her travels.

But even her family in Harmonia could not still her wanderlust. In 1858 she was on the road again through Michigan, into Indiana, Illinois, Wisconsin, and Iowa. Soon those living in remote spots would hear of Sojourner Truth, the preacher and purveyor of her own peculiar brand of "truth."

But not everyone welcomed her. Indiana was then a border state where it was illegal for blacks to enter or be guests of white citizens. Fearless, Sojourner crossed the border into "Copperhead country." At Silver Lake the proslavery forces had packed the United Brethren's meeting-house where she was to speak. The audience did not interrupt her talk, but before she left the platform, a doctor shouted out to her that because her voice was not a woman's, she must be a man. He called for some women in the audience to examine her to see if she had the breasts of a woman. The audience gave its approval. An eyewitness recorded the event:

> Sojourner told them that her breasts had suckled many a white babe, to the exclusion of her own offspring; that some of those white babies had grown to man's estate; that, although they had sucked her colored breasts, they were, in her estimation, far more manly than they (her persecutors) appeared to be; and she quietly asked them, as she disrobed her bosom, if they, too, wished to suck!"[33]

The embarrassed doctor left the meeting as soon as he had paid the $40 wager he had made with a companion regarding Sojourner's sex.

Emancipated but Not Equal.

On November 6, 1860, Abraham Lincoln (1809-65), a candidate supported by the newly-formed Republican party, won the election as the 16th President of the United States. By the time Lincoln was inaugurated, seven southern states had seceded from the Union. The new President condemned secession, but did not call for the use of force. Angry northern radicals and abolitionists criticized Lincoln for neglecting to deal forcefully with the southern states. They called him indecisive and weak. But on April 12, 1861, Fort Sumter off Charleston Harbor was fired upon by southern troops, and the Civil War had officially begun.

As northern troops were mobilized, Lincoln at first refused to allow free blacks to enlist in the army, further frustrating those who wanted to overturn the Confederacy. Lincoln faced dual problems. The North was divided between Free Soilers and abolitionists, and the volatile border states at any time could be provoked into seceding. Above all, Lincoln wanted to preserve the Union; emancipation of the slaves was secondary.

When the war began, Sojourner was in her Michigan home resting her weary, aging body. As she heard criticism of Lincoln, she would counter, "Oh, wait, chile! have patience! It takes a great while to turn about this great ship of State."[34]

Reluctantly Lincoln issued the Emancipa-

tion Proclamation on January 1, 1863. In essence it declared freedom only to those slaves residing in territories in rebellion against the federal government. It did not free those still in bondage in Union states. Despite the limitations of the Proclamation, the Union troops were encouraged, but the infuriated Confederates were emboldened to fight harder. Two years later the 13th Amendment to the Constitution abolished slavery in the entire country.

Although free men of color were serving in the United States Navy, the Army did not allow freed blacks to enlist. In March of 1863 the Enrollment Act was passed permitting free black men to serve. They were, however, to receive no more pay than fugitive slaves doing the most menial labor. In spite of this, many blacks enlisted including Sojourner's grandson, James Caldwell, who signed up with the 54th Massachusetts Infantry, an all-black unit. James never wrote to his family, but later the newspapers reported that 650 soldiers of the 54th had been killed at the battle of Fort Wagner, South Carolina. A brown envelope from the War Department came to Sojourner informing her that her grandson was missing in action. Sojourner learned later that James had been captured the day before the battle. He was held prisoner until 1865.

Not everyone was happy in the North with the arming of black men. The Enrollment Act precipitated the Draft Riots in New York City which brought lynchings, hangings, killing of many helpless blacks, and the burning of homes and a children's orphanage. After four days of violence, federal troops restored order. The riots activated sympathetic men and women to organize relief operations to assist the victims.

While hundreds of thousands of African Americans served both North and South in various noncombatant jobs as spies, messengers, laborers, and skilled workers, thousands more enlisted in the army and served admirably. With the passage of the Conscription Act each state had to draft men if there were not enough volunteers to fill the required quotas. Black recruits were then in demand, and prominent men such as Frederick Douglass became recruiting agents. The segregated black recruits often served with less pay than the white soldiers, were commanded by white soldiers, and if captured were in danger of being killed or returned to slavery. A corporal in the 54th Massachusetts Infantry protested the discrepancy in pay, and his men refused to accept any money until they were guaranteed the same pay as white soldiers. In 1864 Congress awarded them backpay and in the future agreed to give them pay equal to white troops.

Even though she was aging, Sojourner could not sit home while the soldiers suffered. With renewed vigor she set out for Camp Ward in Detroit where the 1st Michigan Volunteer Infantry, a black unit, trained. She arrived with a carriage loaded with food for a Thanksgiving dinner, all donated by the citizens of Battle Creek. She helped serve the food, talked with the men, and sang them a new song she had written to the tune of "John Brown's Body."

In the Presence of a Friend.

In March 1864 Lincoln named Ulysses S. Grant (1822-85) Commander-in-chief of the Union army. During the spring and summer months, the troops of General Grant and General Robert E. Lee (1807-70) were locked in bloody battles in Virginia. In June of that same year Lincoln and his running-mate, Andrew Johnson (1808-75), were renominated on the Union ticket. They handily won the election. By the time Lincoln made his second inaugural address, the war was drawing to a close. Lincoln gave his memorable plea for forgiveness "with malice toward none; with charity for all."

In June 1864 Sojourner made an emphatic announcement—she must go to Washington to see President Lincoln. Friends tried to dissuade the sixty-seven-year-old woman, just recovered from a debilitating illness, from taking another arduous cross-country journey, but Sojourner insisted that she must see the man who had freed the slaves.

Early one morning she and her grandson Sammy Banks were on their way. She had packed into her carpetbag copies of the words of her song and photographs to sell. At the bottom of the photograph was the caption, "I Sell the Shadow to Support the Substance. Sojourner Truth." She also carried her *Book of Life*, to collect autographs from the important people she met. Where there were no trains, carriages, or steamboats, they walked. For Sojourner, it was a retreat back into the past—through Ohio, Pennsylvania and into New York's Hudson Valley where she recalled with a shudder her tortured slave days.

On the way to Washington she stopped to lecture, and sell her songs and photographs. In the east people were shocked to learn that old

Sojourner Truth still lived. An article written by Harriet Beecher Stowe in *The Atlantic Monthly* had helped spread the rumor that the old black campaigner had died. She now was more of a curiosity than ever, and invitations to speak filled her days.

But summer had passed, and she needed to go to Washington. Fortunately with the help of Lucy Colman, an abolitionist friend, Sojourner finally got an appointment to meet Lincoln. She waited patiently in the reception room with other black and white persons. When she was ushered in to see the President at 8:00 P.M., her first words were:

> ... Mr. President, when you first took your seat I feared you would be torn to pieces, for I likened you unto Daniel, who was thrown into the lion's den; and if the lions did not tear you into pieces, I knew that it would be God that had saved you; and I said if he spared me I would see you before the four years expired, and he has done so, and now I am here to see you for myself.[35]

When Sojourner said she thought him the "best president who had ever taken the seat," Lincoln graciously pointed out that several of his predecessors, Washington in particular, would have done the same as he. They exchanged other compliments, and Lincoln showed her the beautiful gold-embossed Bible presented him by the African Americans of Baltimore. Sojourner then asked him to sign her autograph book. She said, "He took my little book, and with the same hand that signed the death-warrant of slavery, he wrote as follows: 'For Aunty Sojourner Truth, Oct. 29, 1864. A. Lincoln.'"

When the visit ended, Lincoln rose, took her hand, and said he would be pleased to have her call again. Sojourner said, "I felt that I was in the presence of a friend, and I now thank God from the bottom of my heart that I always have advocated his cause, and have done it openly and boldly. I shall feel still more in duty bound to do so in time to come. May God assist me." Sojourner said of her visit, "I am proud to say, that I never was treated by any one with more kindness and cordiality than were shown to me by that great and good man, Abraham Lincoln. . . ."[36]

Lucy Colman, who had accompanied her friend to see the President, had a slightly different interpretation of the visit. She said Lincoln appeared to be ill-at-ease and was condescending when he called her "Auntie." When

Sojourner praised him for being the first anti-slavery President, Lincoln had said, "I am not an Abolitionist; I wouldn't free the slaves if I could save the Union any other way."[37]

The Price of Freedom.

When the Civil War broke out, Washington, D.C. had barely recovered from the War of 1812 when the British had captured and sacked most of the public buildings including the Capitol and the White House. Restoration of the city was slow, and fifty years later the city was still a "sea of mud." Although threatened several times by Confederate troops, Washington had withstood the attacks.

After General William Sherman's (1820-91) destructive march to the sea through Georgia and South Carolina in the fall of 1863, and the capture of Richmond, Virginia, the Confederate capital, in April 1865, the war was all but over. When General Lee surrendered to General Grant at Appomattox Courthouse on Good Friday, April 9, 1865, there was jubilation in the North. On April 4 President Lincoln visited the fallen city of Richmond and walked the streets crowded with weeping and cheering black faces. Only eleven days later the cheers turned to tears at the news of Lincoln's death.

The euphoria of the termination of the Civil War and the emancipation of the slaves evaporated rapidly as the nation faced the immense problems of reconstruction. The South was a shambles with about one-third of its male population killed or wounded, cities were gutted and burned, Confederate money was worthless, and there was no black labor force to rebuild or harvest crops. The ex-slaves now faced an uncertain future. Many thought their salvation lay in the North, and they crowded the roadways leading to "Lincoln's city."

In Washington Sojourner witnessed first hand the abominable living conditions of the freed slaves, the "contraband of war," as they poured into the capital. They were homeless, penniless, and unemployed. They roamed the streets and sought shelter in the shacks near the Washington Canal, aptly called "Murder Bay." Here they existed in utter poverty and filth. Temporary camps were set up as shelters.

At General Lee's estate in Arlington, Virginia, the Freedman's Village served for a time as a model refugee community with cabins, a school, a church, a hospital, and a shelter for the elderly. It soon was overflowing with confused and helpless people who had no sense of how to deal with freedom. Sojourner had found another cause.

In December 1864 she was commissioned by the National Freedman's Relief Association to be a counselor to the freed people at Arlington Heights. For over a year she lived at the Village, preaching the Word of God on Sundays and teaching cleanliness and domestic skills to women through the week. But even at Freedman's Village, former slaves were not safe from the treachery of kidnappers who often spirited away black children to be sold in Maryland where the abolition of slavery was still being tested in the courts. Acting upon her own successes with lawsuits, Sojourner urged the reluctant mothers to press charges against the kidnappers. The Marylanders threatened Sojourner, but she confidently retorted that the law was now on her side.

When the war officially ended there were jubilant celebrations at Freedman's Village, but just one week later the cheers turned to cries of mourning at the news of President Lincoln's assassination by John Wilkes Booth at the Ford Theater. Lincoln died at 7:30 A.M. on April 15, 1865. Andrew Johnson became the 17th President of the United States.

In March 1865 Congress had established a Freedmen's Bureau under the jurisdiction of the Army. The Bureau attempted to provide some of the basic needs of the burgeoning black community. Sojourner, with her emphasis on cleanliness, was pressed into service at the Freedman's Hospital. Here she instructed nurses on general sanitation and care of the sick. On Sundays she raised the spirits of the patients with sermons and songs.

It was in Washington that Sojourner had her first encounter with streetcar travel. Conductors accustomed to Jim Crow cars for the blacks, paid no attention to Lincoln's law outlawing discrimination in the capital's public transportation. Streetcars often passed by blacks waiting on street corners. When a conductor left Sojourner standing on the street, she chased the car, boarded, and demanded a ride. At times when she was refused seats beside white passengers, she protested. During a confrontation with a conductor, she was rudely shoved against the door injuring her shoulder. She sued the railway company for assault, and the conductor was fired. From then on she said "the cars looked like pepper and salt.[38]

The efforts of the Freedmen's Bureau scarcely made a dent in solving the problems in Washington. Furthermore, many southern states were passing new restrictive laws called the Black Codes. There was little protection for freed slaves returning to claim members of their families still remaining in the South. Black laborers were often given no pay and were treated no better than slaves. With the passage of the Civil Rights Act of 1866, the Reconstruction Act of 1867, and the ratification of the 14th Amendment in 1868, there was some protection for the southern freed slaves, but abuses continued to abound.

In the winter of 1867 Sojourner left Washington. For a time she traveled through western New York rounding up jobs for ex-slaves, but she soon conceded as Frederick Douglass had observed, it was "like bailing out the ocean with a teaspoon."[39] In 1870 the 15th Amendment gave black men the right to vote, but women of any color were not so fortunate.

Sojourner soon realized the futility of her efforts with legislators in Washington. Missing from any legislation was the mention of giving former slaves land of their own, and without land, there was no incentive and no future. Congress was willing enough to give huge government land grants to railroads, mining companies, and Indians. Why shouldn't land be given to ex-slaves?

Sojourner rested in Battle Creek only six months before she was on the road to the East again, accompanied by her grandson Sammy Banks. Her crusade was to secure land in the West for the freed slaves. With her *Book of Life* in hand, she collected autographs, spoke of her latest project to anyone who would listen, and gathered signatures on the petition she had dictated to be sent to the Senate and the House of Representatives. It read:

Whereas, From the faithful and earnest representations of Sojourner Truth (who has personally investigated the matter), we believe that the freed colored people in and about Washington, dependent upon government for support, would be greatly benefited and might become useful citizens by being placed in a position to support themselves: We, the undersigned, therefore earnestly request your honorable body to set apart for them a portion of the public land in the West, and erect buildings thereon for the aged and infirm, and otherwise legislate so as to secure the desired results.[40]

In Memoriam of Sojourner Truth.

At age seventy-three Sojourner was on the last great mission of her life. In passionate lectures in Philadelphia, New York City, Boston, and other cities, she promoted her cause of land grants in the West for resettlement of the freed slaves and she collected signatures on her petition. Again she added her voice to the women's suffrage movement. In Washington she met with senators and Ulysses S. Grant, then the 18th President of the United States. She pleaded, she begged, and she urged everyone to sign her petition. She and Sammy then moved into Kansas, Iowa, Illinois, and Missouri, all the while gathering more signatures. When she thought she had enough names, she and Sammy returned to Washington to present the signatures to Congress. Before she could find a senator to introduce the petition, she and Sammy were afflicted by Washington's oppressive heat and dust. With the petition still in hand, they left for Battle Creek. Michigan air did not revive Sammy. He died in February 1875 at the age of twenty-four, a loss that Sojourner felt more acutely than the separation from her own children decades earlier. Sojourner went into debt to give him a proper funeral.

During the last years of travel Sojourner's health had been deteriorating, and she suffered from partial paralysis and an ulcer on her leg. After a remarkable recovery she insisted she must return to Washington with her petition. She said, "My good Master kept me, for he had something for me to do."[41] She never completed her Master's work in the capital city.

Her friend and companion, Frances Titus, updated her *Narrative* with newspaper accounts, letters, lectures, speeches, and copies of autographs from her *Book of Life*. The petitions gathered dust on the shelf. But she took one last journey away from her new home on College Street in Battle Creek. Throughout Michigan she spoke of women's rights, prison reform, and temperance. Again she traveled back to Rochester, New York, as a delegate to the Woman's Rights Convention.

Sojourner's petition never reached Congress, and she finally conceded that the job of resettling her people in the West was too big for one woman. But she was encouraged to discover that despite the roadblocks to purchasing land and threats to their lives, ex-slaves were beginning to leave the South to migrate westward to Kansas where they were granted land under the

Homestead Act of 1862.

After three months of intense pain Sojourner died at 3:00 A.M. on November 26, 1883, in her Battle Creek home. All the members of her family, including her grandson James Caldwell, were there to bid her farewell. Her casket was carried by some of Battle Creek's leading citizens to the Congregational and Presbyterian Church. Over 1,000 people viewed her body which was draped with a black veil. As usual she wore her Quaker bonnet, and her white shawl lay folded on her breast. A black-plumed hearse carried her casket to the Oak Hill Cemetery for burial. After the minister's prayer, hundreds of voices joined to sing her favorite hymn "It was early in the morning."

Condolences arrived from friends across the country, and newspapers printed testimonials to her. Frederick Douglass, who was then the Commissioner of Deeds for the District of Columbia, recalled her untimely interruption of his speech with the query, "Frederick, is God dead?" Although he had often disagreed with her and regarded her as uncultured and quaint, he issued a final statement venerating her independence and courage, and her compassion for human causes particularly those of her own race.[42]

During her long lifetime that spanned the election of twenty Presidents, Sojourner Truth witnessed both successes and failures. Fortified by her simple child-like faith and the assurance that her causes were right, she seldom admitted defeat. When she was deceived by men, she learned to trust the voice of God spoken directly to her. She preached her own brand of truth and justice with conviction and simplicity.

For thirty-three years her grave remained unmarked except by lot number. In 1916 the Daughters of the American Revolution had a marble headstone erected. This was replaced some thirty years later by a slim six-foot white marble shaft bearing the words:

IN MEMORIAM
SOJOURNER TRUTH
BORN A SLAVE IN ULSTER COUNTY,
NEW YORK, IN THE 18TH CENTURY.
DIED IN BATTLE CREEK, NOV. 26, 1883.
AGED ABOUT 105 YEARS.
'IS GOD DEAD?"

A historical marker memorializes members of her family buried nearby.

Had she lived sixty years later, she would have wept to see the race riots, the lynchings, the cross-burnings, and the armed confrontations. In the 1960's she would no doubt have been in the front lines of the Civil Rights marches alongside Martin Luther King Jr.

As a black woman Sojourner Truth suffered doubly from the oppressions of society, but even as a mistreated slave she never succumbed to self-pity. Through her life she did not dwell upon her own misfortunes, poverty, sacrifices, or human ailments. Her energies were focused on the bigger issues. She rose above the indignities heaped upon her and passionately fought against injustice wherever she found it. Sojourner Truth was an advocate for all of humanity and was committed to the betterment of unfortunates of all color. As she walked away from Dumont's farm, she embarked on a crusade to help free humanity from bondage. In that she was successful.

Notes

1. Bert James Loewenberg, and Ruth Bogin, eds., *Black Women in Nineteenth-Century American Life* (University Park: The Pennsylvania State University Press, 1976), p. 240. Taken from *The Narrative of Sojourner Truth* by Olive Gilbert. The original dialect has been dropped.

2. Jacqueline Bernard, *Journey Toward Freedom* (New York: W.W. Norton & Company Inc., 1967), p. 11.

3. Loewenberg, p. 241.

4. Ibid.

5. Bernard, pp. 36-37.

6. Loewenberg, p. 241.

7. Bernard, p. 59.

8. Ibid., p. 82.

9. Ibid., p. 85.

10. Loewenberg, p. 241.

11. Arthur Huff Fauset, *Sojourner Truth, God's Faithful Pilgrim* (Chapel Hill, North Carolina: The University of North Carolina Press, 1938), p. 106.

12. Ibid.

13. Ibid.

14. Bernard, p. 122.

15. Hertha Pauli, *Her Name Was Sojourner Truth* (New York: Appleton-Century-Crofts, Inc., 1962), pp. 145-46.

16. Ibid., pp. 150-51.

17. Ibid., p. 154.

18 Benjamin Quarles, *Lincoln and the Negros* (New York: Oxford University Press, 1962), p. 134.

19 Victoria Ortiz, *Sojourner Truth, a Self-Made Woman* (Philadelphia: Lippincott Company, 1974), pp. 92-93.

20 Langston Hughes and Milton Meltzer, *A Pictorial History of the Negro in America* (New York: Crown Publishers, Inc., 1968), p. 44.

21 Ibid., p. 93.

22 Ibid., p. 106.

23 Ibid., p. 129.

24 Ortiz, p. 81.

25 Ibid., p. 60.

26 Ibid., p. 62.

27 Loewenberg, p. 241.

28 Ortiz, p. 63, 65.

29 Loewenberg, pp. 235-36. Excerpts taken from *History of Woman Suffrage* edited by Elizabeth Cady Stanton and others (Rochester, New York: 1881). Parts of the speech were recorded in the original dialect by Frances D. Gage, who presided over the meeting. Here the dialect has been omitted.

30 Ortiz, p. 88.

31 Olive Gilbert, *Narrative of Sojourner Truth* Reprinted by Frances W. Titus (Boston: 1875), p. 304.

32 Frederick Douglass, *Life and Times of Frederick Douglass* (New York: Collier Macmillan Publishers, 1962), p. 275.

33 Gilbert, p. 139.

34 Ibid., p. 174.

35 Ibid., p. 177-78.

36 Ibid., pp. 178-79. Previous quotations found here.

37 Dorothy Sterling, *We Are Your Sisters* (New York: W. W. Norton & Company, 1984), p. 252.

38 Gilbert, p. 187.

39 Bernard, p. 222.

40 Gilbert, p. 199.

41 Bernard, p. 239.

42 Pauli, p. 238.

Chapter 13

Women Recover the Past

EXPERIENCES OF THE PAST should be the starting point for understanding the present. Contemporary women need to know how their foremothers acted out their lives and their destinies. The struggles and suffering of past generations must be kept alive so today's women can judge where they have been, where they are, and where they are going. The past can illuminate the present and add a new dimension to understanding and awareness.

For the most part female histories have been lost or at best have been filtered through male eyes. Men historians have decided what of women's lives to preserve. Those that have survived have been told generally from the male point of view with male biases and prejudices. Women's stories have been placed at the backstage of recorded history. There is little for today's women to look back on to view the parallels that exist between females of all ages.

The histories of past cultures and periods are diverse and flooded by the tides that have swept across former civilizations. To get a true picture of the changing status of women, one must go back to the beginning of history. However, this concluding chapter makes only a few general observations which deal most directly with the twelve women portrayed here. We need to know something of the issues and problems that have surrounded their existence and recognize that some of the same issues still exist today.

These twelve women do speak to contemporary women. For the most part these women of the past functioned within the strictures of oppressive societies that confined them to roles of subordination and inferiority. All of them marshalled their anger or discontent to challenge the status quo. By moral strength, perseverance, and dedication, they accomplished feats that have made their lives admirable. Fortunately some of the twelve women left us portions of their own stories as they either wrote them or related them to others. There are personal accounts to draw on from Perpetua, Teresa of Avila, Juana Inés de la Cruz, Susanna Wesley, Narcissa Whitman, and Sojourner Truth.

Christian and Jewish Feminists.

In the United States the groundwork for present-day women's movements was laid first by feminists in the secular world. The struggle has been slow and obstacle-ridden. Despite opposition and set-backs women activists have continued to work for equal opportunity and pay in the workplace, participation in the political process, membership in male organizations, and equality in educational and social institutions. In addition there are many social issues of great concern to females today—poverty, homelessness, abuse, sexual harrassment, rape, incest, teen-age pregnancy, to name a few.

Women in religious organizations have benefited from the progress made by their sisters in secular and social movements. Concerned women in churches and synagogues have found that Christianity and Judaism have been oppressive, patriarchal, slow to change, reluctant to extend equality to women. Some have left established religious communities vowing never to return; others have joined cults and alternative spiritual movements; still others have remained within their religious traditions and sought to bring about change and reform.

Women theologians of various faiths such as Rosemary Radford Ruether, Phyllis Trible, Letty Russell, Elisabeth Schüssler Fiorenza, Valerie Saiving, Virginia Mollenkott, and Judith Plaskow have led a rising chorus of female voices that express anger, frustration, and disillusionment with women's roles within churches and synagogues today. They have demanded reform.

Progress has been made, but slowly and reluctantly. Although women have had support from some liberal-minded males in the religious hierarchy, women have had to fight their own battles to effect change. Controversy and non-acceptance still exist among both men and women.

One change women have sought is the chance to be ordained into the clergy. Some mainline Protestant Churches and three branches of the Jewish faith have allowed this, but clergywomen have not always been welcomed or accepted by their superiors or their congregations. Roman Catholics, conservative Protestants, and Orthodox Jews do not allow women to be ordained.

Biblical Roots.

To understand the role of women in Jewish and Christian traditions, one should look first at the creation story. Genesis 2 is often cited to prove that women are subordinate to men because Eve was created *after* Adam. Hence she was an afterthought. (In Genesis 1, which was written later, God is said to have created male and female together.)

The hierarchical order was established early—God first, then man, last woman. Christian theologians such as Tertullian (c.160 - c.230), the early church father in North Africa, perpetuated the belief of inferiority of women. He claimed that Eve was responsible for unleashing sin into the world and that she destroyed God's ultimate creation Adam. Tertullian said that because Eve was weak and easy prey to the devil's temptation, all women bear the sin of Eve and are the "devil's gateway."

Those who do not accept the subordinate role of Eve argue that God created man and woman as equals. Furthermore, they claim that as the creation story evolved from the lower forms of life to the higher, Eve, being the last created, was God's crowning achievement. The devil sought her out because she was the more intelligent and persuasive of the two and could easily coax Adam to eat of the forbidden fruit.

It is universally held that God (Yahweh) transcends all human comprehension and definition. Unfortunately, the authors and translators of the Bible have used male terms to image God—God the father, God the warrior, God the king, God the master. Although the term "father" in the Bible is a metaphor, it established early the image of God as a male. And there are no neutral pronouns in the English language for *he* and *him*. To further confuse semantics, the words *man* or *mankind* are used generically to mean *humanity* and also to mean persons of *male* gender.

Artists and sculptors have pictured God as an old man with a white beard, sometimes robed elegantly as a king or a pope. Michelangelo (1475-1564) painted the figure of God on the ceiling of the Sistine Chapel as a male. To today's children, who are especially attuned to visual images, God is a male. Lost are the Biblical references to God as a compassionate mother, as a bearer and caretaker of the young, as a nurturer of the sick and the poor, as a source of strength and life.

In Biblical Palestine Jewish men were the head of the patriarchal family. They studied the Scriptures, performed religious ceremony, and taught in the temple. The most common Biblical images of women were as harlots, temptresses, witches, or cult goddesses. The *good* women tended to the household as dutiful wives and mothers and were the property of their husbands, fathers, or brothers. Their chief role was to bear children, though female functions such as menstruation and childbirth itself were considered unclean. The birth of a son was greeted with celebration and joy, whereas the coming of a daughter was mourned or ignored.

It was not the intent of the early Christian Jews to break from their Jewish heritage, so they followed the established rules and customs of Judaism. But Jesus brought a different message which separated the two faiths. As recorded in the four Gospels, particularly in Luke, Jesus lived out a liberating message which among other things elevated the underclass of society, including women. He treated women as equals, often using them to illustrate his parables. He instructed women and numbered them among his loyal followers. He often referred to the feminine qualities of God, and he, himself, exhibited characteristics normally associated with women—mercy, compassion, gentleness. Women and men, he said, had equal rights and responsibilities in marriage. To the chagrin of the chief priests, he reached out to widows, pagan women, and prostitutes.

When the Apostle Paul, the first great missionary to the Gentiles, wrote his letters to various churches, his words were ambivalent and controversial. Unfortunately, Paul's writings can be cited to prove both subordination and equality of women. There are passages such as Galatians 3:28 that affirm his view that all people, including women, are "one in Christ Jesus." Paul, himself, traveled with women on his many missionary journeys, and he held meetings at their homes.

Yet other passages indicate that Paul believed in the inferiority of women. Often-quoted verses used by opponents of women's ordination are found in I Corinthians 14:34-35 which admonish women to keep silent in church. These verses, however, have been given other interpretations. Some claim that Paul was warning talkative women that they were too noisy in the Corinth church.

Women were the backbone of the early Christian church. They opened their homes for the first Christian meetings and shared leadership roles with men.

As Christianity spread, the church was organized into a hierarchical structure that resembled that of the Jewish synagogue and the Imperial Roman government. Male leaders established doctrine, lead in worship, conducted the sacraments, and interpreted the Word. Popes and bishops became the heads of the church.

Martyrdom for a Cause.

As the christian Church grew more powerful, break-away sects such as the Gnostics and Montanists developed. These mystic sects sought to revive the original charismatic ministry of the early Christians. Women were attracted to the sects because they were accorded leadership roles and with men shared the gift of prophecy.

The mother Church, fearing that divergent beliefs would weaken it, made efforts to stamp out the "heretics." Gnostics and Montanists were not only oppressed by the Church but were also persecuted as Christians by the Roman authorities. Martyrdom became a noble and welcome way to prove one's faith.

Perpetua, thought to be a Montanist, possessed the gifts of prophesy and teaching. Although only 22, she was the leader of the five martyrs who were sacrificed to wild animals in the arena on that fatal March day in 203 A.D.

Another martyr of a later date was Narcissa Whitman. She fulfilled her dream of going West as a missionary to the Cayuse Indians in Old Oregon. Unfortunately, both she and her dream perished during the massacre at the Waiilatpu Mission at Walla Walla in November, 1847.

Sacrifices such as those of Perpetua and Narcissa Whitman are looked on today with skepticism and disbelief. Yet, there are modern examples of martyrdom.

In December, 1980, the citizens of the United States were horrified at the news report of the murder of four American women in El Salvador. The bodies of Maryknoll Sisters Ita Ford and Maura Clarke, Ursuline Sister Dorothy Kazel, and lay missionary Jean Donovan were found along a lonely country road. They had been on their way home from the isolated International airport when all were raped and shot. Their burned van was found near the airport.

The women had been working to rehabilitate impoverished refugees who were fleeing the military massacres. The ensuing investigations by El Salvador and United States officials became mired in a confusion of cover-ups and secrecy. At stake was the financial aid from the United States to the controlling military junta in El Salvador. The final evidence pointed to six men from the Salvadoran National Guard who were assigned to "eliminate the subversive women."

Jean Donovan, 27, had left her affluent lifestyle and comfortable accountant's job in Cleveland, Ohio, to serve the Salvadoran people. There she had found meaning for her life, as had her three companions.[1] The four American women did not welcome martyrdom as had Perpetua, but they had lived each day with the fear that their lives were in danger and expendable. They willingly took the risk.

There have been other martyrs in Central America. As the civil war in El Salvador progressed, missionaries of all faiths have been targets of political violence. Archbishop Oscar Romero was assassinated there earlier in 1980. Six Jesuit priests and two women were murdered in November, 1989. At about the same time two Roman Catholic sisters lost their lives in a bloody ambush in Nicaragua. And no doubt there will be others. Martyrdom is not only an ancient sacrifice.

Celibacy and Virginity.

There are several theories as to when and how monasticism began. Authorities make various claims that the monastic idea was started in pre-Christian Palestine, or with John the Baptist, or by Saint Anthony of Egypt (c.251 - c.350). The Apostle Paul advocated celibacy and virginity. Jerome (c.347 - 420), the early Christian scholar, praised celibate females, although he looked down on women in general. Jerome's female companions organized one of the first convents in Bethlehem.[2]

Convents, often headed by powerful abbesses, gave women protection and offered them alternatives to marriage and childbearing. They escaped the stereotypes heaped on ordinary women as temptresses, shrews, or harlots. Convent life gave them an intellectual and social life. In the Middle Ages the development of convents for celibate females was an important step in the emancipation of women.

As evidenced by the lives of St. Catherine of Siena and St. Teresa of Avila, women in monastic life were accorded respect, dignity, and opportunities not given other women. They exercised considerable power in public and political arenas. They also escaped the indictment that sexuality was a feminine evil. Although Catherine and Teresa were esteemed as holy messengers from God and brides of Christ, they were under the control of male confessors and authorities. Theresa was investigated by the Inquisitors when she proved to be too bold in her pronouncements.

Juana Inés de la Cruz of Mexico entered the convent to seek a safe sanctuary from the evils of Mexican society. The celibate and virtuous life of Kateri Tekakwitha, the Mohawk holy woman, led to her beatification in 1980.

What has been the status of *women religious* in the twentieth century?

The number of women in religious orders reached its peak in the 1930's and 40's. The 1950's witnessed a decline as the first women began to leave the orders. The liberalization of education and relaxed social mores of the 1960s put a strain on the disciplined nun teachers, nurses, and social workers.

As in the priesthood, the number of women in religious orders continues to decline. According to recent surveys there were 78,000 fewer women religious in 1990 than in 1966, and 85% fewer young recruits seeking to enter convents. And the women are aging. In 1990 there were more women in convents over 90 years of age than there were under 30. The average age is 65. The cost of supporting the retired sisters is a financial drain on the Church.[3]

There are several reasons for the decline. As servants of God, the nuns worked long hours for meager pay and little recognition. Their services in education, nursing, and social work have been taken for granted. Some women have left the orders to go into higher paying and more rewarding jobs in colleges, universities, and seminaries.

There is general unrest among the younger sisters who aspire to some day being ordained into the priesthood. The Second Vatican Council of 1965 resulted in many church reforms and efforts at renewal, but the doors to ordination for women remained closed.

In 1979 when Pope John Paul II toured the United States, he met with American representatives of women's orders. At the National Shrine of the Immaculate Conception in Washington D.C., Sister Theresa Kane, president of the Leadership Conference of Women Religious, was invited to speak. She urged the Pope to be mindful of the "intense suffering and pain" that many women in the United States were experiencing. She asked that women "be included in all ministries" of the Church, and that his Holiness be open to the voices of women. Sixty nuns wearing blue arm-bands in protest arose. The Pope ignored the protest and continued his prepared speech.[4]

On his second visit to the United States in 1987, the Pope was generally more positive, but he was faced with more dissent from liberal American priests. Still, he adamantly opposed the marriage of priests and the ordination of women, even though the number of young men entering the priesthood is steadily declining.

In 1988 Pope John Paul spoke to the cardinals about the developments in the Church that had distressed him. He said that the decision of the Anglican Church to ordain a woman bishop (the Rev. Barbara Harris) posed serious obstacles to the reconciliation between Anglicanism and Roman Catholicism.[5] The Vatican's position is firm. Ordination of women is not biblical, and Catholic law clearly states that priests must be baptized males. Females cannot be ordained as priests because women do not bear a natural resemblance to Jesus Christ and his disciples.

Some priests in the United States have supported the efforts of Catholic women for ordination. On August 12, 1990, at two Sunday services in the St. Joan of Arc parish in Minneapolis, three lay women joined the Rev. Roy Bourgeois, a visiting priest, in celebrating mass at the altar. Because the act was in violation of church law, Archbishop John Roach condemned Father Bourgeois and barred him from saying mass in the St. Paul-Minneapolis Archdiocese. The condemnation had a chilling effect on Catholic women feminists.[6]

Not all Catholic women support the position of their sisters who demand equality in the pulpit. Just as with secular women's issues, there are divided opinions and strong feelings on both sides of the issue.

Judaism and Anti-Semitism.

When Gracia Nasi Mendes helped her people escape the Inquisition in Spain and Portugal in the mid-1500s, she was expending her efforts and money in a cause that has plagued Jews throughout history. The 1492 edict that expelled Marranos from Spain was just another of many such world-wide acts of anti-Semitic oppression. No one can talk to World War II without recalling the horrors of the concentration camps of Auschwitz, Buchenwald, Dachau, and Belsen.

Today racism is a growing problem in contemporary America. Anti-Semitism has many faces. It is rampant in the white supremacist organizations whose philosophy is anti-Jew, anti-black, anti-minority, anti-immigrant, anti-homosexual. Hate crimes continue on college campuses. The racist message is proclaimed by a variety of groups including the re-emerging Ku Klux Klan, the Skinheads and other youth gangs of various cities, the right-wing political cult of Lyndon LaRouche, the Posse Comitatus, the Christian Identity Movement, and the White Aryan Resistance.

In one year from 1987 to 1988 there was a 41% increase in anti-Semitic assaults and threats reported by the Anti-Defamation League. In 1988 the New York City Police department reported an increase of 100% in two years in incidents related to race, religion, or sexual preference.[7]

Gracia Nasi Mendes was one of the patrons of Jewish religious, cultural, and educational organizations. Although as a woman she was not allowed to study the Torah, she founded an academy for rabbinic studies and a synagogue in Constantinople. In Salonica, Greece, she established another synagogue and religious academy for the Marranos. She was a sixteenth century woman who would have flourished some 400 years later. With her intelligence and dedication to religious causes, she would have had the opportunity now to become a theologian, a rabbinic scholar, an educator, or even be ordained as a rabbi.

Like Gracia Mendes, the Jewish community continues to be generous in its support of charities and benevolences. Jewish women characteristically exceed non-Jewish women in volunteer work and are unequaled in fund-raising. Here they have found identity and a sense of worth apart from family obligations.

Contemporary Jewish feminists have broken through many barriers. Until recent years women have been excluded from Jewish religious studies. Sons were taught the Torah by their fathers, daughters learned domestic skills from their mothers. For women the inheritance from the past has been one of patriarchal subordination, intellectual inferiority, exclusion from active religious life, and scorn as sexual objects.

Susan Weidman Schneider, founder of *Lilith*, the Jewish feminist magazine, lays out the conflicts for today's Jewish women in non-Jewish American culture. The Jewish woman, she says, not only seeks to fulfill her own individual needs, but is burdened with the preservation of the traditions of her people. The dilemma for Jewish women is how to arrive at equality without destroying Jewish heritage.

Jewish feminists claim that although Judaism emphasizes social justice, benevolence, and philanthropy, women have not always been dealt justice. They have inherited a legacy that has restricted their talents, and limited their opportunities. They have seen their brothers groomed to become leaders in society, professions, and religion. Girls have heard their Orthodox fathers pray each morning that they are thankful God has not created them as women.[8]

Despite criticism from traditional Jewish men and women, Jewish feminists have prompted changes. In three Jewish movements women are now being ordained as rabbis. Only Orthodox Jews do not allow women in the rabbinate.

The Reconstructionists, a break-away segment of Conservative Judaism, have been the most liberal. They were the first to permit women to be ordained.

In the middle of the nineteenth century

the Reform movement decided to accept women as rabbis, but it wasn't until 1972 that Sally Priesand was ordained as the first Reform woman rabbi.

After years of debate and delay, the faculty of the Conservative Jewish Theological Seminary finally voted in 1983 to admit women to the rabbinical program, thus paving the way for women to become rabbis in Conservative synagogues.[9]

But there are hurdles yet to overcome. Some women rabbis have had to settle for small congregations or assistantships in larger synagogues. They are generally paid less than men rabbis and have little chance for advancement. Some congregations hesitate to hire women for fear of antagonizing the older, more conservative members; others hesitate to hire women fearing the cost of maternity leaves; still others believe the authority of male rabbis will be diminished.[10]

There has been a backlash against the Jewish women's movement. Jewish feminists are accused of destroying traditions, threatening the family structure, and weakening Jewish males. However, feminists insist there can be no retreat to the status quo where Judaism was for men only.

From the Pew to the Pulpit.

When Katherine von Bora and Susanna Wesley married clergymen, they learned well what was expected of them as mistresses of Protestant parsonages. They were to be proper wives who subordinated their desires and aspirations to those of their preacher-husbands. It was God's will and their husband's command that they bear children, the primary duty of married women at that time. When children came, they were expected to be good mothers. Katherine and Susanna fulfilled their duties without complaint.

Katherine von Bora, in accordance with her husband's beliefs, presented him with six children in eight and one-half years. Of the six, four lived to adulthood. Martin Luther had remarked that women were given wide hips so they could bear children. In harsher tones he stated that if a woman died in childbirth, it did not matter, for that was why God created her.[11]

Luther believed that God commanded wives to obey their husbands. He said that the husband rules the home, wages war, and defends his possessions while the woman stays at home and looks after the household. Katherine heeded these words, but her story shows that she did much more; she not only had babies and man-

aged the household, but she controlled the finances, she farmed, she nursed her husband's many illnesses, she purchased land, and she even taught foreigners the language. Luther was proud of his capable wife.

Susanna Wesley fulfilled her wifely duties to a greater degree—she bore nineteen children, ten of whom lived. As Katherine, she managed the finances, ran the household, nurtured and taught the children, and became a self-taught student of philosophy, religion, and theology. She, not her preacher-husband, was the mentor and inspiration for her two famous Methodist sons, John and Charles.

However, Susanna made the mistake of leading the church services and preaching sermons during Samuel Wesley's absence. For this impropriety she was sharply reprimanded by her husband.

In America women have consistently outnumbered men at Sabbath services, and women have been the backbone of church activities. They taught Sunday School, worked in women's societies, raised money, and supported missions. Yet in many churches women were not allowed to vote on church matters.

As women became increasingly responsible for the work of the church, it was natural that they would strive to become ordained. The history of women's ordination in both sectarian and mainstream Protestant churches is long and varied. The Quakers were among the first to allow women to preach. The United Church of Christ and Disciples of Christ have ordained women since the middle of the nineteenth century.

Some Methodists claim that John Wesley supported the emancipation of women and allowed females to preach *if* they were sure to preach Methodism. In the United States the Wesley Methodists began to ordain women in the early 1860s, but the reorganized United Methodist Church did not vote to allow women to enter the clergy until 1956.[12]

Although the northern branch of the Presbyterian Church approved the ordination of clergywomen in 1956, the merged Presbyterian Church did not make the final decision to ordain women until 1964. The Southern Baptists allowed women to enter the clergy that same year. In 1990 the Evangelical Lutheran Church of America celebrated its 20th year of ordination of women. Other branches of the Lutheran Church have objected to women's ordination on biblical and theological grounds.

In the Protestant Episcopal Church, after years of debate and contention, the General Convention ruled in 1973 that the priesthood was *not* open to women. One year later in July, 1974, eleven women were "irregularly" ordained by supportive bishops in Philadelphia. The oldest of the eleven was Jeanette Picard, then 79, a retired aerospace consultant and widow of balloonist Jacques Jean Piccard. The ordination became a media blitz. The Church censured the women and the officiating bishops and declared the ordination null and void. In 1976 when the Church voted to accept women into the clergy, the eleven women refused to be re-ordained. The Episcopal Church gave up its insistence on re-ordination.[13]

Generally the same problems exist today for Protestant women entering the ministry as for Jewish women seeking to become rabbis. Initially, there is the difficulty of receiving a first position. Women seminarians often settle for secular jobs or non-ordained church positions before being hired as full-time pastors. As with men just out of the seminary, women are first called to smaller congregations or as assistants or associates in larger churches. Usually women are paid less and advancement is non-existent or slow. Rarely do women move up to positions as senior pastors.[14]

Older lay women in particular feel more comfortable with men clergy, as do executive and professional males. Women clerics realize the problems and work hard to establish rapport with members of their congregations. Studies show that once women pastors are hired, they usually overcome the resentment of certain lay members in the churches they serve.

Relationships with male colleagues vary widely as individuals themselves have different views on sexuality and the roles of men and women. Men are becoming more accepting of women as co-workers, not as competitors or sex-symbols.[15]

Another dimension for women in the clergy, as for women in secular jobs, is balancing their professional duties with those of wife and mother. Supportive spouses are a blessing.

For some women, the ministry is a second career. They may be widowed or divorced with grown children. These women bring maturity and experience to their congregations, attributes often missing in younger men and women just out of the seminary.

Although the numbers are steadily increasing, today's women clergy are still pioneers. In the United States in 1970 there were 6,314 clergy-women, or 2.9% of the total number in the ministry. By 1980 the number had risen to 11,130, or 4.2% of the total.[16] Other statistics show there were about 21,000 ordained women in the United States and Canada in 1987. Between 1977 and 1987 the number of women graduating with Masters of Divinity degrees increased by 224% to 1,496.[17]

The year 2000 should show even greater increases and acceptance if church men and women do not sit back and assume that clergy-women have now "arrived" and there is no more work to be done. Only as lay members and clergy-men aggressively challenge and correct the ingrained preconceptions and biases will clergy-women fully enter "the promised land" as equal partners with men in doing God's work.

Dissenters and Non-Conformists.

When Ralph Waldo Emerson said, "Whoso would be a *man* must be a non-conformist," he was not thinking of *women*, particularly of such women as the twelve whose stories appear in this volume. But Emerson's maxim fits these women. All of them were non-conformists who used their discontent to challenge the status quo. Some dissented for personal reasons, others to advance causes or to correct abuses.

Two of the most outspoken and fearless non-conformists were Anne Hutchinson and Ann Lee. In the early 1600s Anne Hutchinson challenged the entire religious structure of John Winthrop's utopian "city on a hill" in the Massachusetts Bay Colony. Her punishment was excommunication from the Puritan Church and banishment from the colony. One century later when Ann Lee found no peace in England's Anglican Church, she left it, joined a sect, and later founded the American Shaker movement. She was ridiculed and persecuted for her non-conformist ways.

In past church history, women were in part responsible for the growth of religious sects. As they were denied participation in the mainline churches, they sought alternatives. In the early centuries Gnostics and Montanists allowed women to take leadership positions. Later the Quakers welcomed women preachers.

The very fact that women were leaving organized churches to join so-called *heretical* sects provided more fuel for the church hierarchy to claim that women were more susceptible to heresy than men. Hence they were to be watched as troublemakers and witches.

Protest and dissension have always been a way of life in America. The country began with protests against the British, and ever since there have been riots, demonstrations, and marches for assorted causes. In the present media age, protesters hope to appear before the television cameras in nation-wide coverage.

One such protest that received much media attention was the excommunication of Sonia Johnson from the Church of Jesus Christ of Latter-day Saints (the Mormon Church) on December 5, 1980. What first brought the church's attention to Johnson was her support of the Equal Rights Amendment (ERA), which was adamantly opposed by the Mormon Church. She had marched in Washington, had testified before a Senate sub-committee, and had organized a group of feminists called "Mormons for ERA."

The church leaders, fearing she would become a role model for others who might challenge the authority of the Church, ordered her to stand trial before a committee. To avoid the impression that the Church was involved in national politics and the defeat of the ERA, the committee brought charges on only *religious* grounds. Johnson, a life-long member of the Mormon Church, was chastised for her attitude toward the Church, for speaking ill of the church fathers, and for breaking church covenants and rules. Johnson denied all of the charges, claiming that she could only be faulted for her political involvement. In her autobiography Johnson claims that she was the victim of a "kangaroo court."[18]

Through her formative years Sonia Johnson was a loyal member of the Mormon Church, but with the trial came bitterness and disillusionment. It has led her to another life as an articulate feminist lecturer and author.

Since its founding in 1830 the Mormon Church has been a patriarchal church. But the rapid worldwide growth to a membership of 7.3 million has forced the Church to make changes compatible with twentieth century thinking. In 1978 the Church accepted African-American men into the priesthood (women cannot be ordained). In 1990 church leaders made some modifications to their rules. Among them, women were no longer required to pledge obedience to their husbands. Mormon women welcomed the changes, but the Church still has a long way to go before females achieve equality with males.[19]

Ain't I a Woman?

When Sojourner Truth made her famous "Ain't I a Woman?" speech in Akron, Ohio, in 1851, she capsulized the past experiences of African-American women in the United States for almost two centuries. She had been sold as a slave, had worked the fields, had borne children, and had suffered the lash. Yet, she had grown strong through the oppression of slavery and the degradation of racism. She had replaced bitterness and self-pity with an all-consuming passion for human causes.

In the days of slavery, the black woman was at the bottom of the social scale. She had no status, no legal rights, no power. She was easy prey for both black and white men, as well as for spiteful white mistresses. She was expected to work the fields, do the menial household tasks, and breed children. At the same time, she was the glue that held the family together. After working from sunup to dark, she would then tend and feed her own children. Yet, she did dream of better things, and she sometimes translated her dreams into action. Sojourner Truth preached, Phillis Wheatley (c.1753 - 1784) wrote poetry, Harriet Tubman (c.1820 - 1913) escorted slaves north to freedom, and Mary McLeod Bethune (1875-1955) dedicated her life to educating young people.

Today scores of black women have succeeded. Yet for every one who has found success, thousands of African-American women struggle just to exist.

Generally black women have not supported the white feminist movement. They claim that white feminists have been preoccupied with only the problems of white women—especially in the workplace, career opportunities, and affirmative action. Many black women consider these *leisure-time* activities. Their problems are more basic— poverty, housing, health care, education, racism, and unemployment. They are deeply involved with the fight of black men for equal rights. White women, they claim, have taken jobs away from both black men and women. They blame the women's movement and environmental issues for stealing attention away from their fight for racial justice.[20]

The problems of justice and racism have not lessened in recent years. The 1980s saw a sharp increase in the number of black children living in poverty in single-parent households. There was more homelessness, more unemployment, and more sub-standard housing. Civil rights have been rolled back and affirmative action invalidated by the Supreme Court. In 1967 the black family earned 59% of that earned by a white family; by 1985 it had fallen to 57.5%.[21] Added to these were the societal problems of drugs and sexually-transmitted diseases such as AIDS.

Yet there are many success stories. An increasing number of African-American women are succeeding in business, education, entertainment, media, the arts, and politics.

A contemporary counterpart of Sojourner Truth is the Reverend Barbara Harris, who at age 58 was consecrated on February 11, 1989, as the first female bishop in the worldwide Anglican Church. She was not only a female, but she was black.

Harris' appointment was hailed by liberal clergy, women activists, and the black Episcopalians who make up 5% of the church population in America. (Women said it was "like a Pentecost.") Harris brings to the position a wide range of experience. She has been a public relations executive, a civil rights worker, a social activist, a feminist, and a prison chaplain. She led the procession of the eleven Episcopal women priests at the "irregular" ordination in Philadelphia in 1974. Out of the pulpit Harris is a gregarious, flamboyant individual, but when she preaches she is direct and forceful.

The appointment of Harris as Assistant Bishop in the Massachusetts Episcopal Diocese triggered an avalanche of protests from the conservative branches of the Anglican Church. Harris' opponents call her consecration "a blasphemy" and "a sacrilegious imposture." They claim it will deal a fatal blow to reconciliation with the Roman Catholic Church. The Archbishop of Canterbury announced that under current church law he could not recognize Harris nor any clergy ordained by her.[22]

Conservative Episcopalians do not approve of women in the clergy on scriptural grounds. Like the Roman Catholics they regard priests as successors to Jesus Christ's twelve male apostles. And they disapprove of Harris' personal qualifications. She is divorced, does not have an official college or seminary degree, and has little pastoral experience. They claim that her appointment was *sexual politics* engineered by the women-church movement. No man, they say, with her qualifications would have been considered for the episcopate.

The conservative wing of the church has formed the Episcopal Synod of America, a church within a church, to counter liberal trends, while an international commission is trying to work out a compromise that will avoid division in the church.[23]

In the meantime despite death threats and obscene phone calls, Barbara Harris pledges she will continue to work for justice for the oppressed and the unfortunate. Like Sojourner Truth she wants to "turn the world right side up."

A New Community.

This concluding chapter has addressed just a few of the problems facing contemporary American women. But women's concerns are so diverse they cannot be solved by the same solutions. There is great disparity between the problems of the rich and the poor, the black and the white, the educated and the uneducated, the feminist and the anti-feminist, the churched and the unchurched. And the women of the Third World and changing societies of Asia and Europe have far different problems to solve. There are no ready answers.

The goal of feminist theologians such as Elizabeth Schüssler Fiorenza of the Harvard Divinity School is to transform religious institutions into gender-free organizations where the common objective is a reinterpretation of the Gospel. These women want to substitute genderless language and symbols in Scripture and hymns. Theologian Rosemary Radford Ruether of the Garrett-Evangelical Theological Seminary in Evanston, Illinois, claims that women must do more than protest the old; they must form communities where they can discover the new inclusive humanity. She calls on women to make creative changes from within existing institutions.[24]

Women need to form a community *with* men, who together can build a church enriched by inclusiveness and diversity. In creating this new community we need to rediscover and reclaim what was the status of women who once were the backbone of the early church. We need to measure how far we have come and how much farther we still have to go. We can look to the future with hope.

Women today have not traveled this road alone. They have walked arm in arm with strong sisters from the past who have risked themselves to advance women's opportunities. Women of past generations have been empowered by a firm belief in the justness of their causes and by an abiding faith in God. Today's women need nothing less.

Notes

1 Beth Nissen, "The Missionary Murders," *Newsweek*, December 15, 1980, pp. 51-52.

Also: Tim Dutcher-Wells, "Being Evangelized in El Salvador," *The Christian Century*, November 30, 1988, pp. 1084-5.

Ann Carrigan, *Salvador Witness: The Life and Calling of Jean Donovan* (New York: Simon and Schuster, 1984), pp. 263-317.

2 Elizabeth Clark and Herbert Richardson, *Women and Religion: A Feminist Sourcebook of Christian Thought* (New York: Harper & Row, 1977), p. 8.

3 Kenneth L. Woodward with Eleanor Clift and Vicki Quade, "The Graying of the Convent," *Newsweek*, April 2, 1990, pp. 50-51.

4 Sara Maitland, *A Map of the New Country: Women and Christianity* (London: Routledge & Kegan Paul, 1983), p. 83.

Also: Sister M. Theresa Kane, "Be Mindful of the Intense Suffering and Pain," *Redbook*, April 1980, p. 151.

5 Michael McGough, "The Lefebvrite-Feminist Coalition?" *American Spectator*, August 1989, pp. 28-29.

6 Rebecca Sisco, "We're Doing the Eucharist as Women See It," *The Minnesota Women's Press*, October 10-23, 1990, p. 1, p. 10.

Also: Hopfensperger, "Women Celebrate Masses with Priest," *Minneapolis Star-Tribune*, August 18, 1990, p. 1a, p. 8a.

7 Birch Bayh, "Let's Tear Off Their Hoods," *Newsweek*, April 17, 1989, p. 8.

Also: Elinor Langer, "The American Neo-Nazi Movement Today," *The Nation*, July 16-23, 1990, pp. 82-6.

8 Susan Weidman Schneider, *Jewish and Female: Choices and Changes in Our Lives Today* (New York: Simon and Schuster, 1984), pp. 27-38.

9 Ibid., pp. 52-54.

10 Julie Goss, "Women in the Pulpit: Reworking the Rabbi's Role," *Lilith*, Fall 1990, pp. 16-25.

11 Rosemary Radford Ruether, *Women-Church* San Francisco: Harper & Row, 1985), p. 71.

12 Donald W. Dayton and Lucille Sider Dayton "Women as Preachers: Evangelical Precedents,"

Christianity Today, May 23, 1975, pp. 4-7.

13 Teresa Carpenter, "Courage and Pain: Women Who Love God and Defy Their Churches," *Redbook*, April 1980, p. 19.

Also: Rosemary Radford Ruether, and Rosemary Skinner Keller, *Women and Religion in America, volume 3: 1900-1968* (San Francisco: Harper & Row, 1986), pp. 340-46. From chapter "Winning Ordination for Women in Mainstream Protestant Churches" by Barbara Brown Zikmund.

14 Jackson W. Carroll and others, *Women of the Cloth: A New Opportunity for the Churches* (San Francisco: Harper & Row, 1983), p. 138.

15 Ibid., pp. 186-87.

16 Ibid., p. 4.

17 Kenneth L. Woodward, "Feminism and the Churches," *Newsweek*, February 13, 1989, p. 59. Source: Association of Theological Schools in the U.S. and Canada: National Council of Churches.

18 Sonia Johnson, *From Housewife to Heretic* (Garden City, NY: Doubleday & Company, Inc., 1981).

19 "The Mormon Gender Gap," *U.S. News & World Report*, May 14, 1990, p. 14.

20 Harry A. Ploski and James Williams eds., *The Negro Almanac: A Reference Work for the African American*, 5th edition (Detroit: Gale Research Inc., 1989), p. 1371.

21 Janet Dewart, ed., *The State of Black America: 1990* (National Urban League, Inc., 1990), p. 6.

22 Lynn Rosellini, "The First of the 'Mitered Mamas'," *U.S. News & World Report*, June 19, 1989, p. 56.

Also: Richard Walker, "Consecration of Bishop Stirs Episcopal Dissent," *Christianity Today*, March 17, 1989, p. 41, p. 43.

Renée D. Turner, "Festival of Firsts," *Ebony*, May 1989, p. 40, p. 42.

23 Joseph Carey, "A Denominational Gender Gap," *U.S. News & World Report*, June 19, 1989, pp. 56-57.

24 Rosemary Radford Ruether, *Women-Church*, p. 5, p. 39.

Bibliography

Chapter 1 — Perpetua

Bainton, Roland. *The Horizon History of Christianity.* (New York: American Heritage Publishing Co., 1964).

Brewer, E. Cobham. *A Dictionary of Miracles; Imitative, Realistic, and Dogmatic.* (Philadelphia: J. B. Lippincott, 1884, and Detroit: Gale Research Co., 1966).

Butler's Lives of the Saints, volume I. Edited, revised & supplemented by Herbert Thurston & Donald Attwater. (New York: P. J. Kenedy & Sons, 1962).

Deen, Edith. *Great Women of the Christian Faith.* (New York: Harper & Row, 1959).

Delaney, John. *Dictionary of Saints.* (New York: Doubleday & Co., 1980).

Fremantle, Anne ed. *A Treasury of Early Christianity.* (New York: The New American Library of World Literature, Inc., 1953).

Huber, Elaine C. *Women and the Authority of Inspiration; a Reexamination of Two Prophetic Movements from a Contemporary Feminist Perspective.* (Lanham, Maryland: University Press of America, Inc., 1985).

MacHaffie, Barbara. *Her Story: Women in Christian Tradition.* (Philadelphia: Fortress Press, 1986).

Ruether, Rosemary Radford. *Womanguides; Readings Towards a Feminist Theology.* (Boston: Beacon Press, 1985).

Shewring, W. H., translator. *The Passion of SS. Perpetua and Felicity together with the Sermons of S. Augustine.* (London: Sheed & Ward, 1931).

Wright, Elliott. *Holy Company.* (New York: Macmillan Publishing Co., 1980).

Chapter 2 — Catherine of Siena

Bell, Rudolph M. *Holy Anorexia.* (Chicago: University of Chicago Press, 1985).

Buber, Martin. *Ecstatic Confessions.* Translated by Esther Cameron. (San Francisco: Harper & Row, 1985).

Catherine of Siena. *The Dialogue.* Translated by Suzanne Noffke. (New York: Paulist Press, 1980).

_____*The Dialogue of the Seraphic Virgin Catherine of Siena.* Translated by Algar Thorold. (Rockford, IL: Tan Books and Publishers, 1974).

Culver, Elsie Thomas. *Women in the World of Religion.* (New York: Doubleday & Co., 1967).

Cunningham, Lawrence S. *The Meaning of Saints.* (San Francisco: Harper & Row, 1980).

Deen, Edith. *Great Women of the Christian Faith.* (New York: Harper & Row, 1959).

DeWohl, Louis. *Lay Siege to Heaven; a Novel of Saint Catherine of Siena.* (New York: J. B. Lippincott, 1960).

Fremantle, Anne. *Saints Alive.* (Garden City, New York: Doubleday & Co., 1978).

Keyes, Frances Parkinson. *Three Ways of Love.* (New York: Hawthorn Books, 1963).

Perrin, J. M. *Catherine of Siena.* Translated by Paul Barrett. (Westminster, Maryland: Newman Press, 1965).

Ruether, Rosemary and Eleanor McLaughlin eds. *Women of Spirit.* (New York: Simon & Schuster, 1979).

Undset, Sigrid. *Catherine of Siena.* Translated by Kate Austin-Lund. (New York: Sheed & Ward, 1954).

Weinstein, Donald and Rudolph M. Bell. *Saints & Society.* (Chicago: The University of Chicago Press, 1982).

Wright, Elliott. *Holy Company.* (New York: Macmillan Publishing Co., 1980).

Chapter 3 — Katherine von Bora

Bainton, Roland H. *Here I Stand: A Life of Martin Luther.* (New York: Abingdon Press, 1950).

_____*The Horizon History of Christianity.* (New York: American Heritage Publishing Company, 1964).

_____*Women of the Reformation in Germany and Italy.* (Minneapolis: Augsburg Publishing House, 1971).

Clark, Elizabeth and Herbert Richardson, eds. *Women and Religion.* (New York: Harper & Row, 1977).

Dentler, Clara Louise. *Katharine Luther of the Wittenberg Parsonage.* (Philadelphia: United Lutheran Publication House, 1924).

Eckermann, C. V. *Mistress of the Black Cloister.* (Adelaide, South Australia: Lutheran Publishing House, 1976).

Friedenthal, Richard. *Luther: His Life and Times.* Translated from German by John Nowell. (New York: Harcourt Brace Jovanovich Inc., 1970).

Gritsch, Eric W. *Martin—God's Court Jester.* (Philadelphia: Fortress Press, 1983).

Haile, H. G. *Luther, an Experiment in Biography.* (Garden City, New York: Doubleday and Co., 1980).

Harper, Howard V. *Profiles of Protestant Saints.* (New York: Fleet Press Corporation, 1968).

Just, Gustav. *Life of Luther.* (St. Louis: Concordia Publishing House, 1903).

Katterfield, Anna Ilgenstein. *The Morning Star of Wittenberg.* (Washington, D.C.: Review & Herald Publishing Association, 1956).

Kittelson, James M. *Luther, the Reformer.* (Minneapolis: Augsburg Publishing House, 1986).

Kleeberg, M. A. and Gerhard Lemme. *In the Footsteps of Martin Luther.* (St. Louis: Concordia Publishing House, 1965).

Ludwig, Charles. *Queen of the Reformation.* (Minneapolis: Bethany House Publishers, 1986).

Luther, Martin. *Luther's Works,* volume 54. Table Talks. (Philadelphia: Fortress Press, 1967).

MacHaffie, Barbara J. *Her Story: Women in Christian Tradition.* (Philadelphia: Fortress Press, 1986).

Mall, E. Jane. *Kitty, My Rib.* (St. Louis: Concordia Publishing House, 1959).

Manns, Peter. *Martin Luther, an Illustrated Biography.* (New York: Crossroad, 1982).

Nohl, Frederick. *Martin Luther, Hero of Faith.* (St. Louis: Concordia Publishing House, 1962).

Petersen, William J. *Martin Luther Had a Wife.* (Wheaton, Illinois: Tyndale House Publishers Inc., 1983).

Schreiber, Clara Seuel. *Katherine, Wife of Luther.* (Philadelphia: Muhlenberg Press, 1954).

Simon, Edith. *Luther Alive; Martin Luther and the Making of the Reformation.* (Garden City, New York: Doubleday & Co., 1968).

Thulin, Oskar, editor and compiler. *A Life of Luther, Told in Pictures and Narrative by the Reformer and His Contemporaries.* (Philadelphia: Fortress Press, 1966).

Todd, John M. *Luther, a Life.* (New York: Crossroad, 1982).

Walter, Alice E. *Katharine Luther, Liberated Nun.* (St. Louis: Clayton Publishing House Inc., 1981).

Weber, Erwin. *From Luther to 1580: A Pictorial Account.* (St. Louis: Concordia Publishing House, 1977).

Chapter 4 — Gracia Nasi Mendes

Coles, Paul. *The Ottoman Impact on Europe.* (New York: Harcourt, Brace & World, Inc., 1968).

Dimont, Max I. *Jews, God and History.* (New York: Simon and Schuster, Inc., 1962).

Encyclopaedia Judaica, volumes 2, 5, 9, 11, 12, 14. (New York: The Macmillan Company, 1971)..

Fink, Greta. *Great Jewish Women.* (New York: Menorah Publishing Co., Inc., 1978).

Gillon, Diana and Meir Gillon. *The Sand and the Stars.* (New York: Lothrop, Lee & Shepard Company, 1971).

Haliczer, Stephen ed. & trans. *Inquisition and Society in Early Modern Europe.* (Totowa, New Jersey: Barnes & Noble Books, 1987).

Herculano, Alexandre. *History of the Origin and Establishment of the Inquisition in Portugal.* (New York: AMS Press, 1968).

Kamen, Henry. *The Spanish Inquisition.* (New York: New American Library, 1965).

Kim, Young Oon. *World Religions; Living Religions of the Middle East,* volume 1. (New York: Golden Gate Publishing Co., 1976).

Lacks, Roslyn. *Women and Judaism; Myth, History, and Struggle.* (Garden City, New York: Doubleday & Company Inc., 1980).

Lea, Henry Charles. *A History of the Inquisition*

of Spain. 4 volumes. (New York: Ams Press, Inc., 1966).

Loewe, Raphael. *The Position of Women in Judaism.* (London: S.P.C.K., 1966).

Plaidy, Jean. *The Spanish Inquisition; Its Rise, Growth, and End.* (New York: The Citadel Press, 1967). Contains three volumes in one edition.

Priesand, Sally. *Judaism and the New Woman.* (New York: Behrman House, 1975).

Rivkin, Ellis. *The Shaping of Jewish History; A Radical New Interpretation.* (New York: Charles Scribner's Sons, 1971).

Roth, Cecil. *Doña Gracia of the House of Nasi.* (Philadelphia: The Jewish Publication Society of America, 1977).

_____*Gleanings; Essays in Jewish History, Letters and Art.* (New York: Hermon Press, 1967).

_____*A History of the Marranos.* (New York: Schocken Books, 1974).

_____"Joseph Nasi, Duke of Naxos, and the Counts of Savoy." 75th Anniversary Volume of the *Jewish Quarterly Review,* 1967, pp. 460-72.

_____*The Spanish Inquisition.* (New York: W.W. Norton & Company Inc., 1964).

Ruether, Rosemary and Eleanor McLaughlin eds. *Women of Spirit.* (New York: Simon & Schuster, 1979).

Sabatini, Rafael, *Torquemada and the Spanish Inquisition.* (London: Stanley Paul & Co., 1928).

Sachar, Abram Leon. *A History of the Jews.* (New York: Alfred A. Knopf, 1964).

Swidler, Leonard. *Women in Judaism; The Status of Women in Formative Judaism.* (Metuchen, New Jersey: The Scarecrow Press, Inc., 1976).

Turberville, H. S. *The Spanish Inquisition.* (Hamden, Connecticut: Archon Books, 1968).

Universal Jewish Encyclopedia, volume 7. (Universal Jewish Encyclopedia Co., Inc., 1948).

Wagenknecht, Edward. *Daughters of the Covenant.* (Amherst, Massachusetts: The University of Massachusetts Press, 1983).

Wiesenthal, Simon. *Sails of Hope; The Secret Mission of Christopher Columbus.* (New York: Macmillan Publishing Co., Inc., 1973).

Chapter 5 — Teresa of Avila

Beevers, John. *St. Teresa of Avila.* (Garden City, New York: Hanover House, 1961).

Clissold, Stephen. *St. Teresa of Avila.* (London: Seabury Press, 1979).

Delaney, John J. ed. *Saints For All Seasons.* (New York: Doubleday and Co. Inc., 1978).

Dickens, A. G. *The Counter Reformation.* (New York: Harcourt, Brace & World, 1969).

Dicken, E. W. Trueman. *The Crucible of Love; A Study of the Mysticism of St. Teresa of Jesus and St. John of the Cross.* (New York: Sheed & Ward, 1963).

Donze, Mary Teresa. *Teresa of Avila.* (New York: Paulist Press, 1982).

Egan, Harvey D. *What Are They Saying About Mysticism?* (New York: Paulist Press, 1982).

Fremantle, Anne. *Woman's Way to God.* (New York: St. Martin's Press, 1977).

Fülöp-Miller, René. *The Saints That Moved the World.* Translated by Alexander Gode and Erika Fülöp-Miller. (New York: Thomas Y. Crowell Co., 1945).

Harkness, Georgia. *Mysticism, Its Meaning and Message.* (New York: Abingdon Press, 1973).

Hatzfeld, Helmut A. *Santa Teresa de Avila.* (New York: Twayne Publishers, 1969).

Lincoln, Victoria. *Teresa: A Woman.* (Albany, New York: State University of New York Press, 1984).

Petersson, Robert T. *The Art of Ecstasy: Teresa, Bernini, and Crashaw.* (New York: Atheneum, 1970).

Ruether, Rosemary Radford. *Womanguides; Readings Toward a Feminist Theology.* (Boston: Beacon Press, 1985).

Teresa of Avila. *The Collected Works of St. Teresa of Avila,* volume one. (Washington, D.C.: Institute of Carmelite Studies, 1976).

_____*The Collected Works of St. Teresa of Avila,* volume two. (Washington, D.C.: Institute of Carmelite Studies, 1980).

_____*Interior Castle.* (New York: Image Books, Doubleday and Co., 1961).

_____*The Way of Perfection,* second edition. (London: Thomas Baker, 1919).

Wright, Elliott. *Holy Company.* (New York: Macmillan Publishing Co., 1980).

Chapter 6 — Anne Marbury Hutchinson

Adams, Charles Francis. *The Antinomian Controversy.* (New York: DaCapo Press, 1976). Originally published in 1892.

Bacon, Margaret Hope. *The Quiet Rebels; The Story of the Quakers in America.* (Philadelphia: New Society Publishers, 1985).

Baltzell, E. Digby. *Puritan Boston and Quaker Philadelphia.* (New York: The Macmillan Company, 1979).

Battis, Emery. *Saints and Sectaries.* (Chapel Hill: The University of North Carolina Press, 1962).

Bremer, Francis J. ed. *Anne Hutchinson: Troubler of the Puritan Zion.* (Huntington, New York: Robert E. Krieger Publishing Company, 1981).

Crawford, Deborah. *Four Women in a Violent Time.* (New York: Crown Publishers, Inc., 1970).

Ellis, George E. *The Aims and Purposes of the Founders of Massachusetts: Their Treatment of Intruders and Dissentients.* (Boston: Press of John Wilson and Son, 1869).

Emerson, Everett H. *John Cotton.* (New York: Twayne Publishers, Inc., 1965).

Ernst, James. *Roger Williams: New England Firebrand.* (New York: The Macmillan Company, 1932).

Fremantle, Anne. *Woman's Way to God.* (New York: St. Martin's Press, 1977).

Gura, Philip F. *A Glimpse of Sion's Glory: Puritan Radicalism in New England, 1620-1660.* (Middletown, Connecticut: Wesleyan University Press, 1984).

Hall, David D. ed. *The Antinomian Controversy, 1636-1638.* (Middletown, Connecticut: Wesleyan University Press, 1968).

Huber, Elaine C. *Women and the Authority of Inspiration; A Reexamination of Two Prophetic Movements From a Contemporary Feminist Perspective.* (Lanham, Maryland: University Press of America, 1985).

Kerber, Linda K. and Jane DeHart Mathews. *Women's America: Refocusing the Past.* (New York: Oxford University Press, 1982).

Koehler, Lyle. *A Search for Power; The "Weaker Sex" in Seventeenth Century New England.* (Urbana, Illinois: University of Illinois Press, 1980).

Lundin, Roger and Mark A. Noll eds. *Voices from the Heart; Four Centuries of American Piety.* (Grand Rapids, Michigan: William B. Eerdmans Publishing Company, 1987).

Miller, Perry ed. *The American Puritans; Their Prose and Poetry.* (Garden City, New York: Doubleday & Company, Inc., 1956).

———*The New England Mind From Colony to Province.* (Cambridge, Massachusetts: Harvard University Press, 1953).

———*Roger Williams; His Contributions to the American Tradition.* (New York: Atheneum, 1953).

Morgan, Edmund S. *The Puritan Dilemma; The Story of John Winthrop.* (Boston: Little, Brown and Company, 1958).

Ruether, Rosemary Radford and Rosemary Skinner Keller. *Women and Religion in America,* volume 2. (San Francisco: Harper & Row, 1983).

Ruether, Rosemary Radford. *Sexism and God-talk; Toward a Feminist Theology.* (Boston: Beacon Press, 1983).

Vaughan, Alden T. *New England Frontier; Puritans and Indians 1620-1675.* (Boston: Little, Brown and Company, 1965).

Walker, Williston. *Ten New England Leaders.* (New York: Silver, Burdett and Company, 1901).

Williams, Selma R. *Demeter's Daughters: The Women Who Founded America, 1587-1787.* (New York: Atheneum, 1975).

———*Divine Rebel: The Life of Anne Marbury Hutchinson.* (New York: Holt, Rinehart and Winston, 1981).

———*Kings, Commoners, and Colonists; Puritan Politics in Old New England, 1603-1660.* (New York: Atheneum, 1974).

Williams, Selma R. and Pamela J. Williams. *Riding the Nightmare; Women & Witchcraft.* (New York: Atheneum, 1978).

Ziff, Larzer. *The Career of John Cotton; Puritanism and the American Experience.* (Princeton: Princeton University Press, 1962).

Chapter 7 — Juana Ines de la Cruz

Benítez, Fernando. *The Century after Cortes.* (Chicago: University of Chicago Press, 1965).

Blacker, Irwin R. *Cortes and the Aztec Conquest.* (New York: American Heritage Publishing Co., 1963).

Cheetham, Nicolas. *Mexico: a Short History.* (New York: Thomas Y. Crowell Co., 1970).

Flynn, Gerard. *Sor Juana Inés De la Cruz.* (New York: Twayne Publishers Inc., 1971).

Fremantle, Anne. *Woman's Way to God.* (New York: St. Martin's Press, 1977).

González Pena, Carlos. *History of Mexican Literature,* third edition. (Dallas: Southern Methodist University Press, 1968).

Innes, Hammond. *The Conquistadors.* (New York: Alfred A. Knopf, 1969).

Juana Inés de la Cruz. *The Pathless Grove; Sonnets of Sor Juana Inés de la Cruz, 1651-1695, "The Tenth Muse of Mexico."* (Prairie City, Illinois: Decker Press, 1950).

Miller, Robert Ryal. *Mexico; a History.* (Norman, Oklahoma: University of Oklahoma Press, 1985).

The Oxford Companion to Spanish Literature. Edited by Philip Ward. (Oxford: Clarendon Press, 1978).

Prescott, William H. *The Conquest of Mexico; The Conquest of Peru and Other Selections.* (New York: Twayne Publishers Inc., 1966).

Rodman, Selden. *A Short History of Mexico.* (New York: Stein and Day, 1982).

Royer, Fanchón. *The Tenth Muse; Sor Juana Inés de la Cruz.* (Paterson, New Jersey: St. Anthony Guild Press, 1952).

Ruether, Rosemary Radford and Rosemary Skinner Keller. *Women and Religion in America,* volume 2. (San Francisco: Harper & Row, 1983).

Thurman, Judith. *I Became,Alone; Five Women Poets.* (New York: Atheneum, 1975).

Chapter 8 — Kateri Tekakwitha

Brunsman, Gualbert. *I Am Indian; the Story of Kateri Tekakwitha.* (Marty, South Dakota: St. Paul's Indian Mission, 1956).

Buehrle, Marie Cecilia. *Kateri of the Mohawks.* (Milwaukee: Bruce Publishing Co., 1954).

Coffey, Thomas J. *Kateri Tekakwitha.* (Auriesville, New York: Tekakwitha League, 1956).

Dictionary of Canadian Biography, volume 1. (Toronto: University of Toronto Press, 1966).

Donohue, John W., "I Will Love You in Heaven," *America,* June 21, 1980.

Dunbar, David, "The Lily of the Mohawks," *The Catholic Digest,* September, 1980.

Husslein, Joseph, ed. *Heroines of Christ.* (Milwaukee: Bruce Publishing Co., 1939).

Johansen, Bruce E. *Forgotten Founders.* (Ofipswich, Massachusetts: Gambit Inc., Publishers, 1982).

Josephy, Alvin M. *The Indian Heritage of America.* (New York: Alfred A. Knopf, 1968).

Lecompte, Edward. *The Glory of the Mohawks.* (Milwaukee: Bruce Publishing Co., 1944).

McBride, Joseph S. "The Living Spirit of Blessed Kateri Tekakwitha," *Worldmission,* volume 31, number 4, Winter 1980-81.

Maynard, Theodore. *Great Catholics in American History.* (Garden City, New York: Hanover House, 1957).

Notable American Women, 1607-1950, volume III. (Cambridge, Massachusetts: Belknap Press of Harvard University Press, 1971). "Catherine Tekakwitha" by Thomas Grassmann.

The Positio of the Historical Section of the Sacred Congregation of Rites on the Introduction of the Cause for Beatification and Canonization and on the Virtues of the Servant of God Katharine Tekakwitha, the Lily of the Mohawks. (New York: Fordham University Press, 1940.)

Reuther, Rosemary Radford and Rosemary Skinner Keller. *Women and Religion in America,* volume 2. (San Francisco: Harper & Row, 1983).

Sargent, Daniel. *Catherine Tekakwitha.* (New York: Longmans, 1936).

Thornton, Margaret. *Kateri, the Maid of the Mohawks.* (St. Louis: B. Herder Book Co., 1934).

Weiser, Francis X. *Kateri Tekakwitha.* (Caughnawaga, P.Q., Canada: Kateri Center, 1972).

Chapter 9 — Susanna Annesley Wesley

Baker, Frank. "Salute to Susanna." *Methodist History,* volume 7, number 3, April 1969.

Clark, Elmer T. *An Album of Methodist History.* (New York: Abingdon Press, 1952).

Clarke, Eliza. *Susanna Wesley.* (London: W. H. Allen & Co., 1890).

Cook, Alice Isabel. *Women of the Warm Heart.* (London: The Epworth Press, 1954).

Doughty, W. L. ed. *The Prayers of Susanna Wesley.* (London: The Epworth Press, 1956).

Edwards, Maldwyn. *Family Circle, a Study of the Epworth Household in Relation to John and Charles Wesley.* (London: The Epworth Press, 1949).

Ethridge, Willie Snow. *Strange Fires.* (New York: Vanguard Press Inc., 1971).

Harmon, Nolan B. ed. *World Methodism.* (Nashville: United Methodist Publishing House, 1974).

Harmon, Rebecca Lamar, *Susanna, Mother of the Wesleys.* (Nashville: Abingdon Press, 1968).

Harper, Howard V. *Profiles of Protestant Saints.* (New York: Fleet Press Corporation, 1968).

Heitzenrater, Richard P. *The Elusive Mr. Wesley,* volumes I and II. (Nashville: Abingdon Press, 1984).

The Illustrated History of Methodism. (St. Louis: Methodist Magazine Publishing Co., 1900).

Keller, Rosemary Skinner, Louise L. Queen and Hilah F. Thomas eds. *Women in New Worlds,* volume 2. (Nashville: Abingdon Press, 1982).

Kirk, John. *The Mother of the Wesleys.* (Cincinnati: Jennings and Pye, 1865).

Maser, Frederick E. *Susanna Wesley.* (Lake Junaluska, North Carolina: Association of Methodist Historical Societies, no date).

Newton, John A. *Susanna Wesley and the Puritan Tradition in Methodism.* (London: The Epworth Press, 1968).

Snowden, Rita F. *Such a Woman.* (Nashville: The Upper Room, 1962).

Stevens, Abel. *Women of Methodism.* (New York: Carlton & Porter, 1866).

Tuttle, Robert G. *John Wesley; His Life and Theology.* (Grand Rapids, Michigan: Zondervan Publishing House, 1978).

Wallace, Charles. "Susanna Wesley's Spirituality: The Freedom of a Christian Woman." *Methodist History*, volume 22, number 3, April 1984.

Wilder, Franklin. *Father of the Wesleys.* (New York: Exposition Press, 1971).

Chapter 10 — Ann Lee

Andrews, Edward Deming. *The People Called Shakers.* (New York: Dover Publications, 1963).

Andrews, Edward Deming and Faith Andrews. *Visions of the Heavenly Sphere.* (Charlottesville, Virginia: The University Press of Virginia, 1969).

Brewer, Priscilla J. *Shaker Communities, Shaker Lives.* (Hanover, New Hampshire: University Press of New England, 1986).

Campion, Nardi Reeder. *Ann the Word.* (Boston: Little, Brown and Company, 1976).

Clark, Elizabeth and Herbert Richardson. *Women and Religion.* (New York: Harper & Row, 1977).

Desroche, Henri. *The American Shakers from Neo-Christianity to Presocialism.* (Amherst, Massachusetts: University of Massachusetts Press, 1955).

Faber, Doris. *The Perfect Life.* (New York: Farrar, Straus & Giroux, 1974).

Fremantle, Anne. *Woman's Way to God.* (New York: St. Martin's Press, 1977).

Frost, Marguerite. *The Shaker Story.* (Canterbury, New Hampshire: Canterbury Shakers, no date).

Horgan, Edward R. *The Shaker Holy Land.* (Harvard, Massachusetts: The Harvard Common Press, 1982).

Marini, Stephen A. *Radical Sects of Revolutionary New England.* (Cambridge, Massachusetts: Harvard University Press, 1982).

Morse, Flo. *The Shakers and the World's People.* (New York: Dodd, Mead & Company, 1980).

Notable American Women, 1607-1950, volume II. (Cambridge, Massachusetts: Belknap Press of Harvard University Press, 1971). "Ann Lee" by Edward Deming Andrews.

Rice, Edward. *American Saints & Seers.* (New York: Four Winds Press, 1982).

Ruether, Rosemary Radford and Rosemary Skinner Keller. *Women and Religion in America*, volume 2. (San Francisco: Harper & Row, 1983).

Sasson, Diane. *The Shaker Spiritual Narrative.* (Knoxville: The University of Tennessee Press, 1983).

Van Kolken, Diana. *Introducing the Shakers.*
(Bowling Green, Ohio: Gabriel's Horn Publishing Co., 1985).

Whitson, Robley ed. *Shakers, Two Centuries of Spiritual Reflection.* (New York: Paulist Press, 1983).

Chapter 11 — Narcissa Prentiss Whitman

Brandon, William. *The Last Americans.* (New York: McGraw-Hill Book Company, 1974).

Catlin, George. *Episodes From Life Among the Indians and Last Rambles.* (Norman, Oklahoma: University of Oklahoma Press, 1959).

_____*Letters and Notes on the Manners, Customs, and Conditions of the North American Indians*, volume II. (New York: Dover Publications, 1973).

Culver, Elsie Thomas. *Women in the World of Religion.* (New York: Doubleday & Co., 1967).

Dodd, Lawrence. *Narcissa Whitman on the Oregon Trail.* (Fairfield, Washington: Ye Galleon Press, 1986).

Drury, Clifford M. *First White Women Over the Rockies.* Two volumes. (Glendale, California: The Arthur H. Clark Company, 1963).

_____*Marcus and Narcissa Whitman and the Opening of Old Oregon.* Two volumes. (Glendale, California: The Arthur H. Clark Company, 1973).

Dryden, Cecil P. *Give All to Oregon!* (New York: Hastings House, 1968).

Faris, John T. *Winning the Oregon Country.* (New York: Presbyterian Home Missions, 1911).

Haverstock, Mary Sayre. *Indian Gallery; the Story of George Catlin.* (New York: Four Winds Press, 1973).

Hubert, Archer Butler and Dorothy Printup Hulbert eds. *Marcus Whitman Crusader.* Three volumes. (Denver: The Stewart Commission of Colorado College and the Denver Public Library, 1936.)

Idaho Yesterdays, volume 31, numbers 1-2. Spring/Summer Issue, 1987.

Jones, Nard. *The Great Command.* (Boston: Little Brown and Company, 1959).

Mowry William A. *Marcus Whitman and the Early Days of Oregon.* (New York: Silver, Burdett and Company, 1901).

Myres, Sandra L. *Westering Women and the Frontier Experience 1800-1915.* (Albuquerque: University of New Mexico Press, 1982).

Olmsted, Gerald W. *Fielding's Lewis and Clark Trail.* (New York: William Morrow & Co., 1986).

Ross, Nancy Wilson. *Westward the Women.* (San Francisco: North Point Press, 1985).

Sager, Catherine, Elizabeth & Matilda Sager. *The Whitman Massacre of 1847.* (Fairfield, Washington: Ye Galleon Press, 1981).

Saunders, Mary. *The Whitman Massacre.* Reprinted from the original 1916 account. (Fairfield, Washington: Ye Galleon Press, 1977).

Schlissel, Lillian. *Women's Diaries of the Westward Journey.* (New York: Schocken Books, 1982).

Thompson, Erwin N. *Shallow Grave at Waiilatpu: the Sagers' West.* (Portland: Oregon Historical Society, revised edition 1973).

_____*Whitman Mission, National Historic Site.* National Park Service Historical Handbook Series No. 37. (Washington D.C.: Government Printing Office, 1964.)

Whitman, Narcissa. *Coming of the White Women as Told in Letters and Journal of Narcissa Prentiss Whitman.* (Portland: Oregon Historical Society, 1937).

_____*The Letters of Narcissa Whitman.* (Fairfield, Washington: Ye Galleon Press, 1986.)

_____*My Journal, 1836.* (Fairfield, Washington: Ye Galleon Press, 1982).

Chapter 12 — Sojourner Truth

Bernard, Jacqueline. *Journey Toward Freedom.* (New York: W. W. Norton & Company, Inc., 1967).

Cornish, Dudley Taylor. *The Sable Arm; Negro Troops in the Union Army, 1861-1865.* (New York: W. W. Norton & Company Inc., 1966).

Dannett, Sylvia G. L. *Profiles of Negro Womanhood,* volume I, 1619-1900. (Negro Heritage Library). (Yonkers, New York: Educational Heritage, Inc., no date.)

Dillon, Merton. *The Abolitionists: The Growth of a Dissenting Minority.* (New York: W. W. Norton & Company Inc., 1979).

Douglass, Frederick. *Life and Times of Frederick Douglass.* Reprinted from the revised edition of 1892. (New York: Collier Macmillan Publishers, 1962).

Fauset, Arthur Huff. *Sojourner Truth, God's Faithful Pilgrim.* (Chapel Hill, North Carolina: The University of North Carolina Press, 1938).

Filler, Louis. *The Crusade Against Slavery, 1830-1860.* (New York: Harper & Row Publishers, 1960).

_____*Slavery in the United States of America.* (New York: D. Van Nostrand Company, 1972).

Gilbert, Olive. *Narrative of Sojourner Truth, a Northern Slave.* (Boston: Printed for the author, 1850).

_____*Narrative of Sojourner Truth....* Reprinted with an introduction by Harriet Beecher Stowe. (New York: 1853).

_____*Narrative of Sojourner Truth....* Reprinted by Frances W. Titus, with a preface by William Lloyd Garrison and additions from Sojourner Truth's "Book of Life." (Boston: 1875).

_____*Narrative of Sojourner Truth....* Reprinted with further additions. (Battle Creek, Michigan: 1878, 1881, 1884).

_____*Narrative of Sojourner Truth. . . .* (Salem, New Hampshire: Ayer Company, Publishers, Inc., 1967). A reprint of the 1878 edition.

Hughes, Langston and Milton Meltzer. *A Pictorial History of the Negro in America.* (New York: Crown Publishers, Inc., 1968).

Kobrin, Davis. *The Black Minority in Early New York.* (Albany: The University of the State of New York, 1971).

Loewenberg, Bert James and Ruth Bogin eds. *Black Women in Nineteenth-Century American Life.* (University Park: The Pennsylvania State University Press, 1976).

Logan, Rayford W. and Michael R. Winston eds. *Dictionary of American Negro Biography.* (New York: W. W. Norton & Company, 1982).

McManus, Edgar J. *A History of Negro Slavery in New York.* (Syracuse: Syracuse University Press, 1966).

McPherson, James M. *The Struggle for Equality.* (Princeton: Princeton University Press, 1964).

Ortiz, Victoria. *Sojourner Truth, a Self-Made Woman.* (Philadelphia: Lippincott Company, 1974).

Pauli, Hertha. *Her Name Was Sojourner Truth.* (New York: Appleton-Century-Crofts, Inc., 1962).

Quarles, Benjamin. *Lincoln and the Negro.* (New York: Oxford University Press, 1962).

_____*The Negro in the Civil War.* (Boston: Little, Brown and Company, 1953).

Rose, Willie Lee. *Slavery and Freedom.* Edited by William W. Freehling. (Oxford University Press, 1982).

Sorin, Gerald. *Abolitionism, a New Perspective.* (New York: Praeger Publications, 1972).

Sterling, Dorothy ed. *We Are Your Sisters; Black Women in the Nineteenth Century.* (New York: W. W. Norton & Company, 1984).

Thomas, John L. ed. *Slavery Attacked: The Abolitionist Crusade.* (Englewood Cliffs, New Jersey: Prentice-Hall Incorporated, 1965).

Wagenknecht, Edward. *Harriet Beecher Stowe, the Known and the Unknown.* (New York: Oxford University Press, 1965).

Chapter 13 — Women Recover the Past

Baum, Charlotte and others. *The Jewish Woman in America.* (New York: Dial Press, 1976).

Carrigan, Ana. *Salvador Witness: The Life and Calling of Jean Donovan.* (New York: Simon and Schuster, 1984).

Carroll, Jackson W. and others. *Women of the Cloth; A New Opportunity for the Churches.* (San Francisco: Harper & Row, 1983).

Christ, Carol. *Weaving the Visions.* (San Francisco: Harper & Row, 1989).

Christ, Carol P. and Judith Plaskow eds. *Womanspirit Rising: A Feminist Reader in Religion.* (San Francisco: Harper & Row, 1979).

Clark, Elizabeth and Herbert Richardson. *Women and Religion: A Feminist Sourcebook of Christian Thought.* (New York: Harper & Row, 1977).

Clouse, Bonnidell and Robert G. Clouse eds. *Women in Ministry: Four Views.* (Downers Grove, Illinois: InterVarsity Press, 1989).

Culver, Elsie Thomas, *Women in the World of Religion.* (Garden City, New York: Doubleday & Company Inc., 1967).

Daly, Mary. *Beyond God the Father: Toward a Philosophy of Women's Liberation.* (Boston: Beacon Press, 1973).

Dewart, Janet ed. *The State of Black America: 1990.* (National Urban League, Inc., 1990).

Eck, Diana L. and Devaki Jain. *Speaking of Faith: Global Perspectives on Women, Religion and Social Change.* (Philadelphia: New Society Publishers, 1987).

Greenberg, Blu. *On Women and Judaism: A View from Tradition.* (Philadelphia: The Jewish Publication Society of America, 1981).

Gundry, Patricia. *Neither Free nor Slave: Helping Women Answer the Call to Church Leadership.* (San Francisco: Harper & Row, 1987).

Heschel, Susannah ed. *On Being a Jewish Feminist: A Reader.* (New York: Schocken Books, 1983).

Johnson, Sonia. *From Housewife to Heretic.* (Garden City, New York: Doubleday & Company, Inc., 1981).

King, Ursula ed. *Women in the World's Religions, Past and Present.* (New York: Paragon House, 1987).

Loewenberg, Bert James and Ruth Bogin eds. *Black Women in Nineteenth-Century American Life.* (University Park, Pennsylvania: The Pennsylvania State University Press, 1976).

Maitland, Sara. *A Map of the New Country: Women and Christianity.* (London: Routledge & Kegan Paul, 1983).

Marcus, Jacob R. *The American Jewish Woman, 1654-1980.* (New York: KTAV Publishing House, Inc., 1981).

Martin, Faith McBurney. *Call Me Blessed: The Emerging Christian Woman.* (Grand Rapids, Michigan: William B. Eerdmans Publishing Co., 1988).

Miller, Casey and Kate Smith, *Words and Women.* (Garden City, New York: Anchor Press/Doubleday, 1976).

Miller, Jean Baker. *Toward a New Psychology of Women.* 2nd edition. (Boston: Beacon Press, 1986).

Mollenkott, Virginia Ramey. *The Divine Feminine: the Biblical Imagery of God As Female.* (New York: Crossroad, 1983).

Perko, F. Michael. *Catholic and American: A Popular History.* (Huntington, Indiana: Our Sunday Visitor, 1989).

Plaskow, Judith and Carol P. Christ eds. *Weaving the Visions: New Patterns in Feminist Spirituality.* (San Francisco: Harper & Row, 1989).

Ploski, Harry A. and James Williams eds. *The Negro Almanac: A Reference Work on the African American,* 5th edition. (Detroit: Gale Research Inc., 1989).

Rowbotham, Sheila. *Hidden from History: Rediscovering Women in History from the 17th Century to the Present.* (New York: Pantheon Books, 1974).

Ruether, Rosemary Radford. *Sexism and Godtalk: Toward a Feminist Theology.* (Boston: Beacon Press, 1983).

———*Women-Church: Theology and Practice of Feminist Liturgical Communities.* (San Francisco: Harper & Row, 1985).

Ruether, Rosemary Radford and Rosemary Skinner Keller. *Women and Religion in America, volume 3: 1900-1968.* (San Francisco: Harper & Row, 1986).

Schneider, Susan Weidman. *Jewish and Female: Choices and Changes in Our Lives Today.* (New York: Simon and Schuster, 1984).

Smythe, Mabel M. ed. *The Black American Reference Book.* (Englewood Cliffs, New Jersey: Prentice-Hall, Inc., 1976).

Swidler, Leonard. *Biblical Affirmations of Woman.* (Philadelphia: The Westminster Press, 1979).

Watkins, Mel and Jay David eds. *To Be a Black Woman: Portraits in Fact and Fiction.* (New York: William Morrow and Company, Inc., 1971).

Weidman, Judith L. ed. *Christian Feminism: Visions of a New Humanity.* (San Francisco: Harper & Row, 1984).

Index

Grace Stageberg Swenson holds a Masters degree from the University of Minnesota and is a former teacher and librarian. She is the author of several books, including *From the Ashes: The Story of the Hinckley Fire of 1894.* An accomplished storyteller, Swenson gives talks on the 1894 Hinckley Fire and the women about whom she writes in *Women of Faith.*

WOMEN OF FAITH explores the lives of twelve women of diverse historical periods, religions, ethnic origins, and nationalities.

It examines their motivations and commitments, their differences and similarities. Each in her own heroic way overcame the stigma placed on her by society, culture, and religion.

"Each chapter is a fascinating study of the development of a strong and courageous woman. These women live as singular and unique, yet a common profile emerges as well. Each learned to listen to and act on an inner truth that called her to a personal expression of faith beyond the conventions of ordinary religion. The essence of the rich personalities revealed is found in the heart of their various spiritual convictions and in the zest for life with which their faith energized them. Women of Faith is a valuable contribution to the literature of women's spirituality, development, psychology, and history.

I'm touched by a sense of companionship with these women—as if they are fine traveling companions for the spiritual journey. Many of them were already friends, and it was good to come to know them better. Others are new to me, and I feel as if I've made a precious discovery in coming to know them a little."

JANA PREBLE
International teacher and consultant in Spiritual development and a Professor of Applied Psychology and Women's Studies St. Cloud State University, St. Cloud, Minnesota

"Women of Faith" effectively portrays the lives and struggles of twelve heroic women. They range from an early Christian martyr through the lives of European and Mexican Christian and Jewish women on to the brutal murder of a Protestant wife-missionary in America's West and finally to Sojourner Truth's God-impassioned struggle for equality. The women's lives are depicted in the context of the historical issues of their times and demonstrate that God's gift of Faith was the driving force for each of them."

ARLEEN M. HYNES, O.S.B.
Co-author of Biblio/Poetry Therapy—The Interactive Process who chose Benedictine life after marriage and ten children

Perpetua	*early Christian martyr*
Catherine of Siena	*Italian saint*
Katherine von Bora	*Martin Luther's wife*
Gracia Mendes	*Jewish philanthropist*
Teresa of Avila	*Spanish saint*
Anne Hutchinson	*Puritan dissenter*
Juana Inés de la Cruz	*Mexican poet*
Kateri Tekakwitha	*Mohawk holy woman*
Susanna Wesley	*mother of Methodism*
Ann Lee	*founder of the Shaker movement*
Narcissa Whitman	*American missionary*
Sojourner Truth	*slave, itinerant preacher*

ISBN: 0-87839-063-4
$19.95